D1225264

WITHDRAWN

GOD'S LIBRARY

GOD'S LIBRARY

The Archaeology of the Earliest

Christian Manuscripts

===

BRENT NONGBRI

===

Yale

UNIVERSITY PRESS

New Haven and London

Quotations from *Legends of the Centuries*, by Charles Méla (Fondation Martin Bodmer), English translation by David Macey, © 2004 Éditions Cercle d'Art, Paris.

Quotations from Carl Schmidt, "Die neuesten Bibelfunde aus Ägypten." *Zeitschrift für die Neutestamentliche Wissenschaft* 30 (1931): 285–293, De Gruyter, *Zeitschrift für die Neutestamentliche Wissenschaft*, Walter De Gruyter GmbH Berlin Boston, 1931. Copyright and all rights reserved. Material from this publication has been used with the permission of Walter De Gruyter GmbH.

Yale University Press books may be purchased in quantity for educational, business, or promotional use. For information, please e-mail sales.press@yale.edu (U.S. office) or sales@yaleup.co.uk (U.K. office).

Set in Janson type by Integrated Publishing Solutions.
Printed in the United States of America.

Library of Congress Control Number: 2017963318
ISBN 978-0-300-21541-0 (hardcover : alk. paper)

A catalogue record for this book is available from the British Library.

This paper meets the requirements of ANSI/NISO Z39.48-1992 (Permanence of Paper).

10 9 8 7 6 5 4 3 2 1

For Mary Jane Cuyler

Contents

Acknowledgments

I AM GRATEFUL FIRST of all to Alanna Nobbs, Larry Welborn, and the Department of Ancient History at Macquarie University for taking a risk and bringing me out to Australia to work on early Christian manuscripts. This book definitely bears the stamp of the unique environment of Macquarie's Department of Ancient History, where the study of the papyrological and epigraphic record of ancient Christians has been central for decades. I also owe a huge debt to Gill Ellis and the whole Arts Research Office at Macquarie for teaching me how to navigate the Australian grant system, a system to which I am equally indebted. Funding that supported this research came from the Department of Ancient History at Macquarie, the Society for the Study of Early Christianity, a Macquarie University Research Fellowship, and a Discovery Early Career Research Award from the Australian Research Council.

The last revisions on the book took place during an enjoyable stay at Aarhus University. I am obliged especially to René Falkenberg and Kasper Bro Larsen for making that happen. Special thanks are due to Paul Dilley, Melissa Moreton, and everyone at the University of Iowa involved in the Mellon Sawyer Seminar on manuscripts across premodern Eurasia, which was an eye-opening experience that helped to broaden my perspective on the history of book production at a key moment of the project.

Many of the ideas presented in this book were first hammered out in talks presented at Fordham University, Princeton University, Trinity College Melbourne, the University of Manchester, the University of Notre Dame, the University of Sydney, the University of Texas at Austin, and Yale University. The Papyrology and Early Christian Backgrounds group at the annual meetings of the Society of Biblical Literature has become my home away from home for the past decade, and I very much appreciate the organizers, fellow presenters, and audience members at these sessions. I would be remiss not to thank Ann Hanson, who first introduced me to papyri and changed the direction of my research.

Thanks are also due to the curators of the many manuscripts and archives that I was fortunate enough to study. I express my gratitude to the staff at the Bentley Historical Library and the Papyrology Collection at the University of Michigan; the Biblioteca Apostolica Vaticana; the British Library; the Chester Beatty Library; the Houghton Library at Harvard University; the John Rylands Library at the University of Manchester; the Pierpont Morgan Library; the Magdalen College, Sackler, and Bodleian libraries at the University of Oxford; the Scheide Library and the Seeley G. Mudd Manuscript Library at Princeton University; the Special Collections at the Claremont Colleges Library; and the Special Collections at the University of Western Australia. Stasa Bibic, Florence Darbre, and the entire staff of the Fondation Martin Bodmer were especially helpful and accommodating during my visits to Cologny, and David Hogge's guidance in the archives at the Freer Gallery at the Smithsonian Institution was indispensable.

This book has evolved over a number of years and owes much to the patience and guidance of Jennifer Banks, Heather Gold, Susan Laity, and the production team at Yale University Press. Jessie Dolch provided expert copyediting on this challenging manuscript. I am deeply grateful to all these people.

One of the real pleasures of undertaking this project has been benefiting from the boundless enthusiasm and knowledge of Anne-Marie Luijendijk. I have learned a great deal by watching how she frames questions about early Christian book culture, and I'm thankful for her input on the manuscript at several points in the project. I'm also obliged to others who read part or all of the manuscript at various stages: Roger Bagnall, Doug Boin, Josephine Dru, Sean Durbin, Felicity Harley-McGowan, Edwin Judge, Hugo Lundhaug, Dale Martin, Julia Miller, Roberta Mazza, and Gregg Schwendner.

Many other friends have patiently answered questions over the past few years. I single out Malcolm Choat, Cavan Concannon, Stephen Emmel, Larry Hurtado, D. C. Parker, Dan Sharp, and Sofía Torallas Tovar. Their advice saved me from many errors. Those that remain are on me.

I began this project just after I married Mary Jane Cuyler, who has been an inspiring conversation partner through every step of the research, writing, and revision process. Her insightful feedback and admirable lack of tolerance for scholarly "fibs" have made this a much better and more honest work.

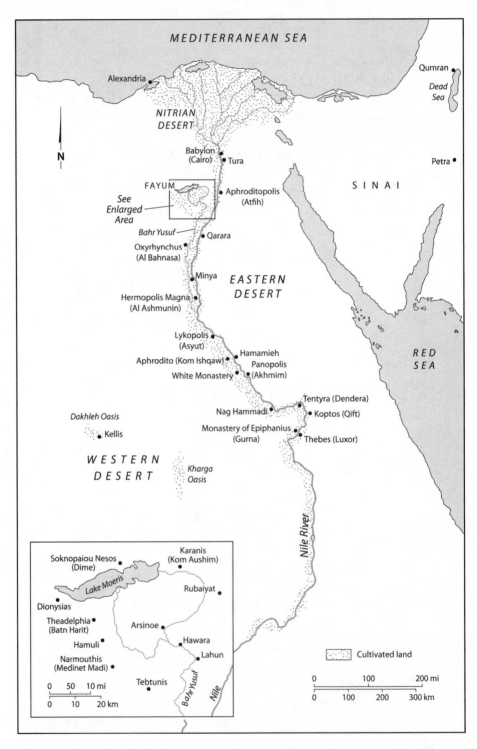

Map showing locations in Egypt mentioned in the text.

(Cartography by Bill Nelson.)

Prologue: Reintroducing the Earliest Christian Manuscripts

LATE IN 1907, IT was publicly revealed that the American businessman Charles Lang Freer (1854–1919) had acquired a group of four early Christian books from an antiquities dealer in Egypt. Freer, who made a fortune from the production of railcars in Detroit during the 1890s, had established himself as a discerning art collector well before he first traveled to Egypt in 1906.[1] Shortly after his arrival there, he spent December 17 and 18 with two Greek scholars looking over a group of manuscripts for sale by a local dealer.[2] His diary entry for Wednesday, December 19, is terse: "Cairo: Bought manuscripts in forenoon & paid for them during afternoon."[3] For the next twelve months, only a select circle of experts knew the significance of what Freer had bought. Then, in December 1907, one of these scholars announced to the world that Freer's purchase had consisted of

—a Greek manuscript on parchment containing Deuteronomy and Joshua datable by its handwriting to the fourth or fifth century CE
—a Greek manuscript on parchment containing the Psalms datable by its handwriting to the sixth or seventh century
—a Greek manuscript on parchment containing the four

I

gospels (in the order Matthew, John, Luke, and then Mark) datable by its handwriting to the fifth or sixth century, enclosed in wooden covers decorated with portraits of the evangelists

  —a Greek manuscript on parchment containing the letters of Paul datable by its handwriting to the fifth century.[4]

The manuscript of the gospels was in an especially fine state of preservation and was considered to be nearly as old as the earliest known Greek copies of the New Testament. It also preserved an unusual ending for the Gospel According to Mark, an ending unknown from other early Greek witnesses that included the ominous line "Christ replied to them, 'The term of years of Satan's power has been fulfilled, but other terrible things draw near.'" This news generated a great deal of interest, not only among biblical scholars and historians, but also among the general public. Newspaper headlines spun the story in a variety of ways:[5]

BIBLE ERRORS TO BE CORRECTED BY NEWLY FOUND MANUSCRIPTS: Valuable Writings Locked Up in Detroit Safety Vault Supply Lost Parts

A NEW VERSE FOR ST. MARK'S GOSPEL: Discovered in Ancient Manuscript Owned by Detroit Man . . . Charles L. Freer, Millionaire Archaeologist Bought Priceless Bit of Vellum From Curio Dealer at Cairo

CHRISTIAN WORLD EAGER FOR FREER MANUSCRIPT: Believed That Important Passages Will Be Supplied by Newly Discovered Scripture

NOT EXCITED OVER C. L. FREER'S FIND: Local ministers do not believe it teaches anything that is new

NEW VERSE IS ADDED TO GOSPEL OF MARK: Contained in an Ancient Manuscript Dug from the Sands of Akhmim. First revealed in Chicago

Marvelous Story of the Discovery of an Authentic Manuscript of the Bible: An American Secures the Precious Relic of the Famous Alexandrian Library; Words of Christ, Lost 1,300 Years, Are Thus Recovered and Officially Declared

The catchwords in the headlines indicate why the manuscripts were thought to be important: They were ancient and might be a conduit to authentic knowledge about Jesus and early Christianity. The headlines also give a sense of the allure of the manuscripts: "Newly Discovered Scripture," "Dug from the Sands," found by a "Millionaire Archaeologist," "First revealed in Chicago," and now kept in Detroit. That is to say, early Christian treasures from Egypt had now been taken to America's heartland—a "Marvelous Story" (Figure 0.1).

Figure 0.1. Newspaper clipping from press cutting book, tentatively identified as from the *Chicago Examiner*, January 5, 1908.

(Charles Lang Freer Papers, Freer Gallery of Art and Arthur M. Sackler Gallery Archives, Smithsonian Institution, Washington, D.C.)

After the excitement of the first announcement came the serious work of editing and publishing the books. This task was given to Henry A. Sanders (1868–1956), a junior professor of Latin at the University of Michigan, who worked with remarkable speed and acumen to produce a study of the text of the Deuteronomy and Joshua manuscript by 1910. Freer supplied the necessary funding to produce a companion photographic facsimile of stunning quality.[6] But it was the release of the study and facsimile of the gospel manuscript in 1912 that brought a second wave of publicity that seems at least as intense as the first.[7] Newspapers across the country reproduced leaves of the manuscript and retold the tale of its purchase. The *New York Times* ran a front-page story on May 13, 1913, and then had a longer feature the following Sunday with illustrations of the book's decorated covers (Figure 0.2).[8] The stories announced the new publications as well as scholars' reactions, and they noted that the gospel manuscript, along with Freer's other ancient books, were to be kept in the art gallery Freer was funding for the Smithsonian Institution in Washington, D.C. Thus the books are sometimes known as "the Washington Manuscripts" and the gospel manuscript as Codex Washingtonensis. With its new name, the codex was in no way inferior, the newspapers claimed, to other famous Bibles around the world: "This happy find of Mr. Freer's places the United States on the list with Russia, which owns the Sinaiticus manuscript at St. Petersburg; with Italy and its Codex Vaticanus at Rome, with England's Alexandrinus at London and Codex Bezae at Cambridge."[9] Freer's gospel manuscript had also, by some accounts, aged significantly since its unveiling as a "fifth or sixth century" manuscript in 1907. According to the *New York Times* of May 18, 1913, the date of the Freer manuscript of the gospels had been established as "the third, or at the latest the early fourth, century."[10] Yet, on May 14, the same paper had cited an article in the *Times* of London stating that the book "probably belongs to the fifth or sixth centuries."[11] Both reports are somewhat curious, since, after an extensive discussion, Sanders himself had concluded that most of the evidence "seems to point to the fourth century, though the beginning of the fifth must still be admitted as a possibility."[12] With regard to the place where the manuscripts were discovered, Sanders offered only mysterious hints: "While I am not as yet allowed to publish the exact spot where

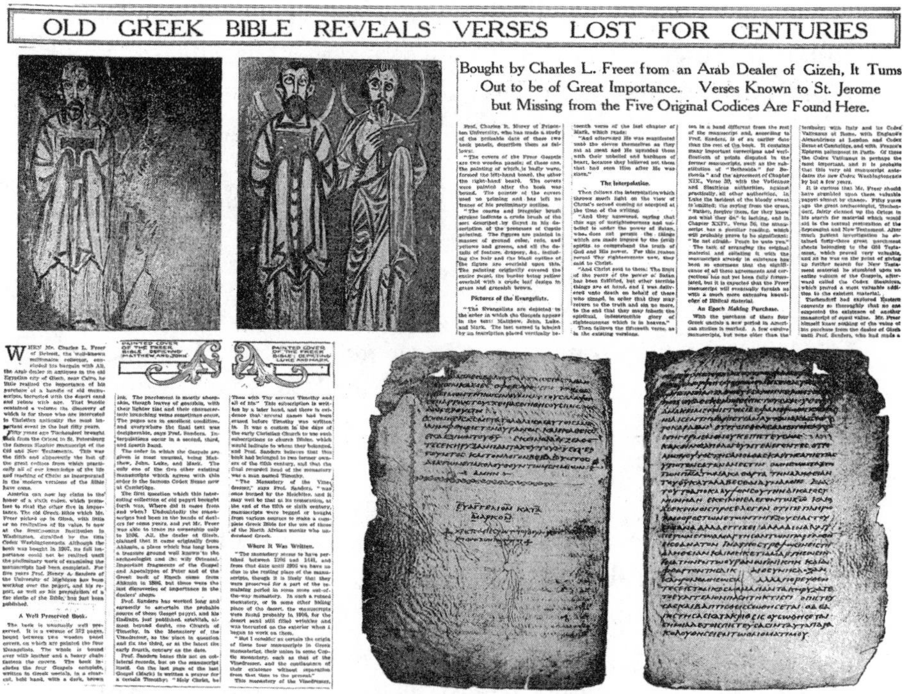
OLD GREEK BIBLE REVEALS VERSES LOST FOR CENTURIES

Bought by Charles L. Freer from an Arab Dealer of Gizeh, It Turns Out to be of Great Importance. Verses Known to St. Jerome but Missing from the Five Original Codices Are Found Here.

Figure 0.2. Article announcing the publication of the Freer gospels, the *New York Times*, May 18, 1913, sec. 7, p. 8.

(Image courtesy of the *New York Times*.)

the MSS were found, the statements made by the finders fix it definitely and are consistent with the evidence gathered."[13]

But even now, more than one hundred years after the publication of Freer's books, what do we actually *know*, both about the age of the manuscripts and about their origins? Paleography, or the determination of the age of a manuscript through the analysis of handwriting, was in its infancy in the early twentieth century, and it still remains a highly subjective exercise to this day. While Sanders ultimately concluded that the Freer manuscript of the gospels was most likely copied in the fourth century, some scholars continued to believe it was a product of the fifth or even the sixth century.[14] The most recent assessment of the age of the gospel manuscript concluded that we are simply not in a position to offer a precise date for the codex on the basis of handwriting and closed with a plea for radiocarbon analysis.[15] The case with the other manuscripts is no clearer.

One highly respected specialist has assigned the Deuteronomy and Joshua manuscript to the sixth century, rather than the fourth or fifth.[16] Another authority places the Psalms codex in the fifth century, instead of the sixth or seventh.[17] Expert opinions can differ by a hundred years or more.

Our knowledge of the provenance of the manuscripts is equally shaky. The first reports said that they had come from Akhmim, a city in southern, or "Upper" Egypt, but this story, like just about every story of the provenance of ancient manuscripts, turns out to be a lot more complicated when we scratch the surface. In that initial public announcement, Sanders described the origin of the manuscripts as follows:

> Mr. Charles L. Freer of Detroit, Michigan, has in his possession four very ancient manuscripts of parts of the Bible. He purchased these early in 1907, in Cairo, from a dealer named Ali Arabi,[18] who stated that the manuscripts came from Akhmîm (the ancient Panopolis). . . . What I have thus far learned of the four manuscripts is not inconsistent with the statement that they came from Akhmîm, and I am now inclined to believe that they once formed parts of a Bible in use in Upper Egypt. Either during or soon after the Moslem conquest in 639 A.D., this Bible ceased to be needed because of the withdrawal of the Greek Christians, and so was either buried or lost.[19]

In the wake of this announcement, Carl Schmidt, an expert in early Christian manuscripts, claimed with utter certainty that the books came from the White Monastery located across the Nile from Akhmim, while a professor at the University of Chicago was equally sure the books had been associated with a monastery in the Nitrian Desert, some six hundred kilometers north of Akhmim.[20] When Sanders published on the topic again a year later, his own views had shifted considerably: "Professor Schmidt has probably been deceived by one of the numerous Arab stories; all are of equal value with the first one told, viz. that the Mss. came from Akhmim. To accept the White Monastery as the last home of the Mss. would imply that this first story was near the truth. Yet any one acquainted with Arab stories would advise us to look in every other direction first, as toward the Nitrian Desert, or the Fayoum, or the region toward Sinai, if we wish to find the last resting place of this ancient Bible."[21]

This change in opinion was probably due to investigations being undertaken by Charles Freer himself. In the winter of 1907–1908, he had returned to Egypt to try to find out more precisely the location of the discovery and to acquire any other manuscripts that might have been part of the find. Upon arrival, he immediately met with the dealer Ali Arabi, who changed his story completely and now told Freer that the books had come from Dime, ancient Soknopaiou Nesos in the Fayum region (see the inset map in the front matter). The area is well north of Akhmim but not so far north as the monasteries of the Nitrian Desert. Furthermore, Ali provided Freer with a detailed story of the discovery of the manuscripts by a man known only as "the digger." Among Freer's papers is a breathless summary of the meeting with Ali Arabi, which reads like a mystery novel:

> The four mss. I bought last year from Arabi, were dug up at night, about one month before I first saw them, by "the digger." . . . The place where these four manuscripts were dug up is called Medinet Dimay. It is in the Fayoum . . . Dimay was once a big city with a big wall around it. Some of the wall still remains. In the middle of the big city stands the ruins of the monastery. . . . The "digger" was the first man to dig there and during his first digging he found the four bibles you have. Found them all in one place, only a little digging, one corner of all the big place, many more papyrus must be there.[22]

Freer, along with the scholars working on the publication of the manuscripts, did not disclose this news and deliberately allowed the spread of misinformation regarding the location of the find. Questions about the place of discovery were referred to Schmidt's article about the White Monastery.[23] If other manuscripts from the same find were available, Freer wanted to be the one to get them. And Dime was the place he expected to find them.[24]

The most recent and thorough investigation of the provenance of the Freer books undertaken by Kent D. Clarke (published in 2006) offers a qualified acceptance of Ali Arabi's story: "Many of the details pertaining to both the general region and specific location where the Washington Manuscripts were supposedly discovered reveal close similarities to independent descriptions of Dimai and its environs. . . . If the Washington Manuscripts were not actually discovered at this location, a great deal of thought and effort went into correctly describing Dimai and the surrounding area."[25] But a number of problems remain. For one thing, Ali Arabi's accurate knowledge of Dime by no means necessitates that Freer's books were found there, only that the dealer or his informant had visited the site. Also, "the digger" could not have been the first person to set a spade to Soknopaiou Nesos. The site already had a reasonably well-documented history of excavation, especially during the second half of the nineteenth century. The famous British manuscript hunters Bernard P. Grenfell and Arthur S. Hunt had dug there at the turn of the century.[26] Sanders himself would visit the site of Soknopaiou Nesos in 1913 and find that it did not at all meet his expectations. There were no visible remains of a monastery. By 1920, at least one experienced Cairo dealer, Maurice Nahman, was certain that the Freer manuscripts were found not at Dime but farther south in the Fayum at Batn Harit (ancient Theadelphia).[27] Nevertheless, the University of Michigan carried out excavations at Dime during 1931–1932 and concluded that the area "appeared to have been abandoned about the middle of the third century," well before the Freer manuscripts were copied.[28] More recent and extensive archaeological investigations at the site have uncovered a single fragmentary Coptic papyrus perhaps datable to the sixth century and three ostraca, or potsherds, with Coptic writing, as well as one ostracon that may display a roughly drawn Christian symbol. These findings, along with the presence of later ceramics and other signs of later human and animal occupation of the site, led the excavators to conclude that after the site was abandoned, its main temple may have become a remote monastic hermitage.[29] While it is of course possible that the Freer books were found at this site, this is not exactly the setting where one would imagine the production or use of luxurious books like the Freer volumes.[30] At the end of the day, the only real connection between the books and the town of Dime is the word of an antiquities dealer who had also claimed that the manuscripts were found elsewhere. Nobody involved with the books—the dealer, the buyer, and to a degree even the scholars who studied and published the manuscripts—was completely forthcoming about provenance. The result is an obfuscation of origins at every level. Thus, we don't know exactly how old the books are, and we don't know where in Egypt they came from.[31]

This is not to say that we have no secure knowledge about these books. We know a good deal about the texts they carry, especially the very peculiar text of the gospel manuscript, which captivated textual critics of the New Testament for decades after its discovery.[32] But the books themselves quite quickly faded from public view. The Freer manuscripts have rarely been on display.[33] Subsequent high-profile purchases of ancient Christian manuscripts from Egypt were either larger than Freer's set of books (such as the wealth of Coptic books acquired by J. Pierpont Morgan in 1911; see Chapter 3) or even older than the Freer manuscripts (such as the Greek papyrus books bought by Chester Beatty in 1930; see Chapter 4). Then in the 1940s, not just a forgotten verse, but whole texts that had been lost from view showed up on the antiquities market and were said to have come from Nag Hammadi, a site whose very name now conjures up the idea of "secret gnostic heresies." In the 1950s another collection of well-preserved books emerged. These were mostly purchased by the Swiss collector Martin Bodmer and included Greek papyrus copies of the gospels of Luke and John that were thought to date from perhaps as early as the second century (see Chapter 5). The appearance of these manuscripts was surely a key reason why Freer's books, despite the excitement they generated early on, have fallen into what one prominent scholar has described as a state of "comparative neglect" such that academics do not often pay serious attention to them, and "the general public today scarcely knows of them."[34]

I have opened with this extended consideration of Freer's books because their story is instructive in a number of ways. First, it illustrates how little we know with any certainty about the dates and provenance of many early Christian manuscripts. Second, it emphasizes that our lack of knowledge is often the result of the operations of the antiquities market. Third, we can see how academic publications and the popular media can provide both information and misinformation about early Christian manuscripts. Fourth, only through a combination of archival research, archaeological exploration, and the use of newer technologies such as radiocarbon analysis can we begin to increase our knowledge of these artifacts. Finally, even the scholarly loss of interest in the Freer manuscripts is illuminating. Historically, the value of ancient Christian manuscripts has been gauged primarily in relation to their ability to provide access to authentic knowledge about the "original text" of the Bible, especially the New Testament. When seemingly older Christian books appeared on the scene, Freer's manuscripts receded into the background. A related issue is the fact that Freer's manuscripts were copied on parchment, that is, animal skin, rather than papyrus, a writing surface manufactured from the reeds of the *Cyperus papyrus* and related plants. The subsequent finds associated with Chester Beatty and Martin Bodmer mentioned above included papyrus books thought to be very old, which has tended to give Christian manuscripts preserved on papyrus an air of prestige in both the popular and academic imaginations.

To state flatly that Christian manuscripts have been understudied would be inaccurate, especially as regards those that preserve parts of the New Testament. First and foremost, papyrologists have made important contributions to the study of early Christian manuscripts. The academic division of labor is such that papyrologists generally edit and publish the earliest Christian manuscripts and therefore usually have the first word about any newly discovered books. Papyrological specialists have also frequently been intrigued by the apparent Christian preference for the codex (the modern form of a bound book with pages) as opposed to the roll, which had been the medium of choice for the transmission of literature for centuries.[35] At the same time, generations of biblical scholars have expended an enormous amount of time and energy using ancient manuscripts to try to determine the "original text" of the documents of the New Testament. Even though the goal of establishing a single, original text has come to seem more and more problematic in recent years, this work continues.[36] Manuals of New Testament textual criticism will thus often introduce a selection of early Christian books in relation to their value for reconstructing the early text of the New Testament, but the details of the ancient manuscripts themselves are often sparse in such works, and they are, naturally, limited to manuscripts containing parts of the New Testament.[37] As an outgrowth of the text-critical task, a number of scholars have come to pay close attention to the "scribal habits" of the copyists of individual manuscripts.[38] These studies often illuminate physical features of manuscripts in a helpful way with close descriptions of the written page, but they ultimately function in service to the text-critical enterprise.[39] Other scholars have undertaken in-depth studies of the copyists of Christian books and used the manuscripts to think further about issues regarding church history, such as the formation of the New Testament canon.[40]

Thus, while biblical scholars have for the most part focused intently on the texts contained within our earliest Christian manuscripts and papyrologists have exploited these manuscripts for the study of certain historical phenomena, the same kind of attention has not been paid to the books themselves as three-dimensional archaeological artifacts worthy of study in their own right. Many of our most important early Christian manuscripts were apparently found, like the Freer manuscripts, as parts of ancient collections of books. The contours of those groups are sometimes unclear, but even the parts of the broader context that we *do* know tend to be neglected in favor of the isolated study of individual manuscripts, or even of individual texts within a manuscript. This lack of consideration of the books as physical objects has resulted in implausibly precise (and often implausibly early) dates being assigned to a number of important manuscripts. In fact, despite the useful data sometimes provided by factors such as the archaeological context of the collections, the codicology of the manuscript (its size and layout), the binding techniques used to assemble the books, and the availability of technology like radiocarbon analysis, early Christian manuscripts are most frequently dated by means of only paleography, which is, as we will see again and again, a deeply problematic practice. What we need is greater attention to the books themselves as artifacts, to the archaeology of early Christian manuscripts.

In saying this, I do not mean to imply that no work at all has been done in this area. Conferences and collections of essays dedicated to studying manuscripts in context have been appearing for several years now, and detailed studies of individual manuscripts continue to be produced.[41] Three synthetic studies written over the past quarter century need to be mentioned at the outset, as they especially help to frame my own project. Published in 1995, Harry Gamble's *Books and Readers in the Early Church* brought together a wealth of evidence for the production and consumption of books by ancient Christians. Who made early Christian books? Who read them? What did "publication" mean in an ancient context? Gamble addressed these questions by mining the literature written by early Christian authors for references to books and reading practices and weaving together a rich history of the place of the book in early Christian groups. While the extant remains of ancient books do occasionally feature in Gamble's discussions, he drew mainly from literary evidence, with the physical artifacts playing a secondary role. I have written the present book in part to complement Gamble's excellent work by turning attention to the surviving books themselves and what we can know about their age and their histories, both ancient and modern.

In 2006, the field received a second strong push in the right direction with the publication of Larry Hurtado's collection of essays *The Earliest Christian Artifacts: Manuscripts and Christian Origins.*[42] Pointing out that a large portion of professional scholars of the New Testament lack familiarity with the manuscripts of the New Testament, Hurtado presented a series of studies on the contents, forms, and scribal features of the earliest Christian manuscripts (those he recognized as predating the fourth century). I very much share Hurtado's sense that the field of biblical studies would be well served by an improved knowledge of Christian manuscripts. Yet, although Hurtado's book has a good deal of useful information in it, some features of its organization tend to obscure what I am calling the archaeology of the manuscripts. For instance, when Hurtado first introduces "The Texts," he does so by dividing them into "Old Testament Texts," "New Testament Texts," and "Other Early Christian Writings." Hurtado rightly flags the potential anachronism involved in such an approach (and the tacit reinforcement of modern canonical divisions should also be noted).[43] What concerns me more, however, is the decontextualization that this framework causes. That is to say, such an organizational scheme makes it more difficult to see the fact that what we call "Old Testament" and "New Testament" texts sometimes occur in the same physical book or that such "biblical" books seem to have been found together not only with what we would now call "apocryphal" books but also with non-Christian writings. It is my hope that the present book will supplement Hurtado's studies with more detailed discussions of the major groups of early Christian manuscripts *as groups*, to the degree that such groups can be established.

Whereas Gamble and Hurtado have approached early Christian books from within the field of biblical studies, Roger Bagnall has recently given a bird's-eye view of the study of Christian manuscripts from the perspective of a papyrologist. The published version of a set of lectures, Bagnall's *Early Christian Books in Egypt*, appeared in 2009 and laid down a series of challenges. Observing what he characterized as "the excessively self-enclosed character and absence of self-awareness" in the scholarship on early Christian books, Bagnall charged that much of what we think we know about them is "profoundly at odds with fundamental social realities of the ancient world and with basic probability."[44] Bagnall provided an updated treatment of topics perennially interesting to papyrologists, such as the economics of book production (How much did books cost? How many Christians owned books?) and the spread of the codex (Might the phenomenon be as much Roman as Christian?), but the largest portion of the book is dedicated to a problem Hurtado also raised: the uncertain nature of paleographic dating.[45] Bagnall emphasized that these paleographic judgments about the ages of early Christian manuscripts deserve more scrutiny than they have generally received because of the key role they play in historical questions concerning the growth of Christianity in Egypt and the development and spread of the technology of the codex. What I attempt to do is offer this scrutiny by way of taking seriously "the character of written texts as archaeological artifacts."[46]

And when we think of early Christian manuscripts as archaeological artifacts, one of the first things we notice is that they rarely have a definitive archaeological context. Most of them were not excavated by professional archaeologists using modern methods of precisely and accurately recording the place of the find and the surrounding material. Many were instead discovered by accident, looted and sold on the antiquities market, or even just excavated by scholars before the advent of "scientific" archaeology. Thus, accurate archaeological information about early Christian books is not easily available. This absence of secure knowledge about these manuscripts creates a vacuum that is often filled by what I would call an "imaginary archaeology" of Christian manuscripts (or, less charitably, a "fake archaeology" of Christian manuscripts). According to this imaginary archaeology, Christian manuscripts are discovered from the sands of Egypt and are essentially self-interpreting. They have secure dates, and they clearly confirm or disconfirm some fact about early Christian history. Whether it is the "reliability" of the biblical text at stake or "lost Christianities" supposedly restored by the discovery of so-called heretical texts, early Christian books are often characterized as providing clear evidence of the past: revealing, unveiling, demonstrating, and confirming. This kind of imaginary archaeology seduces even competent biblical scholars, who regularly speak of "the archaeological discovery" of Christian manuscripts that have no clear archaeological context and proceed to use these manuscripts confidently as the basis for their reconstructions of various aspects of Christian history.[47] Even when the role of the antiquities trade is acknowledged, it is usually in the form of the repetition (and embellishment) of one particular form of a discovery or acquisition story, with seemingly no awareness of, or concern for, the existence of equally plausible divergent or contradictory accounts. My intention is to make this sort of scholarly error less frequent by "reintroducing" the earliest Christian books as archaeological artifacts.

The present book, then, is a double-edged sword. On one hand, I want to establish what we are able to know about these manuscripts as archaeological artifacts. And there is a certain amount that we *can* learn about them. We can look closely at some of the best-preserved examples in order to better understand the ancient technologies of book production (Chapter 1), take seriously all our options for establishing dates for these books (Chapter 2), and try to trace the histories of these books, whether that means examining archaeological sites and practices (as in the case of Oxyrhynchus in Chapter 6) or following the sometimes complicated series of buyers and sellers of manuscripts to establish which items might actually have belonged to a given ancient collection of manuscripts (as in the case of the Beatty Biblical Papyri [Chapter 4] and the Bodmer

Papyri [Chapter 5]). On the other hand, I cannot provide the "real history" of these books to displace the imaginary archaeology. Instead, the overall effect of my research is to raise consciousness about how messy and fragmentary our knowledge about these books is. In order to appreciate how these manuscripts can help us know something about the *ancient* world, we first have to learn as much as possible about the *modern* history of these books. In the pages that follow, I frequently direct attention toward antiquities dealers and popular media reception, topics that are not always on the radars of students of early Christian manuscripts. I am convinced that these factors must be considered if one is to gain an adequate understanding of how knowledge about these manuscripts is produced.

In the course of my discussion, I often call into question the credibility of information solicited from dealers and local Egyptians about discoveries of early Christian books. Professional antiquities dealers are out to make a profit, and everyone agrees that their word should be taken with a grain of salt. But those scholars who have cast doubt upon reports from the finders of manuscripts have sometimes been accused of imperialism or orientalism.[48] It is important to be attuned to such possibilities, but it is equally important to be aware of the ways in which imbalances of power in colonial settings can affect the production of knowledge. For example, even well into the second half of the twentieth century, European and American scholars in Egypt were in the habit of offering locals *baksheesh*, tips or bribes, for information about manuscripts and other discoveries.[49] It is thus not surprising to find locals telling scholars what they believe the scholars want to hear. I view this less as dishonesty per se and more as an example of "everyday forms of resistance," attempts by locals to make the best of a situation of unequal power.[50] Thus, to simply take the statements solicited from locals at face value is a dubious policy. My own position is that all accounts, both those of scholars and those of nonscholars, ought to be subjected to critical evaluation. Just as often as I question the reliability of reports from Egyptians, I challenge the reports of "Western" scholars when they seem to lack a basis in evidence.

Before getting under way, I should say a few words about spelling conventions, terminology, resources, and methodology. Most of this book deals with manuscripts found in Egypt, where the arid climate helped to preserve papyrus and parchment. My sources employ a variety of transliterations of Arabic toponyms and personal names, and I have not tried to systematize them. Egyptian cities and towns mentioned in the book can be identified on the book's maps (in the front matter, Figure 4.1, and Figure 5.1).

Papyrus manuscripts are usually named using a set of conventional abbreviations in the form "P.xxx." followed by one or more numbers. For example, P.Oxy. 2.208 (or P.Oxy. II 208) refers to the remains of a single papyrus sheet of the Gospel According to John found in the Egyptian city of Oxyrhynchus and published in the second volume of the series *The Oxyrhynchus Papyri*. P.Bodmer II refers to a nearly complete papyrus codex of the Gospel According to John published in the *Papyrus Bodmer* series. For the most part, I follow the key to these abbreviations that can be found online at http:// papyri.info/docs/checklist. I occasionally deviate from these guidelines for various reasons. For example, most scholars know the Chester Beatty codex of Numbers and Deuteronomy as "Chester Beatty Codex VI," but according to the checklist, it would be P.Beatty V (because it appeared in the fifth volume published in the series). To avoid confusion, I refer to the Beatty Biblical Papyri by their traditional numbering rather than using any "P" abbreviations. I also use Arabic instead of Roman numerals for publications with many volumes (thus P.Oxy. 78.5129 instead of P.Oxy. LXXVIII 5129).

The bibliography on many of these manuscripts is quite large, especially concerning those manuscripts that preserve substantial portions of the documents of the New Testament. Citing all the relevant literature for every manuscript I mention would be cumbersome, so when I refer to manuscripts, I also provide a reference to the relevant entry in the Leuven Database of Ancient Books (http:// www.trismegistos.org/ldab/) in the form "LDAB xxxx." The Washington codices, for example, are LDAB numbers 3288 (Deuteronomy-Joshua), 3220 (the Psalms), 2985 (the gospels), and 3044 (the Pauline letters). The bibliography in the Leuven Database is not exhaustive, but it provides a good start for curious readers who may want to follow up with specific manuscripts I cite.

Although I have provided Leuven Database numbers in order to cut down on my references, this book still has a lot of notes. This was a considered choice on my part. One of the things I am trying to highlight and combat in this book is a certain sloppiness that plagues the study of early Christian manuscripts, that is, a tendency to simply repeat the assertions of earlier writers without checking to see whether any actual evidence exists to back up the claims (Chapter 7 is in fact a case study of the negative consequences of this ubiquitous practice). For that reason, I opted for thoroughness rather than concision in the notes, especially when it comes to questions of dating. If I say an artifact dates to a certain year or period, I provide the evidence in the notes to show how I reached that conclusion, or at the very least I try to refer accurately to the source from which I obtained the date (I was surprised by how often people *don't* do this). Not every reader will be interested in every date and every note, but it's my way of keeping myself honest.

It should already be clear that I want to be relentless in my focus on these manuscripts *as objects*. At the same time, I also want to avoid losing sight of the fact that it is groups of people that imbue these objects with special meaning. Despite the current trend in some circles toward investing inanimate objects with agency, I remain convinced with Simon Goldhill and many others that "things require people to make them talk, even and especially within the rhetoric which insists that 'things speak for themselves.' . . . Things do not have a life of their own, simply awaiting the excavator's spade, but always take shape and meaning within a cultural milieu, a cultural milieu which is reciprocally created and moulded by things. Things take on cultural authority because they can be taken to express value, ideology, history; things can lose their authority because this invisible, soft power is not integral to them."[51]

At one level, the human agency behind manuscripts is obvious: Whoever inscribed these manuscripts did so for a reason and brought them into existence. Similarly, ancient users wrote corrections and notes and made repairs. But it's not just these ancient copyists and users whom I want to highlight. The perceived importance of these manuscripts has a lot to do with the modern systems of classification that scholars use to organize them. For example, biblical scholars call a number of the pieces we will be examining in this book "New Testament papyri" and invest them with a great deal of value. Textual critics of the New Testament regularly refer to manuscripts containing New Testament documents written on papyrus by using a Gothic letter "P" (𝔓) followed by a number (for example, 𝔓1 or 𝔓66).[52] Within New Testament studies, the very word "papyrus" carries a certain aura of antiquity and authority.[53] At first glance, this seems logical enough. These manuscripts contain parts of the New Testament, and they are written on papyrus. Yet, both parts of the description are problematic.

For one thing, it is not immediately obvious why texts copied on one particular writing surface should be segregated from texts written on other surfaces.[54] In fact, this was not always the case. Before the early twentieth century, the few known papyrus manuscripts carrying texts of the New Testament were simply grouped together with the more numerous parchment manuscripts containing either continuous texts of the New Testament books or manuscripts with selected readings (lectionaries).[55] The placement of the papyri in a separate list is usually said to originate with the 1908 handbook of Caspar René Gregory (1864–1917).[56] In fact, the idea goes back to at least 1901, when Frederic G. Kenyon (1863–1952) proposed a list for papyri (Pap.[1], Pap.[2], Pap.[3], etc.) that was to be separate from the traditional list of parchment manuscripts of the New Testament. The parchment manuscripts had long been abbreviated using letters of the alphabet—A for the Codex Alexandrinus, B for the Codex Vaticanus, and so on. Kenyon wanted a separate list for the papyri on the grounds that letters, which were in short supply, should not be wasted on small, scrappy fragments of papyrus.[57] Gregory preferred to keep a single list and simply reserve the letter "P" for all papyrus manuscripts, which would be individually identified with a number (P1, P2, P3, etc.), just as some letters of the alphabet already did double or triple duty (for example, D[ea] for Codex Bezae of the gospels [*evangelia*] and Acts; D[p] for a different book, Codex Claromontanus, that contains Paul's letters). Eventually, however, Gregory agreed to Kenyon's suggestion to establish a separate list for papyri. But as the twentieth century progressed, more substantial papyrus remains came to light, including nearly complete books containing works from the New Testament. Kenyon's original reasoning for establishing an independent classification for papyri thus became less and less compelling. Nevertheless, disciplinary inertia has kept the lists separate with the result that texts preserved on papyrus tend to enjoy an unearned prestige.

The "New Testament" in "New Testament papyri" is no less problematic. If some scholars are correct that a few Christian papyri were copied as early as the second century (as we will see, none can actually be dated with any certainty to that period), then the designation of any such manuscript as "New Testament" would be highly ambiguous, if not totally meaningless. The very phrase "New Testament" (Greek: *kainē diathēkē*) was still only tentatively being applied to Christian writings at the end of the second century.[58] And even after that time, it was not at all a settled question exactly *which* books would be included under such a heading. That problem would be debated for centuries. Furthermore, as best we can tell, none of our extant manuscripts copied on papyrus contains even half of the twenty-seven documents that would come to be called "the New Testament" in later centuries. Thus, one can in all honesty say that there isn't really any such thing as "a New Testament papyrus."

I draw attention to this system not because I think it is useless or unhelpful, but rather because I want to emphasize that our systems of classification are not in any sense natural or neutral. They create meanings and provide certain artifacts with importance and power while at the same time directing attention away from other artifacts and generally distracting us from the archaeology of the manuscripts. For instance, consider the designation 𝔓72. For biblical scholars, this sign refers to a Greek manuscript containing Jude and the two letters of Peter. But the codex that contained these works (LDAB 2565) also contained several other early Christian writings, including the Nativity of Mary, the "apocryphal" correspondence of Paul and the Corinthians, the eleventh Ode of Solomon, and the paschal sermon of Melito of Sardis. What is more, the "New Testament" texts, Jude and the letters of Peter, appear to have originally been parts of different books before being bound together secondarily. Referring to these three works in isolation as the "New Testament papyrus" 𝔓72 is at best confusing and at worst misleading.[59] The use of Gregory's "𝔓" numbers tends to flatten manuscripts into a single dimension— their usefulness in the text-critical enterprise. For these reasons, I for the most part avoid Gregory's "𝔓" numbers in this book. I refer to the manuscripts using the usual papyrological abbreviations or other customary designations, which, I think, do a better job of keeping us as aware as possible of the archaeological contexts and/or modern collection histories of the manuscripts.[60]

Finally, having made this critique, I am not unaware of the irony that this book focuses on the Beatty Biblical Papyri, the Bodmer Papyri, and the Oxyrhynchus Christian materials—groups of manuscripts that have gained fame in large part because they have been regarded as including several of the "earliest New Testament papyri." And because of the nature of these collections, my focus is mostly limited to Greek and Coptic books to the exclusion of, for example, early Christian books copied in Syriac.[61] That broader contextualization would be useful, but I must draw lines somewhere, and coming from a background in biblical studies, I hope that a focus on these three corpora will provide the type of critical introductory book I wish had existed back when I first began my own work on early Christian manuscripts.

CHAPTER ONE

The Early Christian Book

T HE MAJORITY OF CHRISTIAN books copied before the
fifth century CE survive in the form of a single fragmentary
leaf, or, if we are lucky, fragments of multiple leaves. Some
books, however, survived antiquity completely intact, or
nearly so. Of these, many that were discovered before the middle of
the twentieth century were either rebound in modern bindings or
disassembled by placing the individual pages between glass plates,
with little or no attention paid to recording the details of how they
were originally put together. We are fortunate that in a few cases,
records of varying quality were kept, and in a few very exceptional
cases, ancient Christian books survive for us today in roughly the
condition in which they were discovered. Over the decades, scholars
have been able to use this evidence to reconstruct how ancient books,
including early Christian books, were originally assembled.[1] In this
chapter, I try to provide sufficient information for a good working
knowledge of early book production, which will be helpful in understanding some of the arguments in Chapter 2 and elsewhere about
the dates assigned to early Christian books.

But I should begin by posing the question: What exactly do we
mean by an "early Christian book"? We should first examine the
noun. Before about the third century CE, the word "book" (*biblos* or
biblion in Greek, *volumen* in Latin) invariably referred to rolls. They
were the main vehicle for the transmission of literature up until the

early Christian period, when the codex overtook the roll as the chief medium for literature. Using the Leuven Database, we can get a rough sense of the change over time.[2] For the first century, codices account for virtually zero percent of surviving books. Codices make up about 5 percent of books assigned to the second century, about 24 percent of books assigned to the third century, about 79 percent of books assigned to the fourth century, and about 96 percent of books assigned to the fifth century. The major shift seems to have occurred over the course of the third and fourth centuries, the same period when many Christians transitioned from being members of a persecuted minority to positions of political power in the Roman Empire. Although we will encounter a few Christian rolls in the following pages, "the book" in the early Christian centuries was almost always the codex.

The adjective "early" also merits attention. Studies of ancient Christian manuscripts are frequently limited to the period before the fourth century, or, if the "great majuscules" are to be included, the period before the end of the fourth century.[3] I draw evidence from a wider time frame on two grounds. First, for reasons that will be outlined in Chapter 2, it is in most cases impossible to differentiate a book produced in the third century from a book produced in the fourth century. Thus, restricting oneself to "pre–fourth century" manuscripts is somewhat arbitrary because the criteria used to determine what should be placed in that category doubtless color the resulting set of data. Second, the primary foci of this book are the Beatty Biblical Papyri, the Bodmer Papyri, and the fragmentary Oxyrhynchus Christian books. These assemblages include books that were made perhaps as early as the second century to perhaps as late as the seventh century. I therefore draw comparative evidence freely from this whole period. It is true that changes affecting the production of Christian books took place over that time span. The reign of Constantine was surely an important turning point, after which we may imagine that Christian books were produced in greater numbers and more lavish formats. Yet it is clear that there was also continuity in the techniques of book production throughout Late Antiquity, and if the experts who assign dates are even close to correct, it is also the case that synchronic variation in the construction of

Christian books was just as wide as diachronic variation in the early centuries of the Christian era.

Last but not least, we need to consider the modifier "Christian."[4] This is deceptively simple: A Christian book is a book containing text that we identify as Christian. Fair enough. But what about a book containing literature that only *might* be Christian (such as a copy of the Jewish scriptures in Greek)? How do we distinguish between a Jewish book and a Christian book? Or what about a book containing what we might call "pagan" (or, better, "classical") material that is found among a collection of books that also includes gospels, letters of Paul, and other identifiably Christian compositions? Surely, in some important way, such copies of "classical" literature are also "Christian" books. Or what about a work that has no specifically Christian content but is composed by an author we know to be a Christian? We will encounter each of these situations in the following chapters. Fortunately, most of the books I discuss are not so ambiguous; a majority of scholars would agree that they are "Christian books."

The claim that Christians demonstrated a preference for the codex format well before others in the Roman world rests in large part upon the early dates often assigned to Christian codices.[5] It is perhaps more prudent to say simply that the vast majority of Christian books that have survived are in the codex rather than the roll format. The exact origins of the codex and the reasons for its eventual replacement of the roll are matters of debate.[6] Papyrologists unanimously see the codex as a derivation from joined sets of wooden tablets used for memoranda and educational purposes.[7] But at what point did parchment and papyrus codices begin to be used for the more permanent preservation and transmission of literature? The Roman poet Martial mentions parchment codices, apparently large enough to contain at least the *Iliad* in a single volume, near the end of the first century CE.[8] In a recently rediscovered text written in the late second century, the Roman physician Galen recounts the loss of his medical recipes kept in deluxe parchment codices that were burned in a fire at Rome. While these codices did not contain literature, they were not simply ephemeral notebooks. Galen reports that they were extremely expensive and the type of item that was passed from one generation to the next.[9] We also possess a papyrus document from Egypt probably from the second century describing the purchase of what seem to be parchment codices (*membranai*) that the buyers had "collated" (*antebalomen*), which suggests the sale of inscribed parchment codices.[10] So, the parchment codex seems to have been known in both Rome and Egypt by the second century. Papyrus codices, on the other hand, do not appear to be mentioned in literary sources during this early period, but they are better represented in terms of actual extant examples (if the dates assigned to these artifacts are correct). The LDAB presently assigns twenty-eight papyrus codices to the period before 200 CE but only one parchment codex.[11] Of these, seven are identified as Christian, which does represent a sizable percentage, but with such small numbers of extant books and the uncertainties of dating assignments, it is hard to know what to make of this statistic. But in whatever way we assess the role of Christians in the spread of the codex, the fact remains that when we speak of early Christian books, we almost always mean codices.

Materials

Most of the books that form the focus of the present study were constructed from papyrus or parchment and inscribed with ink. Papyrus was made by first cutting thin strips from the stem of the papyrus plant and then placing them closely side by side (without overlapping) on a flat surface.[12] Then a second layer of strips was placed in the same fashion on top of the first but oriented at a right angle to the first layer of strips. The two layers were pressed together and dried. The two sides of the resulting surface, a *kollēma* (plural *kollēmata*), would have papyrus fibers running at a perpendicular angle. Several *kollēmata* constructed in this way, usually twenty to twenty-five centimeters wide, were then pasted together to form long rolls.[13] The overlapping area of a few centimeters where the pasting occurred is known as a *kollēsis* (plural *kollēseis*). According to a recent analysis, blank rolls usually consisted of twenty such pasted *kollēmata* (if copyists required longer rolls, they could simply glue a new roll to the end of another). These rolls would usually be about twenty-five to thirty-three centimeters high. They would be rolled up from right to left with the horizontal fibers on the inside of the roll and the vertical fibers on the outside.[14]

Before the third century, and the increased popularity of the codex, works of literature would usually just be copied on to one or more such rolls. The roll was thus a simple production relative to the more complicated codex. The standard roll was inscribed on the horizontal fibers because it is easier to write along the horizontal fibers rather than against the vertical fibers and because the written surface, being on the inside of the roll, was protected. In some cases, a work would continue to be copied on the back side (that is, the side with vertical fibers). Scholars call such a roll an "opisthograph." In other cases, a roll would be used for one work, and then later, the blank back side with vertical fibers would be used to copy something else, possibly another work of literature, but more usually some sort of everyday document.[15] When codices came to be produced, the sheets were usually cut from blank rolls, as we can see from the frequent presence of *kollēseis* on leaves of codices.[16] It seems that only in exceptional cases were papyrus sheets not cut from a roll but instead were "custom made" for a codex.[17]

Parchment is animal skin that has been processed to create a surface amenable to writing.[18] It is most often produced from the skin of sheep, calves, or goats. The term "vellum" is occasionally reserved for writing surfaces produced from calf skin, but it is also sometimes used interchangeably with "parchment." Parchment is prepared by removing the hair from the flayed animal hide using various methods, including mechanical removal (scraping) and chemical baths, and then stretching and drying the processed hide under tension (as opposed to the production of leather, which involves soaking the depilated hide in tanning agents and a drying process that does not involve a high degree of tension). The result of the parchment-making process is an animal membrane that is fixed in a taut, stretched form that is durable, although it is much more liable to water damage than is leather. Additional scraping while the skin is under tension brings the parchment to the desired thickness. The surfaces of the two sides of the skin differ in color and texture, with the external surface (the hair side) being more porous and slightly darker than the internal surface (the flesh side). The natural shape of a flayed animal hide combined with the stretching and drying pro-

cess leads to irregularly shaped pieces of parchment. Rectangular
sheets could be cut from them in any dimensions, depending upon
the original size of the pelt. It is hypothesized that for a large Bible
like Codex Sinaiticus, a single calf or sheep pelt might have yielded
only two sheets (or even just one sheet), which were about eighty-six
centimeters wide and thirty-six centimeters high. Sinaiticus is estimated to have originally contained some 370 sheets. Doing the math
shows that the number of animals required to produce a large, high-
quality parchment Bible could be staggering, although it should be
remembered that complete Greek Bibles were a rarity in antiquity
(only four survive).[19] While a few parchment fragments from Egypt
are sometimes assigned to quite early dates, most of the codices considered to be the earliest extant books were constructed from papyrus. Parchment codices became more popular in the fourth century
and came to be much more common than papyrus codices in the fifth
century and beyond.

Books were inscribed using different types of inks. A recent
analysis of black inks used in the Roman era divides them into three
broad groups: (1) carbon inks, which consisted of soot; (2) mixed
inks, which consisted of soot mixed with metallic salts; and (3) iron
gall inks, which consisted of oak galls and iron sulfate. All three
types were mixed with a liquid (usually water) and a binding agent
(usually gum arabic). Although there are few detailed studies of the
chemical composition of surviving examples of inks, it seems that in
general carbon inks were the most frequently used in Egypt in the
Roman period. During the third and fourth centuries, we begin to
see more inks containing metallic compounds (aging can cause these
inks to appear more brown than black, which allows them to be identified without chemical analysis). The shift to metallic inks seems to
roughly coincide with the shift from papyrus to parchment, which
makes sense, as metallic inks tend to adhere more readily to parchment than do strictly carbon-based inks.[20]

At this point, it will be helpful to properly define several key
words, some of which I have already used. A *sheet*, also called a bifolium (plural bifolia), is the basic unit of a codex. When folded, it
forms two leaves. A *leaf*, also called a folium or folio (plural folia),
is one half of a sheet. It has two *sides*, each of which is a page. A *page*

is one face of a leaf. When a codex lies open, the page on the left is called the *verso*, and the page on the right is called the *recto*.[21]

A *quire* (sometimes called a "gathering") is a stack of folded sheets, which yields double that number of leaves and quadruple that number of pages. Thus a quire of four sheets will have eight leaves and sixteen pages. Codices can be formed either by folding a large stack of sheets into one quire (a single-quire codex) or by folding and then joining smaller individual stacks of folded sheets (a multi-quire codex). The term *bookblock* refers to the folded stack of sheets (in the case of a single-quire codex) or to the stack of quires (in the case of a multi-quire codex).

Stacking the Sheets

As the sheets were cut from the papyrus rolls, they could be stacked in different ways. They might be stacked with the horizontal fibers facing up, or they might be stacked with the vertical fibers facing up. Another method was to stack the sheets in an alternating pattern (one sheet with horizontal fibers facing up, the next sheet with vertical fibers facing up). Papyrus sheets stacked in that way, when folded, will yield a quire in which facing pages will always have the same fiber orientation (Figure 1.1). We see a related phenomenon in the quires of parchment codices, in which facing pages are usually both hair side or both flesh side. Such parchment codices are sometimes described as conforming to "Gregory's Rule," since Caspar René Gregory was allegedly the first person to note the practice in a classic article.[22]

Single-quire papyrus codices could be composed of a surprisingly large stack of sheets. A codex containing the books of Ezekiel, Daniel, Susanna, and Esther in Greek, parts of which are held in several different institutions (LDAB 3090), had at least fifty-nine sheets, or 236 pages.[23] Such thick single-quire codices are rare, and for good reason. Large quires can be difficult to keep closed; they tend to spring open. More importantly, as a single stack of identically sized sheets increases in height, the folded quire tends to bulge, and the central-most leaves protrude. Our existing samples of large single-quire codices show that this excess was either trimmed off

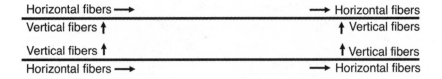

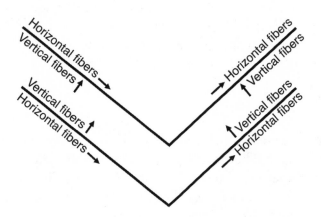

Figure 1.1. Papyrus stack with alternating horizontal and
vertical faces up, before and after folding.

after binding or avoided altogether by cutting sheets that gradually
decreased in width. The result is that the central leaves of large
single-quire codices have a progressively smaller space for writing.[24]

The multi-quire codex escapes these difficulties. Multi-quire codices were generally composed of smaller groups of sheets, especially
groups of three sheets (a *ternio*, six leaves, twelve pages), four sheets
(a *quaternio*, eight leaves, sixteen pages), or five sheets (a *quinio*, ten
leaves, twenty pages).[25] The formation that came to be preferred
was the *quaternio* or quaternion (from which English "quire" is derived). The earliest codices, however, were often composed of quires
containing differing numbers of sheets. For example, a parchment
codex containing Jeremiah, Lamentations, the Epistle of Jeremiah,
and Baruch in Coptic (LDAB 108176) is reported to be composed
of nine *quaterniones* and one *ternio*, while a Coptic codex in the British Library (LDAB 107763) containing an intriguing mix of works

(Deuteronomy, Jonah, and the book of Acts) is reported to be composed of a mix of *quiniones* and *seniones* (quires of six sheets).[26]

Joining the Sheets: Single-Quire Codices

Single-quire codices could be bound different ways. Most of the Coptic codices discovered near Nag Hammadi in 1945 were single-quire constructions. The folded papyrus quire was placed into a leather cover. In most cases, an extra strip of leather (the spine lining strip) lay between the leather cover and the spine of the quire. The sheets were bound using two separate tackets (cords of leather or vegetal fibers) that pierced through the sheets of the quire at the central fold of the codex and through the spine strip and were tied at the back of the spine, either inside or outside the leather covers that encased the quire (Figure 1.2).[27] The tackets also passed through leather stays that rested between the tacket and the central papyrus sheet in the quire, thus protecting the papyrus from rubbing against the tacket. One of the two small rectangular stays in the center of Nag Hammadi Codex VI is visible in Figure 1.3. Alternatively, a single-quire codex could be sewn by "stabbing," that is, sewing the spine through a series of holes punched through the folded quire

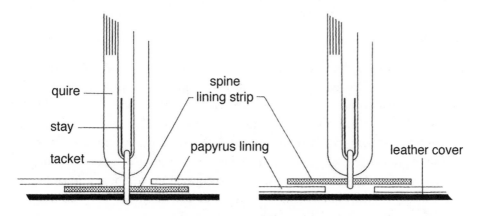

Figure 1.2. Two methods of binding and cover attachment
found among the Nag Hammadi codices.

(Image adapted from Figure 1.3 in *The Archaeology of Medieval Bookbinding* by J. A. Szirmai,
© 1999, Ashgate. Reproduced by permission of Taylor & Francis Books UK.)

Figure 1.3. Nag Hammadi Codex VI opened to the center of the quire,
showing lower leather stay still in place.

(Photo by Jean Doresse. Image courtesy of the Institute for Antiquity and Christianity
Records, Special Collections, Claremont Colleges Library, Claremont, California.)

from front to back at a slight remove from the central fold itself.
This method could be carried out with a single thread or with separate threads, one near the top of the codex and one near the bottom.
Another method, the "whipstitch" ("overcasting" or "oversewing")
involves sewing the thread through holes in the quire punched at a
slight remove from the central fold and wrapping the thread around
the outside of the spine in a helical pattern. Both stabbing and overcasting seem to have been employed on a small codex found in the
Monastery of Epiphanius containing acrostic hymns in Greek and
Coptic (LDAB 6416, Figure 1.4). As Figure 1.4 indicates, sewing
by the stabbing method or overcasting method leaves a pattern of
holes in the individual sheets that straddles the central fold. Codices
bound in the manner of the Nag Hammadi books described above

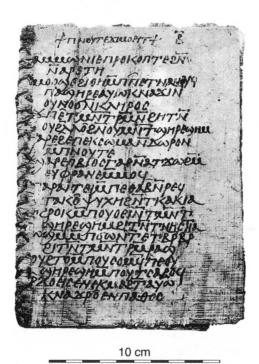

10 cm

Figure 1.4. P.Mon. Epiph. 592, a Greek-Coptic papyrus codex bound by
overcasting and stabbing, found at the Monastery of Epiphanius at Thebes.

(Detail of Walter E. Crum and H. G. Evelyn White, *The Monastery of Epiphanius at
Thebes, Part II* [New York: Metropolitan Museum of Art, 1926], Plate I.)

would show a pattern of holes pierced directly through the central
fold itself.

Sewing the Quires: Multi-Quire Codices

Multi-quire codices were made of several independently folded stacks
of sheets. The usual manner of binding for the earliest multi-quire
codices was sewing by the "link-stitch" or "chain-stitch" method.[28]
The link-stitch also appears in a wide variety of formations, sometimes using one thread, sometimes using more. But the basic movement of the thread is standard and can be described as follows: The
thread enters a sewing station, that is to say, a hole punched through
the central fold of the quire; the thread proceeds within the central
fold; and then it goes back through to the outside of the spine at the

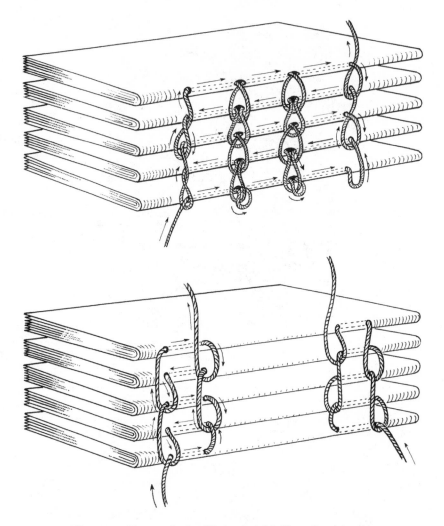

Figure 1.5. Two methods of link-stitch binding of multi-quire
codices, using a continuous thread (top) or two separate threads at two
independent pairs of sewing stations (bottom).

(Image adapted from Jean Vezin, "La réalisation matérielle des manuscrits latins pendant le
haut Moyen Âge," in Albert Gruys and J. P. Gumbert [eds.], *Codicologica 2: Éléments pour
une codicologie comparée* [Leiden: Brill, 1978], Figures 1 and 2.)

next sewing station, at which point it drops and loops though the
length of thread that links the previous two quires. The thread then
goes back up and in, either through the same sewing station from
which it exited (Figure 1.5, top) or through the proximate sewing
station in the quire above (Figure 1.5, bottom). The thread then pro-

Figure 1.6. P.Bodmer XVI, codex in leather cover with stitching exposed.
(Image courtesy of the Fondation Martin Bodmer, Cologny-Geneva.)

ceeds within the central fold to the next sewing station, and so on, climbing up to the next quire when it reaches the head or tail of the spine.[29] Two common variations of the link-stitch are illustrated in Figure 1.5. The first shows a codex bound using a continuous thread passing through all the sewing stations. The second shows a codex bound by two separate threads sewn at two independent pairs of sewing stations. Ancient Greek and Coptic codices whose bindings have survived intact show a number of variations on these basic themes.[30] One example in which we can see the extant stitching quite clearly is P.Bodmer XVI, a Coptic codex of Exodus (LDAB 108535) that was assigned by its editor to the fourth century. The leather cover is damaged in the area of the spine with the result that the stitching of the quires is visible. The book was composed of six parchment quires sewn using the link-stitch at two independent pairs of sewing stations. Figure 1.6 shows this codex closed with the stitching exposed; Figure 1.7 shows the codex open to the center of the fifth quire. When, as is more usual, the binding structures of codices have not been so nicely preserved, the method of binding can still sometimes be determined by examining any bits of the binding threads that may have survived in place or by examining patterns of rubbing and wear in the center of each quire. As a comparison of Figure 1.3 and Figure 1.7 indicates, the centers of the quires in multi-quire codices can have an appearance very similar to that of the centers

Figure 1.7. P.Bodmer XVI opened at the center of the fifth quire,
showing lower parchment stay.

(Image courtesy of the Fondation Martin Bodmer, Cologny-Geneva.)

of single-quire codices in that they also often employ parchment or
leather stays that sit between the binding cords and the central sheet
of each quire to prevent chaffing. In other respects, however, the
sewing of the multi-quire codex is considerably more complicated
and less intuitive than the relatively simple tackets or stabbing used
to bind single-quire codices.

The Relationship Between Single-Quire Codices and Multi-Quire Codices

This difference between the sewing techniques typically used for
single-quire codices and the link-stitch of multi-quire codices raises
the question of the relationship between the two types of construction. That the multi-quire codex developed from the single-quire
codex is not to be doubted.[31] We can even see some likely intermediary stages in that development, such as Nag Hammadi Codex I
(LDAB 107741), a papyrus codex that contains quires of twenty-two

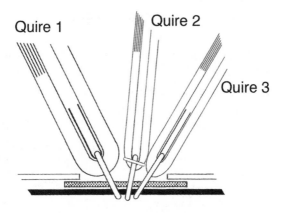

Figure 1.8. Reconstruction of a cross section of Nag Hammadi
Codex I, showing the three quires.

sheets (= eighty-eight pages), eight sheets (= thirty-two pages), and six sheets (= twenty-four pages).[32] As Stephen Emmel has observed, "Codex I is more like three single-quire codices bound into a single cover than it is like the usual multi-quired codices."[33] That is to say, rather than having several smaller quires bound by a continuous thread that passed through each of the quires, Codex I consisted of one large quire and two smaller quires, each of which seems to have been pierced with a single independent tacket that attached it to the cover. Only two of the three quires appear to have been attached to each other, and this was accomplished by gluing the inner edge of the last leaf of the second quire to the inner edge of the first leaf of the third quire (Figure 1.8). The result seems to have been a functional book that was somewhat awkward to use. The limitations of this kind of construction are fairly obvious. Quires joined to the cover by a single tacket are not entirely secure and are free to move within the covers, putting stress on the papyrus leaves at the point at which they are pierced by the tackets. Furthermore, adding a second tacket to each quire would double the number of holes piercing the leather cover. Leather is a very sturdy material, but an increasing number of quires would mean an increasing number of tackets piercing the cover, possibly leading to structural instability. The advantages of the link-stitch process are evident. The same threads that move through the centers of quires also link the quires at the multiple sewing stations and provide strength to the structure of the spine. The multi-quire codex could thus accommodate more material with greater stability.

These observations do not, however, have any bearing on the dates of our surviving codices. That is to say, it is not at all the case that single-quire codices are invariably older than multi-quire codices. Rather, the variety of construction techniques of surviving codices from Egypt suggests that the rise and spread of the codex format was a drawn-out process involving both diffusion of the technology from one locality to another and independent experimentation at the local level. Refinement of construction techniques at any given time would have varied widely from place to place. In fact, it would not surprise me if the parchment codices of books such as the *Iliad* mentioned by Martial in the first century were multi-quire constructions. Barring the use of extremely small handwriting or an unusually large format, the 15,693 lines of the *Iliad* would make for a quite large single-quire codex.[34]

Inscribing the Pages

Copyists prepared their writing surfaces in different ways. Pliny informs us that papyrus sheets were smoothed with a piece of ivory or a shell. If papyrus surfaces have been expertly smoothed, it can be difficult to distinguish the face of the leaf with horizontal fibers from the face with vertical fibers.[35] Parchment leaves would usually be ruled by gently incising guidelines into the writing surface using a straight-edge, while papyrus leaves were sometimes pricked at four corners to define the written area of the page and provide guidance in keeping the margins consistent. More detailed discussions of page preparations and scribal practice are readily available, so I mention only one mechanical question and one peculiar scribal feature of Christian manuscripts.[36] First, the mechanical question: Were the leaves inscribed before or after they were bound? In the case of later medieval codices the answer is almost always copying before binding. The presence of quire signatures tends to suggest that the individual quires would be copied while unbound and then at a later point be bound together. Otherwise, why would it be necessary to keep blank quires in any particular order? Among our earliest codices, however, we can often observe copyists fairly obviously adjusting the size and spacing of their writing when they have realized they might have either too few blank leaves remaining or too many blank leaves remaining, which suggests that the addition or removal of extra sheets or quires was either not possible or was a less attractive option than altering the spacing of the writing on the later pages.[37] Does this mean that such codices were already bound before copying? It is difficult to say, but I suspect that codices displaying these features were in fact bound and then copied. On occasion, other pieces of evidence are more decisive. In a small papyrus codex containing the Greek version of Psalms 72–88 now in Dublin (LDAB 3158), we find a stroke of a letter written over the binding thread, which indicates that this single-quire codex was bound before it was copied.[38] Similarly, when different copyists are responsible for inscribing the two halves of the same bifolium, it is reasonable to suppose that the copyists were not working simultaneously and that the quires were bound before the copying. Such is the case in an intriguing papyrus codex at the Fondation Martin Bodmer (LDAB 4120, discussed in Chapter 5 and illustrated in Figure 5.9). With more lavish codices, the process almost always involved inscribing before binding. We can see that this was the case with, for example, Codex Sinaiticus, the great parchment Bible (LDAB 3478), the leaves of which were inscribed by at least four different copyists. Important divisions in the text start at the beginnings of quires regardless of whether the preceding quire had been completely inscribed, and the resulting blank leaves were cut out.[39] This is a good indication that several copyists were working simultaneously on different parts of the book before it was bound.[40] Absent this kind of clear evidence, however, it is difficult to know the order of events with certainty.

The only scribal feature I mention here is the peculiar Christian method of abbreviating certain words such as ιηϲΟΥϲ (Jesus), θεΟϲ (God), κΥριΟϲ (Lord), and χριϲτΟϲ (Christ). In Christian manuscripts, these words are generally shortened by contraction. Only selected letters of the word are written, and the abbreviated form was marked with a horizontal stroke above the letters. For instance, the word "God," θεΟϲ, would appear in manuscripts as $\overline{\text{θϲ}}$. On occasion, some words are shortened by suspension. Thus, ιηϲΟΥϲ (Jesus) can be seen as both $\overline{\text{ιϲ}}$ (contraction) and $\overline{\text{ιη}}$ (suspension). Other words, such as πνεΥμα (spirit), ανθρωπΟϲ (human), ΥιΟϲ (son), πατηρ (father), ΜΗΤΗΡ (mother), ΙϹΡΑΗΛ (Israel), ΙЄΡΟΥϹΑΛΗΜ (Jerusalem), and even ΜШΥϹΗϹ (Moses), are also similarly abbreviated, though with less regularity than the first four epithets. It is a scholarly custom to call such a shortened word a *nomen sacrum* (plural *nomina sacra*).[41] The execution of these abbreviations varies considerably, but the practice is almost universal among extant Christian manuscripts, so much so that the presence of a *nomen sacrum* is usually regarded as sufficient evidence for declaring that a given manuscript was a Christian production. By the same token, the absence of *nomina sacra* in, say, a codex of Genesis, is enough to persuade some scholars that such a manuscript is a Jewish rather than a Christian production.[42] The origins of the practice are obscure, and no theory commands wide assent among specialists.[43]

Covers

Early Christian books display different sorts of covers, and some books may not have had a cover at all. We can place the surviving examples into two groups: covers of wood and covers of leather. As we saw, two wooden panels decorated with portraits of the evangelists served as the cover of the Freer gospel codex at the time of its purchase.[44] Such wooden covers could be attached to each other by a single strip of leather running the length of the spine (a spine strip or back strip) and/or several smaller pieces of leather crossing the spine at intervals (spine slips or hinging thongs). The bookblock could be attached to the covers either through the use of adhesives (pastedowns on the inside of the cover and glue along the spine), sewing (such as incorporating the spine slips into the stitching of the bookblock itself), or both. Covers constructed of leather were usually stiffened by wrapping the leather around stacks of blank papyrus or waste papyrus before attaching the bookblock.[45] The cover could be attached to the bookblock either by means of pastedowns on the inside of the cover or by incorporating one or more leaves from the beginning and end of the bookblock into the cover itself (that is, by actually folding the leather of turn-ins of the cover over some of the leaves of the bookblock; this method was used on P.Bodmer XVI; see Figure 1.6).[46] Leather covers can sometimes provide

Figure 1.9. Inside of the leather cover of Nag Hammadi Codex I after the removal
of the bookblock but before the removal of all the waste papyrus lining the cover.
Two leather stays and three tackets are visible at the spine. (The cover is now MS
1804/1 in the Schøyen Collection.)

a means of giving a relatively secure date for the construction of a
codex (or at least the construction of the covers). The papyrus used
to stiffen the covers often included old documents, which occasionally carry dates. This type of construction was used for the covers of
some of the Nag Hammadi codices (Figure 1.9). The covers were
disassembled, and the latest dated document (348 CE) was found in
the cover of Codex VII (LDAB 107747), which gives us a *terminus
post quem*, that is, the earliest possible date, for the construction of

the codex in the middle of the fourth century. Both wooden and leather covers were sometimes equipped with strips of leather (wrapping bands) that wrapped around the codex to keep it closed.

Ancient Repairing of Codices

The preceding discussion indicates that a considerable amount of work went into the production of papyrus and parchment codices, especially multi-quire codices. That being the case, it is not surprising that we find different kinds of repairs made to codices. They seem to have been important possessions, used for relatively long periods of time, and subject to wear and tear.[47] Repairs could take various forms. Papyrus sheets sometimes broke at the central fold. This kind of damage could be repaired by using a vertical strip of papyrus as a patch. We see this phenomenon in P.Bodmer II, a papyrus codex of the Gospel According to John (LDAB 2777).[48] Any portion of a papyrus leaf could also split horizontally or vertically along the fibers of the plant. Such damage was sometimes repaired by tying a loop of thread through the damaged area. P.Bodmer XXI, a papyrus codex containing Joshua 1–6 and other material (LDAB 108537), has been repaired in this fashion in several places (Figure 1.10).[49] In parchment codices, we sometimes see patches added to fix damaged leaves. Figure 1.11 shows a leaf of P.Bodmer XIX, a parchment codex containing part of the Gospel According to Matthew and part of Romans (LDAB 107759), which has been patched at its outer edge. Makers of parchment codices sometimes applied patches during the initial preparation of the sheets to cover over holes or other imperfections in the treated skins. The patches visible on the leaves of P.Bodmer XIX are found on the edges of leaves, areas that would be especially liable to damage due to heavy usage. For that reason, I assume that such patches in this codex are later repairs. The same codex also nicely illustrates the phenomenon of rebinding, which appears to have been quite common.[50] As it exists now, the book contains only a portion of Matthew and three leaves of Romans. The last leaf of Romans is pasted to a wooden panel that would have been the back cover of the book. The first inscribed leaf at the beginning of the codex contains only the words "Last Part of Matthew" in a hand distinct from that of the rest of the codex. It

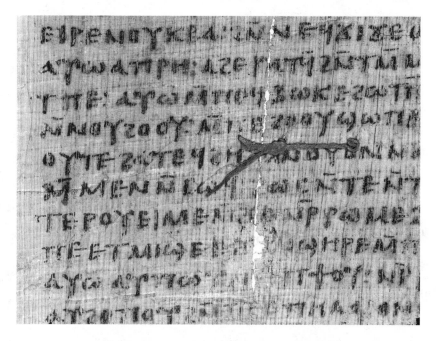

Figure 1.10. P.Bodmer XXI, showing ancient repair of a
damaged papyrus leaf using a loop of thread.
(Image courtesy of the Fondation Martin Bodmer, Cologny-Geneva.)

seems to be functioning as a title for this rebound codex, the leaves
of which were once part of a larger codex.[51]

Modern Conservation of Early Christian Codices

The early Christian codices fortunate enough to survive the ravages
of time have come to us in widely varying states of preservation.
The vast majority of the earliest codices are represented by just
fragments of a single leaf or perhaps two leaves. Generally, these
scraps are flattened and mounted between panes of glass. And in
fact, even those books that did survive in better states of preservation have often been disassembled after their discovery. In the late
nineteenth and early twentieth centuries, conservators like the renowned Hugo Ibscher (1874–1943) would take apart even reasonably well-preserved codices and place the individual leaves between
panes of glass (Figure 1.12). The benefit of this type of conservation

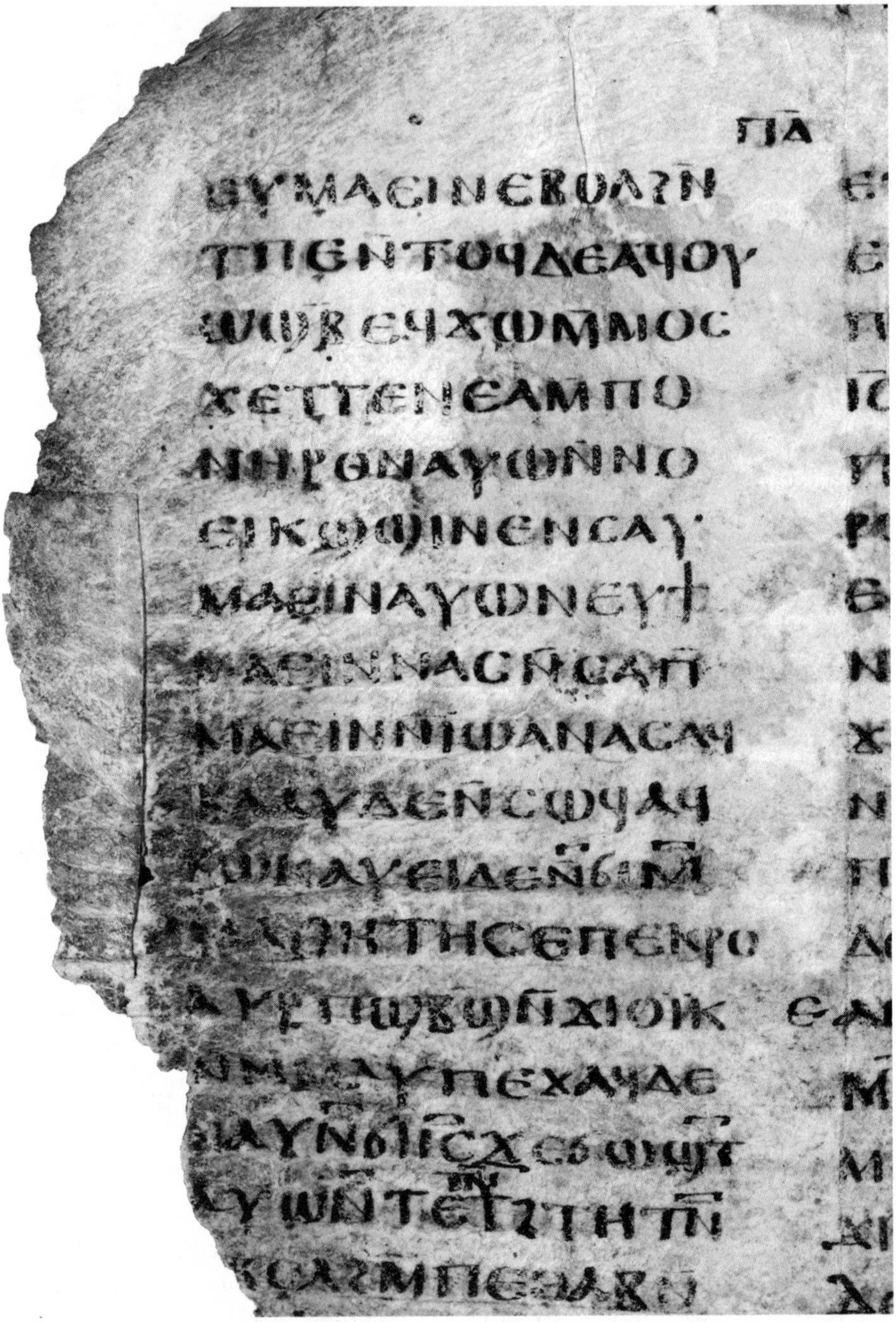

Figure 1.11. P.Bodmer XIX, showing ancient repair of the damaged edge of a parchment leaf using a parchment patch.

(Image courtesy of the Fondation Martin Bodmer, Cologny-Geneva.)

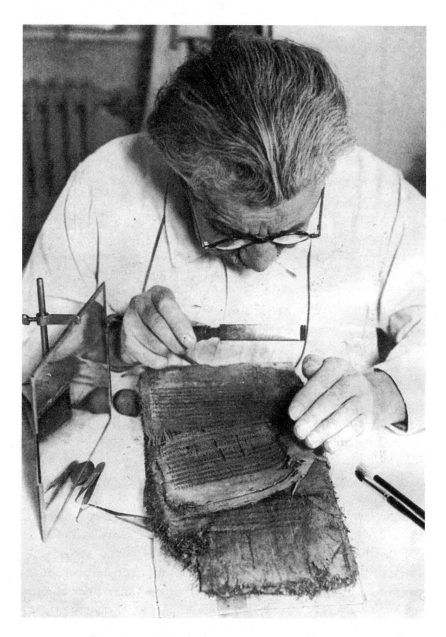

Figure 1.12. Hugo Ibscher at work on the Manichaean
codices from Medinet Madi in 1934.
(Image originally published in *Illustrierter Beobachter*, February 10, 1934, p. 186.)

is that it permits close study of individual folia or bifolia with a lower risk of further damage to the leaves. Early scholars were understandably interested in making the most careful possible study of the texts carried on the manuscripts. The drawback is the loss of the sometimes crucial information that could have been provided by the intact binding structures. Also lost is simply the sense of the ancient book as a three-dimensional object. For this reason, the writings of Ibscher and other conservators can be excellent resources for those interested in the construction of Christian books. Ibscher's desk in Berlin was an early stop for many of the most important early Christian codices found between the 1890s and the 1930s, including the Chester Beatty Biblical Papyri and the Manichaean codices from Medinet Madi. As he took apart these bookblocks and framed the individual leaves, Ibscher often recorded his observations about various aspects of book production.[52] Although his descriptions are not as detailed as we might like, they nonetheless provide valuable evidence, given that he had the benefit of seeing many codices in a state near to that in which they were discovered.

Only a very few of the earliest Christian codices exist today in something like that condition. One example is a parchment codex now in Barcelona that contains the Gospels According to Luke, John, and Mark in Coptic (LDAB 107904, 107905, and 107760; Figure 1.13). This book is not especially large (16.5 cm by 20 cm), but it is a quality production written on parchment in a spacious two-column layout. It is usually assigned on the basis of its handwriting to the fifth century. Its wooden covers and parts of its leather binding structures are very well preserved. It was bound by the link-stitch method using two separate threads sewn at two independent pairs of sewing stations (see Figure 1.5, bottom). In its present form, the book helps us to imagine ancient Christian codices in something approaching their original state. Yet, the excellent appearance of the book now is at least a bit deceptive, for this book is a product of the antiquities market, and when it emerged from that market in the 1970s, it did not look this good. Many of the leaves were detached, and the whole object had to be reassembled through the efforts of dedicated scholars and conservators.[53]

Unlike the conservators of this codex, their predecessors working during the first half of the twentieth century were essentially

Figure 1.13. P.PalauRib. inv. 181–183, parchment codex containing the Gospels According to Luke, John, and Mark in Coptic bound in wooden covers, shown here closed and open.

making up the craft as they worked. Thus, some earlier techniques of preservation (such as the use of clear adhesive tape, which became popular for a period in the middle of the twentieth century) are now recognized as less than ideal. Twenty-first-century conservators often spend a good deal of their time undoing the conservation efforts of their early-twentieth-century forerunners.[54] Still, the increased knowledge of recent decades has not entirely prevented further destruction of early Christian books, especially those that have been badly handled after their discovery. Most recently, one can look at the case of the antiquities dealer Bruce Ferrini, who did irreparable damage to the so-called Tchacos codex (LDAB 108481), which contains the famous Gospel of Judas, by placing it in a freezer.[55] This action was devastating to the papyrus leaves of the codex, as the moisture in the fibers expanded in the freezing process and left the thawed papyrus highly liable to crumbling. This is just one of the many horror stories that could be told about books on the antiquities market. When we turn to books that have been properly excavated and immediately conserved, however, we can often see the latest scientific knowledge put to good use in preserving extremely fragile books that might not have survived had they been discovered a century ago.[56]

Each area I have discussed in this chapter could be, and on occasion has been, the topic of its own book. The overview that I have presented here should provide a sufficient orientation for readers to appreciate the discussions of books in the following chapters. I have not delved into questions of who produced these codices.[57] Were they all written by Christians? Did the same person who manufactured a codex also inscribe it? How much training and what type of training did the copyists have? The answers will of course vary from book to book, and other scholars have pondered these questions in great detail.[58] My focus is on the artifacts themselves, but I hope that close attention to the books will at least help us better frame our questions about who made them, used them, preserved them, and, eventually, got rid of them.

CHAPTER TWO

The Dating Game

OW DO WE KNOW how old an ancient manuscript is? The answer depends on the type of manuscript. What papyrologists call "documents," that is, receipts, deeds, tax returns, official government proclamations—in short, nonliterary texts—often preserve the dates on which they were copied, just as such documents still do today. In Roman Egypt, it was common practice to date documents by combining the regnal years of emperors with the traditional system of Egyptian months. P.Amh. 2.78 is a typical example. It is a petition to a centurion detailing complaints against one Hekusis Euporas, and it carries a date of "the twenty-fifth year of Marcus Aurelius Commodus Antoninus Augustus, Thoth 30," which in terms of the Gregorian calendar would be September 26 of the year 184 CE.[1] So we can often know the dates of documents like these down to the very day that they were copied.

But we are interested in manuscripts that contain early Christian *literature*, which would have no occasion for including such specific dates. Beginning around the ninth century, some copies of Greek biblical manuscripts do give us dates in the form of colophons, that is, short notes to the reader from the scribe who copied the manuscript. Figure 2.1 shows a manuscript of the four gospels. The book is open to the last page of the Gospel According to John, and at the bottom of the page we find a short message from the copyist: "Writ-

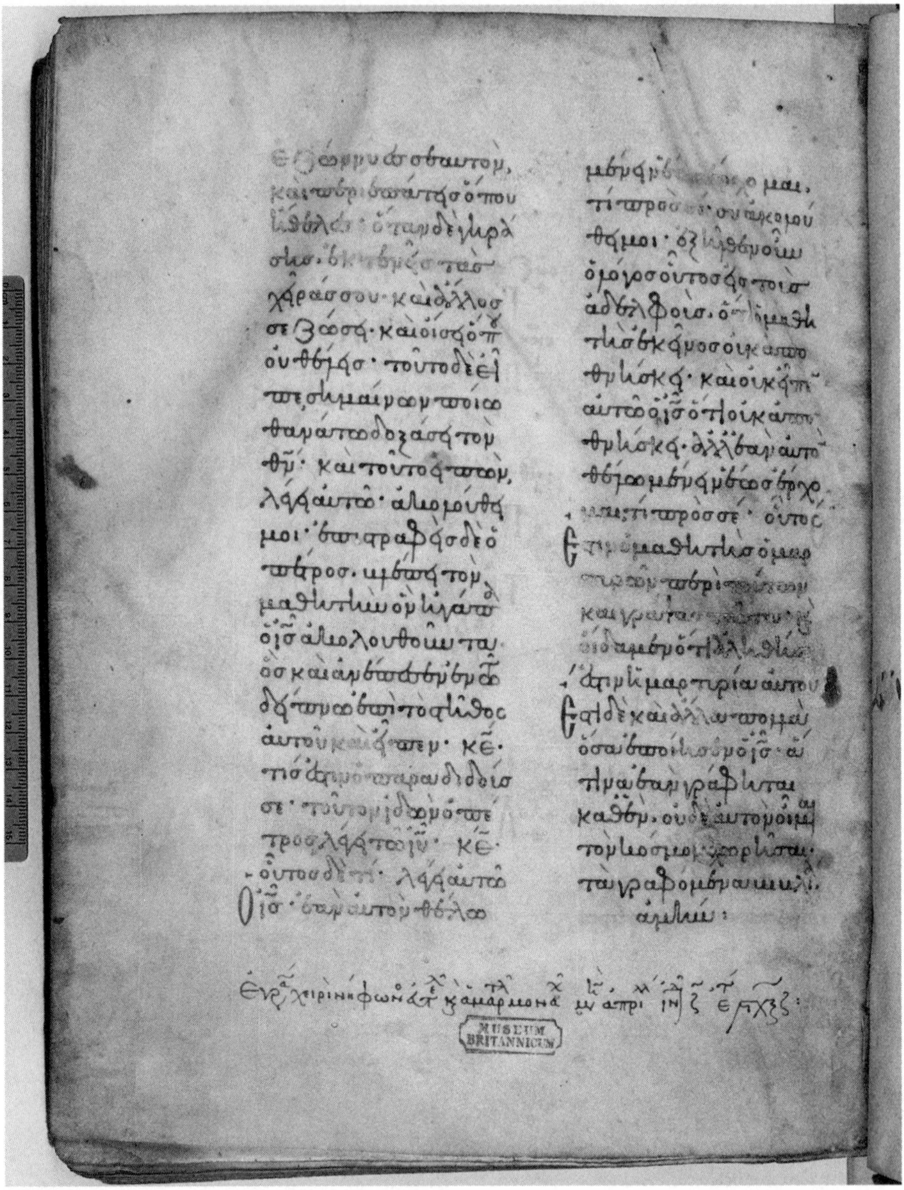

Figure 2.1. British Library, Add. Ms. 5107, a parchment codex of the four gospels. The colophon at the base of the page indicates that the book was copied in 1159 CE.

(Image by permission of the British Library, London, UK/Bridgeman Images.)

ten by the hand of Nepho, worthless and sinful monk, in the month of April, in the seventh indiction, in the year 6667." This method of dating was based on the (still alarmingly common) assumption that the world was created in September of 5509 BCE, so we can simply do the math: 6667–5509 (+ 1, because of the difference in how new years were reckoned) = 1159 CE.[2] If only it were always so easy! But colophons with dates like this begin to become common in Greek biblical manuscripts only in the ninth century. How do we assign dates to literary papyrus and parchment books from earlier periods? Again, it depends on the specific manuscript. We can almost never be so precise as to know the exact year, or even the exact decade, that a manuscript was copied, but certain features of some manuscripts can help us narrow the window of possible dates. The following discussion introduces a variety of methods that we can use to estimate the date of undated manuscripts: by looking at their contents, by studying their reuse, by comparatively analyzing the handwriting used to copy the manuscript (paleography), and finally by deploying more technologically involved methodologies such as radiocarbon dating and ink analysis.

Establishing Limits

Different sorts of circumstances can on occasion allow us to discern the earliest possible date a manuscript was copied (what scholars call the *terminus post quem*, "point after which") or a latest possible date at which it was copied (the *terminus ante quem*, "point before which"). For instance, the contents of a manuscript may establish a *terminus post quem*. Among early Christian texts, good examples of this phenomenon are copies of martyrdoms. They are set at precise moments in time, usually ascertainable by the Roman official who is prosecuting the Christians. P.Bodmer XX (LDAB 220465) is a copy of the *Apology of Phileas*, which recounts the trial of the bishop Phileas under the Roman prefect of Egypt, Clodius Culcianus. Figure 2.2 shows a leaf from this codex. Other versions of this text in fact tell us the exact date of the martyrdom: the twenty-first year of Diocletian, that is, 305 CE.[3] The composition of this text, and hence the copying of the Bodmer manuscript, happened at some point after that. How long after Phileas was martyred might this particular manu-

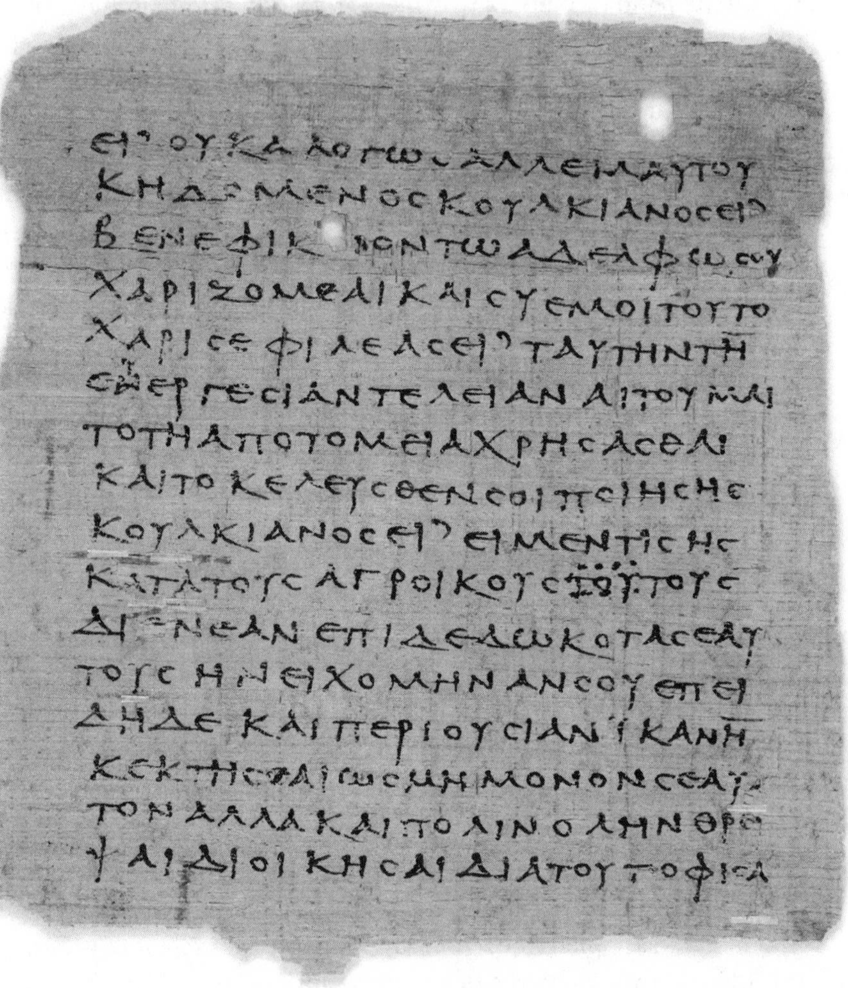

Figure 2.2. P.Bodmer XX, the *Apology of Phileas*. Since Phileas was killed
in 305 CE, we know this codex was copied sometime after that date.
(Image courtesy of the Fondation Martin Bodmer, Cologny-Geneva.)

script have been copied? This is an open question.[4] The only thing
we can say with certainty is that this manuscript was copied after 305.

Another instance in which a limit for dating can be established
is when a manuscript is reused. Recall that for ancient users of papyrus rolls, the "front" surface is almost always the side on which the
fibers of the papyrus plant run horizontally. On the "back" surface,

the papyrus fibers run vertically.[5] On occasion, pieces of papyrus that had already been written along the horizontal fibers were turned over and reused. This kind of reuse can be helpful for dating an undated literary manuscript in two different ways. First, a literary manuscript can be reused for a dated document. Such is the case of P.Ryl. 1.16 (LDAB 2661), a fragment of a roll of an unknown comedy written along the horizontal fibers (Figure 2.3). It was reused for a letter written in either January 253 or January 256 CE.[6] This fact gives us a *terminus ante quem* for P.Ryl. 1.16, which must have been written earlier than 256 CE. How much earlier? Again, it is difficult to say. To propose an answer, we must resort to analyzing the handwriting. Acknowledged experts in the field disagree by seventy-five years, with one renowned scholar claiming that P.Ryl. 1.16 was copied "about 150 CE" and another equally respected authority saying it was copied between 220 and 225.[7] This wide range of possibilities, even for such a relatively "datable" piece as P.Ryl. 1.16, highlights the difficulty of using handwriting to try to assign specific dates to undated manuscripts.

The second way reuse can be helpful for establishing a date for a literary manuscript is essentially the opposite situation—when a dated documentary roll is reused for a piece of literature. For example, P.Oxy. 12.1444 is a portion of a report concerning payments of grain from 248–249 CE written along the fibers. At some point after that, the documentary roll was turned over and upside down, and its reverse was reused for a copy of some orations, published as P.Oxy. 11.1366 (LDAB 2432, Figure 2.4). Thus, the handwriting of the orations has a *terminus post quem* of 248–249 CE. How much later were the orations copied? Again, we cannot know for sure.[8]

On rare occasions, a combination of these scenarios allows us to date a literary manuscript with a reasonably high level of precision. A good example of this phenomenon is a manuscript of a work called the *Kestoi*, which, although it lacks specifically Christian content, was in fact written by a Christian author, Julius Africanus.[9] Africanus was a polymath active during the third century who exchanged letters with the theologian Origen. P.Oxy. 3.412 (LDAB 2550) is the tail end of a papyrus roll that contained Book 18 of the *Kestoi*, which was a sprawling compendium of all sorts of technical knowledge and entertaining anecdotes. With this literary papyrus, contents and reuse

Figure 2.3. P.Ryl. 1.16 (left), a fragment of a papyrus roll containing an unknown comedy, and its reverse, P.Ryl. 2.236 (right), a letter written in either 253 or 256 CE. Note the contrast between the types of writing.

(Images courtesy of the John Rylands Library, University of Manchester, copyright of the University of Manchester.)

Figure 2.4. Ghent University Library BHSL.PAP.oooo51/1 and 2.
The front of this papyrus roll was published as P.Oxy. 12.1444 (left), a report
concerning payments of grain from 248–249 CE. The back was published as
P.Oxy. 11.1366 (right), a copy of unidentified orations.

combine to provide a fairly narrow window of possible dates that
this manuscript was copied. The text mentions the "Baths of Alexander" near the Pantheon in Rome. These would be the Baths of
Nero, which came to be known as the baths of the emperor Severus
Alexander only after a major expansion of the complex apparently
completed in 227 CE.[10] Thus, the *Kestoi* must have been composed
sometime *after* that year. If we turn this manuscript over (to the side
with vertical fibers), we find that the back side of the roll was later
reused for a copy of the will of a certain Aurelius Hermogenes written in a neat cursive hand (Figure 2.5). The will states that it was
both made and opened during the reign of the Roman emperor Marcus Claudius Tacitus.[11] This emperor ruled for only less than a year,
so we can tell that the will was originally written in 276 CE and that
Hermogenes died during that year. Therefore, this manuscript of
the *Kestoi* of Julius Africanus was copied after the construction of the
Baths of Alexander but before the copying of the will on the reverse.
We thus can date this literary manuscript with confidence to some-

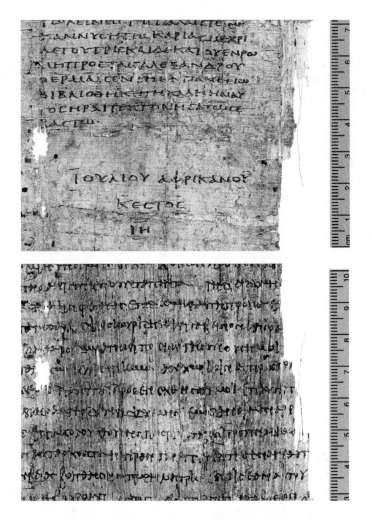

Figure 2.5. Detail of the front and back of British Library Papyrus 2040.
The front of this papyrus roll was published as P.Oxy. 3.412 (top), a copy of
the *Kestoi* of Julius Africanus, written after 227 CE. The back was published
as P.Oxy. 6.907 (bottom), a copy of the will of Aurelius Hermogenes,
probably copied in 276 CE or shortly thereafter.

(Image by permission of the British Library, London, UK/Bridgeman Images.)

time between 227 and probably 276 CE. I say "probably" because
even in this special case, there is a degree of uncertainty. The copy
of the will on this particular papyrus was actually made at some point
after the opening of the original will in 276. We assume it was made
during the lifetime of one of the heirs and in all probability at some

time close to the date Aurelius Hermogenes died.[12] It would be wonderful if we had more literary manuscripts of the Roman era that could be dated with this level of precision, but this copy of the *Kestoi* is a truly exceptional item.

The papyrus fragment of the *Kestoi* was found in one of several trash heaps in and around the Egyptian city of Oxyrhynchus. As we will see in Chapter 6, thousands of papyri were found in those ancient rubbish dumps. And even this fairly vague statement of provenance is more than what we know about the origin of many early Christian manuscripts, which can be traced back no further than the antiquities market.[13] But because trash heaps are open to blowing winds, and because the record keeping of Grenfell and Hunt's excavations of Oxyrhynchus was not as thorough as we might like, the archaeological context of a piece like the *Kestoi* cannot tell us as much as we might hope. In some cases, however, archaeology can be very useful in establishing limits for dating manuscripts. The story of another early Christian book illustrates how.

The Syrian city of Dura-Europos on the eastern frontier of the Roman Empire was sacked and abandoned in 256 CE. The ancient remains were excavated from 1928 to 1937 by Yale University and the French Academy of Inscriptions and Letters.[14] These archaeologists uncovered an amazing array of artifacts and monuments, including a synagogue decorated with elaborate paintings and a Christian building with paintings of scenes from the gospels. These buildings were well preserved because, during the last siege of the city, the structures and the street next to them were filled high with dirt and rubble in order to reinforce the western wall of the city. While removing the debris used to fill the street, excavators discovered a crumpled piece of parchment not far from the Christian building, P.Dura 10 (LDAB 3071; Figure 2.6).[15] Upon inspection, it turned out to be a gospel harmony, or combination of the four canonical gospels copied in a neat Greek hand. The roll from which the fragment came must have been copied before the sacking of the city in 256. How much earlier it was copied, again, is a point of disagreement among scholars.[16] But we can say with confidence that this piece has a secure *terminus ante quem* of 256 CE. Unfortunately, finds of manuscripts in such precisely datable archaeological contexts are the exception rather than the rule.[17]

Figure 2.6. P.Dura 10 (P.CtYBR inv. DPg 24), a fragment of a
parchment harmony of the gospels. Because it was found at Dura-
Europos, we know it was copied before 256 CE.

(Image courtesy of the Yale Papyrus Collection, Beinecke Rare
Book and Manuscript Library, Yale University.)

Paleography

In the vast majority of cases, then, scholars attempting to assign a
date to literary papyri of the Roman era rely on paleography, the
comparative analysis of handwriting. Paleography, broadly speak-
ing, is the study of ancient forms of writing. The field of Greek
paleography encompasses everything from the earliest examples of

recognizably Greek letters carved in stone to the elaborate Greek cursives in use when the printing press was introduced in Europe.[18] The academic field of paleography concerns all aspects of writing and its production and aims at comprehensively describing writing, documenting the social settings in which writing takes place, and tracing lines of influence among different types of scripts and even among scripts in different languages.[19] From the perspective of the contemporary academic field of paleography, the use of handwriting analysis to assign dates is really a secondary matter. Nevertheless, the chief interest of Greek paleography for most biblical scholars is in fact its role in the process of trying to establish dates for otherwise undated examples of Jewish and Christian writing.[20] The usefulness of paleography for assigning dates to undated samples rests upon a key assumption: Graphic similarity generally equates to temporal similarity. Thus, the procedure of paleographic dating is deceptively simple: First, compare a sample of handwriting of unknown date with the relatively small set of more securely dated examples (that is, with dated documents written in literary hands or with those literary manuscripts that can be dated more objectively using the various methods outlined above). Next, assume that close graphic similarity means that the samples were produced at roughly the same time. Describing the procedure in this way raises several questions: What is meant by "similarity"? How is "comparison" to be carried out? And just how "rough" are the dates generated by such a process?

To begin to answer these questions as they relate to Greek writing of the Roman era, it will be helpful to introduce one important way that scripts are classified. Papyrologists generally divide handwriting into two broad categories, sometimes described as literary and documentary, but probably better thought of as capitals and cursives.[21] Specimens of these types are nicely contrasted in Figure 2.3. Documentary writing (so-called because it is most often used for letters, tax records, receipts, and so forth) consists of quickly and competently written cursives, with letters often written without lifting the pen and connected to one another with ligatures. Greek literary writing (generally used for copying works of literature) is characterized by capital letters separated from one another and formed with multiple strokes and relatively few ligatures, yielding an impression of regularity. Figure 2.7 shows capital, intermediary, and fully

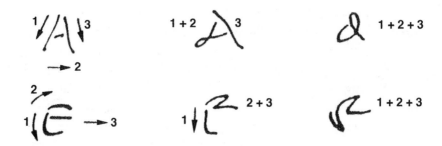

Figure 2.7. Capital, intermediary, and cursive methods of writing.
(Image adapted from Eric G. Turner, *Greek Manuscripts of the Ancient World,*
2nd. ed. [London: Institute of Classical Studies, 1987], 2.)

cursive examples of the formation of alpha and epsilon. Although this distinction between capitals and cursives is fundamental, it is best not to be dogmatic about the division, because "the gradations between the most elegant book hand and the most fluent cursive are almost infinite."[22] This point is nicely illustrated by comparing Figures 2.3 and 2.4. If we imagine a spectrum with well-defined capitals at one end and flowing cursive at the other end, the samples in Figure 2.3 would be at the poles of that spectrum, whereas those in Figure 2.4 would be nearer to the center. Furthermore, on some occasions, literature is copied in documentary hands, and, conversely, dated documents are sometimes written using literary styles.[23] And some documents, although written in flowing cursives, clearly aim at a formal style.[24]

These points are important when it comes to the question of assigning dates to undated manuscripts. A manuscript can be dated by means of paleography most confidently when it can be compared with a large number of similar manuscripts with secure dates.[25] Thus, there are some grounds for being cautiously confident about assigning paleographic dates to samples of Greek documentary writing of the Roman era, since the pool of securely dated tax records, deeds, receipts, and other documents is quite large.[26] By contrast, there are relatively few securely dated examples of literary Greek writing of the Roman era, so it is correspondingly much more difficult to paleographically date literary manuscripts with precision. Fortunately, many copies of Jewish and Christian texts are written in styles that contain cursive elements making them suitable for comparison with some cursively written dated documents. And the handful of dated documents written in more literary styles can give us reference points for thinking about the possible dates of undated manuscripts composed in more formal capitals.

So how does paleographic dating work in practice? When presented with an undated literary manuscript, paleographers first attempt to assign the writing to a broad grouping of similar looking examples, usually called "styles."[27] Grouping manuscripts by writing styles involves scrutinizing various characteristics of the script. Such characteristics include (but are not limited to) the "module" or "modulus" of the letters (that is to say, the ratio of width to height), the number of strokes used to produce the letter, whether the writing is angular or curved, the shading (alternation of thick and thin strokes in the letters), the inclination or "lean" of the letters, and the use of ligatures to connect letters. Reference is also frequently made to the "ductus," the imagined movement of the hand required to produce the forms we see on the page. This quality is usually characterized as either "fluid" or "slow" but also can refer to the direction and sequence of strokes used to produce letters. Beyond the shapes and formation of individual letters, paleographers take into consideration such features as bilinearity (the degree to which the writing adheres to parallel upper and lower notional lines), the vertical and horizontal spacing of letters, and the use of various diacritical indicators such as breathing marks, diaireses, and apostrophes.

Using selections of these qualities, paleographers have designated several different groupings (styles) of handwriting. Some of these groups are universally recognized by paleographers; others are the subject of debate. For this discussion, I rely on the classification system of Eric G. Turner, who divides literary writing of the first four centuries CE into three broad groups.[28] His most clearly articulated group is what he calls "Formal Round" writing. Within this group, Turner includes three distinct styles, the Rounded Majuscule (sometimes called the Roman Uncial), the Biblical Majuscule (something of a misnomer, as it was often used for nonbiblical texts), and the Alexandrian Majuscule (sometimes called the Coptic Uncial). These styles are illustrated in Figure 2.8. The Rounded Majuscule is characterized by letters in a square modulus and strict bilinearity, with only phi and psi protruding above and below the notional lines.

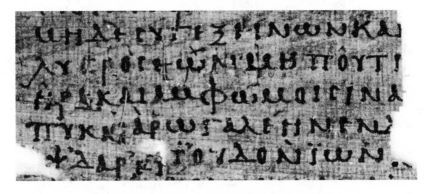

Figure 2.8. Examples of Turner's "Formal Round" classification.
Top: Rounded Majuscule (the Hawara Homer, Bodleian MS. Gr. Class. A.1 [P]);
middle: Biblical Majuscule (Codex Sinaiticus, British Library Add. MS. 43725,
Scribe A); bottom: Alexandrian Majuscule (P.Oxy. 15.1820).

(Images courtesy of the Bodleian Libraries, the University of Oxford; the British Library,
London, UK/Bridgeman Images; and the Egypt Exploration Society and Imaging Papyri
Project, University of Oxford, the Centre for the Study of Ancient Documents, University of
Oxford, the Cairo Museum, the Association Internationale de Papyrologues,
and Dr. Adam Bülow-Jacobsen.)

There is very little discernable differentiated shading in the strokes, which often end with decorative serifs.[29] The Biblical Majuscule, by contrast, shows a well-defined difference in shading with few or no serifs, while maintaining a square modulus, with phi, psi, upsilon, and rho regularly breaking bilinearity.[30] The Alexandrian Majuscule shows rounded letters and a tendency to join strokes with loops, with fewer sharp angles than the Rounded Majuscule or the Biblical Majuscule.[31] The adherence to a square modulus is sometimes less strict in examples of the Alexandrian Majuscule, and the letter xi may be added to the list of those that breach the upper and lower lines.

Turner's next most coherent grouping is the "Formal Mixed" style, which includes samples of what other paleographers would call the "severe style" and the "sloping ogival majuscule."[32] These scripts show a mixture of narrow and broad letterforms, as illustrated in Figure 2.9. As the examples show, the breadth of some letters of the Formal Mixed group can be exaggerated (see especially the mu, nu, and pi of P.Oxy. 17.2098, LDAB 1145), while the omicron is generally smaller than other letters and elevated to a position just below the upper notional line. This style occasionally shows serifs at the ends of some strokes (as in P.Oxy. 60.4055, LDAB 90). Some samples of the Formal Mixed group, such as P.Herm. 4, a personal letter, are documentary rather than literary.

More nebulous is Turner's third and final grouping, the "Informal Round" hands. Included in this classification are a number of different types of writings in capitals that do not achieve the regularity of formation and the precise bilinearity of the Formal Round scripts. A sampling of these is illustrated in Figure 2.10. As the examples indicate, this classification covers a wide assortment of graphic types, and it ought not be understood as a particular style.[33]

When it comes to the question of establishing dates for undated manuscripts, these groupings are usually treated somewhat differently. For the Formal Round and Formal Mixed groupings, a manuscript of unknown date is usually assigned to a style within one of these groups (or its affinities with one or more styles are noted). The earliest and latest securely datable samples of each style will provide the range within which the sample of unknown date can be placed. Because of the presence of more cursive elements in samples of the Informal Round types, the establishment of dates for these pieces

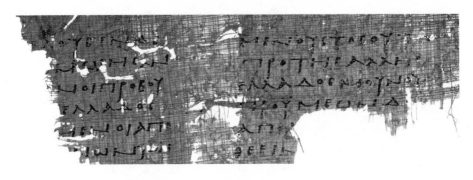

Figure 2.9. Examples of Turner's "Formal Mixed" classification.
From the top: P.Oxy. 17.2098, P.Oxy. 60.4055, P.Bodmer XLVI, and P.Herm. 4.

(Images courtesy of the Egypt Exploration Society and Imaging Papyri Project, University of Oxford; the Fondation Martin Bodmer, Cologny-Geneva; and the John Rylands Library, University of Manchester, copyright of the University of Manchester.)

Figure 2.10. Examples of Turner's "Informal Round" classification.
Top: P.Lond. 2.141 (British Library Papyrus 141, left) and P.Oxy. 50.3531 (right);
bottom: P.Oxy. 50.3533 (left) and P.Oxy. 9.1182 (right).

(Images courtesy of the British Library, London, UK/Bridgeman Images; the Egypt
Exploration Society and Imaging Papyri Project, University of Oxford, the Centre for the
Study of Ancient Documents, the University of Oxford, the Cairo Museum, the Association
Internationale de Papyrologues, and Dr. Adam Bülow-Jacobsen.)

more frequently involves reference to dated documents with similar
types of handwriting.

All competent paleographers agree on this general approach,
but there are differences among them about the degree of chronological precision one can attain using this method.[34] According to a
highly influential group of scholars, one can trace with great chronological precision the rise, perfection, and decline of a particular type
of writing.[35] These paleographers believe that they can not only

assign an undated manuscript to a general stylistic group but also to a particular chronological point in the "evolution" of that style of writing. Such paleographers often feel confident in providing a date range as narrow as twenty-five years or even ten years and in linking types of handwriting very closely to particular historical eras. Others, however, are highly suspicious of such developmental constructs and tightly restricted date ranges. They point out that the frameworks of the alleged rise, perfection, and decline of styles of writing are based on precious few securely dated anchor points.[36] They also stress that slight differences in the formation of letters, rather than showing chronological development or decline, may instead be the result of geographic difference or of the competence, age, or personal inclinations of individual copyists and thus not at all indicative of a relative date.[37] This second group of paleographers would emphasize that copyists could have relatively long working lives (twenty-five to thirty years is not uncommon).[38] They would also note the persistence of writing styles among teachers and students across generations.[39] Finally, this second group of paleographers would highlight the demonstrated ability of copyists to write in styles generally associated with different time periods.[40] This last point especially gives pause, because it challenges the key assumption I mentioned at the outset—that graphic similarity necessarily equates to chronological similarity. Paleographers attuned to these types of complexities hesitate to give precise dates for undated manuscripts and will provide a broader range of dates.

The best way to appreciate these nuances is by looking at a couple of examples. I begin with a case study of the Rounded Majuscule (or Roman Uncial), whose story takes us back to the early days of Greek papyrological paleography and illustrates some of the precarious aspects of paleographic dating. At the turn of the twentieth century, the paleography of Greek papyri was in its infancy. The almost complete absence of datable samples of Greek literary handwriting before the ninth century meant that opinions about dates of any given manuscript of the Roman era could diverge wildly. Before the masses of papyri from Oxyrhynchus and elsewhere in the late 1890s provided a corpus of comparative material to establish a more solid sequence of dated samples of Greek writing, comparisons were made and dates were assigned largely on the basis of a particu-

Figure 2.11. From the top: The Hawara Homer (Bodleian MS. Gr. Class. A.1 [P])
with comparanda: the Ambrosian *Iliad*; P.Oxy. 1.20 (two fragments; British
Library Papyrus 742); and P.Lond. 2.141 (British Library Papyrus 141).

(Images courtesy of the Bodleian Libraries, the University of Oxford; the British
Library, London, UK/Bridgeman Images; the image of the Ambrosian *Iliad* is adapted
from Aristide Calderini, *Ilias Ambrosiana: Cod. F. 205 P. Inf. Bibliothecae Ambrosianae
Mediolanensis* [Bern: Urs Graf, 1953], fol. 31r.)

lar set of Victorian aesthetics (the "handsomeness" of a hand or the
presence or absence of "character"). We can see these processes at
work in the dating of the so-called Hawara Homer (LDAB 1695; see
Figure 2.8 and Figure 2.11), now considered the prime example of
the Rounded Majuscule. Its discovery in 1888 was sensational:

> It is not often that an explorer is so fortunate as to discover
> a prize like that which fell to the lot of Mr Flinders Petrie

last winter. Under the head of a mummy excavated by him at Hawara he found a large roll of papyrus, which, when unfolded, turned out to contain the greater part of the second book of the Iliad. The roll had belonged to a lady with whom it had been buried at death. The skull of the mummy showed that its possessor had been young and attractive-looking, with features at once small, intellectual, and finely chiseled, and belonging distinctively to the Greek type. Through the generosity of Mr Haworth, both skull and papyrus are now in the Bodleian Library at Oxford, along with a tress of the unknown Hypatia's black hair. The papyrus is assigned to the fifth century by Mr Maunde Thompson. The text is written in large beautifully formed capitals.[41]

Edward Maunde Thompson (1840–1929) was the principal librarian of the British Museum and generally acknowledged as the foremost British expert of his day in Greek and Latin paleography. In an 1893 publication, Maunde Thompson described the Hawara Homer as dating from "perhaps as late as the fifth or sixth century."[42] His assignment of the piece to that time period was based upon the similarity of its writing to that of such well-known parchment manuscripts as the "Ambrosian *Iliad*," a richly illustrated but now fragmentary codex in Milan (LDAB 2215, see Figure 2.11). But in 1899, Frederic Kenyon, at that time assistant keeper of manuscripts at the British Museum, published a book on Greek paleography that challenged Maunde Thompson's dating of the Hawara papyrus.[43] Describing the manuscript as having "a strong claim to be regarded as yet handsomer than any that has hitherto been mentioned," Kenyon conceded that features of the writing—letters in a square modulus, "well-rounded curves," a high cross-bar on the alpha, and a deeply curving mu—are indeed found in vellum manuscripts of the fifth and sixth centuries, but he pointed to more recently published papyri datable to the first and second centuries as even more illuminating parallels. He referred in the first instance to P.Lond. 2.141, a lease on papyrus written in 88 CE, but this sample is clearly less formal than the Hawara Homer (see Figure 2.11).[44] More compelling was Kenyon's reference to P.Oxy. 1.20 (LDAB 1630), another copy of the *Iliad* published in 1898, the reverse of which was reused for a cursive document probably written in the late second or early third century. Thus, the *Iliad* on the front was copied before that time, likely in the second century. Pointing also to the presence of cursive notes in the margins of the Hawara Homer that appeared to be written in a hand attributable to the third century, Kenyon assigned the Hawara Homer to the second rather than the fifth century CE. So convincing was Kenyon's case that Maunde Thompson himself came to consider the Hawara Homer as (literally) a textbook example of a second-century hand. In his monumental introduction to Greek and Latin paleography published in 1912, Maunde Thompson featured the Hawara Homer as a prototypical example of literary writing of the second century.[45] The redated Hawara Homer even inspired Maunde Thompson to endorse a reassignment of the Ambrosian *Iliad* to the third century on the basis of its likeness to the Hawara Homer![46]

The proposal of a third-century date for the Ambrosian *Iliad* has not stood the test of time. It is now routinely assigned to the fifth century or the early sixth century.[47] The Hawara Homer, however, has retained its position as a prototypical second-century hand in more recent guidebooks.[48] And the Rounded Majuscule or Roman Uncial, of which the Hawara Homer is the parade example, has been declared to have a date range that is basically limited to the second century. But it is worthwhile to examine the argumentation that led to this conclusion, for it is as much metaphysical as it is paleographic. Guglielmo Cavallo has made the case as follows:

> The elegant harmony of the forms, moreover, certainly recalls a period of intense cultural life in the Greek world. It is well known that the passionate philhellenism of Hadrian promoted the "Renaissance of Hellenism" that assured Greek culture pride of place in the empire; thus the foundations were laid for that blossoming of Hellenism that characterizes the Antonine period. Because graphic manifestations are intimately linked to cultural phenomena inasmuch as, inevitably, they constitute a reflection of them, it is certain that the calligraphic impulse that so thoroughly pervades the literary writing of the second century is in general due to the revival of the values of Greek civilization. The "Roman

uncial" in its most perfect forms is perhaps the highest ex-
pression of this impulse. . . . It is therefore almost certain that
manuscripts such as [P.Oxy. 1.20 and the Hawara Homer]
should be attributed to the age of the Antonines. . . . With
the closing of the second century, different cultural factors
and changing technical trends and tastes signal the decline
and then the disappearance of the "Roman uncial." To document the phase of decline, one can cite . . . above all P.Oxy.
32.2624[, which] shows the impossibility of preserving a
canon when it no longer corresponds to the cultural climate
that expressed it.[49]

Thus, this proposed cultural setting determines the limits for dating
undated papyri of this style. For instance, the papyrus said to most
embody the phase of "decline," P.Oxy. 32.2624 (LDAB 3923), was
in fact assigned by its original editor, Edgar Lobel, to the *first half*
of the second century on the basis of cursive writing on the back
that Lobel thought dated to the second half of the second century.
In order for the papyrus to fit his developmental scheme, Cavallo
reassigned the Rounded Majuscule writing on the front of the papyrus to the late second century and the cursive on the reverse of the
papyrus to the third century.[50]

Yet, if the Rounded Majuscule is to be so strictly associated with
the second century, how do we account for its appearance in manuscripts sometimes assigned to the fifth century, such as the Ambrosian *Iliad*, P.Duk. inv. 5 (Plato's *Parmenides*, LDAB 3827), P.Ant.
2.78 (Plato's *Theaetetus*, LDAB 3830), and PSI 7.748 + 749 (the *Iliad*,
LDAB 2109)? The most widely accepted understanding is that these
later manuscripts are examples of "archaizing," that is, deliberately
mimicking an obsolete script out of antiquarian interests. Indeed,
Cavallo has proposed a very specific cultural setting and reason for
the reappearance of the Rounded Majuscule in the fifth century.
Noting the supposed absence of Christian texts copied in the most
formal Rounded Majuscule script, Cavallo posited that its appearance in later manuscripts represented a "revival" that came about
"in a pagan and conservative environment . . . to create an ideal continuity with the book of the classical tradition in an age when that
tradition was drawing near to its tragic death. The Ambrosian *Iliad*

shows that the designated function, between the fifth and sixth centuries, of the Rounded Majuscule was that which brought back to
life, in a graphic way, the Antiquity against which the Byzantine was
destined to triumph."[51] Yet again, however, matters of actual evidence
and paleography might not be so tidy. A fragment of a papyrus roll
published in 1980 known as PSI 11.1200 bis (LDAB 4669) is regularly classified as a specimen of the Rounded Majuscule script, but
it employs the *nomina sacra* abbreviations characteristic of Christian
manuscripts, showing that this script was used for Christian manuscripts and not just non-Christian ones.[52] Furthermore, P.Duk.
inv. 5, which on Cavallo's theory ought to be an artifact of the fifth
century, was assigned by its original editor to the second century
(on the basis of what he perceived as closer similarity to the Hawara
Homer than to the Ambrosian *Iliad*).[53] Eric Turner assigned the
Duke parchment to the third or fourth century.[54] Such assignments
raise the possibility that examples of this script might be more evenly
spread across the period from the early second century, through the
third and fourth centuries, and into the fifth century.

It is worthwhile to think a little more about this phenomenon of
archaism (or is it persistence?) of related hands. One of the samples
mentioned by Cavallo as showing letterforms that anticipate the
second-century emergence of the Rounded Majuscule is P.Oxy. 2.246,
a record of a transaction involving livestock with an explicit date,
the twelfth year of Nero, or 66 CE.[55] The papyrus is written in what
its editors called "a fine uncial hand of a literary type." A sample of
its writing is placed side by side in Figure 2.12 with another Oxyrhynchus papyrus, P.Oxy. 50.3529 (LDAB 5716). The editor of P.Oxy.
50.3529 made explicit reference to its similarity with P.Oxy. 2.246
and noted that its script "is large, upright, and gawky; this awkward-
ness, and some letter-forms, especially the narrowly-pointed alpha,
might suggest the early Roman period."[56] The identity of the work
on the papyrus, however, makes such a date impossible, for P.Oxy.
50.3529 is a copy of the Martyrdom of Dioscorus, who was killed
under the prefect Culcianus in the twenty-third year of Diocletian
(306–307 CE). Thus P.Oxy. 50.3529 was copied after that point,
demonstrating that this type of writing could still be used as much
as two to three centuries after the time it was used in P.Oxy. 2.246.
Is this an instance of a copyist of Christian literature deliberately

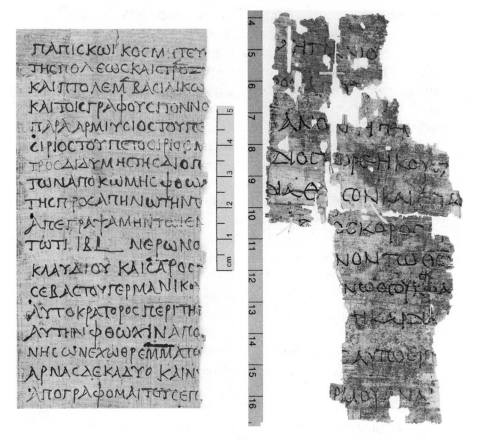

Figure 2.12. P.Oxy. 2.246 (Cambridge University Library Add. MS. 4052),
a transaction involving livestock (66 CE) (left), and P.Oxy. 50.3529, a copy of
the Martyrdom of Dioscorus (after 306–307 CE) (right).

(Images courtesy of Cambridge University Library; the Egypt Exploration
Society and Imaging Papyri Project, University of Oxford.)

imitating a form of writing that had been obsolete for centuries, as
Cavallo had proposed for the copyist of "pagan" literature in the
Rounded Majuscule? Or is it simply a form of writing that persisted
through the centuries but which, because of accidents of survival,
has so far not appeared in samples securely datable to the second
and third centuries? Both possibilities are disconcerting for the
paleographer.

    If we are dealing with archaism in the case of the Rounded Ma-
juscule and related scripts, we are left with the question of how com-

mon this kind of phenomenon was. Because of the relatively small pool of securely dated examples, it is difficult to know. The following summation by Peter Parsons is sobering and concludes with a real stinger for those of us who study early Christian manuscripts: "We do not know whether archaism was a matter of personal choice or the habit of certain scriptoria or the requirement of certain patrons, or whether it was more likely at certain periods or places or in the copying of certain genres of text (say, scriptural texts)."[57]

A second (and much briefer) case study reveals further difficulties, although it in many ways represents an ideal situation. Lucio Del Corso, an expert paleographer, has generated a list of all the examples of the "severe style" published in the first seventy volumes of the P.Oxy. series.[58] So we have a group of samples all found (though not necessarily copied) at a single location. Out of this corpus of 248 examples, sixteen have either a reasonably secure *terminus post quem* or a *terminus ante quem* established by one of the methods already discussed. The earliest of these datable samples was probably copied in the second half of the second century, the latest in the second half of the third century. Therefore, it is not surprising that undated manuscripts written in the severe style are usually assigned to the second or third centuries.

But matters are not quite so simple. First of all, what counts as the severe style? Del Corso states that he has been "inclusive" in his determination, but his list names only three papyri containing Christian material. Other equally respected paleographers have described the writing of many more Christian pieces from Oxyrhynchus as belonging to the severe style.[59] This observation just highlights the very subjective nature of paleographical assignments. More important is an interesting conundrum presented by Del Corso's database: All the datable samples on his list are rolls rather than codices. On one level, the point is obvious. As we have seen, rolls have a blank side that could be reused and thereby sometimes provide a secure *terminus post quem* or *terminus ante quem* for samples of literary writing on the rolls.[60] Yet, this fact has implications for the dating of the *codices* in Del Corso's list (there are at least ten of them, mostly assigned to the third century).[61] The third and fourth centuries CE are generally recognized as the period during which the decisive shift from roll to codex as the vehicle for the transmission of literature occurred.[62] But the pool of datable samples of the severe style comes exclusively from rolls, and these samples have been used to assign dates even to the codices that also display this type of handwriting. It may be the case that all of these codices were in fact produced during the third century. Yet, it is equally possible that the severe style persisted beyond the second half of the third century, but we have a dearth of examples *datable* to this later period because the medium of choice had shifted to the codex, which cannot easily incorporate used dated documents or be itself reused for documents.[63] If so, dates assigned to codices on the basis of datable samples obtained from rolls may tend to skew early. And this is not just an issue for the severe style of writing.[64] In fact, the many new datable samples of Greek literary handwriting of all styles of the Roman era that have come to light over the past 120 years are overwhelmingly derived from rolls rather than codices.[65] But it is this database of samples *from rolls* that has been used to assign dates both to rolls *and to codices*. This fact has special importance for the dating of early Christian manuscripts, which tend to be copied in the codex format.[66] It may be the case that much of the corpus of early Christian codices has been dated too early.

In the following chapters, we will see several examples of early Christian manuscripts, especially those containing what would come to be designated as "biblical" material, that have been dated within quite narrow limits (and quite early) solely on the basis of paleography. I offer alternative analyses that bring to bear other factors beyond paleography, such as archaeological provenance and codicology. Although paleography, when practiced in a disciplined manner involving close comparison with securely dated examples of handwriting, can establish a range of possible dates for an undated literary manuscript, it can never be conclusive. Paleographic comparison is by its very nature a subjective undertaking, and oftentimes, especially when early Christian manuscripts are concerned, paleographic dating can devolve into little more than an exercise in wishful thinking.[67]

Radiocarbon Analysis

If paleography is so subjective and problematic, radiocarbon analysis stands out as potentially bringing a welcome dose of hard science to the question of dating ancient manuscripts. It is true that radio-carbon analysis does provide us with extremely helpful data, but it is not quite the magic bullet that it is sometimes imagined to be when it comes to dating manuscripts. The crucial point (often missed when the results of radiocarbon analysis are publicized) is that radiometric dates are expressed not in exact years (say, "circa 250 CE") but rather in terms of ranges of years and probabilities. To understand why this is the case, it is helpful to take a moment for a somewhat simplified discussion of the process that gives us these dates.[68]

The majority of carbon atoms on earth have an atomic weight of 12, but when cosmic rays interact with nitrogen atoms in the upper atmosphere, the unstable (radioactive) carbon-14 isotope is produced. These isotopes form carbon dioxide molecules and disperse into the lower atmosphere. During the process of photosynthesis, a small percentage of the carbon dioxide that plants absorb contains the carbon-14 isotope. When animals consume plants, they acquire carbon-14 as well. Thus all living things regularly absorb carbon-14 and maintain rough equilibrium with the content of carbon-14 present in the atmosphere until they die. At that point, they cease to acquire new carbon-14. Because carbon-14 decays at a regular rate, decreasing by half every 5,730 years (its "half-life"), the amount of carbon-14 present in dead organic material functions as a kind of clock, ticking away until the unstable isotope is completely decayed.

Scientists can measure the amount of carbon-14 in a sample and use an equation to determine the age of the material in "radiocarbon years" before the present ("BP"), where "present" is understood to be the year 1950.[69] This age in radiocarbon years is accompanied by a number representing the level of uncertainty in the calculation, indicating the precision of the measurement. These results, however, are based on the assumption that the amount of carbon-14 in the atmosphere has remained constant, which it has not. Because the percentage of carbon-14 has varied, these results in radiocarbon years BP must be converted into calendar years through a process of calibration that accounts for the variation of the amount of carbon-14 in the atmosphere. This calibration is accomplished in large part by using a simple fact that we all learn as children: You can tell how old a tree is by counting its rings. The science of dendrochronology provides us with a long, continuous series of organic specimens of known ages, namely tree rings.[70] Once a tree ring is formed, it no longer takes in new carbon-14. Each annual ring thus carries the signature of the carbon-14 content of the atmosphere for the year in which it was produced. Droughts and periods of intense rain alter the sizes of tree rings in a given region, and thus over a period of time, clear patterns of rings emerge. These patterns of rings in younger trees have been carefully matched with the overlapping patterns of rings in older trees going back thousands of years. The age of these rings in radiocarbon years BP can then be coordinated with their known ages in calendar years to produce a calibration curve. This curve can then be used to convert radiocarbon years BP to a range of calendar dates with degrees of probability. Figure 2.13 is the segment of a recent calibration curve for the first few centuries of the common era. Note that the curve is not a fine line but rather a swath, which reflects the uncertainty of the radiocarbon age determinations. Also, note that the "wiggles" at some points in the calibration curve illustrate that some radiocarbon years BP will correspond to more than one set of calendar years. Thus, the calibrated results of radiocarbon analysis will provide a range (or ranges) of possible dates with degrees of probability that the actual date falls somewhere within the range(s).

I should pause here to emphasize this key point: The results of radiocarbon analysis give us *ranges* of possible dates, ranges within which any date is just as probable as any other date. It is worth quoting a geochronologist on this important nuance: "Dates reported in the scientific literature are typically given in the form '5,000 years, plus or minus 300 years.' This simply means that, to a high degree of probability (which is usually specified precisely when a date is reported), the true age of the sample lies between 4,700 and 5,300 years. It is as likely to be 4,795 years, or 5,123 years, or anything else in that range, as to be exactly 5,000 years."[71] Thus, when we read, for example, that a papyrus dates to 250 CE ± 50 years, no special significance should be placed on that "central" year. Any year within the range would be equally likely. So, a better way of expressing such dates would be to use the earlier and later limits (in this case, 200–300 CE) in order not to give the impression of undue precision.

The technology used to carry out these fairly accurate radiocarbon datings has existed since the late 1960s, but it is only in more

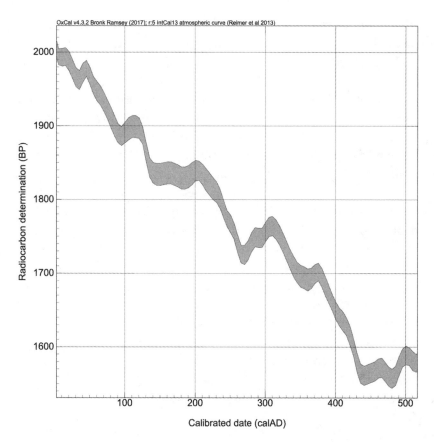

Figure 2.13. A recent calibration curve for the first five centuries CE showing radiocarbon years on the vertical axis and calendar years on the horizontal axis.
(Image from OxCal v4.3.2, https://c14.arch.ox.ac.uk/oxcal/OxCal.html.)

recent decades that radiocarbon analysis has become practical for the study of papyrus and parchment manuscripts. While such artifacts in theory could have been tested during the 1950s and 1960s, older methods of measurement required that relatively large samples of the artifacts be destroyed in the process of acquiring a sufficient mass of carbon-14. With the development of accelerator mass spectrometry (AMS), results can be attained with much smaller samples. In the case of papyrus, analysis can sometimes be performed successfully on just a few fibers taken from the empty margins of a manuscript.

The most compelling results of radiocarbon analysis emerge

when an object's date is disputed by a matter of several centuries or more. The so-called Shroud of Turin provides an ideal example. The earliest secure historical record of the shroud is a letter written in 1389 from Pierre d'Arcis, the bishop of Troyes, to Pope Clement VII in Avignon. The bishop had complained to the (anti-)pope that the shroud, a "cleverly painted" cloth, was falsely being presented as the actual burial cloth used to wrap Jesus.[72] Although the bishop believed this cloth was a recently produced fraud, many others, both in his era and even in our own day, have regarded it as the authentic shroud used to cover the body of the crucified Jesus, and thus an artifact of the first century. In the late 1980s, radiocarbon analysis of small portions of the shroud was carried out at three separate facilities at the University of Arizona, Oxford, and Zürich. The three analyses were in very close agreement: "The results . . . yield a calibrated calendar age range with at least 95% confidence for the linen of the Shroud of Turin of AD 1260–1390 (rounded down/up to nearest 10 yr)."[73] It is telling that these results align so closely with the earliest certain appearance of the shroud in the historical record in the fourteenth century. The radiocarbon analysis of the shroud has thus proved to the satisfaction of sober observers that the shroud is a product of the thirteenth or fourteenth century and not the first century.[74]

Radiocarbon analysis has produced somewhat less clear verdicts when it comes to ancient papyrus and parchment dating from closer to the early Christian period. Part of the problem is that the historical questions we wish to answer usually deal with smaller intervals of time. With the Shroud of Turin, the question was, Does this cloth date from the Roman era or the late medieval period? With papyrus and parchment manuscripts, the questions are more along the lines of, Was this manuscript most likely produced in the middle of the second century or the early fourth century? For these sorts of questions, radiocarbon analysis is still helpful but considerably less decisive. Methods of reporting results and the possibility of even slight contamination take on greater importance.

A good example of the complexity of the issues can be found in the efforts to use radiometric dating on the Dead Sea Scrolls. Discovered in the vicinity of the site of Qumran on the shores of the Dead Sea in the 1940s and 1950s, the Dead Sea Scrolls consist of a collection of more than nine hundred Jewish texts on parchment, leather, and papyrus in varying states of preservation.[75] Although scholars from early on broadly agreed that the scrolls likely emerged from the Hellenistic and Roman eras, they disagreed about when, precisely, the scrolls were copied.[76] In 1990, portions of several scrolls were subjected to radiocarbon analysis in Zürich.[77] A second set of tests was carried out a few years later at Arizona.[78] The results of these tests showed that some of the samples could be as early as the third century BCE and some as late as the end of the first century CE, with many of the ranges clustering in the first century BCE. This outcome thus did not end the debates about the precise time that the scrolls were copied, and in fact the analysis may have created as much controversy as it resolved.

The first difficulty had to do with the way the results of the analysis were reported. The initial presentation of the results used phrases like "good agreement between radiocarbon and paleographic dates" and "ages determined from carbon-14 measurements [are] in reasonable agreement with paleographic estimates."[79] Many scholars took this language to mean "Carbon 14 datings of Dead Sea Scrolls have confirmed the dates assigned to them by paleographers."[80] Yet, such claims are highly misleading. For one thing, the radiocarbon dates of some of the samples barely overlapped or did not overlap at all with the suggested paleographic dates.[81] More importantly, even when there was overlap, the radiocarbon dates still cannot be said to "confirm" the correctness of the paleographic dates because most of the proposed paleographic ranges are incredibly narrow.[82] For instance, one copy of the book of Isaiah (1QIsaᵃ) was assigned a paleographic date of 150–125 BCE. The results of the Arizona radiocarbon analysis of that roll yielded a date range of 250–103 BCE at 76 percent probability. So, if the radiocarbon analysis "confirmed" or "was in agreement with" a paleographic date of 150–125 BCE, then it also would have "confirmed" or "been in agreement with" a paleographic date of 250–225 BCE, a full century earlier.[83] Because paleographic dates are so often proclaimed in unrealistically narrow ranges, a given radiocarbon date range can actually "confirm" several contradictory sets of paleographic dates. The whole language of "confirmation" should thus be dropped in these contexts. A more useful (and accurate) way of describing the relationship would be to say that a given range of paleographic dates *is not inconsistent* with the results of radiocarbon analysis.

A second difficulty arose with the recognition that even the rigorous cleaning treatments used by the labs may not have been sufficient to remove contamination from castor oil and other organic products applied to the parchment scrolls during the years after their discovery.[84] Thus, the radiocarbon dates of some of the parchment pieces may be skewed. In the case of the papyrus material analyzed, contamination also seems to have been an issue. One of the papyrus pieces tested as part of a control group was a deed of sale written in Aramaic that carries a date of "year 3 of the freedom of Israel," that is, 134 or 135 CE.[85] The results of radiocarbon analysis returned a range of 144–370 CE with a probability of 95 percent.[86] What has happened here? The most likely explanation is contamination by modern carbon-14. Because this sample carries a precise date, we can clearly see that the radiocarbon analysis has yielded a range of dates that is not correct. This observation should prompt us to always remember the flip side of these percentages: In this case, the results of the radiocarbon analysis inform us that there is a 5 percent chance that the actual date of the papyrus *does* fall outside the 144–370 CE window. Sometimes improbable things happen.

A different but related set of issues surrounds the radiocarbon analysis of the so-called Codex Tchacos (LDAB 108481), which contains the Gospel of Judas. When the National Geographic Society published a translation of the gospel with much fanfare during the Easter season of 2006, the fact that the codex had been subjected to radiocarbon analysis was widely reported in the media.[87] The society's official publication said this about the carbon-14 dating:

> Four samples were papyrus pieces from the codex, while a fifth was a small section of leather book binding with papyrus attached. No portion of the text was damaged in this process. In early January 2005, scientists at the AMS lab completed their radiocarbon-dating testing. While individual samples' calibrated ages varied, the mean calendar age for the collection was between CE 220 and 340, with an error margin of +/– sixty years. According to AMS Lab Director Dr. Tim Jull and research scientist Greg Hodgins, "the cal-

ibrated ages of the papyrus and leather samples are tightly
clustered and place the age of the Codices within the Third
or Fourth centuries A.D."[88]

This is the extent of the information that the National Geographic Society provided in its official publication of the Gospel of
Judas. As I write these words in 2017, the full results have not yet
been published in a scientific periodical. My request for a copy of
the results received no response.[89] Some further information on the
radiometric testing is available in a second volume produced by the
society, a popular account of the discovery and marketing of the codex
written by journalist Herbert Krosney.[90] One must handle Krosney's
report with caution, however, for it contains a number of errors.[91]
What we are able to learn is that "the mean calendar age" reported
by the National Geographic Society was determined by calculating
the results from the samples taken from the codex pages *and* samples
taken from the papyri used as stuffing for the leather cover of the
codex.[92] As we have seen, such papyrus from the covers of books is
usually waste, and its creation would predate its use as stuffing for the
leather cover by an indeterminate amount of time. The inclusion of
these pieces in the production of the statistical mean has skewed the
reported date of the codex too early. An analysis that omits the papyrus taken from the cover would produce a range of dates from the
late third century to the very end of the fourth century.[93] This corrected radiocarbon range has more overlap with paleographic analysis of the Tchacos codex, which tends to assign the writing to the
fourth or fifth century.[94]

The date of "280 CE ± 60 years" for the Tchacos codex that one
frequently sees reported as fact is therefore highly suspect. Yet, an
early date placing the codex in the third century fits a certain narrative of the history of early Christianity. This is nicely captured in a
comment by one of the scientists who carried out the radiocarbon
analysis: "All five samples, remarkably, are the same age. . . . All date
to the third to fourth century, clearly before the Council of Nicaea,
which presumably would have suppressed such a document."[95] But
as I outlined above, the results of the radiocarbon analysis in fact
do not rule out a date after the Council of Nicaea (which took place
in the year 325). Rather, a set of preconceptions about Nicene

Christians and "heretical" literature appears to have been a guiding influence in the reporting of the results. It seems that even scientists can get caught up in the sensationalism of ancient Christian manuscripts.

I wish to be clear. Radiocarbon analysis is a very useful tool that has revolutionized archaeology. The examples I have cited here may leave the impression that it cannot help us date early Christian manuscripts, but that is not at all my purpose. I have drawn attention to these incidents in order to show that when it comes to ancient manuscripts, radiocarbon analysis is not necessarily the panacea it is sometimes thought to be. Like the results of all other dating methods, the results of radiocarbon analysis need to be treated with caution. When carried out properly and reported accurately, however, this kind of analysis adds important data to be considered along with available archaeological, codicological, and paleographic evidence when trying to establish dates for early Christian manuscripts.

Ink Analysis

Before closing this discussion, I turn to the analysis of ink, which is occasionally invoked in the discussion of dating ancient Christian manuscripts. As I mentioned in Chapter 1, the black inks of the Roman era were usually composed of soot and gum arabic. In the third and fourth centuries, we see more examples of inks containing metallic compounds. These metallic-based inks tend to fade to brown over the centuries and can often be identified simply by examining a manuscript with the naked eye.[96] More advanced techniques can analyze samples of ink to determine exactly what chemical components they contain.[97] As we have seen in the cases of paleography and radiocarbon analysis, claims that ink analysis can provide precise dates for manuscripts are sometimes rather exaggerated. The Gospel of Judas can again help to illustrate the pitfalls. In early 2013, several news outlets circulated a story stating that ink analysis of the Gospel of Judas was "consistent with a date of approximately A.D. 280."[98] Some biblical scholars seized on the round number. In a blog posting, one prominent scholar of the Gospel of Judas provided a link to a Fox News story on the topic and commented, "Apparently the ink has been studied in depth and it has been definitively dated to

280 CE. Now that is early!"[99] Of course, the ink analysis by no means "definitively" dated the codex. The news story was derived from a study carried out by the firm McCrone Associates, which stated in its report: "McCrone Associates determined the components used to create the ancient ink were consistent with ingredients in known inks from the third and fourth centuries A.D. One ink included a carbon black constituent, in the form of soot, bound with a gum adhesive. The other ink found in the document was an iron-based ink, which is thought to be [an] intermediate between the ancient world's carbon-based inks and the modern iron gall formulations that became popular in early medieval times."[100] In the current state of research, what ink analysis can tell us is whether certain chemical components are present or absent in a sample. These data can be compared with the profile of ink samples of known ages to find out whether the composition of the ink in question is consistent or inconsistent with the composition of the dated samples of ink.[101] For the Gospel of Judas, the report concluded that the makeup of its ink was "consistent with ingredients in known inks from the third and fourth centuries" (though one might add that carbon-based inks with metallic compounds were also commonly in use from the fifth century to the seventh century as well).[102] Thus, at present, the usefulness of ink analysis for assigning a precise date to a Roman-era manuscript is somewhat limited.[103] Very recent developments may change this situation, however. A 2016 study published by scientists at Columbia University has raised the possibility that Raman spectroscopy may be able to track oxidation in components of ancient ink and thus provide a possible nondestructive means of estimating dates for ancient manuscripts.[104] These results are intriguing and potentially revolutionary, but they await further testing and confirmation. For now, analysis of ink simply provides another piece of useful data to add to the mix, but it is not (yet) a "definitive" dating criterion.

Assigning a date to Greek literary manuscripts of the Roman era is a difficult task. In some cases, we are lucky enough to have clues that can give us a firm *terminus post quem* or *terminus ante quem*, but most of the time, especially with fragmentary Christian manuscripts, we are forced to resort to the inexact art of paleography to assign a date. If the institutions that own the manuscripts have the money and willingness to subject pieces to radiocarbon testing and ink analysis, we may be able to gain further insight from these techniques, though these results must also be regarded critically. The bottom line is that if you see reports of dates like "circa 150 CE" or "about the year 200" in reference to an early Christian manuscript, you should be very suspicious. Chances are good that the sources of such reports simply do not understand the complexities of how these manuscripts are dated. These sorts of issues need to be constantly kept in mind as we move on to survey the earliest Christian manuscripts.

CHAPTER THREE

Finding Early Christian Books
in Egypt

I N THE EARLY HOURS of October 23, 1731, a devastating fire
swept through the Ashburnham House in London, which had
recently become home to both the royal collection of manuscripts and the large collection of books amassed by Sir Robert Bruce Cotton (1571–1631) and his descendants. Many of the
holdings were destroyed or severely damaged, but some escaped.
According to the official inquiry into the disaster, "The Fire prevail-
ing, notwithstanding the Means used to extinguish it, Mr. *Casley* the
Deputy-Librarian took Care in the first Place to remove the famous
Alexandrian MS. and the Books under the Head of *Augustus* in the
Cottonian Library, as being esteemed the most valuable amongst the
Collection."[1] The "Alexandrian manuscript" reportedly rescued by
David Casley (1681–1754) is now best known as Codex Alexandri-
nus (LDAB 3481), a parchment codex of the Greek Bible generally
assigned to the fifth century. Among the manuscripts that fared less
well in the fire were those shelved under the bust of the emperor
Otho. These included the so-called Cotton Genesis (LDAB 3242),
a richly illustrated parchment codex containing the book of Genesis
in Greek usually thought to have been copied in the late fifth century. It was badly burned and reduced to "a charred ruin."[2]
  What is interesting for our purposes is that both the Codex Al-

83

exandrinus and the Cotton Genesis had already been known to British and European scholars for more than a century at the time of the great fire of 1731. The first certain appearance of Codex Alexandrinus in the historical record is its presentation as a "gift" from the patriarch of Constantinople to the British crown in the late 1620s.[3] The presence of the Cotton Genesis in England can be traced back to a period at least a half century earlier. One of its leaves bears the signature of Thomas Wakefeld, the first Regius Professor of Hebrew at Cambridge, who died in 1575. Exactly how and when the codex got to England in the first place remains a mystery.[4]

There is even earlier evidence for the presence in Western Europe of other ancient Christian books, like the famous fourth-century Greek Bible, Codex Vaticanus (LDAB 3479), and Codex Bezae, the Greek-Latin diglot copy of the gospels and Acts (LDAB 2929), probably copied in the fifth century.[5] Ancient Christian books with material outside the typical biblical canon were also known at quite early dates. In the second half of the eighteenth century, two Coptic codices containing Christian "gnostic" texts came to light. The noted traveler James Bruce (1730–1794) acquired a papyrus book in Thebes sometime around 1769.[6] Known as the "Bruce Codex" (LDAB 107927), it was probably produced in the fourth century and included three texts in Coptic, one of which carries a title, "The Book of the Great Logos Corresponding to Mysteries." Also in the eighteenth century, the physician and book collector Dr. Anthony Askew (d. 1774) was able to acquire "at a book shop" a fourth- or fifth-century parchment codex (LDAB 107926), which contained an extended dialogue between the resurrected Jesus and his disciples on "gnostic" themes.[7] Although the nature of their contents seems to have held more interest for Theosophists than for church historians, the antiquity of these unorthodox Christian books was recognized early on.[8]

So, several ancient Christian books were known already in the eighteenth century, but it is the nineteenth and twentieth centuries that are generally regarded as the golden age of discoveries of Christian manuscripts. And rightly so. Whether it was the sheer number of Christian manuscripts that came to light from a site like Oxyrhynchus, or the strange forgotten Christian texts that were uncovered such as the Gospel According to Peter from Akhmim or the ending of Mark in the Freer codex of the gospels, or the acquisition of complete or nearly complete biblical books thought to come from the second and third centuries, the discoveries of Christian books in the century between 1860 and 1960 were of a different order and fundamentally altered the landscape of biblical scholarship.

Why did so many manuscripts emerge from Egypt at this time? There were many reasons. Increasing travel to Egypt by Europeans created demand for portable antiquities, including books. That period also saw a growing number of organized excavations of ancient sites in Egypt. And as we will see, many early Christian manuscripts from Egypt are said to have been discovered by local Egyptians who were "digging for fertilizer," a practice sometimes characterized as an age-old tradition, which it may well be. But this practice also has a fairly specific history in the second half of the nineteenth century. During the American Civil War, U.S. cotton exports plunged, with the result that cotton production in Egypt exploded to fill the void in the global cotton market.[9] Demand for cultivatable land in Egypt thus increased greatly, which brought about a corresponding need for fertilizer. A natural source was available in the form of what Egyptians call *sebakh*. This material consists of the remains of ancient buildings composed of mud-brick (Nile silt mixed with straw) along with centuries' worth of plant and animal refuse that accumulated in huge mounds surrounding ancient cities.[10] The high concentration of nitrates in *sebakh* made it useful for fertilizer and also for the manufacture of gunpowder. The second half of the nineteenth century thus saw the large-scale destruction of many ancient sites in Egypt as groups of local workers (*sebakhin*) dug out ancient sites and transported the *sebakh* to be spread on fields near and far. So it is no accident that the great age of manuscript discoveries in Egypt began in the second half of the nineteenth century, and many books no doubt were accidentally discovered while people were digging for *sebakh*. At the same time, because the gathering of *sebakh* was an activity regulated by the government, it often seems to have provided a convenient cover for the intentional looting of ancient sites.

In order to establish some context for the Beatty, Bodmer, and Oxyrhynchus materials to be discussed in detail in the following chapters, here I give a broad overview of discoveries of early Christian manuscripts in the sands of Egypt over the past two centuries. I thus omit discussion of such spectacular discoveries outside Egypt as that of the Faddan More Psalter (LDAB 128980), a ninth-century parchment codex with covers made of leather and papyrus that turned up in an Irish bog in 2006.[11] I also leave aside the well-documented stories of manuscripts acquired from the holdings of active monasteries, most (in)famously Constantine von Tischendorf's procurement of a substantial portion of a fourth-century Greek Bible, the Codex Sinaiticus, from Saint Catherine's Monastery at Mount Sinai in the 1840s and 1850s.[12] My focus instead is on Christian manuscripts unearthed through licit and illicit excavation in Egypt over the course of the past century and a half.[13] What can we know about the histories of these books? In what contexts were Christian manuscripts discovered?[14] How did they come to be known? Although some of these "discovery" stories are quite familiar within the guild of biblical scholars, the fragility of the evidence that supports them is less frequently discussed. I proceed by first giving some previously unpublished data about a quite well-documented find of Christian books from Hamuli in the Fayum. I then discuss the various contexts in which Christian books have been reportedly found, namely, tombs, caves, houses or buildings, and areas in and around monastic dwellings. I close with a discussion of what is easily the most famous discovery of Christian books, the hoard of Coptic codices found near Nag Hammadi.

The Anatomy of a Chance Find: The Coptic Codices from Hamuli

Only a few of the important finds of ancient Christian books in the nineteenth and twentieth centuries were the result of professional archaeological excavation. In most cases, we are dealing with treasure hunting or chance finds. Thus, discoveries of early Christian manuscripts are often shrouded in mystery, with little more than hearsay and the tales of antiquities dealers to connect us to the archaeological context of the finds. We are fortunate, however, to have an account of one manuscript find produced just a few years after the time of the discovery by someone who was both a close observer of, and a participant in, the initial sale of the discovered

books. David L. Askren (1875–1939) was an American medical missionary in the Fayum region.[15] He arrived in Egypt in 1899 at the
United Presbyterian Hospital in Asyut and started his own practice
farther north in the Fayum in 1904. He continued working in the
Fayum as a doctor until 1939. He regularly treated the Egyptian
workers (*fellahin*), who often uncovered ancient manuscripts, and his
name will reappear at several points in this book, especially in regard
to manuscripts that ended up being exported to the United States.

In a letter to Francis W. Kelsey (1858–1927), professor of Latin
language and literature at the University of Michigan, Askren described in some detail the discovery and marketing of a collection of
Coptic books eventually bought by J. Pierpont Morgan in 1911.[16]
The Hamuli codices are a collection of about fifty books of biblical, extrabiblical, and liturgical content. Some of them are richly
illustrated, and some have leather bindings that are still intact.
They mostly date from the ninth and tenth centuries. Thus, while
these codices come from a time several centuries removed from the
very earliest Christian books in Egypt, the circumstances of their
discovery are nevertheless instructive because they are exceptionally
well documented. Askren's letter about the Hamuli find provides a
good example of the challenges one encounters when trying to ascertain the exact archaeological conditions of a chance discovery
like this one:[17]

Steamship "CANOPIC"
February 11th, 1915.

My dear Mr. Kelsey,

In accordance with your request, I have the pleasure to
give you a brief history of the discovery of the Coptic Manuscripts near Hamooli, Fayoum, Egypt.

During the winter 1909 and 1910 a German excavator
by the name of Dr. Zuker was working in Fayoum district.[18]
He excavated about a month in an ancient Roman city near
Rubiyatt but finding nothing he crossed over the lake Dimé
but not finding anything he left Dimé and walked along the
western side of the Fayum to an old Roman ruin called in
Arabic Medinet el Maadi (City of the past) where he arrived
about the first of January 1910.

At this site he found some pottery and Papyri but of no great value and late in January Typhus fever appeared among his workers and I was forced to break up his camp.

During Dr. Zuker's walk along the western desert at a point near Hamooli he noticed a small mound of ancient ruins, but owing to its insignificance he did not stop to excavate it.

At this time the Fellahin (farmers) were beginning to dig in this mound to obtain dust for fertilizer and owing again to its insignificance, they were permitted to work without the usual Government Antiquities Guard.

This ancient mound covered the ruins of a building of some size and was evidently the remains of an old Coptic Convent, the natives using the word Kineesa (church) to describe it.

One day early in February, as I remember about February 10, 1910, the Fellahin opened up a room, and in this room they found a receptacle (Arabic sanduk) full of books of parchment.

They considered they had made a big find but could not keep it secret, so there was an immediate division of the spoils and the books were scattered among the villagers, and in some instances in the subdivision the books were even divided into single pages.

The first books brought into the Fayoum were sold to a Greek merchant by the name of Stomati Scopelitis for two hundred dollars for two books, which were purchased from the Fellahin by Fanous Monsour for one-hundred and twenty-five dollars at Hamooli, both being personally known to me as they are among my clientèle.[19]

As such a find must at once be reported to the Government the local mayor of the town of Hamooli attempted to obtain the books but failing he called in the aid of a higher police official who used force and searched many houses frightening the natives very much, and naturally all denied any knowledge of them to prevent confiscation though they maintained quite a traffic among themselves often at the price of ten dollars per page.

Two days after Stomati Scopelitis purchased his books Dr. Zuker happened into my clinic so I took him to Stomati's and showed him the books; after looking them over he told us they were formulae, etc. of alchemy, and that he did not consider them of great value, perhaps one hundred and twenty-five dollars per book.

About five days after the discovery, I was informed that a large Greek dealer from Cairo and also a native dealer, Ali Arabi of Gizeh,[20] were out at Hamooli buying the books and were paying five hundred dollars per book, and two or three days later a native friend brought one complete and part of a second book to me to sell for him.

Some days later I took my books to Cairo and attempted to sell them to various dealers who placed the price at one hundred and twenty-five dollars for the ones without a frontispiece and two hundred dollars for the ones with a picture. One of the dealers informed me that this was the price that had been placed upon them by various savants at the time in Cairo, among them British Museum experts.

I then took my books to Mr. Nahman[21] of the Credit Foncier and there saw the Greek antiquity merchant who had been in Fayoum.

I sold my books to Mr. Nahman, who told me at the time that he had acquired quite a number of them, but that he was afraid he would not be able to realize on them.

Later, I do not remember how long afterward, the story got out among local dealers, that Mr. Nahman had sold the books to Mr. Pierpont Morgan in Paris for a million dollars, and that it was a very bad bargain for Mr. Morgan.[22]

It was and is yet common gossip that there were about two hundred volumes found by the natives, but as only fifty were eventually acquired by Mr. Nahman, I am inclined to believe that they are all that were found and that the two hundred estimate is only a grossly exaggerated native story.

I know that there were a number of books bought by the native from Gizeh, Ali Arabic [sic], but I presume that he and Mr. Nahman came to some agreement and Mr. Nahman took the entire find to Paris.

In view of your interest in the discovery of manuscripts in this region I will make inquiry from time to time of the Fellahin who come to me as patients and if I can get track of any manuscripts now in hiding or hereafter discovered I will try to get possession of them, and hold them till I can send you an account of them with photographs or one or more sample pages and this I will do with the understanding that if you desire the manuscripts you will come or send for them within a reasonable period, making a price which shall bear a fair relation to the price which I shall have to pay the Fellahin.

I am practicing medicine at Fayoum, Egypt, and expect to remain there. My address is the American Mission, Fayoum, Egypt.

I have the honour to be,
Yours,
(signed) David L. Askren

This account highlights several reasons why the exact details of a discovery of ancient books (the number of books involved, the precise location and archaeological context of the find) can be very difficult to reconstruct after the fact: Finds of books can be divided almost immediately upon discovery and dispersed among those present. Books can be further subdivided by intermediaries. News of a discovery can quickly attract antiquities dealers from out of town who can purchase and further scatter parts of a find while at the same time mixing the materials from the new discovery with their existing inventories. The fear of confiscation by the government can lead to the suppression of accurate information and the production of false stories. It all adds up to a great deal of difficulty generating accurate knowledge about a find.

The Hamuli codices, however, constitute a somewhat unusual case even beyond having this early testimony from Askren. Several of the manuscripts preserved colophons that gave precise dates for the copying of many of the books (ranging between 823 CE and 914 CE). The notes from the copyists also let us know that several of the books were copied for or transferred to the Monastery of the Archangel Michael, and thus both confirm that the manuscripts belong together and provide us with a very likely identification of the ruined building in which they were allegedly found. Even more remarkably, after the initial dispersal of the books early in 1910, the discovery was largely reassembled in Cairo thanks to the presence there of two scholars, Émile Chassinat (1868–1948) and Henry Hyvernat (1858–1941), who found out about the books and apparently persuaded dealers to consolidate the materials, if Askren is correct, through Nahman.[23] Thus, within a few months of the find the bulk of it had been reconstituted before it was transported to Paris and eventually purchased there by Morgan in December 1911.[24]

Yet, even under these "favorable" circumstances, some of the Hamuli materials were not included in the lot Morgan purchased. These other books and leaves ended up in other repositories both within Egypt and in Europe and the United States.[25] At the same time, material almost certainly *not* originating from the Hamuli find was mixed in with Morgan's 1911 purchase.[26] Were the Hamuli codices not so distinctive in their colophons and level of preservation, determining which books were part of the find could have presented serious problems. And indeed, the reasonable degree of confidence that we can have both in the inventory of this find and in its provenance is exceptional. In a few other cases, painstaking detective work has produced even more detailed accounts of discoveries of Christian manuscripts, but as we will see, even in these cases, some frustrating ambiguities persist.

Christian Books Found with Bodies

With these caveats in mind, I turn to reports of Christian books found in cemeteries and tombs or otherwise associated in some way with corpses. Although there is some evidence for this practice among Christians in Late Antique Egypt, it was not nearly as widespread as is sometimes claimed.[27] Perhaps the most famous example of a Christian book being found with a corpse is the discovery in the winter of 1886–1887 of a codex containing portions of the Apocalypse of Enoch, the Gospel According to Peter, the Apocalypse of Peter, and the Martyrdom of Julian of Anazarbus (LDAB 1088). The book is now generally believed to have been produced in the sixth or seventh century. It was said to have been found "in a tomb" in a cemetery in Akhmim.²⁸ The editors provide a very rough location of the tomb and give no description of the tomb or its contents beyond the passing remark that the texts could be more ancient than "the monk" in whose tomb they were deposited.²⁹ What factors, beyond the presence of this book, identified the body as that of a monk? We are not told. Indeed, we know nothing else of the circumstances of the find. Yet, both scholarly and popular interest in the find, which focused largely on the previously lost text of the Gospel According to Peter, generated many retellings of the discovery. These reports rarely failed to note that the book came from a tomb, and some accounts placed considerable emphasis on this point. The *Times* of London, for example, began its story on the codex as follows: "The Egyptian tombs, which have preserved so many records of antiquity, this time give us new and valuable documents illustrating the early history of the Church. In the winter of 1886–1887 a parchment manuscript was found in a tomb at Akhmim, in Upper Egypt." Other treatments of the codex show a similar interest.³⁰

Indeed, fascination with "the Egyptian tomb" ran high in England and elsewhere in the late nineteenth century and increased after the sensational discovery of Tutankhamun's tomb in 1922. It is perhaps not surprising, then, that other finds of Christian books could become associated with tombs even when no real evidence suggested that the books came from graves. For instance, in 1903, the Coptologist Carl Schmidt published a portion of the so-called Berlin Gnostic codex, a papyrus book probably of the fifth century containing the Gospel According to Mary, the Secret Book of John, the Sophia of Jesus Christ, and the Acts of Peter (LDAB 107765). He described the provenance of the codex as follows: "On the basis of my personal research, the manuscript first surfaced with an Arab antiquities dealer in Akhmim. It was, as I further learned, found wrapped in feathers in a wall niche. Hence we may safely assume it comes from the tombs of Akhmim or at least from the town's surroundings."³¹ Yet, the suggestion that the book came from a tomb in Akhmim seems more than a little speculative. In an earlier report announcing the discovery of the codex, the story is different in a couple of small but important ways. According to that earlier account, the book was indeed "found in a wall niche" but was purchased "*in Cairo* from an antiquities dealer *from Akhmim*."³² Nothing more is said regarding the location of the find. Is Schmidt's later claim that the book originated with a dealer *in* Akhmim simply a deduction from the fact that the dealer in Cairo was said to be *from* Akhmim? Schmidt does not say. And the assumption that the book was from a tomb seems to have no basis at all, or at least not one that Schmidt reports. It does not seem too far-fetched to suppose that the sensational reception of the Gospel According to Peter from a tomb in Akhmim a decade earlier may have influenced Schmidt's speculation.[33]

A second case of an early Christian book possibly being found in a burial context provides considerably more detail and is instructive on a number of levels. In the course of describing one of his many trips to Egypt to acquire items for the British Museum, the orientalist E. A. Wallis Budge (1857–1934) wrote that in 1909 and 1911, he had "urged the natives to search for more unopened graves in ancient Coptic cemeteries, and to try to find me more texts." In January 1911, Budge received word that the native workers had met with success at a tomb near Al Ashmunin (ancient Hermopolis), where he states that they found

> several mummies of the Roman Period and a long rectangular wooden coffin, the sides of which were decorated with paintings of serpents and figures of gods in the style of the second or third century A.D. In this coffin was the body of a man wrapped in coarse Akhmîm linen, with an iron chain round his waist. Between his feet was a linen-covered bundle, which, when untied, was found to contain a papyrus book. When the finder of this MS. brought it to me it was still in the linen wrappings in which he discovered it. The MS., which measured about 11 inches by 6 inches, was in a very dilapidated state; . . . The leaves were very brittle, and when turned over portions of the letters flaked off them, but without disturbing them greatly, I was able to find out that the MS. contained a copy of the Coptic version of Deuteronomy, the Book of Jonah, and the Acts of the Apostles in the dialect of Upper Egypt. I therefore agreed to buy and take possession of it. I questioned the finder of the MS. very closely, and then went at once with him to look at the tomb and the coffin in which he had found the MS., and I was

convinced that the coffin was made in the Roman Period.
From what I could see in and about the tomb I assumed:
(1) That the man who was in the coffin with the MS. was a
Christian, and probably a "solitary" or anchorite of especial
holiness; (2) that the MS. found between his feet was his
own property; (3) that he had copied it with his own hands,
and valued it highly, and always had it with him or near him
during his lifetime; (4) that he had been buried by his disciples, who either found the coffin empty—which was most
probably the case—or had turned out its occupant to make
room for their master; (5) that the man with whom the MS.
was buried lived either towards the end of the fourth or early
in the fifth century of our Era at the latest. I arrived at the
last conclusion after a careful examination of the mummies
that were in the tomb, for all of them certainly belonged to
the period when the coffin was made, and this period was the
second or third century; and this Christian could not have
been buried there for some considerable period after that. I
was able to see enough of the Coptic text of the MS. to sat-
isfy me that the writing and style of page were different from
anything of the kind I had ever seen before, and I therefore
took careful note of everything in the tomb which might
help me to date the MS.[34]

There are several points to highlight here. On one hand, if the book
was indeed found with the corpse, then Budge's use of the contextual data from the tomb to estimate the date of this codex (i.e., that
it was produced by someone in the late fourth or early fifth century)
was reasonably effective. When scholars at the British Museum studied the codex (LDAB 107763), they found it to be one of those rare
papyrus books that can be dated with some confidence. The papyri
used to stiffen the leather cover were mostly accounts and contracts
written in cursive hands that were judged as "unlikely to be of a later
date than about 320, and may probably be as much as ten or twenty
years earlier," which provides a *terminus post quem* for the construction of the book, or at least its covers.[35] Furthermore, the presence
in the codex of a cursive script in use in the fourth and fifth centuries
provides a loose *terminus ante quem* for the copying of the main text.[36]

Thus, the book was probably copied at some point in the fourth or fifth century.

But these observations are counterbalanced by more problematic aspects of the narrative. The inference that the person in the tomb had himself copied the book is, of course, dubious to say the least. More seriously, although early forms of stratigraphic excavation had by this time been pioneered in Egyptian archaeology by William Flinders Petrie (1853–1942), Budge's work did not proceed according to those principles.[37] Indeed, it would be wrong to suggest Budge's activities in Egypt constituted archaeology in any modern sense of the term. He simply established agreements with locals that he would buy items that he happened to fancy from what they unearthed.[38] His narrative leaves unclear just how much time elapsed between his request for papyri from cemeteries, the discovery of this book, and his own first inspection of it. We have no notion of how much may have been removed from (or brought into) the tomb before Budge saw it. Budge tells other stories of visiting sites, asking for particular objects, and then returning after a year or more to find that just such objects had come to light.[39] It is somewhat suspicious that the locals seemed to regularly supply Budge with exactly what he was looking for. Budge had requested papyri from tombs, and that is what he was delivered. There is thus a degree of uncertainty about whether this book actually was found with a corpse. Ultimately, the connection of the codex to the tomb is nothing more or less than a claim made by the sellers of the codex, and it is a claim that very likely increased the perceived value of the item being sold. Whether or not we regard this as an instance of a Christian book being found in a tomb with a corpse is really a question of how much we trust the word of the sellers of the codex.

We find ourselves in a similar situation with the so-called Qarara codices, a group of four papyrus codices, two in Greek (LDAB 8121 and 10719) and two in Coptic (LDAB 108481 and 108582), that appeared on the antiquities market in Geneva in the early 1980s. While the existence of these books had been known to a handful of scholars since 1983, it was not until 2006 that these books, or rather one of them, became widely known, for among the works it preserved was the Gospel of Judas in Coptic. A popular book by Herbert Krosney that accompanied the National Geographic Society's

highly publicized translation of the Gospel of Judas related a colorful story of the discovery of these codices in limestone "catacombs"
in Egypt. The most informative part was this small section: "The
burial cave was located across the river from Maghagha, not far from
the village of Qarara in what is known as Middle Egypt. The fellahin
stumbled upon the cave hidden down in the rocks. Climbing down
to it, they found the skeleton of a wealthy man in a shroud. Other
human remains, probably members of the dead man's family, were
with him in the cave. His precious books were beside him, encased in
a white limestone box."[40] This report has been frequently repeated
both in the popular media and by specialists.[41] It is rarely noted that
Krosney's account, generated almost thirty years after the alleged
date of the discovery, is wholly unreliable.[42] He did not interview the
people who supposedly found the codex. His source was "Joanna
Landis," a pseudonym for an antiquities dealer who wished to remain anonymous. She claimed to have been taken to the site of the
find in 1978, guided by one "Am Samiah," another pseudonym for a
local villager said to have had a hand in the early marketing of the
books. The tale of the visit to the cave is replete with unnecessary
embellishments ("Standing in that cave, Joanna experienced a sud-
den feeling of fear and foreboding, almost mystical in its depth").[43]
More seriously, though, the story is also contradicted later in the
account. When "Landis" tried to return to the alleged site of the
find in 2005, "Am Samiah" had long since died. She found instead
"Mahmoud," who had been a government worker and a driver for
"Am Samiah." "Mahmoud" also claimed to have visited the site of
the find but stated that "the texts were found in Jebel Qarara, but
not exactly where Joanna had been. . . . The real cave was some five
kilometers away."[44] In fact there is no good reason to believe any of
this story. When the codices appeared on the antiquities market in
Geneva and were shown to the Coptologist Stephen Emmel in 1983,
all that the owner told him was that they were found somewhere
"near the village of Beni Masar, about 8 km. south of Oxyrhynchus
(modern Behnasa)."[45] The claim that these books were found in a
tomb is thus dubious, and even the claim that they were all found
together is not completely secure, as they may have first come together in the inventory of a dealer.

A more recent discovery is less open to doubt but still frustratingly vague. In 1984, during excavations in a cemetery about forty-five kilometers north of Oxyrhynchus, a small but thick parchment codex of the Psalms in Coptic was reportedly discovered. The so-called Mudil Psalter (LDAB 107731) was likely copied in the fourth or fifth century. It is said to have been found either "under the head of a young girl" or simply "near the head of a young girl" in a tomb, or, most elaborately, "placed open as a pillow beneath the head of an adolescent girl in a humble cemetery."[46] The codex was found during work supervised by the Egyptian Antiquities Organization, but no analysis was undertaken on the human remains or other material in the tomb. Nor is there any photograph or drawing of this discovery showing either the corpse or the book in situ before removal. Thus we are left to wonder what was the exact relationship between the book and the corpse and what the date of the burial might have been.

More precise information and documentation would definitely be helpful because there do appear to be occasions in which books were buried in or near cemeteries but not, at least as far as we can tell, in association with a corpse. The discovery south of Asyut of a single-quire Coptic codex of John's gospel (LDAB 107755) probably copied in the fourth or fifth century provides a good example: "When Mr. Guy Brunton was clearing [an area near the village of Hamamieh] in March 1923 for the British School of Archaeology, a broken crock was found, buried 18 inches under the surface, in the neighbourhood of the Roman or early Coptic graves. The pot is of red pottery painted pale buff, with a decoration in black of bands and spots, which cannot unfortunately be closely dated. Mr. Brunton's assistant, Mr. Starkey, in emptying the dust from the pot found that it contained a little package of papyrus wrapped in rag, and tied with thread."[47] The book was found "in the neighbourhood" of graves, but there is no mention of any association with a body or of disturbance indicative of the removal of a body. The reason for the burial of a book in this manner is unclear.

What we learn from all of these cases is that there is very little credible evidence for the burial of Christian books in tombs with corpses in Egypt. Aside from these three cases (the Akhmim Enoch and Peter codex, Budge's Coptic Deuteronomy codex, and the Mudil

Psalter), I am not aware of other credible reports of early Christian books being found in tombs in Egypt.[48] Burial with books was more common in pre-Roman Egypt, but there is not a great deal of evidence for the practice during the Roman period.[49] As we will see, a tomb context is sometimes claimed for the Nag Hammadi codices as well as the Chester Beatty codices, but there are competing hypotheses in both cases.

Christian Books Found in Caves

At least one important collection of Christian books was found in a cave, or, more accurately, an abandoned quarry.[50] Late in 1941, it was announced that earlier in the year, a collection of early Christian books had come to light in Tura, about ten kilometers south of Cairo.[51] The Egyptian government had allowed British soldiers to store munitions in a quarry that had been mined for building materials in antiquity. In early August, before the munitions were deposited, local workers who were clearing out the quarries and tunnels found a pile of papyrus books and unbound quires. The fullest account of the circumstances of the find was published in 1946 by the Assistant Keeper at the Cairo Museum, Octave Guéraud (1901–1987):[52]

> I visited the quarry shortly after the discovery with Mr. Drioton, Director General of the Egyptian Antiquities Service.[53] We interviewed the European foreman, the Egyptian *raïs* (supervisor) and one of the workers who had witnessed the discovery. They showed us where the papyrus was found: in one of the tunnels 20 or 25 meters from the opening of the rotunda. The slow disintegration of the rock over the centuries led to an accumulation in the tunnels of dust and rock debris that formed an embankment along each wall. It is, we were told, in clearing out this accumulation at a level of about a meter, the workers came upon a mass of papyrus deposited almost at the foot of the wall, crammed together (and not dispersed in the debris), but without any kind of protection or anything that implied they had been hidden with any care.[54]

The fate of the books in the immediate period after they were dis-covered is more difficult to reconstruct. The workers gave their version of events: "When questioned about what they did at the mo-ment when the papyri were discovered, the workers said that they had alerted the *raïs*, who alerted the foreman, who called the police. The police came and found all the papyrus, which nobody had touched. The police took them, and we do not know what they did after that."[55]

Other rumors circulated that much of the find was destroyed when workers used the papyri to make a fire to heat their coffee. As Guéraud noted at the time, such a story is "wholly improbable" be-cause it would be difficult "these days to find, ten kilometers from Cairo, anyone ignorant of the market value of papyri."[56] Rather, it seems that a substantial portion of the find was dispersed at the point of discovery and entered the local antiquities market. By Au-gust 10, 1941, a scrap from the find had reached the Cairo Museum. On the following day, the inspector for the Egyptian Antiquities Service responsible for the area that included Tura showed up in Cairo with a suitcase full of papyri, about half of what eventually ended up at the museum.[57] It was clear from the beginning that the language of the manuscripts was Greek, and upon examination, these books turned out to be dialogues and previously unknown bib-lical commentaries by the early Christian writers Origen and Didy-mus the Blind, probably copied in the sixth and seventh centuries (LDAB 771–777 and 3509).[58] Some of the leaves show clear evidence of being palimpsests, with traces of earlier erased writing still visible to the naked eye.

When King Farouk I was informed of the find and its impor-tance, he dispatched his own agent to Tura, who was able to buy a significant amount of papyrus, which was then presented to the museum. The museum tried to work through dealers, primarily Maurice Nahman, to acquire the rest of the find, but prices rose too quickly, and parts of the discovery made their way to Germany, Spain, Switzerland, Italy, Great Britain, and the United States.[59] Many leaves are still missing.[60] Some have appeared in surprising places. As recently as the 1980s, ten leaves of Didymus's *Commentary on the Psalms* turned up in the attic of a house in New England. They had been obtained by an American engineer in Egypt in 1941 and given to a relative, who placed the papyrus leaves in the back of a book where they sat forgotten for decades.[61]

Nevertheless, because at least part of the find was quickly taken to the museum and entrusted to the care of specialists, we have the rare opportunity to ascertain some things about the physical state of the materials when they were discovered (Figure 3.1).[62] Some leaves were apparently found lying flat and in excellent condition. Others were severely damaged by insects or the rubble that had fallen and covered the codices. Some of the quires were found rolled up together and tied with a papyrus strip. Others were found in a similar state but apparently torn in half in antiquity. It is interesting to see these varying levels of preservation within a single find. Guéraud reported seeing no evidence of either habitation or burial in the cave, but he noted that any such evidence may have been removed by the workers who cleared the area (as much as two months may have elapsed between the time of the discovery and Guéraud's inspection of the cave). Nevertheless, he concluded that this cache of books probably did not represent an active library of a hermit but rather "a clandestine deposit" possibly taken from a larger collection from a monastery, hastily left in the ancient quarry, and then forgotten.[63]

Christian Books Found in Houses or Buildings

A few early Christian books are reported to have been found in buildings. We have already noted that a dealer stated that the Berlin Gnostic codex (LDAB 107765) was found in a "wall niche," but Carl Schmidt did not believe that report, claiming instead that the book was likely found in a tomb. A few decades later, however, Schmidt was prepared to believe that an important collection of recently unearthed papyrus books had indeed come from a house. In the early 1930s, seven Coptic papyrus codices appeared on the antiquities market in Egypt. They were divided up and sold, with the bulk of the material being purchased by Schmidt and Chester Beatty, each working through the Cairo dealer Maurice Nahman.[64] Most of the find is now split between Berlin and Dublin, with a few leaves in Warsaw and Vienna. When the discovery of the codices was made public, it aroused considerable attention.[65] The books contained writings by Mani, a prophetic teacher of the third century whose ideas

Figure 3.1. Papyrus codices of the works of Didymus and Origen found at Tura
before restoration, showing varying states of preservation.

(Images originally published in Octave Guéraud, "Note préliminaire sur les papyrus
d'Origène découverts à Toura," *Revue de l'histoire des religions* 131 [1946], 85–108,
Plates I–V; courtesy of *Revue de l'histoire des religions.*)

had been condemned by what we would call more "orthodox" Christians.[66] The contents of the codices are as follows: A collection of Manichaean Psalms (LDAB 107976); a collection of Mani's letters (LDAB 108139); a collection of homilies (LDAB 108112 + 108140); a book of Acts (LDAB 108138); two volumes of dogmatic material, the *Kephalaia* (LDAB 107977 and LDAB 108111); and a volume of commentary, the *Synaxeis* (LDAB 108137). The codices, despite being beautifully produced on very fine papyrus, are poorly preserved. They were already damaged when they were first offered for sale, and since their discovery they have suffered a good deal, both because of events of global significance, such as World War II, and because of more mundane circumstances, such as an ill-timed sneeze that destroyed a fragile leaf of one of the codices.[67] Schmidt gave the most detailed account of the discovery of the books. Although he initially appears to have associated the books with Akhmim, a report from an anonymous informant changed his mind:[68]

> The whole find must have come before the eyes of my informant, because according to a passing remark that he now made to me in March of 1932, the papyrus books, each enclosed in bare wooden covers, lay in a wooden box found in what had been a domestic dwelling. The wooden box was said to have disintegrated, so retaining it was not worthwhile. It looks as though the whole discovery was offered by the Arab finders to the antiquities dealer of the Fayum, but he did not dare invest his money alone in these unsightly papyrus books, and so he divided the find with other dealers. This confirms an observation by Dr. Ibscher that the Manichaean manuscripts were, because of their damp storage, in danger of disintegration in the near future; they could not have been in the dry desert soil. Because the cellars of the houses in Medinet Madi were exposed to moisture from above and below, the papyri could be completely penetrated by salt crystals.[69]

The account raises questions: Does Schmidt's reference to "cellars" mean that the books were found under a floor? If so, were they deliberately placed there? Or were the books simply abandoned by someone in a room that was built over as the ground level rose (a common practice in Roman Egypt)?

These kinds of questions were put into sharper focus with the discovery in the late 1980s and early 1990s of another cache of Manichaean materials in Egypt. This time the books and fragments came to light as the result of controlled and well-documented excavations, and there is no doubt that the books came from houses and other buildings. What is interesting for our purposes is the specific archaeological contexts within which the books were found. These books come from the town of Kellis, located in the Dakhleh Oasis some 350 kilometers due west of Luxor. Among the Roman-era remains of the town were three churches, so other indications of a Christian presence were to be expected.[70] One of the areas excavated was a block of domestic buildings (Figure 3.2). The datable materials so far obtained indicate that this residential area was probably occupied from the second half of the third century and abandoned at the end of the fourth century or the beginning of the fifth. The finds in the domestic areas included large numbers of inscribed papyri and wooden boards, some containing literary material. Among the finds in House 3 were two wooden "codices," slabs of wood bound along the edge with cords, which were found "tied together with string and buried in mineralized floor deposits in the south-east corner of Room 4" (LDAB 108331 and 108332).[71] While not much in these bound wooden slabs is legible, one panel contains a collection of Manichaean psalms. What this tablet was doing embedded in the floor is an open question, but it suggests that the book was out of use in the final phases of occupation at the site and probably dates to an earlier period. Two other bound wooden tablets (one containing a book of accounts from the late third or early fourth century and the other, LDAB 2524, containing orations of Isocrates) were found not far away in Room 9 of the adjacent House 2. These were discovered next to a jar in a layer of sand, chaff, and ash, sitting atop a distinct deposit of sand, which was itself above a layer containing donkey droppings and other indications of the presence of animals (Figure 3.3).[72] The area seems to have been used as a stable. Again, why the books would have been left there is a mystery. Documentary papyri and woodworking implements found elsewhere in House 2 suggest that its occupant in the middle of the fourth century was a carpenter

Figure 3.2. Domestic spaces in Area A of the Kellis excavations.
(Image courtesy of Colin A. Hope, Dakhleh Oasis Project.)

who produced wooden tablets. It is tempting to suppose that at least
some of the inscribed wooden tablets found at the site were also
produced there, but this cannot at present be proved. Other literary
materials at Kellis were found in different contexts. Parts of a papyrus book containing Manichaean psalms and a version of the Acts of
John were found strewn across the area, with some fragments in the
so-called North Building, some in House 1, and some in House 3
(LDAB 5667).[73] The fragments in the North Building were found in

Figure 3.3. The Kellis Agricultural Account Book and Kellis Isocrates
codex in situ, in the southeast corner of Room 9 of House 2.

(Image courtesy of Colin A. Hope, Dakhleh Oasis Project.)

deposits that seem to have been deliberately dumped there in antiquity. The fragments found in House 1 came from a floor-raising fill in the large courtyard, which had been used to stable animals. The pieces in House 3 were found with other papyri in a deposit over the floor of Room 1. The excavator concluded that "all of the fragments may once have been contained within material dumped into the west rooms of the North Building at different times and this in itself may indicate that they originated elsewhere on the site."[74] Thus, this codex appears to have been discarded as trash. In fact, many of our earliest fragmentary Christian texts were discovered in trash contexts, not just those discovered in the famous garbage heaps in the city of Oxyrhynchus. The implications of this fact have been explored recently in a landmark study by AnneMarie Luijendijk.[75] I discuss the Oxyrhynchus discoveries in some detail in Chapter 6. For now, it is enough to note that much of the Manichaean literature from Kellis comes from fill contexts, suggesting that these books were discarded in antiquity. Yet, even though the Manichaean books found in the houses of Kellis were uncovered in secondary deposition, just knowing the general archaeological context of the site gives us a strong indication of the dates of the books (providing at the very least a good *terminus ante quem* at the end of the fourth century). Also, because of the rich collection of documentary materials found in some of the same contexts as the books, we get a good sense of the social milieu in which the books were most likely used.

Christian Books Found in and Around Monastic Dwellings

As we already saw, the Coptic books discovered at Hamuli were almost certainly found at the Monastery of the Archangel Michael. Given that monastic rules encourage literacy and reading, it is not surprising that books or the fragmentary remains of books might be found among the ruins of old monasteries. What we would like to know is in exactly what sorts of contexts within monasteries books are found. Two excavations from the area of western Thebes shed interesting light on the question. The first project, sponsored by the Metropolitan Museum of Art in New York, took place from 1912 to 1914 and excavated the pharaonic Tomb of Daga, which had been reused by Christian monks during the sixth and seventh centuries. In what has come to be known as the Monastery of Epiphanius, excavators recovered a great deal of material relating to the daily lives of the monks who had inhabited the area. In addition to a wealth of documentary texts on papyrus and ostraca, this excavation yielded several books and remains of books and literary material in Greek and Coptic.[76] Literary texts were even copied on potsherds or pieces of limestone. Reconstruction of the contexts of many of the finds is somewhat challenging because of the limitations of the archaeological processes of the times. These are laid out with admirable self-consciousness and honesty in the excavation report. The editors note that the area had been disturbed in the nineteenth century by previous diggers and that many of the ostraca and other items were found in the modern waste piles of those earlier endeavors (and that their own workers often missed inscribed ostraca that were only later discovered in their own waste piles). They also note that the monks themselves upset the stratigraphy of the site when they renovated the area in antiquity.[77] Nevertheless, many of the items they discovered did have secure, specific archaeological contexts. For instance, a small (12.5 cm wide by 17 cm high) papyrus codex of eight leaves containing Greek and Coptic acrostic hymns copied in a neat hand (LDAB 6416, see Figure 1.4) was found in a rubbish hole in one of the rooms, which seems to have been used as a dwelling in the earliest phase of monastic occupation of the site. Also found in the hole were personal papers of Apa Epiphanius.[78] Thus, again we have an informative context for the discovery of a Christian book—it was discarded along with personal papers. That is to say, it was trash. And because this trash pit was a compact, indoor locus rather than a dump open to the winds, we may assume that these items were discarded together and represent the property of Epiphanius.

More recent excavations outside a hermitage near the Monastery of Epiphanius have uncovered additional Christian books from the area. Polish excavators working at a hermitage in a reused pharaonic tomb in Gurna uncovered three Coptic books in 2005. The excavator described the circumstances of the find: "In the southern part of the hermitage, on the outer edges of a dump of ashes and rubbish from an oven or kitchen, three books were discovered" (Figure 3.4).[79] These included two papyrus codices in leather covers, one containing the *Canons* of Pseudo-Basil (LDAB 113913) and one containing an encomium for Pisenthios (568–632), bishop of Koptos (LDAB 113914). The third book was a parchment codex bound between wooden boards with portions of the book of Isaiah and, copied in a different hand, the Martyrdom of Peter (LDAB 113915). Like the book of acrostic hymns from the Monastery of Epiphanius, these books were discarded whole and as such were probably not subject to movement by blowing winds even though they were in an open rubbish dump. It is almost certain that they were discarded by the residents of the nearby hermitage. As a final note, it is worth pointing out that these books might well be described as having come from a "tomb," insofar as the nearest structure is the pharaonic tomb that was being reused as a hermitage. This is all the more true of the books from the Monastery of Epiphanius that actually did come from inside the pharaonic tomb. But, of course, these books were not at all burial goods. The lesson here is that, without know-

Figure 3.4. The Gurna Coptic codices in situ in a rubbish mound.
(Image courtesy of Tomasz Górecki.)

ing the precise archaeological context in which a book was found, a general location, even if it happens to be technically accurate, may still mislead.

The Coptic Codices of Nag Hammadi

Finally, the story, or rather the stories, of the most famous discovery of early Christian manuscripts displays elements that by now will be quite familiar: a clandestine find, dispersal in the antiquities market, and the resulting questions about the exact circumstances of the discovery and the extent of the materials found. When scholars speak of the Nag Hammadi codices, they refer to twelve papyrus books and one loose tractate that appeared on the antiquities market in 1946 (LDAB 107741–107753, Figure 3.5). The books are written in Coptic and contain a variety of Christian material, including a complete copy of the famous Gospel According to Thomas. From early on, it was recognized that the codices came from the area near Nag

Hammadi. The French scholar Jean Doresse was able to establish that the find likely came from somewhere at the base of the cliffs of the Jabal al-Tarif near the village of Hamra Dum, although it is not clear exactly where. Doresse's clearest description of the area of the find comes in a caption to a photograph used as the frontispiece of the English edition of his major work on the Nag Hammadi codices, *The Secret Books of the Egyptian Gnostics*. There the spot of the find is located at "the south-east flank of the Gebel et-Tarif . . . at the foot of the wall of rock," where "overturned earth in front of the cliff . . . marks the site of the ancient cemetery where the jar containing the manuscripts was buried."[80] This description has no parallel in the French edition of the book, in which a different photograph carries only the brief caption "Le lieu de la découverte" (Figure 3.6).[81] Doresse elsewhere indicates that a tomb in the "overturned earth in front of the cliff" was the location of the discovery: "Was it in one of these tombs that the papyri were found? Certainly, one cannot, even if one

Figure 3.5. The Nag Hammadi codices in 1948.

(Image adapted from Jean Doresse and Togo Mina, "Nouveaux textes gnostiques coptes découverts en Haute-Égypte: La bibliothèque de Chenoboskion," *Vigiliae Christianae* 3 [1949], 129–141, Figure 1; image appears courtesy of the Institute for Antiquity and Christianity Records, Special Collections, Claremont Colleges Library, Claremont, California.)

Figure 3.6. Doresse's photographs of the site of the discovery
from the French (left) and English (right) editions of his book.

(Images originally published in Jean Doresse, *Les livres secrets des gnostiques d'Égypte:
Introduction aux écrits gnostiques coptes découverts à Khénoboskion* [Paris: Librairie Plon,
1958], opposite p. 137; and Jean Doresse, *The Secret Books of the Egyptian Gnostics: An
Introduction to the Gnostic Coptic Manuscripts Discovered at Chenoboskion* [New York:
Viking, 1960], frontispiece; images courtesy of the Institute for Antiquity and Christianity
Records, Special Collections, Claremont Colleges Library, Claremont, California.)

searches very far around, see any other place—any ruin or sepulcher—
from which they could have come." He did not provide any more
specific locale: "As to the exact location of the find, opinion differed
by some few dozen yards; but everyone was sure that it was just about
here."[82] The various words Doresse used to describe the find spot
(*cavités; les sépultures se dispersent même jusqu'à une centaine de mètres
du pied de la montagne; l'antique cimetière; vaste mais pauvre nécropole*)
leave it unclear whether he was referring to the pharaonic tombs cut
into the cliff itself, the talus (rubble embankment) at the foot of the
cliff, or the plain beyond the talus. Nevertheless, there seems to be
no question that Doresse was describing a find spot in a burial con-

text at the southeastern end of the Jabal al-Tarif. And although different, the photographs in the French and English editions of Doresse's book both depict portions of the cliffs in this area.[83]

That was the state of knowledge about the find until the 1970s. At that time, James M. Robinson undertook an investigation and uncovered a great deal more information regarding the circumstances of the discovery and marketing of the codices.[84] Robinson was even able to identify Muhammad 'Ali al-Samman, the man who allegedly first found the codices in 1945. Muhammad 'Ali spoke about the discovery himself in a television interview in 1987:

> I was digging [near the cliffs at Jabal al-Tarif] for *sebakh*, for fertilizer, with my pick-axe and carrying it back to the fields on the camel. Then I came across this big earthenware pot which was buried in the sand. I had a feeling that there might be something inside . . . [so] I came back later the same day and I smashed the pot open. I broke it open exactly where I had found it. I thought there might be an evil spirit inside, a *jinni*. I had never seen anything like it before. I smashed the pot on my own and inside I found these old books. Then I brought the others over to see. They said, "We don't want anything to do with these books. They belong to the Christians, the Copts." They said, "It's nothing to do with us." . . . It was all just rubbish to us. Yes, my mother did burn some in the bread oven. . . . One of the people from the village of Hamra Dum killed my father so it was decided that I should kill his murderer, in revenge. I did kill him and with my knife I cut out his heart and ate it. I was in jail because of the killing and when I got out of jail I found that my mother had burned a lot of those old papers. Later on I sold one book. All the others had gone. I got eleven Egyptian pounds for it.[85]

Despite the somewhat gory details, the story of the discovery is fairly straightforward: Muhammad 'Ali found the jar and later the same day smashed it open by himself and discovered the books, which he then showed to others. But this account is complicated by the fact that Robinson's interviews produced stories in which the details vary considerably from the version of Muhammad 'Ali's story given above. In some accounts, between one and seven other people were present with Muhammad 'Ali at the discovery of the jar. The number of codices said to have been found varies between twelve and thirteen.[86] Was a codex in this instance *actually* burned? In some versions, Muhammad 'Ali is said to have found the jar with the books in proximity to a corpse, while others denied this: "Muhammad Alī maintained that a fresh corpse with abnormally elongated fingers and teeth lay on a bed of something like charcoal beside the jar, and that it was left there. But he denied a rumor or speculation from earlier years that a staff and a rug were at the site, and his younger brother Abū al-Majd denied that anything other than the jar was found."[87]

But there is more. Muhammad 'Ali actually identified two *different* locations as the spot of the find. Early on in Robinson's questioning, Muhammad 'Ali asserted that he found the books in a tomb in the cliffs (Figure 3.7): "A clandestine drive past the cliff . . . resulted in the identification by Mohammed Ali of the tomb of Thauti as the cave just inside of which he had discovered the codices in a sealed four-handled jar some 60 cm. high and 30 cm. wide buried beside a corpse or mummy which he reburied where he found it. By this time the caves had been numbered in black paint 1–158, from south to north; this is T 73."[88] This alleged find spot is consistent with the earliest reports of the find in the 1940s, which placed the discovery in a "tomb" or a "cave."[89] On the basis of this identification, Robinson and his team conducted extensive excavation ("to bed rock") at the tomb of Thauti (T 73), but their efforts did not provide any evidence to confirm the tomb as the site of the find. Robinson confronted Muhammad 'Ali with this lack of evidence and asked him

> to reconsider his identification. He changed his identification to the northern side of the fallen broken boulder visible in Doresse's photo, where the boulder forms an overhanging slab at some 45°. On 14–15 December this and the adjoining areas were cleared to bed rock, without finding evidence of a burial or reburial, or of sherds from the jar. The excavation of places associated with the site of the discovery (Areas A–D, T 1 and T 73) included the sifting of the debris first

with a 1 by 1 cm. mesh, then by the finer mesh of a window screen, in view of the report by Mohammed Ali that he
broke the jar near the site of the discovery and saw flying
into the air what must have been papyrus fragments; none
were found. Nor were sherds found that could be readily
associated with the jar in which the codices were discovered.
Nor was it possible to locate the corpse or mummy Mohammed Ali said he reburied where he found it, beside the jar
on a bed of charcoal. According to the memory of Regheb
Andrawus 'El-Kes' Abd El-Said, a neighbor of Mohammed
Ali who acquired Codex III, Mohammed Ali told him at the
time that a staff lay beside the jar, a detail later denied by
Mohammed Ali; in any case, it was not found. Thus the excavation produced no archeological confirmation of the precise site of the discovery.[90]

It seems, then, that although scholars of early Christianity often
speak as if we know the exact circumstances of the discovery of the
Nag Hammadi codices, in fact we know only the general area in
which locals assert the books were found. They may or may not have
been found with a corpse. Of all the places near the area of Doresse's
photos, one of the caves in the cliff would be the most likely place of
discovery, as only these areas yielded evidence of human activity in
the probable period of the deposition of the books.[91]

    This is not to say that the detailed information that Robinson
unearthed is unhelpful. Indeed, the real value of Robinson's labors is
the history of the books on the antiquities market once they reached
the hands of the dealers. This story is reasonably well known and
not in dispute. I will only mention that one of the main dealers involved was Phocion J. Tano (1898–1972), a Cairo-based antiquities
trader of Cypriot ancestry who would also handle a large portion of
the Bodmer Papyri in the 1950s. Tano reportedly made a trip to the
site of the find in March 1946 and was able to acquire several of the
Nag Hammadi codices through various channels.[92] One of the codices that escaped Tano (Codex I, the "Jung Codex") left Egypt and
was purchased by the Jung Institute of Zürich in May 1952. In that
same month, Tano's codices were "nationalized" and became the
property of the Coptic Museum in Cairo. Almost all the remaining

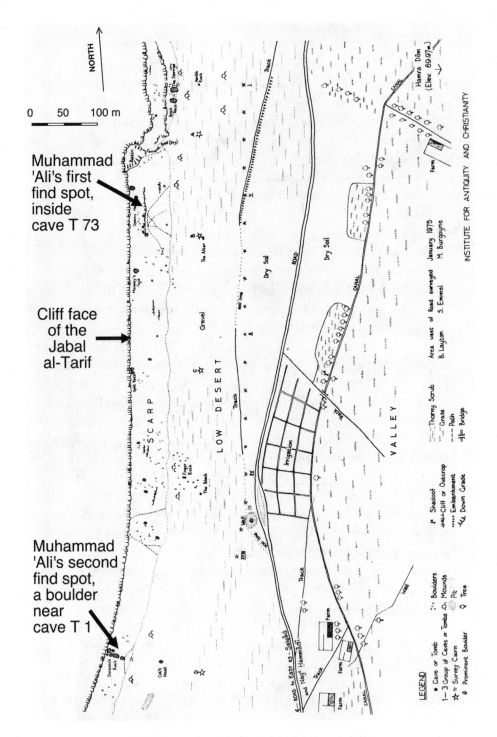

Figure 3.7. Proposed locations of the point of
discovery of the Nag Hammadi codices.

(Image adapted from a map in the Institute for Antiquity and Christianity Records, Special Collections, Claremont Colleges Library, Claremont, California. Original map prepared by Bentley Layton, Stephen Emmel, and Michael Burgoyne. Used by permission of Stephen Emmel.)

parts of the find would eventually be acquired by the Coptic Museum, although it was not until October 1975 that the last portions of Codex I finally returned to Egypt.[93]

The main thing to be learned from this overview is that reliable knowledge about discoveries of early Christian books is extremely difficult to come by. In most situations, we are dealing with materials that were found by people who are not professional archaeologists. The information they provide may be based on misunderstandings or might equally be complete fabrication. Finders, dealers, buyers, and (as we saw in the case of Freer's books) even scholars all have reasons to be less than forthcoming about the locations of finds. The antiquities market essentially erects a wall between us and secure knowledge about manuscripts not unearthed through proper archaeological excavation. For that reason, we should always be open to questions about such discoveries of early Christian manuscripts: What is the extent of the collections? When and where were they discovered? When were the books copied? In what context might they have been used? These questions will face us repeatedly in the following chapters.

CHAPTER FOUR

A Discovery "Which Threw All Others in the Shade"

The Beatty Biblical Papyri

I
N THE WINTER OF 1931–1932, Arthur Boak (1888–1962), a professor of history at the University of Michigan, was in Egypt working on the university's excavation of the ancient city of Karanis (modern Kom Aushim). On December 20, he wrote a letter informing a colleague back at Michigan of some unusual and exciting news:

> We had the Askrens as our guests for Christmas dinner last night and, somewhat to my surprise, the doctor brought with him six leaves of a Biblical codex which had been sent to him by the man from whom we secured our Biblical fragments two years ago and who supplied the Beatty collection. The leaves were written on both sides in a good hand which, as far as I can judge, is the same as that of the fragment from the Beatty collection published in the London Times as from Philippians (it is really from Romans). . . . The appearance of these leaves suggests that part of the previous find has been withheld either by the finders or by this dealer. I rather think by the former, as the latter would have sold all that he

could to Beatty. I was told that the natives had burned part
of the codices, but it was evident that some escaped.[1]

We meet here again the same Dr. David Askren who had been involved in the early marketing of the Hamuli codices in 1910 and had
assisted both J. P. Morgan, Jr., and Charles Lang Freer in the purchase of Coptic and Greek books in 1915.[2] By the early 1930s, Askren
was working closely with the Michigan team excavating Karanis and
using his local connections to provide the Michigan scholars with
access to antiquities that surfaced for sale. In this case, the find was
a set of well-preserved leaves from a codex containing the letters of
Paul. The *Times* article to which Boak refers had appeared a month
earlier. Sir Frederic Kenyon, who had recently retired as director of
the British Museum, had announced Chester Beatty's acquisition to
the world:[3] "I have now . . . the privilege of making known a discovery of Biblical manuscripts which rivals any of these in interest and
surpasses all of them in antiquity. . . . Among them are the earliest
manuscripts of the Greek Bible yet known. The exact dating of literary hands on papyrus is seldom possible, but approximate datings
may be given, often with considerable security. The earliest of these
manuscripts can be assigned with confidence to the second century
of our era, and not to a very late period in it."[4] The report was syndicated in newspapers throughout Europe and North America, and
the headlines heaped superlatives upon the importance of the find.
As Kenyon would later put it, these codices constituted "a discovery
. . . which threw all others in the shade."[5] While several important
finds of early Christian books had emerged from Egypt during the
preceding decades, the manuscripts that Beatty and the University
of Michigan had acquired were something new. If Freer's codices
took us back perhaps as far as the fourth century, here was a collection of early Christian books from a century earlier and including
at least one item, a papyrus codex containing the books of Numbers
and Deuteronomy (LDAB 3091), that Kenyon would claim was as
old as the early second century.[6]

    This collection of books has come to be known as the Chester
Beatty Biblical Papyri. The name can be slightly confusing. Although
the Chester Beatty Library holds other papyrus manuscripts containing biblical texts (some of which we will encounter in the next

chapter), the label "Chester Beatty Biblical Papyri" generally refers only to this group of eleven Greek papyrus codices that Beatty purchased between 1930 and 1934 and designated by Roman numerals:[7]

I. Gospels and Acts (LDAB 2980)
II. Pauline letters (LDAB 3011)
III. Revelation (LDAB 2778)
IV. Genesis (LDAB 3160)
V. Genesis (LDAB 3109)
VI. Numbers and Deuteronomy (LDAB 3091)
VII. Isaiah (LDAB 3108)
VIII. Jeremiah (LDAB 3084)
IX + X. Ezekiel, Daniel, Susanna, and Esther (LDAB 3090)
XI. Ecclesiasticus (LDAB 3161)
XII. Letter of Enoch, Melito's *On Passover*, and the Apocryphon of Ezekiel (LDAB 2608)

At the same time, other parts of these books have ended up in several different institutions in Europe and the United States. The bulk of the find that had surfaced in the 1930s was edited and published with astounding efficiency by Kenyon in a lavishly produced set of editions and plates subvented by Beatty.[8]

The Beatty Biblical Papyri immediately became famous because of their age and their state of preservation. Fragments of early Christian writings on papyrus had been known for decades, but the Beatty Biblical Papyri were much more extensive, and their perceived antiquity made them crucial evidence for the textual traditions of the Greek scriptures. The gospels codex especially challenged the reigning theory of the development of the text of the New Testament. They also played an important role in discussions of the history of the book, establishing a date for the use of the papyrus codex in Egypt considerably earlier than had been believed previously. Thus, these books have had no shortage of scholarly attention over the decades since their discovery. Yet, questions about the provenance of the manuscripts have never been answered in a satisfactory way, and the dating of the codices, which was based only on paleography, is open to some question. There is also the possibility that additional material exists that may belong to the same cache of manuscripts. There is still more to learn about these books.

The Acquisitions of the Beatty Biblical Papyri

Alfred Chester Beatty (1875–1968) was an American whose wealth stemmed from the mining business, first in the western United States and then through the copper and diamond mines of Africa.[9] He immigrated to London in 1913, but eventually, in 1950, he moved to Dublin in search of a more favorable tax climate. By the close of World War I he had already become known as an avid collector of books and art.[10] In the 1920s and 1930s, he regularly spent his winters in Egypt (he had a villa built near the pyramids of Giza), and he acquired a number of important papyrus manuscripts during these visits. We have already encountered the Coptic Manichaean codices that Beatty and Carl Schmidt bought in the early 1930s. At about the same time, in January 1930, Beatty also began to purchase a cache of Christian papyri in Greek.

Archival correspondence in the Chester Beatty Library provides details of the transactions.[11] It was either very late in 1929 or early in 1930 that Beatty found out the books were for sale. In January 1930, Beatty sent a telegram to the Department of Manuscripts at the British Museum written in a code that, naturally enough for Beatty, referred to mines. He seems to have also sent photographs that experts at the British Museum could evaluate. The text of the telegram that the museum sent in response in early February is preserved:

SILVER MINE IS VERY RICH HAS 3 SHAFTS (STOP)
GOLD MINE RICH HAS FOUR SHAFTS (STOP)
SHOULD BUY BOTH WITHOUT FAIL ESPECIALLY THE SILVER MINE[12]

"Mines" stood for manuscripts, "rich" meant old, and the number of "shafts" referred to the estimated century. In fact, the "silver mine" was a set of leaves containing the book of Daniel in Greek (LDAB 3090) estimated to be of a third-century date, and the "gold mine" was a copy of Genesis in Greek (LDAB 3160), believed to be of the fourth century. By September, Beatty had acquired parts of all of the eleven codices that would become the Beatty Biblical Papyri, but he would continue to make purchases.[13] Most, if not all, of Beatty's acquisitions of these books came from the Cairo dealer Maurice Nahman, with whom he was also negotiating for the Coptic Manichaean books.[14]

Other buyers were also active at this early stage. In early 1930, the Vienna papyrus collection acquired small fragments of the gospels codex (LDAB 2980).[15] Also in 1930, a portion of the Isaiah codex (LDAB 3108) was purchased in a mixed lot of papyri for the Florentine papyrus collection.[16] In the same year, Wilfred Merton acquired two leaves of the same codex for his personal collection.[17] It was also at this point that the University of Michigan entered the story. Once again, its conduit was Dr. Askren. In a letter of March 9, 1930, Enoch E. Peterson (1891–1978), the director of Michigan's project at Karanis, wrote to colleagues at Michigan to ask about money for buying papyri:

> When Winter was here in the Fayoum there was a certain dealer, whom Dr. Askren knows, who came to Doctor's home with some fragments. Among the fragments were some that at first glance seemed to be Biblical. He told us that a dealer in Beni Suef had six complete sheets, that is pages, with writing on both sides and that these fragments were from the same lot. He asked twenty five pounds for the fragments. At that time we did not buy—as the man asked L.E. 150.00 for each sheet. . . . Now after receiving your letter I have come into Fayoum and we have bought the fragments for L.E. 25.00. These we enclose for your examination. . . . I grant that L.E. 25.00 is a big sum to pay for these small fragments but we did so for one very good reason, namely, to get in closer touch with this dealer. He claims to have sold some sheets to Nahman.[18]

Upon examination, these fragments turned out to be leaves from a papyrus codex of Numbers and Deuteronomy (LDAB 3091). Encouraged by this development, and mistakenly believing he was buying more parts of this codex, Peterson paid the dealer for additional material in April 1930. When he received the new leaves, it was clear that they were part of a different codex, later identified as containing parts of the book of Enoch and the paschal sermon of Melito of Sardis (LDAB 2608). By the end of May, the Michigan scholars had learned that Chester Beatty had also bought portions of the same manuscripts and indeed had acquired much more from the same find. Michigan made no more acquisitions until Dr. Askren's Christmas dinner surprise late in 1931. After purchasing those six leaves of the Pauline Epistles codex, the Michigan team in January 1932 was offered a second, larger batch of material, which was described in a letter that also clarifies the number of dealers involved in these transactions and aspects of the provenance:

> The dealer who markets these papyri lives at Beni Serêf, but the papyri come from near Assiût. The dealer told Dr. Askren that through Nahman he had sold Beatty 17 pages at L.E. 100 each, and directly 22 pages at L.E. 80 a piece. He sold us previously 6 at L.E. 70 and now the present six at the same price. It is obvious that some were marketed by other channels since Peterson bought our first six from someone else, still the man in question controls the bulk of the supply. He states that they came from a tomb where they were found along with a corpse. If this is true, there has been no large library find and we cannot expect an indefinite supply coming in from time to time. Our friend claims that [there] are some twenty-two sheets still to be had, but that is all, and professes to be able to get these and sell them to us, but at not less than L.E. 70 a piece, which made a total of L.E. 1540 (or considerably less than $ 6160.00, at current rates). Do you think we could raise this sum or any part of it? If you think it worthwhile to try to get the 22 pages or fragments you had better cable me how much I may spend, and have the sum put to Peterson's credit, when I cable in return that I have used it.[19]

By late February 1932 or shortly thereafter, the Michigan team had raised the money and bought both the well-preserved leaves (which turned out to be more of the codex of the Pauline letters) and the fragments. Beatty helped Michigan export the material from Egypt to London, and Michigan in turn sold the fragments (but not the leaves of Paul) to Beatty at the cost that they had paid. This concluded Michigan's purchases from this find.[20]

Beatty thus had been able to acquire the majority of the find by the middle of 1932, but pieces continued to appear on the market for the next three years. Some forty-six additional leaves of the codex of Paul's letters were still for sale in 1934 along with a substantial part of the Ezekiel-Daniel-Susanna-Esther codex (LDAB 3090). Beatty would end up purchasing the additional leaves of the codex of Paul's letters, but he passed on the portion of the Ezekiel codex, finding the dealer's price too high. The leaves were instead purchased in the summer of 1935 by representatives of John H. Scheide in Egypt, apparently through the agency of Dr. Askren, and subsequently became part of the Scheide Library at Princeton University.[21] No further material from the find seems to have come on the market for about twenty years. Then, in the 1950s and 1960s, portions of the Ezekiel-Daniel-Susanna-Esther codex again appeared on the antiquities market, and these were purchased by collections in Madrid, Barcelona, and Cologne.[22]

The Provenance of the Find

In his first announcement and early publications on the Beatty find, Kenyon did not have much to say about the provenance of the books: "The source of the find has not been disclosed but it is evident that it must come from the library of a Christian Church or monastery in Egypt."[23] In the introductory volume to his edition of the Beatty Biblical Papyri, Kenyon offered some speculation but little additional information: "Their place of origin is unknown, since they reached [Beatty] through the hands of natives and dealers, whose statements as to *provenance* are not always reliable. From their character, however, it is plain that they must have been discovered among the ruins of some early Christian church or monastery; and there is reason to believe that they come from the neighbourhood of the Fayum."[24] Shortly after Kenyon's initial public announcement of Beatty's purchase in the *Times*, a second story of the origins of the codex emerged from the Coptologist Carl Schmidt.

When in the spring of 1930 . . . I had a short stay in Cairo, dealers there showed me numerous splendid partially preserved papyrus sheets in Greek language, which upon closer inspection turned out to be pieces of Old and New Testament biblical manuscripts. A purchase by me was, of course, ruled out from the start due to the fantastic asking prices. . . . Apparently the whole find, as also the case elsewhere, had been distributed among the different dealers, so that a purchase required disproportionately large funds just to secure a significant share. This regrettable scattering was confirmed during a visit in the Faiyum, where additional pages were offered to me for still more exorbitant prices. The risk that the find would be scattered to the winds was eliminated when I happily received the news that A. Chester Beatty, a well-known private collector, had acquired most of the leaves and transferred them to London.[25]

Schmidt then summarized the information in Kenyon's article before offering his own account of the origins of the codices:

Determination of provenance is always very difficult, since both the finder and the dealer have a great interest in covering all their tracks, so as not to be brought to account by the authorities or the museum administration. Nevertheless, I have continued the investigation of the mysterious location of the discovery during my last stay, and I was able, through my old familiar informant, who himself had possessed a number of [the codex] leaves, first to get the admission that the Faiyum, the first place one would first think of, did not come into consideration. A find spot in Upper Egypt is ruled out by the group of dealers into whose possession the leaves had come. In any event, the location of the discovery could not be far from the Faiyum. I believe I got an important clue in the statement of my source when he described how to reach the find spot: that I must go east from Bush, a railway station between Wasta and Benisuêf (115 km from Cairo), to the shore of the Nile and cross the Nile to the village

'Alâlme. 'Alâlme is the location from which a road goes to the monastery of Anthony and Paul on the Red Sea, and north of which is the old Monastery of Anthony, and still farther north also on the east bank the village of Aṭfîḥ, ancient Aphroditopolis, from which Antony, the founder of Egyptian monasticism, hailed. Here churches and monasteries must have been present which in antiquity had owned Christian scriptures on papyrus and copied them on parchment when [the papyrus copies] were worn out.[26]

In 1933, Schmidt again wrote of the origins of the codices. Somewhat annoyed that Kenyon's introductory volume had not taken notice of his earlier report, Schmidt reiterated and elaborated his claims:

Kenyon has unfortunately made no comment on my investigation of the find spot; indeed, he does not mention my article. Again this spring I have questioned the Faiyum dealer and received the same information, according to which 'Alâlme, a village on the east bank of the Nile in the area of Aṭfîḥ, ancient Aphroditopolis, is to be regarded as the find spot. A dealer would not have come to this remote area unless the finder had traveled from there to the Faiyum. I know well the information of a Cairo middleman can mislead. The dealer remarked in passing that the papyrus books were found in a pot. Thus was my thesis fully confirmed: that this find consists of worn out, broken codices, which, as holy writings could not be destroyed, but rather were committed to the earth in pots, as it was customary to store important documents in jars. Such discoveries of books in containers are not uncommon in Egypt. . . . The finders have apparently gathered up the smallest scrap out of the pot and not discarded anything as worthless—as we are given notice by Dr. Ibscher that countless pieces defy assembly. We shall probably have to do without a further increase in material, apart from about six leaves that are still in the possession of a dealer because his demands are too exorbitant. To my knowledge, these are Old Testament pieces.[27]

Schmidt thus remained convinced that the find had emerged from the village of 'Alâlme near Aphroditopolis and that the worn books had been disposed of in something like the style of a Jewish *genizah*, a repository for old and damaged books, the most famous example of which was associated with the Ben Ezra synagogue near Cairo, from which thousands of manuscripts were taken in the 1890s.[28] All of this is deduced from the report of a person characterized as "an old familiar informant" and "a Faiyum dealer." Although Schmidt offers his conclusions with his usual confidence, there are at least a few reasons to pause before taking the story at face value. First, Schmidt's local agents were not always the most reliable individuals. In 1928, it was discovered that one of them was, wittingly or unwittingly, a purveyor of forgeries.[29] Second, very little seems to be known about any Christian remains in the immediate vicinity of this village.[30] If one crosses the Nile at Bush, the nearest village on the other side is Naj al Alalimah (alternatively spelled Nagaa al Aslalmah). This village is about fourteen kilometers south of the area identified as Pispir, the traditional site of Antony's first seclusion (Figure 4.1), today the village of Dayr al Maymun.[31] Aphroditopolis is a further twenty-three kilometers north and seems to be mentioned by Schmidt only as a relatively well-known point of reference.[32] If there are early Christian remains in the area of 'Alâlme, they are not very well documented. Third, the practice of *genizah*-style deposition of manuscripts is not well attested in the early Christian period.[33] Finally, there are other versions of the find story that seem to have been forgotten, which should at least make us hesitate before accepting Schmidt's account.

In addition to Kenyon's general localizing of the find in "the neighbourhood of the Fayum," Henry Sanders, who edited the leaves of the Pauline Epistles codex acquired by Michigan, mentioned that according to "current gossip in Egypt," the Beatty codices "were found in a Coptic graveyard." Later he added in passing that "the Beatty fragments were found" in the region of "the upper Nile."[34] Archival records at the University of Michigan already cited above provide a bit more specificity concerning the Michigan team's working assumptions about the origins of the codices: "The dealer who markets these papyri lives at Beni Serêf, but the papyri come from near Assiût. . . . He states that they came from a tomb where they

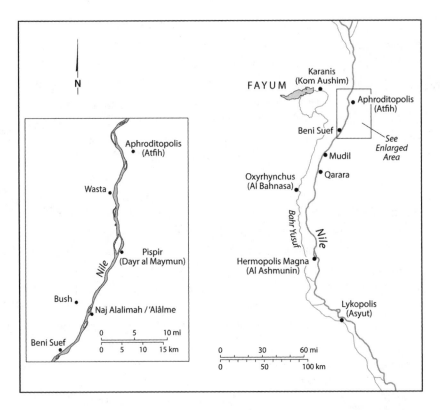

Figure 4.1. Areas of the proposed find spots of the Chester Beatty Biblical Papyri.
(Cartography by Bill Nelson.)

were found along with a corpse."[35] Thus, according to this version, the books came from considerably farther south, in Asyut (ancient Lykopolis) and emerged from a funerary context rather than the *genizah*-style deposit that Schmidt had proposed.[36]

Another seemingly related story was recently uncovered by Charles Horton, former curator of the Western Collections of the Chester Beatty Library. In 1934, Beatty himself had become more interested in determining the exact provenance of the books, and he commissioned an investigation. The result was a four-page typed report complete with diagrams titled "MEMORANDUM re Discovery of Early Biblical Papyri, Based on conference with Shaker Farag on March 17th & 18th, 1934" (Figure 4.2).[37] However, the key details about the location of the find have been redacted. We

MEMORANDUM re Discovery of Early Biblical Papyri.

Based on conference with Shaker Farag on March 17th & 18th,1934.

    The Papyri in question were found in three earthenware jars about 1928-1930 by some Arabs that were digging near the Monastery of   in Egypt about   miles south of Cairo on the   bank of the Nile (Some brief notes in reference to the Monastery will be found attached to this memo).

    The jars in which the Papyri were found, were found a few feet below the surface in the sand. They were on top of a wooden coffin.^x From the description they were in approximately the position shown in the sketch below:

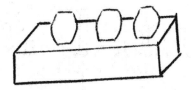

x
  Very often Mss were actually buried in the coffin. There are cases where a copy of the Gospels was buried with an Arch-bishop, the Mss being placed in his hands.

Figure 4.2. Memorandum of March 18, 1934, describing the alleged circumstances of the discovery of the Beatty Biblical Papyri (Chester Beatty Library Archives, CBP 1566, Page 1). Note the diagram of ceramic jars on a coffin.

(Image © The Trustees of the Chester Beatty Library, Dublin.)

find only blank spaces where the crucial information should be. The beginning of the memorandum reads as follows:

> The Papyri in question were found in three earthenware jars about 1928–1930 by some Arabs that were digging near the Monastery of _____ in Egypt about ____ miles south of Cairo on the _____ bank of the Nile (Some brief notes in reference to the Monastery will be found attached to this memo).[38]
>
> The jars in which the Papyri were found, were found a few feet below the surface in the sand. They were on top of a wooden coffin. From the description they were in approximately the position shown in the sketch below.

The author of the report then writes of efforts to recover one of the jars before moving on to describe the books themselves:

> They were placed upright in the jars. They were shoved in rather loosely and there were no bindings. The leaves, however, were held together in some cases by the binding cord[,] the holes of which are shown in the margins of many of the papyri leaves. There are a series of pages from the New Testament that seem to have had originally about 26 lines and they were in pretty good condition[,] the bottom margin and a few lines being missing. These apparently were found in one of the jars. The other jar contained a portion of the Old Testament on very long sheets of papyri.[39]

The last page of the memorandum contains a drawing of a codex page labeled "Text of the Prophets Old Testament" with sets of measurements showing the size of the page (about 12.5 cm by 35.5 cm), the block of writing, and the margins.

Thus, most of the description of the actual books is fairly general. Detailed information about the books is limited to just two codices, each of which is readily identifiable. The leaves of the "New Testament" with twenty-six lines per page showing damage at the bottoms could only be the Pauline Epistles (the gospels codex was not in "pretty good condition," and the leaves of Revelation are more damaged at the top than the bottom). The drawing of "The Text of the Prophets of the Old Testament," a tall, narrow codex with dimensions of about 12.5 by 35.5 centimeters, must be the codex containing Ezekiel, Daniel, Susanna, and Esther, which measures about 12.8 by 34.4 centimeters and has just over fifty lines per page. And it is no accident that the informant could give information about only these two books, for it was parts of these two codices that were still on the market in early 1934. As indicated above, Beatty ended up buying the leaves of the Pauline Epistles, but the price of the Ezekiel leaves was too high for him. Those leaves were bought by Scheide. The information in the memorandum may well have been generated by combining rumors in order to provide an attractive "backstory" for the sale of the rest of a dealer's inventory.

By 1936, Kenyon had incorporated aspects of Schmidt's story of the discovery, but he also seems to have included information either from the brief comments of Sanders or, more likely, from the report commissioned by Beatty:

> The circumstances of the find have never been fully revealed; indeed they are known only to the natives who made it, and their statements, for obvious reasons, are not very dependable. The first reports spoke of the district of the Fayum, to the west of the Nile; but information given to Dr. Carl Schmidt was to the effect that the actual site was on the opposite side of the river, near the remains of the ancient city of Aphroditopolis. The papyri are said to have been found in a Coptic graveyard, enclosed in one or more jars, which is very probable, for other papyri have from time to time been similarly found, jars or buckets having been frequently used as receptacles for books in antiquity.[40]

Kenyon also noted that the codices themselves may provide one clue to the provenance. The Isaiah codex (LDAB 3108) contains marginal glosses in an early form of Coptic; that is to say, the glosses are written entirely in Greek letters without employing any of the supplementary Coptic letters that became customary.[41] The dialect of the glosses is Fayumic, which suggests an association with the region of the Fayum, but dialect is not an infallible guide to provenance, as is illustrated by the Bodmer Papyri, which show that books written in a variety of Coptic dialects could all be found together in one place.[42]

And it was the appearance of the Bodmer Papyri in the 1950s that occasioned still another suggested provenance. Early on, the Bodmer Papyri were thought to have come from Panopolis (modern Akhmim), and it was once a popular idea that the Bodmer Papyri and the Beatty Biblical Papyri were actually from one and the same find, but this connection no longer seems plausible.[43] No sales records link the Beatty Biblical Papyri to Akhmim, and each collection considered as an independent entity shows internal coherence. Ultimately, it is very difficult to know anything for certain about the provenance of the Beatty Biblical Papyri. The fact that the Michigan leaves appear to have come from a dealer from Beni Suef and that Schmidt located the site of the find just fifteen kilometers from there may mean that the books at least passed through that area, but the further suggestion that the books came from Asyut complicates matters. Considerably more Christian manuscripts are traceable to that region than to the area around Aphroditopolis. But a single statement from a dealer is tenuous evidence indeed for establishing provenance. The point to take away from this exercise is that it will no longer do to just repeat the account of either Schmidt or Kenyon as fact.[44] The existence and early attestation of an alternative, equally plausible story relativize the suggestions of Schmidt and Kenyon.

The Beatty Biblical Papyri as a Group

The eleven codices are all papyrus and in varying states of preservation, from more than 75 percent complete (86 of a probable 104 leaves of the Pauline Epistles codex survive) to just two damaged leaves (all that remains of the codex of Jeremiah and the codex of Ecclesiasticus). The books vary in size and layout. They have been assigned dates ranging from the second (or possibly third) century to the late fourth or early fifth century. I summarize the basic data about the codices in Table 4.1. The headings of the columns are for the most part self-explanatory. In the final column ("Proposed Dates"), I have resisted the urge simply to assign the date that I think most likely. Instead, I use that column to illustrate the variety of opinions in the literature. The estimations of dates are drawn from Kenyon's original editions (which occasionally included the views of Arthur S. Hunt), Eric G. Turner's *The Typology of the Early Codex*, and other studies that are noted in the analysis that follows. The lists of proposed dates in the table are not exhaustive. In Table 4.2, I include data for a set of papyrus leaves in the collection of Martin Schøyen published in 2005 and 2010. I argue later that there is a chance that these papyri may also belong to the Beatty find (the dates for the Schøyen manuscripts are those given in the original editions).

In terms of contents, we find a book containing the four canonical gospels, although this volume held the book of Acts as well (LDAB 2980). We also have a codex with a collection of the Pauline Letters, although this collection apparently did not include the Pastoral Letters (LDAB 3011). There is also an independent codex of Revelation (LDAB 2778). At least some of the codices, then, have something resembling, but not quite matching, the shape of what would become the standard codex subcollections of "the New Testament" in the medieval period—namely, the gospels, the Pauline Letters, Acts and the Catholic Epistles, and Revelation.[45] Seven of the codices contain various pieces of Hebrew scriptures in Greek translation. The only item that we might designate as "nonbiblical" is a codex containing the Letter of Enoch, Melito's paschal sermon, and the Apocryphon of Ezekiel (LDAB 2608). Aside from the few Coptic glosses on the Isaiah leaves (LDAB 3108), the collection is entirely in Greek.

The linguistic uniformity stands in contrast to the appearance of the books, which are striking for their variety in size, shape, and construction. The range of sizes and shapes is most easily appreciated in a scaled depiction of all the codices (Figure 4.3). The sizes vary, but none of the codices has a height of less than 21 centimeters, and some of the codices (Codex VI and Codex IX + X) could be classified as "large format," that is, more than 30 centimeters in height. Codices II, III, VI, and VII are roughly proportional (width about 58 percent of height), but their absolute dimensions are quite different, ranging from a height of 24.2 centimeters for Codex III to a height of 33 centimeters for Codex VI. Before further observations

Table 4.1. The Chester Beatty Biblical Papyri

Designation(s)	LDAB No.	Language	Contents	Page Dimensions (w × h) [Reconstructed]
Beatty Codex I P.Vindob. G. 31974	2980	Greek	Matthew, John, Luke, and Mark; Acts	[20.4 cm × 25.4 cm] (Turner)
Beatty Codex II P.Mich. inv. 6238	3011	Greek	Romans, Hebrews, 1 and 2 Corinthians, Ephesians, Galatians, Philippians, Colossians, 1 Thessalonians	[16 cm × 28 cm] (Ebojo)
Beatty Codex III	2778	Greek	Revelation	[13–13.5 cm × 23.5–24.5 cm] (Malik)
Beatty Codex IV	3160	Greek	Genesis	[18 cm × 28 cm] (Turner)
Beatty Codex V	3109	Greek	Genesis	[17 cm] × 21 cm (Turner)
Beatty Codex VI P.Mich. inv. 5554	3091	Greek	Numbers, Deuteronomy	[18–19 cm × 33 cm] (Turner)
Beatty Codex VII PSI 12.1273 P.Merton 1.2	3108	Greek (with Coptic glosses)	Isaiah	15.3 cm × [26] cm (Turner)
Beatty Codex VIII	3084	Greek	Jeremiah	[15.2 cm × 30.5 cm] (Turner)
Beatty Codex IX + X Scheide MS 97 P.Köln Theol. 3–13, 15–40 P.Matr. Bibl. 1 P.Monts.Roca 4.46–47	3090	Greek	Ezekiel, Daniel, Susanna, Esther	12.8 cm × 34.4 cm (Turner)
Beatty Codex XI	3161	Greek	Ecclesiasticus (Sirach)	[17.8 cm × 26.7 cm] (Turner)
Beatty Codex XII P.Mich. inv. 5552 and 5553	2608	Greek	Letter of Enoch, Melito *On Passover*, Apocryphon of Ezekiel	14 cm × [27] cm (Turner)

Material	Quires	Extant Folia (Estimated Total Folia)	Binding	Proposed Dates
Papyrus	Ca. 55 (single-sheet quires)	31 (ca. 110)	Stabbing	First half 3rd cent. (Kenyon) "200–250" (Orsini) Sec. half 3rd cent. (Hunt) End of 3rd cent. (Cavallo)
Papyrus	1	86 (104)	Not preserved; remains consistent with two tackets	Late 1st cent. (Kim) End of 2nd cent. (Cavallo) "200–225" (Orsini) First half 3rd cent. (Kenyon) Sec. half 3rd cent. (Sanders) 3rd or 4th cent. (Pickering)
Papyrus	Not known	10 (ca. 32)	Not preserved	Late 3rd cent. (Kenyon) 3rd cent.? (Turner) "200–300" (Orsini) "250–325" (Malik)
Papyrus	Not known	50 (ca. 66)	Not preserved	4th cent. (Kenyon) 4th cent. (Turner)
Papyrus	9[?]	27 (ca. 84)	Not preserved	Sec. half 3rd cent. (Kenyon) 3rd to 4th cent. (Turner)
Papyrus	Not known	54? (ca. 108)	Not preserved	First half 2nd cent. (Kenyon) Late 2nd or 3rd cent. (Hunt) 2nd to 3rd cent. (Turner)
Papyrus	1	33 (ca. 112)	Not preserved	First half 3rd cent. (Kenyon) 3rd cent. (Turner)
Papyrus	Not known	2 (difficult to estimate)	Not preserved	Late 2nd cent. (Crisci) 2nd or early 3rd cent. (Kenyon) 4th cent. (Turner)
Papyrus	1	100? (118)	Not preserved	2nd cent. (Wilcken) First half 3rd cent. (Kenyon) 3rd or 4th cent. (Turner)
Papyrus	Not known	2 (at least 54)	Not preserved	4th cent. (Kenyon) 4th cent. (Turner)
Papyrus	Probably 1	At least 15 (28)	Not preserved	4th or possibly 5th cent. (Kenyon) 4th cent. (Turner)

Table 4.2. Possible additional material from the Beatty Biblical Papyri find

Designation(s)	LDAB No.	Language	Contents	Page Dimensions (w × h)
P.Schøyen 2.26	8120	Greek	Leviticus	10.5 cm × 21 cm (De Troyer)
P.Schøyen 1.23	8119	Greek	Joshua	11 cm × 20 cm (De Troyer)

are made about the codices as a group, it is helpful to discuss the individual books briefly in turn, paying special attention to the dates that Kenyon assigned, which in large part formed the basis for the sensation that the manuscripts caused.

The Individual Books

The first of the Beatty Biblical Papyri to be fully published was the codex containing the gospels in the so-called Western order (Matthew, John, Luke, and Mark) and also Acts (LDAB 2980).[46] If the assigned third-century date is correct, Codex I would be a very early example of the four gospels being bound together in a single volume. The combination of the gospels and Acts as a unit is curious by later medieval standards, when Acts was more usually grouped with the so-called Catholic Epistles. The texts of the books preserved in this codex were also remarkable in that they did not align well with any of the known "families" of texts that scholars of the nineteenth century had established on the basis of the great parchment codices such as Codex Vaticanus, Codex Sinaiticus, and Codex Bezae, among many others. At the time Kenyon was editing the Beatty papyri, a chief question among textual scholars was whether or not the Codex Vaticanus preserved an especially early version of the texts of the New Testament. The evidence of Beatty Codex I was, in Kenyon's view, clear: "It points, perhaps decisively, to the conclusion that the Vatican MS. does not represent a text of original purity dominant in Egypt throughout the second and third centuries; that other texts, with many minor variations, existed during that period in Egypt as well as elsewhere; and that the Vatican text represents the result, not

Material	Quires	Extant Folia (Estimated Total Folia)	Binding	Proposed Dates
Papyrus	Not known	8 (ca. 73)	Not preserved	Late 2nd or 3rd cent. (Cavallo)
Papyrus	Not known	6 (ca. 36)	Not preserved	Late 2nd or 3rd cent. (Cavallo) 210–215 CE (Cavallo)[?]

of continuous unaltered tradition, but of skilled scholarship working on the best available authorities."[47] The Beatty codex was thought to show that the texts of the New Testament were more fluid during the second and third centuries than had previously been imagined. This view would be the norm for the next quarter century.[48]

For Kenyon, then, the textual importance of the Beatty gospels codex lay at least in part with its early date. Kenyon assigned the gospels codex to the third century. His statement of the date is worth quoting at length, as it gives insight into the common procedure for dating undated manuscripts in the 1930s:

> The hand is in the sequence between that which is to be found, for example, in the Herodas papyrus of the first or second century, and that of the magical papyri which are generally assigned to the fourth. It has none of the characteristics of the vellum uncial hands of the fourth and later centuries. It has some resemblance to the Freer or Washington codex of the Gospels, but appears to be earlier. Its sloping character is in accordance with the general practice of the third century. The date which I should assign to it is the third century, and the first half of it rather than the second. In a matter of such importance it would be unsatisfactory to rely on a single opinion: but precisely the same estimate was independently formed by papyrologists of the experience of Mr. H. I. Bell and Dr. W. Schubart. Prof. A. S. Hunt, who has been good enough to give an opinion on a photograph of a page of the papyrus, also assigns it to the third century, though he is inclined to place it in the second rather than

Figure 4.3. Scale image of the Chester Beatty Biblical Papyri.
Top (left to right): Codex I, Codex IV, Codex V, Codex III; middle (left to right):
Codex II, Codex VII, Codex VIII; bottom (left to right): Codex XI, Codex VI,
Codex XII, Scheide MS 97 (= Beatty Codex IX + X).

10 cm

the first half of the century. I do not think that he, any more than I, would wish to dogmatize on such a point; indeed, no competent papyrologist would on the available evidence care to be positive within a generation or two. A date in the third century may, however, be assigned with some confidence and the primitive method of quire-formation, described above, and the early type of some of the abbreviations are also arguments in favour of an early date.[49]

For Kenyon, the assignment of a date presumed a regular, linear development of writing (a "sequence"). The only comparative material Kenyon mentioned was "the Herodas papyrus," an undated papyrus roll containing the Mimes of Herodas copied in a plain hand usually assigned to the first or second century CE (LDAB 1164), unnamed magical books, and the Freer codex of the gospels (LDAB 2985). There is no reference to any securely dated manuscripts. Nevertheless, Kenyon's third-century dating has not yet been seriously challenged. Some modern paleographers have described the writing of this codex as a species of the severe style and accordingly assigned it to the first half of the third century.[50] Guglielmo Cavallo, however, has classified the writing of the Beatty codex as an example of "the inclining ogival majuscule" and followed Hunt in assigning Codex I to the end of the third century.[51] The third-century assignment is not unreasonable, but I do hesitate because of the phenomenon I identified in Chapter 2, namely, that our corpus of datable samples is taken almost entirely from rolls, and our concern here is a codex. The unstated working assumption is that the datable rolls give a full representation of the span of time that this type of writing was in use, even though the roll format was largely supplanted by the codex by the end of the fourth century.

As to Kenyon's statement about the construction technique, it is not so much that the method of quire formation is "primitive"; rather, it is anomalous. To my knowledge, there is no other "literary" codex constructed and bound like the Beatty gospels. The lucky preservation of two sets of consecutive conjoint leaves with the continuous text of Luke 10:6–13:24 shows that the book was made up of single-sheet quires. As Figure 4.4 shows, pairs of holes straddle the central folds of these sheets, indicating that some variety of the

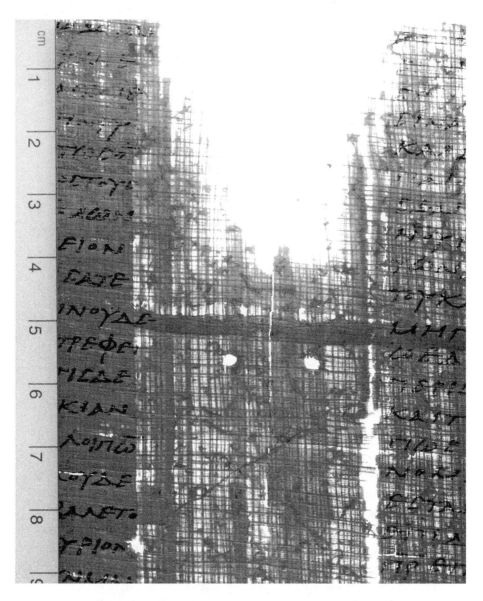

Figure 4.4. Chester Beatty Codex I, detail of folios 13–14,
showing pairs of binding holes straddling the central fold.

(Image © The Trustees of the Chester Beatty Library, Dublin, photographed by the Center
for the Study of New Testament Manuscripts.)

stabbing method of binding was employed. Codices that show similar patterns of holes slightly removed from the central fold are usually classified as "notebooks" by papyrologists.[52] Codices made up of single-sheet quires are generally documentary in nature and date as late as the eighth century.[53] The Beatty gospels codex is much larger (that is to say, thicker) than either these "notebooks" or the documentary codices. From the extant thirty leaves known to him, Kenyon was able to calculate that Codex I originally would have consisted of about fifty-five sheets (110 leaves, 220 pages). Books with that number of very fine parchment leaves are about 2.5 centimeters thick.[54] We are thus asked to imagine a stack of single, independently folded sheets of papyrus at least 2.5 centimeters high bound only by being stabbed through from front to back using two strands of cord (or four strands, if each cord passed around the spine). A book constructed in such a manner cannot have been easy to use. It is not difficult to understand why we have not found more widespread use of this technique of construction for literary codices.

The Beatty codex of the Pauline Epistles (LDAB 3011), on the other hand, is a common construction of a single quire. Kenyon calculated that there would have been 104 sheets, of which 86 have been preserved.[55] The leaves originally would have been about 27–28 centimeters high, and the width varies because the central leaves, which would have protruded when the codex was folded, were either made slightly shorter when they were originally cut from the roll or trimmed off after the codex was made. Thus, the outer leaves of the quire may have been up to 16 centimeters wide, while the central leaves of the quire were probably closer to 13.5 centimeters wide.[56] The method of binding is not entirely clear. Like the other Beatty codices, this one has been disassembled and the individual leaves placed between glass. Looking at single leaves, it is difficult to determine a regular pattern of holes along the central fold, but by superimposing images of several successive leaves with the use of photo-editing software, patterns emerge. Basically, along the central fold there is reasonably clear evidence of three holes, at about 2.0, 11.5, and 17.0 centimeters from the top of the page. Just looking at individual leaves, one might take these as simple jagged edges, but when multiple leaves are superimposed, the pattern is unmistakable. I would expect another hole about 24 centimeters from the top of the page (that is, about 4 cm from the bottom of the page), but the bottoms of the leaves are too damaged to preserve such evidence. A second set of holes in the margins is visible at 7.0, 13.5, and 17.5 centimeters from the tops of several of the leaves. Not all of the holes are visible in all of the leaves, both because of damage and because the holes seem to have been punctured rather than cut. The result is that some holes have been flattened out between the plates of glass. This pattern of holes is consistent with an initial binding of the quire in the style of the Nag Hammadi codices (an upper and lower tacket through the central fold), and the second set of marginal holes raises the possibility of a secondary binding by stabbing at some point.

The writing of the codex is perhaps the most "calligraphic" of the Beatty codices. It is clear and neat with serifs decorating the ends of strokes. The pages are numbered in a hand distinct from that of the copyist. A cursive hand (assigned to the early third century by Kenyon) has placed a count of the *stichoi*, or line counts, at the end of each text, although these numbers do not match the actual number of lines in the papyrus. For instance, Galatians, which occupies 311 lines, has a stichometrical notation of 375—a sign of a slightly dishonest professional copyist paid by the line? The codex also shows signs of use in the form of reading marks, small ticks in a different ink from the text itself that seem to mark sense units in some of the epistles.

Codex II has been a source of debate with regard to both its date and its contents. Kenyon originally assigned the handwriting of the codex to the first half of the third century, a date for which he found confirmation in the short cursive stichometrical notes. He cited no comparative evidence.[57] The great German papyrologist Ulrich Wilcken (1862–1944) proposed a date of "about A.D. 200," or perhaps even moving into the second century, although he did not propose any precise comparanda either.[58] Sanders, who edited the Michigan leaves of the codex, preferred the second half of the third century, but he too offered no actual dated parallels for the hand.[59] In 1975, Guglielmo Cavallo classified the writing of Codex II as a precursor to the "Alexandrian Majuscule" and suggested a date in the second half of the second century on the basis of a comparison with P.Fay. 87, a receipt for money paid to a bank in 155 CE.[60] Interestingly, though, the original editors of that papyrus singled out its writing as distinctively *uncharacteristic* of the second century, observing that "the papyrus is written in a remarkable hand, which presents at first sight an almost Byzantine appearance"![61] Turner accepted a date in the third century without, to my knowledge, naming any comparanda.[62]

In 1988, however, an article appeared that made the incredible claim that Codex II "was written sometime before the reign of the emperor Domitian," that is, before 81 CE.[63] And if the previous discussion of the date of the Pauline Epistles codex lacked sufficient reference to specific comparative papyri, this article suffered from the opposite problem. In the space of just ten pages, the author cited dozens of individual papyri to try to establish a first-century date for the Pauline Epistles codex. Unfortunately, not a single one of the mass of dated manuscripts cited in the article provides anything close to a good comparandum for the writing of the Beatty codex. The reason for this is that the article proceeds by isolating single, particular features of the script in the Pauline Epistles codex (such as a supposed tendency to emphasize the upper notional line) and then piling up examples of first-century papyri that allegedly also show one of these features. No images are given other than the author's own drawings. The whole exercise is thus one of obfuscation. Although some of these references are easy enough to check, especially now during an age in which more and more papyri are digitized and available online, some of them are to be found only in libraries with specialized papyrological resources. In any event, the piecemeal approach to comparison is exposed as unhelpful simply by looking at the parallels proposed in the article. For instance, P.Med. inv. 70.01 (SB 12.11012), a document dated to 55 CE, is said to be "in the exact style" of the Beatty Pauline Epistles codex (Figure 4.5). But the writing of this papyrus is not at all in "the exact style" of that of the Pauline Epistles codex. Individual letters are formed differently (note especially the alpha, epsilon, mu, pi, and phi), and the overall effect of the writing is quite distinct. In a patient unpacking and debunking of this argument, Stuart Pickering aptly observed that the main problem in this method of comparison is that "it is in fact fairly easy to find similar letter shapes in hands many centuries apart which have no stylistic connections apart from a common heritage of the

Chester Beatty Codex II, page 28

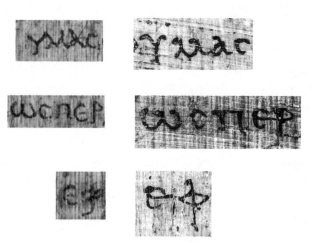

P.Med.inv. 70.01

| P.Med.inv. 70.01, detailed samples of writing | Beatty Codex II, samples from pages 28-29 |

Figure 4.5. Comparison of the writing in P.Med. inv. 70.01, a document of 55 CE, and the writing of Beatty Codex II of the Pauline Epistles.

hand-written letter shapes of the Greek alphabet."[64] Pickering himself followed Cavallo's method of comparing the writing of the Pauline Epistles codex with samples of writing generally agreed to be a part of the Alexandrian stylistic class. Without committing himself to a specific date for Codex II, Pickering placed an "emphasis on the third and fourth centuries" as a locus for seeking to place samples of writing like that of Codex II. Yet, the difficulty of this method becomes clear when we turn to the recent work of Orsini and Clarysse, who employ the same basic method as Pickering and place the writing of Codex II into the Alexandrian stylistic class. But rather than staying with Pickering's third- and fourth-century time span, they restrict the range of possible dates for Codex II within the narrow confines of a twenty-five-year period (200–225 CE).[65] This is an unrealistically small range of dates for any literary papyrus of the Roman era. As we have seen, we have professional writers attested in the record who had active careers longer than this. It appears that at the end of the day, we must admit that no truly compelling securely dated parallels for the script of the Pauline Epistles codex have been proposed.

On the question of contents, the problem may be stated succinctly. The extant remains show that the codex contained the following Pauline letters in this unusual order: Romans, Hebrews, 1 Corinthians, 2 Corinthians, Ephesians, Galatians, Philippians, Colossians, and 1 Thessalonians. The pages are numbered, and the numbering sequence commences with the beginning of Romans. From the surviving leaves, it can be calculated that, if the codex began with Romans, seven leaves must be missing from the beginning of the quire. Because the codex is a single quire, seven leaves must also be missing from the end of the codex. The difficulty is that these seven leaves (fourteen pages) would not be enough space to accommodate the rest of the letters attributed to Paul (2 Thessalonians, 1 and 2 Timothy, Titus, and Philemon). If 2 Thessalonians was included, as seems likely, only Philemon would also fit. Some scholars have suggested, then, that this codex did not contain the so-called Pastoral Epistles (1–2 Timothy and Titus), while others have argued for the possibility of an additional quire that has been lost. These discussions are sometimes interesting, but beyond the evidence of the leaves that actually exist, we cannot know the contents of the final leaves.[66] Fortunately, this codex forms the subject of a recent very thorough doctoral dissertation that promises to shed more light on all the problems discussed here.[67]

The Beatty codex of Revelation (LDAB 2778) has also been treated in a recently published doctoral dissertation.[68] When Kenyon edited these ten leaves in 1934, he was able to show that they formed five bifolia and constituted either an entire quire of twenty pages or the center of a larger quire. If this was the center of a single-quire codex, Kenyon posited a quire of about sixteen sheets (sixty-four pages), which would account for the complete text of the book of Revelation with a few blank leaves at the end. If it was a multi-quire codex, he posited quires of six sheets, five sheets (that is, the five existing sheets), and six sheets, which would contain all of Revelation with a blank leaf at the beginning and the final leaf having only half a page inscribed. In regard to the date of the codex, Kenyon said only that "there is nothing in the hand to suggest a later date than the third century, but it is likely to be late in the century."[69] More recent paleographers have agreed with this general assessment, although Turner has occasionally included the fourth century in the range of possible dates. And, according to the latest and most detailed analysis, which brings datable comparanda to the table, the codex is said to belong to the period between 250 and 325 CE.[70]

Between them, the two codices of Genesis among the Beatty Biblical Papyri account for nearly the entire text of that book, but the codices are quite different in character.[71] Codex IV (LDAB 3160) consists of fifty leaves out of an estimated sixty-six leaves. The pages were likely about eighteen centimeters wide and twenty-eight centimeters high and were laid out in double columns. Because of heavy damage to the inner margins, the quire structure cannot be easily determined. The codex is written in an example of the Biblical Majuscule assigned by general consensus to the fourth century. Kenyon also points out a cursive note written on one of the pages that he assigns to the early fourth century.[72] A different hand also added page numbers.

Among the twenty-seven extant leaves of the other codex of Genesis (Codex V, LDAB 3109), Kenyon was able to identify two quires of five sheets each. He posited that nine quires would suffice for all of Genesis (one quire of two sheets, plus eight quires of five sheets),

with a few leaves at the beginning and end either left blank or containing other material. Kenyon thus estimated the whole book would
have consisted of eighty-four leaves (168 pages). Page numbers were
added to this codex by a hand different from that of the copyist.
Some letters of the text were also copied over in a hand similar to
that of the paginator of the codex.[73] The main text is written in what
Kenyon calls "a good documentary hand."[74] After suggesting multiple parallels from documents securely dated to the period between
216 and 345 CE, Kenyon assigned Codex V to the second half of the
third century. More recent analyses have diverged from that point,
with Guglielmo Cavallo preferring a date toward the beginning of
the third century and Turner opting for a third- to fourth-century
date, or, on one occasion, simply a fourth-century date.[75]

Codex VI, the Beatty manuscript of Numbers and Deuteronomy
(LDAB 3091), is an impressive book laid out in double columns with
a page size of 18–19 by 33 centimeters. The vertical margins are
especially generous, accounting for fully 42 percent of the height of
the page (6.4 cm for the upper margin and 7.6 cm for the lower margin). About half of the estimated 108 leaves survive, with the pages
numbered in a distinct, cursive hand. Its construction is indeterminate. Because the inner margins of most leaves are damaged, it
is difficult to tell which were conjoint. The codex could be either a
single quire or a multi-quire construction. Both Kenyon and Turner
suggested it might have been composed of single-sheet quires like
Codex I, but I think this unlikely.[76] In one sequence of well-preserved
leaves (the pages numbered 21–22, 23–24, and 25–26), I was unable
to trace any horizontal continuity of the papyrus fibers across the
leaves.

The Numbers-Deuteronomy codex is generally believed to be
the oldest book in the collection. That the codex is a Christian,
rather than a Jewish, production seems assured by the regular use of
the *nomen sacrum* contraction of the name "Joshua," which in Greek
is identical to the name "Jesus" (*Iēsous*). In his edition of the text
published in 1935, Kenyon provided his most detailed discussion of
the date:

> The point of special interest about this manuscript is its very
> early date. The evidence of this is purely palaeographical,

but does not appear to admit of doubt. It is written in a rather small, upright hand, square in build (i.e. with height and width of letters about equal), with well-rounded curves, and light, flowing strokes. It is a type of hand easily recognizable as belonging to what is known as the Roman period of papyrus palaeography. It is akin to, but probably rather later than, the long Hyperides papyrus in the British Museum, which is assigned on fairly good evidence to the end of the first century after Christ. It does not seem possible to date it later than the second century, or even, in my opinion, after the middle of that century. This also is the opinion of Mr. H. I. Bell and Prof. Schubart, and is confirmed by Prof. Wilcken (*Archiv für Papyrusforschung*, xi. 113), who speaks of the reign of Hadrian; but it should be noted that Prof. Hunt, while thinking it may well be of the second century, added that this type of hand continued into the third century, and that therefore "late 2nd or early 3rd" would be a cautious date for it. I think this dating is almost certainly over-cautious.[77]

The early date assigned to the codex, then, is the result of a mixture of appeals to evidence and appeals to authority. The only relatively datable comparative evidence Kenyon presented is the famous Hyperides roll (LDAB 2423), which has been variously dated between the second century BCE and the second century CE, with recent opinion settling on the later end of that spectrum.[78] In subsequent years, Kenyon would come to describe the Beatty Numbers-Deuteronomy codex without qualification as a product of the "first half of the second century," and Hunt's wider range of dates was soon forgotten.[79] Kenyon's opinion would be repeated regularly in the following decades, and this early dating of the codex was significant in making it not only one of the oldest known Christian books, but also the oldest known well-preserved codex. It thus played an important role in discussions of the development of the codex and its early adoption by Christians.

It is worth noting, however, that in the 1970s Eric Turner brought some methodological discipline to the paleographic discussion by offering four securely dated samples of handwriting for comparison with the script of the Numbers-Deuteronomy codex.[80] All of them

Figure 4.6. P.Oxy. 17.2105, fragment of a papyrus roll
containing an edict of a prefect.

(Image courtesy of the Egypt Exploration Society and Imaging
Papyri Project, University of Oxford.)

fall in the third century, some as late as the middle of the century.
Individual letters in each of the pieces resemble those of the Beatty
codex, often quite closely, but overall, none of them constitutes a
compelling parallel.[81] Colin H. Roberts revisited the question in
1979. After surveying a series of dated documentary parallels ranging from the late first century to Turner's third-century proposals,
Roberts offered an additional possible comparative sample that does
seem to me to be informative, P.Oxy. 17.2105, an edict of a prefect
from sometime between the years 231 and 236 (Figure 4.6).[82] The
basically square modulus of the letters, the shapes of the individual
letters, and the relative spacing of the letters yield a similar overall
appearance, even if P.Oxy. 17.2105 seems less neat and bilinear. This
is to be expected in the copying of a document rather than a piece
of literature. The similarities can be better appreciated by placing

P. Oxy. 17.2105, line 4

Samples
from Chester Beatty
Codex VI

Figure 4.7. Detail of the scripts of P.Oxy. 17.2105 and Chester Beatty Codex VI.

(Image of P.Oxy. 17.2105 courtesy of the Egypt Exploration Society and Imaging Papyri Project, University of Oxford. Image of Beatty Codex VI © The Trustees of the Chester Beatty Library, Dublin, photographed by the Center for the Study of New Testament Manuscripts.)

strings of letters side by side (Figure 4.7). The theta that sometimes tends toward a slightly triangular shape, the elongated crossbars of the epsilon and theta, the vertical compactness of the omega, and the horizontal spacing between letters are all quite similar in the two pieces. After examining all the data, Roberts offered this verdict: "I know of no dated papyrus that provides a consistently close parallel to this hand and on present evidence a second century date, though possible or even probable, is not necessary and a provisional verdict should be second/third century."[83] Thus even Roberts, who was not shy about assigning very early dates to Christian manuscripts, provided a formulation very similar to that recommended by

Hunt in opposition to Kenyon's restriction of the date to the first half of the second century. The heart of the problem is summed up by Turner: "It seems to me that champions of a second century date (especially a date around A.D. 150) must show not that the handwriting *may* be as early as that, but that it *must* be as early."[84] In framing the challenge this way, however, Turner set the bar impossibly high. Because types of handwriting remain in use through time, exact dating strictly on paleographic grounds is not a feasible goal. Thus, pending new evidence, we must allow for a date in either the second or the third century. Greater precision on the basis of paleography alone is simply not possible.

Codex VII consists of the remains of several leaves containing parts of the book of Isaiah (LDAB 3108), split between the Beatty Library and other holding institutions. They are universally assigned to the third century. Kenyon, comparing the cursive marginalia to a document dated to 236 CE (B.G.U. 4.1062) added that "the first half of the century seems more probable than the second."[85] I have already mentioned the marginal glosses in an early form of Coptic that appear in this codex but, curiously, in none of the others. The existence of four pairs of conjoined leaves and the preservation of page numbers on some of the surviving leaves demonstrate that the codex was a single quire that originally would have been 224 pages long, with Isaiah ending at about page 208. The original dimensions of the pages have been calculated as 15.2 by 26.7 centimeters (Turner estimated a slightly shorter height of 26 cm).

All that remains of Codex VIII are two very fragmentary leaves of the book of Jeremiah (LDAB 3084). Kenyon reconstructed dimensions of about fifteen by thirty centimeters. The handwriting Kenyon described as "clear, rather large, but not very regular." In terms of date, he classified the codex as "probably late second or early third century."[86] Edoardo Crisci has assigned it to the end of the second century.[87] Eric Turner, however, assigned the hand to the fourth century on the basis of similarities to undated magical codices assigned to the fourth century (LDAB 5760 and 5653).[88] As neither Kenyon nor Crisci has cited parallels, and Turner's proposed comparanda are themselves paleographically dated, we have no real grounding for a date for this codex.

Containing the books of Ezekiel, Daniel, Susanna, and Esther, Codex IX + X (LDAB 3090) is notable for its size. With dimensions of 12.8 by 34.4 centimeters, it is unusually tall and narrow. It also represents an especially large (thick) example of a single-quire codex, with its estimated fifty-nine sheets. The bifolia, conjoined leaves, in the Beatty Library are too damaged to show an obvious pattern of holes for binding. There is one pair of small holes 2.4 centimeters apart along the central fold through which a tacket may have passed.

The history of the acquisition and publication of these leaves makes for yet another demonstration of the perils of paleographic dating. Beatty's leaves consisted of eight bifolia containing Ezek 11:25–17:21 and Esth 2:20–8:6. Kenyon described the handwriting of the Ezekiel and Esther leaves as "probably of the latter part of the third century." Initially, he believed that the leaves of Daniel were part of a separate codex and assigned their handwriting to a period "apparently not later than the first half of the third century."[89] When the plates were published in Kenyon's *General Introduction* in 1933, Hunt recognized that they were in fact parts of a single codex. At the same time, the German papyrologist Ulrich Wilcken published a review of Kenyon's *Introduction* and suggested that several of the dates Kenyon assigned were too late, especially that of the Esther manuscript, which Wilcken would place in the second century.[90] In his edition of the leaves published in 1937, Kenyon identified two copyists in the codex: one responsible for Ezekiel, and one writing both Daniel and Esther. Citing Wilcken's opinion on the date of the Esther leaves, Kenyon settled on this formulation: "There is at any rate no reason to place it later than the first half of the third" century.[91] Thus, Kenyon had been prepared to assign the work of a single copyist (that of Daniel and Esther) to different halves of the century.

When the leaves that Scheide purchased in 1935 were published, the editors pointed out a few small notes in a cursive hand that Harold Idris Bell assigned to the third century.[92] Guglielmo Cavallo has made a passing reference to the leaves of Ezekiel as "third or fourth century."[93] Yet, in 1979 Colin H. Roberts reported that Hunt, who is usually regarded as quite cautious when it comes to assigning dates, "put a note in his copy of the *Archiv* against Wilcken's article on the Chester Beatty collection (xiii. p. 114), agreeing with Wilcken's comment on the Esther-Daniel-Ezekiel codex that Kenyon's dating was too late."[94] Thus, again, recognized experts disagree by more than a century (and even individual paleographers have expressed more than one opinion about the date of the codex). And again, there is no reference in the discussion to dated manuscripts.

The remains of Codex XI (LDAB 3161) consist of only one damaged but relatively complete leaf and two small fragments of a second leaf.[95] The better-preserved leaf carries the page numbers 73 and 74 and contains parts of chapter 36 and 37 (of a total of fifty chapters) of Ecclesiasticus, meaning that it is not unreasonable to conclude that the first numbered leaf of the codex likely contained the beginning of Ecclesiasticus. Kenyon extrapolated that the whole book would occupy twenty-seven sheets (= fifty-four leaves, 108 pages). The inner margin is mostly missing, so nothing can be said of the binding and quire structure of the codex. Kenyon had little to say about the script: "The hand is large and sloping, rather coarse in character, and may probably be assigned to the latter part of the fourth century."[96] Turner also placed this codex in the fourth century, while Cavallo and Maehler compared it to the hand of P.Herm. 4 and 5 and placed it in the early part of the fourth century, classifying it as a species of the "sloping ogival majuscule."[97]

Codex XII (LDAB 2608) is split between the Beatty Library and the University of Michigan.[98] At the time of its publication, this book represented the only known Greek text of all three books it contained: the Letter of Enoch, Melito's paschal sermon, and the Apocryphon of Ezekiel.[99] In addition to fragments of one or more leaves, fourteen nearly complete leaves survive from the center of a quire, and the pages are numbered in a cursive hand preserving numbers between 17 and 36. The second surviving leaf contains pages 17 and 18. Thus, if we are dealing with a single-quire codex with this single sequence of page numbering, the book would have consisted of an additional seven sheets, for a total of fourteen sheets, or fifty-six pages. Kenyon initially assigned the codex to "the fourth or possibly fifth century" but later restricted the range to the fourth century on the basis of comparison with an undated magical papyrus assigned to the fourth century (LDAB 5590).[100]

Additional Material from the Find?

Beyond these eleven books, no other texts are generally considered as part of this find. There is, however, a small chance that some material in roll form was part of the discovery and possibly one or two other codices. The evidence for documentary rolls being part of the find is slim. Among the archival records in the Chester Beatty Library is a note from Harold Idris Bell dated April 11, 1930, giving an assessment of Beatty's early purchases: "As regards the non-literary documents, they are so brittle that I have not ventured to handle them much before they are dampened out, but they too are good papyri. One roll contains copies of two first century documents (from the period of Titus and Vespasian). If these should prove to be part of the same find as the Christian texts it might be very interesting."[101] I do not know if this material remains a part of the Beatty collection. The relatively early dates mentioned by Bell make an association with the Beatty Biblical Papyri unlikely, but it would be good to know the contents of the documents more precisely and what, if any, additional information exists surrounding their acquisition.

The possibility of additional codices belonging to the find is somewhat more promising, but still highly circumstantial. Purchased in 1998 from an unnamed "private collection" in Zürich, P.Schøyen 2.26 (LDAB 8120) and P.Schøyen 1.23 (LDAB 8119) preserve portions of Leviticus and Joshua, respectively (see Table 4.2).[102] The former consists of eight papyrus leaves of Leviticus (10.5 cm wide by 21 cm high) reconstructed from fragments, and the latter consists of six leaves of Joshua (11 cm wide by 20 cm high), also reconstructed from fragments. The manuscripts were assigned by their editor to the same copyist but to different codices (the pages of both manuscripts being numbered in two separate sequences).[103] The books are said to have originated from Oxyrhynchus, but their extent of preservation is better than the typical scraps from the Oxyrhynchus trash heaps.[104] Furthermore, the editor of these texts has pointed out their paleographic similarity to the Chester Beatty codex of Numbers and Deuteronomy. I think this a good comparison, and I find the writing of the Schøyen leaves also quite similar to that of the Beatty Ezekiel-Daniel-Susanna-Esther codex, especially the script of the leaves of Esther. Thus, in terms of the age of the Schøyen papyri, recall that the Beatty Ezekiel-Daniel-Susanna-Esther codex has been assigned dates ranging from the second to the fourth centuries.[105] Samples of writing from the Beatty Codex VI and the Schøyen Joshua codices are given in Figure 4.8 and show similarities among both individual letters and overall appearance. In addition, the Schøyen manuscripts were said to have been originally purchased in Egypt in 1930, the same year that the Chester Beatty Biblical Papyri first appeared on the market. A more detailed knowledge of the ownership history of the Schøyen leaves might be able to establish or rule out a connection with the Beatty Biblical Papyri, but I nevertheless want to raise the possibility that the Schøyen pieces, given their state of preservation, paleographic features, and alleged original circumstances of purchase, might have been part of the Beatty find. These kinds of questions are always difficult to answer firmly. In fact, in the next chapter, I will be quite critical of some efforts to associate a number of different manuscripts with the Bodmer Papyri. Each proposal must be evaluated on its merits, and the establishment of the contours of these collections of early Christian books will always be subject to revision in light of new evidence and analyses.

What emerges from this overview of the Beatty Biblical Papyri is the fragility of our knowledge about them. Although they have been known and studied for more than eighty years, their provenance and dates are far from settled. The best prospects for gaining knowledge of the provenance of the codices is continued "museum archaeology," that is, attempting to find more records, especially of dealers like Maurice Nahman and intermediaries like David Askren. And even if a definite provenance is likely to remain elusive, pursuing these questions will also help to integrate these books into the history of the Egyptian antiquities trade in the early twentieth century. Nahman's trade in ancient jewelry has recently been treated in a fascinating study, and many of the characters involved are the same ones who were purchasing manuscripts (such as Freer and Morgan).[106] Tracing these transactions more thoroughly is certainly a desideratum.

The way ahead with better determination of dates of the codices is also clear. The repeated discussions of paleographic opinions that I have offered can generate a feeling of simply going around in circles. And, when paleographic analysis proceeds without reference

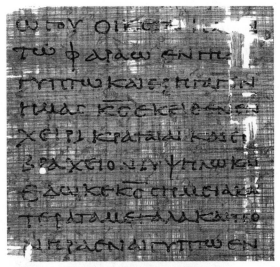

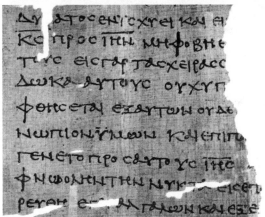

Figure 4.8. Comparison of the scripts of Beatty Codex VI (top)
and P.Schøyen 1.23 (Schøyen MS 2648).

to securely dated parallels, going around in circles is exactly what we
are doing. This is not to say that useful insights cannot be garnered
from the comparison of multiple manuscripts with unknown dates.
For instance, it is noteworthy that among the few comparative manuscripts cited in relation to the writing of the Beatty Biblical Papyri,
magical codices appear with relative frequency, a phenomenon that

would bear further exploration.[107] Yet, until such time as compelling, securely dated comparanda are presented, or, better yet, the books are subjected to radiocarbon analysis, we are unlikely to get past a fairly general sense that the books might have been produced for the most part in the third to fourth centuries.

These types of problems are not unique to the Beatty Biblical Papyri, although the lack of any truly well-defined anchors to place the collection either in time or in space is more pronounced for the Beatty biblical material than it is for either the Bodmer Papyri (which include pieces that at least have a secure *terminus post quem*) or the Christian books from Oxyrhynchus (which, of course, have a known provenance—for the most part). And as we will see, these latter sets of books present their own difficulties.

CHAPTER FIVE

An Elusive Collection
The Bodmer Papyri

LTHOUGH SOME QUESTIONS LINGER about the provenance and extent of the find that included the Beatty Biblical Papyri, the situation with the Bodmer Papyri is vastly more complicated. In my experience, although most biblical scholars are familiar with the term "Bodmer Papyri," few could actually tell you exactly what they are. And there is good reason for this. The designation "Bodmer Papyri" generally refers to a group of Greek, Coptic, and Latin papyrus and parchment books that began to emerge from a number of private collections during the 1950s. Included in this group are some of the earliest well-preserved ancient Christian codices. Most of the books ended up in the library of the Swiss collector Martin Bodmer, but some parts of the cache were purchased by several other institutions or have subsequently been sold or donated to new owners.[1] The publication of the manuscripts began in the 1950s and is ongoing. A dedicated *Papyrus Bodmer* series contains some of these books as well as other material that probably was not part of the ancient collection. At the same time, some manuscripts that probably were part of the ancient collection have also been published in a number of other series and journals.[2] The result of this history of publication is that not everything that carries the name "P.Bodmer" was part of the find, and many items that do not have a "P.Bodmer" designation may well have been part of the find.[3] Furthermore, the "P.Bodmer" designations sometimes refer to individual texts, not whole codices, so in some instances, several "P.Bodmer" items are all part of a single codex. To make matters even more complicated, scholars disagree considerably about which pieces (both those with and those without the "P.Bodmer" designation) actually made up the find. One of the goals of this chapter is to lay out the evidence as clearly as possible and to reach some tentative conclusions about the extent of the find.[4] Only at that point will we be in a position to try to get a sense of the physical characteristics of the manuscripts in the ancient collection.[5]

Closely related to the problem of the extent of the collection is the question of provenance. The manuscripts are from Egypt, but where in Egypt did they come from? It seems that as the books were being acquired, they were thought to have been found near Asyut (ancient Lykopolis; Figure 5.1). Yet, when the pieces were first published in the 1950s and 1960s, an early consensus coalesced around Akhmim (ancient Panopolis) as the find spot. More recent work by James M. Robinson placed the find spot still farther south, close to Dishna, not far from Nag Hammadi. The connection to Asyut was not publicly revealed until 1988, and it has gained no support. Among biblical scholars, Robinson's account is largely accepted, while in papyrological circles, Panopolis is often still preferred as the location of the find. Tied up with the problem of the place of the discovery is the equally difficult issue of who brought these books together in antiquity. Are they the remains of a monastic library? Or might they have originated in an urban educational setting? I will touch on all these problems, but an adequate treatment would require (at least) an entire book.

In trying to untangle the problems associated with these manuscripts, I make frequent reference to the work of Robinson, who has carried out the most detailed investigations of this collection as a whole. His book on the Bodmer Papyri contains a wealth of valuable data.[6] At the same time, it has a number of shortcomings. Although it was published in 2011, the contents mostly reflect research that was carried out during the 1970s and early 1980s. Some publications from the 1990s are treated, and the odd item from the present millennium is occasionally mentioned, but the book basically reflects

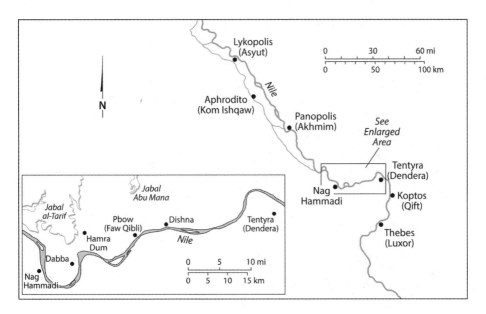

Figure 5.1. Areas of the proposed find spots of the Bodmer Papyri.
(Cartography by Bill Nelson.)

the state of research in the mid-1980s and ignores many crucial new developments. Robinson's book was also apparently prepared from unpolished notes, with the result that there is a good deal of repetition and even some contradictions.[7] Building on the many helpful parts of Robinson's work and wading through the rumor and hearsay, I seek in the present chapter to elucidate the important but confusing corpus known as the Bodmer Papyri.

The Stories of the Find and Acquisition of the Books

The items we now call the Bodmer Papyri began to appear on the antiquities market in Egypt in the early 1950s, and, yet again, that market has obscured the exact circumstances of the find. It was clear already in the 1950s that the Swiss collector Martin Bodmer (1899–1971) had acquired a group of ancient Christian books of considerable importance, but information about the possible source of those books has trickled out only very slowly over the years. Meanwhile, it became known that other repositories possessed parts of some of the books that Bodmer had acquired. As of 2003, we know that Bodmer's

assistant, Odile Bongard (1918–2003), conducted most of the transactions that brought the main part of the find to Geneva. Bodmer
was born into a wealthy family and had already become known as a
prominent collector by his early thirties.[8] Beginning in the years
after World War II, Bodmer set out to assemble a library of *Weltliteratur* (world literature), a concept that for him centered on, but was
by no means limited to, Homer, the Bible, Dante, Shakespeare, and
Goethe.[9] Bongard played an important role in this undertaking. Just
before her death in 2003, she recounted some of the details:

> One day, in the course of an animated discussion about the
> Ancient World, Martin Bodmer spoke to me in these terms:
> "Just find me a fragment of pottery from the fifth or sixth
> century with, say, a text by Homer!" At this juncture, Henri
> Wild visited the library in 1951. He was a Swiss Egyptolo-
> gist from the Institut Francais in Cairo. . . . I asked him the
> same question Martin Bodmer had asked me. "But there's a
> dealer in Cairo who has something much better than that:
> it's a papyrus roll, probably from the third or fourth century,
> with a text from the *Iliad*, but it's in a fairly poor state." I
> begged him to send that papyrus to my home at any cost. A
> few days later, on 17 July 1951, I received a small parcel that
> had been sent business rate. It contained the famous roll. . . .
> Wild had also sent me the address of a Greek Cypriot dealer.
> Phocion Tano, an Orthodox believer who was originally
> from Famagusta, was an antiquities dealer in Cairo and a
> supplier to collectors such as Chester Beatty and Pierpont
> Morgan.[10]

Tano was the same dealer who had handled the bulk of the Nag
Hammadi find just a few years before.[11] On Tano's advice, Bongard
traveled to Egypt in 1953 and set about acquiring more manuscripts.
She reported a private conversation with Tano while she was in
Egypt: "He told me about an interesting discovery, and we agreed
that he would let me have everything that he could collect. When I
asked him where the discovery had been made, he told me it was
in Mina or Minia, near Assiout, and begged me not to divulge that
information for twenty years." Bongard then traveled to Asyut to

investigate, but she found nothing. I am not aware of a town called Minia in the vicinity of Asyut, and I have found no indication that Bongard actually attempted to visit the city of Minya, which sits some 130 kilometers north of Asyut. In any event, she continued visiting dealers in Cairo and Luxor trying to collect parts of this find. How she identified which items from the dealers' inventories were in fact part of the find is left unsaid. She summarized the arrival of the manuscripts in Geneva as follows:

> These acquisitions have come to be surrounded by lots of legends. But, as I know from the packaging I have kept, *all the* [manuscripts] were sent in several small packages to my home address and in various different ways (often between two pieces of card, or wrapped up in such a way that they could be inserted into a newspaper and so on). There were two notable exceptions. The Bodmer Codex II was brought by the dealer in person on one of his trips to Europe. When Martin Bodmer was passing through Cairo on his way back from New Delhi, which he visited on 9 September 1957 for the International Red Cross and Red Crescent International Conference, he was given a small collection of sheets of papyrus at the airport. It was meant as a kindly gesture. The most important were the Menander and part of the *Psalms*. He was given them by an Egyptian from Luxor.[12]

Thus, we have a statement from the purchaser of the bulk of the find (but based only on the word of the dealer) asserting that it originated near Asyut, or ancient Lykopolis. In fact, Bongard's placement of the find near Asyut (without any of the details given above) had already been related in 1988 by Rodolphe Kasser (1927–2013), the Swiss scholar who edited most of the Coptic material from the Bodmer find.[13] But there is also a second story attributed to Bongard. William H. Willis (1916–2000), an American classicist who had a hand in acquiring some of the find for the University of Mississippi, reported that Bongard "told me (in confidence!) that . . . she 'had reason to believe' that the codices were found in the ruins of a iv-cent church at Dishnā," in Upper Egypt.[14] If either of these stories were true, one would never know it from the publications of the papyri, in which the editors told quite different stories. The first items in the *Papyrus Bodmer* series—Books 5 and 6 of the *Iliad* (P.Bodmer I, LDAB 7335 + 2073), copied on the back of a papyrus roll originally used for a land register—were published in 1954.[15] Then followed in quick succession a number of the new acquisitions. P.Bodmer II (LDAB 2777), a papyrus codex of the Gospel According to John in Greek, was first published in 1956.[16] P.Bodmer III (LDAB 107758), a papyrus codex of the Gospel According to John and Genesis in Coptic, appeared in 1958. In the same year, P.Bodmer IV (LDAB 2743), another piece of classical literature, the *Dyskolos* of the comic playwright Menander, was published, along with several parts of a mixed codex of Christian literature in Greek (LDAB 2565).[17] Early on, most of the manuscripts published in the *Papyrus Bodmer* series were thought to be part of the same find. Most, but not all. P.Bodmer XVII (LDAB 2894), a papyrus codex containing Acts and the Catholic Epistles in Greek, was said to be of a different provenance. So also P.Bodmer XXIV, a papyrus codex containing the Psalms in Greek, was declared by its original editors to be of distinct origin from the other codices in the collection, although this opinion seems to have changed over the years for unknown reasons.[18] But the majority of the ancient books being published in the *Papyrus Bodmer* series were thought to be part of a single find. Moreover, the document on the back of which the *Iliad* texts (P.Bodmer I) were copied mentions the Panopolite nome, so it was thought that these items may have originated in Panopolis (modern Akhmim).[19] Many papyrologists continue to entertain this hypothesis, usually positing that the material originated in an educational setting in Panopolis where both classical and Christian authors formed part of the curriculum.[20] According to one variant of this theory, both the Bodmer Papyri and the Chester Beatty Biblical Papyri originated as part of a single find in Panopolis.[21]

Others, however, expressed doubt that Panopolis was the source of the codices. In general, Kasser was very guarded about their provenance, but he was adamant that P.Bodmer I, the chief piece of evidence connecting the material to Panopolis, was not part of the find.[22] In the 1960s, Kasser described the provenance of the codices simply as "Upper Egypt" or "near Thebes." By the early 1970s, however, Kasser began describing the provenance of the Bodmer Papyri as the area just northeast of Nag Hammadi, although he did not immediately disclose his basis for this claim.[23] In a 1981 publication, however, his source was revealed to be the dealer who had sold Bodmer most of the codices, Phocion Tano. Tano had told Kasser this information just before he died in 1972.[24] In 1988, Kasser made a more precise identification of the site of the discovery as the village of Dabba and the date of the discovery as "about 1950 or 1951," citing the dealer as his source; Kasser persisted in accepting Dabba as the site of the find in later years.[25]

But Kasser's revelations were outdated even before they were announced. The ground had already shifted in the mid-1970s, when, as an unanticipated result of his attempt to trace the acquisition history of the Nag Hammadi codices, James M. Robinson learned from local informants in Upper Egypt of a separate discovery of books allegedly made about twelve kilometers from the Jabal al-Tarif, the probable site of the discovery of the Nag Hammadi codices.[26] Robinson then undertook a two-pronged research agenda. First, he followed the rumors in Egypt and interviewed figures allegedly involved in the discovery and marketing of the books. Second, he checked the records of the depositories known to hold material from the Bodmer find to see whether further information about provenance could be found and whether other material at these institutions might belong to the same discovery. From his interviews in Egypt, Robinson asserted, with characteristic confidence and color, that he had identified the finders and established a more precise date and location for the find:

Ḥasan Muḥammad al-Sammān, a tall, dull peasant, and Muḥammad Khalīl al-ʿAzzūzī, an ignorant one-eyed peasant perhaps in family origin from the hamlet Naj Azzūz seven kilometers to the southwest of Abū Manāʿ . . . found a jar containing books about 300 meters out from the foot of the Jabal Abū Manāʿ, at al-Qurnah, "the corner" of the cliff. . . . Ḥasan found the jar buried a couple of meters deep when he was digging *sabakh* to fertilize the fields. He called over to Muḥammad al-ʿAzzūzī "to see what the poor find." Then Ḥasan broke the jar with his mattock and left the pieces where they lay. Then he pulled out the books from the jar

and put them in the skirt of his *jallabīyah*. Some that were
torn and in very bad condition were burned on the spot.
As Ḥasan was carrying the rest home, he gave away some
to passersby, since he was told that they were the books of
giants, which aroused fear in him. There was also in the jar
a square mirror some twenty centimeters across with a
wooden back; Muḥammad Khalīl al-ʿAzzūzī took it. . . . The
date of the discovery was toward the end of the year of the
coup that deposed King Farouk and ultimately brought
Nasser into power. The date of that event, July 26, 1952, is
for Egypt what the Fourth of July is for the U.S.A. and the
Quatorze Juillet is for France—an unforgettable date. . . .
With the help of this reference point, the discovery may be
dated with some confidence late in 1952.[27]

Robinson proceeds to narrate a story of the various local brokers
who handled the find before the main part of it ended up with Tano.
The story is nearly as dramatic as Robinson's account of the Nag
Hammadi books. In the case of the marketing of the Bodmer Papyri, we meet with two additional incidents of burning parts of the
find, police raids, and even a kidnapping "in the dark of night" gone
wrong. Robinson's story is pieced together from interviews with locals conducted mostly in 1975 and 1976, some twenty years after the
events in question. To his credit, Robinson presents the conflicting
stories of his interviewees, and a close reading of the account shows
that his conjectures are clearly marked as such: "one may well assume," "one may hence conjecture," "may well have," etc. In light of
some of the discrepancies in the story, though, the details are certainly open to question.

The most important of these details for our purposes are descriptions of the items that were said to be found in the jar. When
the bulk of the find reached the city of Dishna, the books that remained (after the alleged burnings, spontaneous gifts to passersby,
etc.) were counted out. There were, according to Robinson's informants, at that point "thirty-three books . . . plus three or four rolls
some twenty-five centimeters or more in height, plus two to four
roughly triangular-shaped leaves about fifteen centimeters high, and
about ten small rolls the size of one's finger, later said by Tano to be

letters."[28] Elsewhere, Robinson mentions that one informant reported "a wooden board found in the jar, on which was inscribed in black ink a list by number and title in Coptic and Greek, but not in Arabic, of forty-three items, taken to be an inventory of the contents of the jar."[29] If this list is indeed to be understood as the contents of the jar, then Robinson's Egyptian sources reported either

> a find consisting of forty-eight to fifty-one items (after some were already destroyed or separated)

or

> a find consisting of forty-three items (before any would have been destroyed or separated).

The memory of these exact numbers twenty years after the fact is quite remarkable, and the disparity between the two sets of numbers gives me pause. This hesitation is only increased by a third account that Robinson elicited from Louis Doutreleau (1909–2005), a French scholar who had been involved in editing the papyrus codices found in the quarries at Tura during World War II. Bodmer had enlisted Doutreleau's help in evaluating the materials that Tano had for sale, and Doutreleau also corresponded with Victor Martin, who edited several of the Bodmer books. According to Doutreleau, the find consisted of "some thirty codices" and originated in "the region of Nag Hamadi, like the Gnostic papyri."[30] The ultimate source of Doutreleau's information is Tano, who, he claims, had withheld this information from Bodmer.[31] What is important for the present investigation is that we hear nothing from Doutreleau of rolls or indeed of any material aside from "some thirty" codices.

The second aspect of Robinson's research involved working through archival material associated with the purchases of the items in the find. Although the records of the Bodmer collection were inaccessible to him, Robinson searched the archives of other institutions known to hold material from the find. For instance, about half of P.Bodmer XXII (a Coptic parchment codex of parts of Jeremiah, Lamentations, the Epistle of Jeremiah, and Baruch; LDAB 108176) and most of what is now usually called the Crosby-Schøyen codex

(Schøyen MS 193, a Coptic papyrus codex of mixed contents; LDAB 107771) were bought on behalf of the University of Mississippi in 1955.[32] Bodmer's purchase included the other half of this parchment codex and fragments of the papyrus codex, suggesting that the books traversed the same network of dealers and brokers and probably had a common origin. The situation is similar for a small square papyrus codex containing a mix of classical and Christian material in Greek and Latin (LDAB 552). Most of this codex was purchased in 1955 in Cairo by Ramón Roca-Puig (it is now housed in the Abbey of Montserrat), but Bodmer acquired portions of the book as well.[33] So also the Chester Beatty Library in Dublin acquired in 1956 half of a papyrus codex containing the book of Joshua in Coptic (Ac. 1389, in the Beatty Library's records).[34] Bodmer had bought the other half of this codex (P.Bodmer XXI, LDAB 108537). And it was in the course of research in Dublin that Robinson made a key discovery. The Beatty Library kept a registry of acquisitions, which contained some quite revealing information. The entry for Ac. 1389 stated that this portion of the book was "bought from Phocion J. Tano, 53 Sharia Ibrahim Pasha, Cairo. Summer. 1956 with a.c. 1390 and 2 boxes of loose leaves £835." The book known as "Ac. 1390" (LDAB 2763) is a papyrus codex containing mathematical exercises in Greek and a portion of the Gospel According to John in Coptic. Thus, this book, also purchased from Tano, should probably be considered as part of the Bodmer find as well. But there is more. The entry in the registry of acquisitions for Ac. 1390 contained a short typewritten note:

> Small Village
> DESHNA
> just after NAGH HAMADI
> about 2 hours before LUXOR by train.
> Probably from a Library of a Monastery.
> Found in a Jar in a cemetery.[35]

Whether or not the note was typed by Tano, as Robinson suspected, the information is likely to have come from him as the one who sold the manuscripts to Beatty.[36] Taken together, this information suggests the possibility that other books acquired by Beatty from Tano at that time may also be part of the Bodmer find, which again is lo-calized near Dishna.

What are we to make of all these conflicting data? The sugges-tion that the books were found at Asyut has been universally re-jected. The case for Panopolis is weak, as I demonstrate momentar-ily. There does appear to be a cluster of early evidence placing the spot of the find near Dishna in the region of Nag Hammadi, but much of this information is second-hand and seems to derive ulti-mately from the main dealer involved, Tano.[37] Furthermore, bring-ing the find into the proximity of Nag Hammadi would have poten-tially increased the monetary value of the books by drawing them into association with the already famous Coptic codices discovered there in 1945, a point that had been noted as early as the 1950s.[38] More concerning still is the fact that, unless there was miscommu-nication, Tano also seems to have at various times proposed three different find spots: Dishna, the region of Asyut, and the village of Dabba.[39] It would appear that Tano was lying about (at least) two of the three find spots he seems to have affirmed. Robinson's inter-views among the locals also place the find near Dishna and seem independent of Tano's influence. Yet, as we have seen, the informa-tion that Robinson gathered from locals was conflicting in regard to the extent of the find and seems suspiciously precise for recollec-tions twenty years after the fact. Are we thus again left to pick and choose among details in the varying reports of dealers and third par-ties? Not quite.

Fortunately, one additional piece of the puzzle has very recently come to light. Like the Nag Hammadi codices, some of the Bodmer books were preserved with their leather covers at least partially in-tact. The cover of P.Bodmer XXIII (LDAB 108542), a papyrus codex containing the book of Isaiah in Coptic, which everyone agrees is part of the main find, contained inscribed papyri, both literary and documentary. The pieces extracted from the cover have been desig-nated as follows:[40]

P.Bodmer LI, fragment of a roll with an educational ex-ercise (LDAB 5269), reverse used for a medical or ethno-graphic treatise (LDAB 699689)

P.Bodmer LII, a leaf from a Greek papyrus codex of Isocrates, *Ad Nicoclem* (LDAB 2508)

P.Bodmer LIII, blank papyrus with traces of ink on one
side

P.Bodmer LIV, fragments of a leaf of a papyrus codex
containing a land register

P.Bodmer LV, fragments of a leaf of a papyrus codex containing a tax register

P.Bodmer LVI, fragment of a leaf of a papyrus codex
containing a tax register

In 2015, P.Bodmer LIV–LVI were published, and the financial information they contain establishes that they were most likely written
during the first half of the fourth century, which incidentally provides a *terminus post quem* for the construction of this codex.[41] More
importantly, P.Bodmer LVI mentions a man with a relatively rare
name that also occurs in another papyrus (P.Ryl. 4.705), which identifies the man as "from Tentyra," that is to say, Dendera, which is
about twenty-five kilometers east of Dishna (see Figure 5.1). While
this indication is not definitive, it does tip the balance of evidence
toward the region around Dishna as the most likely spot of the find.[42]

Why is this important? The almost exclusive focus among papyrologists on Panopolis as the setting for the Bodmer Papyri has
probably hindered research on the manuscripts. Their reluctance to
accept some of the more daring aspects of Robinson's arguments
about the Bodmer Papyri, namely that they constitute the remains of
the library of the monastic order founded by Pachomius in the early
fourth century, is understandable. Nevertheless, the combination of
the more reliable material amassed by Robinson (the acquisition data
from the Chester Beatty Library) and the new evidence of the papyri
extracted from the cover of P.Bodmer XXIII indicates that future
research on the milieu of the Bodmer Papyri should probably focus
farther south, on the region between Nag Hammadi and Dendera.

The Contents of the Find

After all the work of determining the most likely place the books
were found, what can we say about the contents of the discovery?

Unfortunately, determining what books were part of the find is just as challenging as figuring out where the books were discovered. There is general agreement about a central core of items that Bodmer purchased in the 1950s. But as we have seen, despite Bongard's claim to have collected the entire find, it was already evident in the 1950s that other institutions had purchased material from this find, for other libraries had parts of some of the books that Bodmer had bought. As Robinson searched the records of these libraries, he checked their inventories to see when those items were purchased and what other items were bought along with them. In this way, Robinson compiled inventories of ancient books that he thought were probably part of the same find. He published the resulting lists in a series of different outlets, and as his research progressed, these lists changed.[43] Robinson's final book on the topic appears to have mixed the various lists, which causes considerable confusion for anyone trying to use his most recent work.[44] In what follows I try to systematize Robinson's data before subjecting them to analysis.

Tables 5.1–5.7 present information about all the material that Robinson has proposed as belonging to the Bodmer find. A few additional items proposed by other scholars have been included. For the sake of ease in presenting the data, I have arranged the codices and rolls separately. I present the codices first, since there is a broad consensus that the first group of codices (Table 5.1) formed the main part of the find. Tables 5.2–5.4 represent codices that Robinson has at one time or another assigned to the Bodmer find with differing levels of certitude. Table 5.5 consists of two codices with "P.Bodmer" designations that are definitely not from the Bodmer find and two codices with "P.Bodmer" designations that are universally excluded from the find, though for less clear reasons. Table 5.6 includes the rolls with classical material that Robinson and others have regarded as part of the find, and Table 5.7 contains another set of rolls associated with the monk Pachomius and his followers, which Robinson also assigned to the find.[45] The headings of the columns are mostly self-explanatory. I have again used the "Proposed Dates" column to illustrate the variety of opinions in the literature. And even this listing of proposed dates is not exhaustive (again, the use of paleography to assign dates has led to widely varying assessments in some instances). When there is no dispute about the date,

Table 5.1. Codices universally regarded as part of the Bodmer Papyri

Designation(s)	LDAB No.	Language	Contents	Page Dimensions (w × h) [Reconstructed]
P.Bodmer II P.Köln 5.214 Chester Beatty Ac. 2555	2777	Greek	John	14.2 cm × 16.2 cm (Martin)
P.Bodmer III	107758	Coptic (Bohairic)	John and Gen 1:1–4:2	15 cm × 21.5 cm (Sharp)
P.Bodmer XXV + IV + XXVI P.Köln 8.331 P.Monts.Roca inv. 45 ("Bodmer Menander")	2743	Greek	Menander (*Samia, Dyskolos*, and *Aspis*)	13 cm × 27.5 cm (Turner)
P.Bodmer V + X + XI + VII + XIII + XII + VIII (the Bodmer "composite" or "miscellaneous" codex; P.Bodmer VIII now at Vatican Library)	2565	Greek	Nativity of Mary, correspondence of Paul and the Corinthians, 11th Ode of Solomon, Jude, Melito *On Passover*, liturgical hymn, 1–2 Peter	14.2 cm × 15.5 cm and 14.6 cm × 16 cm (Turner)
P.Bodmer VI	107761	Coptic ("archaic" Sahidic)	Proverbs	12 cm × 14.5 cm (Kasser)
P.Bodmer XX + IX	220465	Greek	*Apology of Phileas*, Pss 33–34	14 cm × 15.5 cm (Martin)

Material	Quires	Extant Folia (Estimated Total Folia)	Binding	Proposed Dates
Papyrus	8 (Kasser)	75 (78)	Link-stitch, 2 pairs of stations (rebound with single thread)	2nd cent. (Hunger) Ca. 200 (Martin) 200–250 (Turner) 3rd–4th cent. (Orsini) 4th cent. (Nongbri)
Papyrus	7	72 (at least 80)	Link-stitch, 2 pairs of stations	4th cent. (Kasser)
Papyrus	1	26 (32)	Two tackets? (only holes remain; rebound by stabbing)	3rd cent. (Kasser) 4th cent. (Turner) Late 4th cent. (Orsini)
Papyrus	13 (Nongbri)	85 (87)	Link-stitch, 2 pairs of stations (apparently rebound with added material by stabbing)	3rd–4th cent. (Kasser) 4th cent. (Turner) 4th cent. (Orsini)
Parchment	9	64 (at least 72)	Link-stitch, 2 pairs of stations	3rd–4th cent. (Choat) 4th–5th cent. (Kasser)
Papyrus	At least 3	9 (2 leaves known to be missing; extant pages are numbered up to 136)	Not preserved	4th cent. (after 305 CE, date of Phileas's death)

(table continues)

Table 5.1. Continued

Designation(s)	LDAB No.	Language	Contents	Page Dimensions (w × h) [Reconstructed]
P.Bodmer XIV–XV (now at Vatican Library as Hanna Papyrus 1, Mater Verbi)	2895	Greek	Luke and John	13 cm × 26 cm (Turner)
P.Bodmer XVI	108535	Coptic (Sahidic)	Exod 1:1–15:21	13.5 cm × 16 cm (Kasser)
P.Bodmer XVIII	108536	Coptic (Sahidic)	Deut 1:1–10:7	14 cm × 14.5 cm (Kasser)
P.Bodmer XIX	107759	Coptic (Sahidic)	End of Matthew and beginning of Romans	12.5 cm × 15.5 cm (Kasser)
P.Bodmer XXI Chester Beatty Ac. 1389	108537	Coptic (Sahidic)	Joshua (and Tobit?)	12.5 cm × 18.5 cm (Kasser)
P.Bodmer XXII Mississippi Coptic Codex II (Mississippi Codex II now part of the Van Kampen Collection, VK 783)	108176	Coptic (Sahidic)	Jeremiah, Lamentations, Epistle of Jeremiah, Baruch	11.9 cm × 14.8 cm (Willis) 12 cm × 14 cm (Kasser)
P.Bodmer XXIII	108542	Coptic (Sahidic)	Isa 47:1–66:24	[13.5] cm × 21 cm (Kasser)
P.Bodmer XXIV (now at Museum of the Bible, MS.000170)	3098	Greek	Pss 17–118	[13 cm × 24 cm] (Turner)

Material	Quires	Extant Folia (Estimated Total Folia)	Binding	Proposed Dates
Papyrus	1	51 (72)	Two tackets? (only holes remain; rebound, method unclear)	2nd–3rd cent. (Kasser) 3rd–4th cent. (Orsini) 4th cent. (Nongbri)
Parchment	6	42 (42)	Link-stitch, 2 pairs of stations	4th cent. (Kasser) 5th cent. (Orsini)
Papyrus	6	48 (48)	Link-stitch, 3 stations	4th cent. (Kasser) Sec. half 4th cent. (Orsini)
Parchment	7 (in an earlier binding at least 12)	48 (48 in present binding; in an earlier binding at least 120)	Original not preserved (rebound by link-stitch, 2 pairs of stations)	4th–5th cent. (Kasser)
Papyrus	At least 3	39 (at least 62)	Link-stitch, 2 pairs of stations	Early 4th cent. (Shore) 5th cent. (Kasser)
Parchment	10	73 (at least 74)	Link-stitch, 2 pairs of stations	4th cent. (Kasser) 4th–5th cent. (Orsini)
Papyrus	6	41 (42)	Link-stitch, 2 pairs of stations (?)	4th cent. (Kasser) 4th–5th cent. (Orsini)
Papyrus	1	49 (at least 82)	Original not preserved (rebound, method unclear)	2nd cent. (Roberts) 3rd–4th cent. (Kasser) 3rd–4th cent. (Turner) AMS radiocarbon analysis is forthcoming

(*table continues*)

Table 5.1. Continued

Designation(s)	LDAB No.	Language	Contents	Page Dimensions (w × h) [Reconstructed]
P.Bodmer XLV + XLVI + XLVII + XXVII	4120	Greek	Susanna, Daniel 1, moral exhortations, Thucydides Book VI	15.5 cm × 18 cm (Carlini)
P.Bodmer XXXVIII + XXIX–XXXVII (the "Codex of Visions")	1106	Greek	Visions of Hermas, Vision of Dorotheos, hexameters	[17.5 cm × 28.5 cm] (Kasser)
P.Bodmer XL	108548	Coptic (Sahidic)	Song of Songs	15.6 cm × 19.6 cm (Kasser and Luisier)
P.Bodmer XLI	108121	Coptic (Subakhmimic)	Acts of Paul	14.1 cm × 22.7 cm (Kasser and Luisier)
P.Monts.Roca inv. 126–178 + 292 + 338 (the Barcelona-Montserrat "Miscellaneous" Codex)	552	Latin and Greek	Cicero *In Catilinam* 6–8, 13–30, acrostic hymn, drawing, euchologium, Latin hexameters on Alcestis, story about Hadrian, list of words	11.4 cm × 12.3 cm (Gil and Tovar)
Schøyen MS 193 (formerly Mississippi Coptic Codex I) Chester Beatty Ac. 2026	107771	Coptic (Sahidic)	Melito *On Passover*, 2 Macc. 5:27–7:41, 1 Peter, Jonah, liturgical exhortation	15.2 cm × 14.6 cm (Willis)

Material	Quires	Extant Folia (Estimated Total Folia)	Binding	Proposed Dates
Papyrus	At least 2	10 (at least 12)	Not preserved	3rd cent. (Cavallo) 3rd–4th cent. (Kasser) 4th cent. (Turner)
Papyrus	1	22 (24)	Original not preserved (rebound with two separate upper and lower thread tackets)	4th or 5th cent. (Cavallo and Kasser) Early 5th cent. (Orsini)
Parchment	Not known	8 (at least 79; extant pages are numbered up to 157)	Not preserved	5th cent. (Kasser) 6th cent. (Orsini)
Papyrus	Not known	7 (at least 18)	Not preserved	Late 4th cent. (Kasser)
Papyrus	1	52 (at least 56)	Two separate thread tackets	Sec. half 4th cent. (Gil and Tovar)
Papyrus	1	68 plus 2 stubs (68 plus 2 stubs)	Single-thread tacket	2nd cent. (Willis) 2nd–3rd cent. (Roberts) 3rd–4th cent. (Turner) 4th cent. (Orsini) 4th cent. (Kasser) 5th–6th cent. (Orlandi) AMS radiocarbon analysis is forthcoming

The Bodmer Papyri

Table 5.2. Additional codices accepted by Robinson as being part of the Bodmer Papyri

Designation(s)	LDAB No.	Language	Contents	Page Dimensions (w × h) [Reconstructed]
Chester Beatty Ac. 1390	2763	Greek and Coptic (Subakhmimic)	Mathematical exercises, John 10:7–13:38	14.2 cm × 25.5 cm (Robinson)
Chester Beatty Ac. 1499	3030	Greek and Latin	Blank pages, Greek grammar, Greek-Latin lexicon of Pauline epistles	13.6 cm × 16.8 cm (Wouters)
Chester Beatty Ac. 1501 (= P.Chester Beatty XIII)	3158	Greek	Pss 72–88	11.1 cm × 14.5 cm (Pietersma)
Chester Beatty Ac. 1501 (= P.Chester Beatty XIV)	3159	Greek	Pss 31, 26, 2	[Too fragmentary to estimate accurately]
Chester Beatty Ac. 1493 (= P.Chester Beatty 2018)	108402	Coptic (Sahidic)	Apocalypse of Elijah	16.7 cm × 19.9 cm (Pietersma and Comstock)
P.PalauRib. inv. 181–183	107904, 107905, 107760	Coptic (Sahidic)	Luke, John, and Mark	16.5 cm × 20 cm (Quecke)
Chester Beatty Ac. 2556 (= Cpt 54)	108078	Coptic (Sahidic)	Letters of Pachomius 11b, 10, 11a, 9a, 9b	[13.5 cm] × 16.5 cm (Quecke)

I have given the opinion of the original editor. In most instances where dates differ, I have cited the original editor, Kasser's 1991 assessment from *The Coptic Encyclopedia*, Eric G. Turner's opinions from *The Typology of the Early Codex* (1977), and/or Pasquale Orsini's reevaluations in the 2015 issue of *Adamantius*. Items with widely disputed dates are discussed below in the section "Physical Aspects of the Bodmer Books." References to specialist studies can be found

Material	Quires	Extant Folia (Estimated Total Folia)	Binding	Proposed Dates
Papyrus	Not known	8 (at least 8)	Not preserved	Sec. half 4th cent. (Shore)
Papyrus	6	48 (50)	Link-stitch, 2 pairs of stations	4th cent. (Wouters)
Papyrus	Not known	8 (at least 8)	Two separate thread tackets (1 lost)	4th cent. (Pietersma)
Papyrus	Not known	1 (not possible to determine)	Not preserved	4th cent. (Pietersma)
Papyrus	Not known	10 (at least 10)	Not preserved	4th–5th cent. (Shore)
Parchment	29	230 (230)	link-stitch, 2 pairs of stations	5th cent. (Quecke) Late 5th cent. (Orsini)
Papyrus	Not known	4 (at least 4)	Not preserved	6th cent. (Quecke)

in the notes or in the bibliography on the LDAB. All dates are CE, unless otherwise noted. Robinson was clear that his lists were works in progress and not meant to be the final word. And I wholeheartedly agree with his judgment that "by the very nature of the case absolute certainty is hardly attainable and degrees of probability are all that can be reasonably achieved."[46] Nevertheless, I am convinced that some items he tentatively includes as a part of the find may be

Table 5.3. Additional codices sometimes (but not always) included by
Robinson and others as part of the Bodmer Papyri

Designation(s)	LDAB No.	Language	Contents	Page Dimensions (w × h) [Reconstructed]
P.Chester Beatty XV	3530	Greek	*Apology of Phileas* and Pss 1–4	[Too fragmentary to estimate accurately]
P.Chester Beatty XVI	5622	Greek	Jannes and Jambres	16.2 cm × [22.5 cm] (Pietersma)
Chester Beatty school exercises (no number)	5508	Greek	School exercises	14.5 cm × [21 cm] (Clarysse and Wouters)
Chester Beatty Ac. 2554 (P.Panop. 19 = reuse of P.Panop. Beatty 1–2)	16164 (TM no.)	Greek	Tax receipts from Panopolis and blank pages	[17.5–20 cm] × 25.1 cm [width of individual pages varies]
P.Bodmer XLII (in publication)	None	Coptic (Sahidic)	2 Corinthians	[15.5 cm × 16.5 cm] (Sharp)
P.Bodmer XLIII	113751	Coptic (Sahidic)	Zostrianos	12.1 cm × 25 cm (Kasser and Luisier)
P.Bodmer XLIV (unpublished)	None	Coptic (Bohairic)	Daniel	[Not known]

decisively excluded. Other items cannot be categorically excluded but seem very doubtful. Also, there is material in the list that may represent a "phase" in the life of the collection distinct from that of the bulk of the codices. That is to say, some of this material seems to consist of older works at some point reused in the construction of the covers of the codices. I discuss this material first.

As Table 5.6 indicates, some of the pieces described as "rolls" are in fact just small fragments of rolls that resemble the scrappy remains found in the trash heaps of Oxyrhynchus. One of the first of these highly fragmentary classical texts to appear in print was a small

Material	Quires	Extant Folia (Estimated Total Folia)	Binding	Proposed Dates
Papyrus	Not known	14 (at least 14)	Not preserved	4th cent. (Pietersma)
Papyrus	Not known	11 (at least 12)	Stabbing	Early 4th cent. (Turner) Late 4th cent. (Pietersma)
Papyrus	Not known	3 (at least 6)	Not preserved	Late 3rd or early 4th cent. (Clarysse and Wouters)
Papyrus	1	Not known, leaves dismembered	Not bound	4th cent. (339–346 CE, dated by contents)
Parchment	Not known	1 (difficult to esti- mate, possibly originally associated with P.Bodmer XIX)	Not preserved	4th or 5th cent. (Sharp)
Papyrus	Not known	1 (difficult to estimate)	Not preserved	4th or 5th cent. (Kasser and Luisier)
Parchment	Not known	Not known	Not known	10th–12th cent. (Funk)

part of an unknown play published as P.Bodmer XXVIII (LDAB 7072). Its date of purchase is not known, so it may not be associated with the main find at all. But there is a second possibility. The editor noted that these fragments may have been removed from the cover of one of the codices, pointing out that a portion of one side of one of the fragments was "covered by a whitish powder which could be remaining traces of paste."[47] This theory has become somewhat more plausible with the discovery that the covers of P.Bodmer XXIII contained a literary papyrus of a classical author (the leaf of Isocrates mentioned above, published as P.Bodmer LII; LDAB 61364).[48]

Table 5.4. Codices regarded by Robinson as "possibly" being
a part of the Bodmer Papyri find

Designation(s)	LDAB No.	Language	Contents	Page Dimensions (w × h) [Reconstructed]
Papyrus Vatican Copt. 9	107766	Coptic (Bohairic)	Minor prophets	15 cm × [22 cm] (Bosson)
P.Mil.Vogl. V	107795	Coptic(Oxy-rhynchite)	Pauline letters (Romans, 1–2 Corinthians, Hebrews, Gala-tians Philippians, Ephesians, 1–2 Thessalonians, Colossians)	16.5 cm × 27.5 cm (Orlandi)
Glazier Codex	107756, 209	Coptic(Oxy-rhynchite)	Acts 1:1–15:3	10.6 cm × 11.9 cm (Depuydt)
Scheide Codex	107734	Coptic(Oxy-rhynchite) and Greek	Matthew	10.5 cm × 12.0 cm (Sharpe)

Table 5.5. Codices with "P.Bodmer" designations but regarded by no one
as part of the Bodmer Papyri find

Designation(s)	LDAB No.	Language	Contents	Page Dimensions (w × h) [Reconstructed]
P.Bodmer XVII	2894	Greek	Acts and Catholic Epistles	[20 cm × 32 cm] (Kasser)
P.Bodmer L	2968	Greek	Matthew	[Too fragmentary to estimate accurately]
P.Bodmer LVII P.Köln inv. theol. 1+53–60 Cairo Tura Codex V British Library Pap. 2921 P.BYU Did.	776	Greek	*Commentary on the Psalms* by Didymus the Blind	24.4 cm × 27 cm
P.Bodmer LVIII (formerly Phillipps 18833)	107785	Coptic (Sahidic)	Dialogue of Cyril of Alexandria, Letters of Theophilus of Alexandria, Works of Agathonicus	14.7 cm × 19.1 cm

Material	Quires	Extant Folia (Estimated Total Folia)	Binding	Proposed Dates
Papyrus	7	72 (72)	Not preserved	4th cent. (Kasser)
Papyrus	1	49 (about 150)	Not preserved	4th or 5th cent. (Cavallo)
Parchment	15	112 (112)	Link-stitch, 3 stations	5th–6th cent. (AMS radiocarbon, reported in Sharpe)
Parchment	30	238 (238)	Link-stitch, 3 stations	5th cent. (Schenke)

Material	Quires	Extant Folia (Estimated Total Folia)	Binding	Proposed Dates
Papyrus	17	124 (132)	Not fully preserved	6th–7th cent. (Kasser)
Papyrus	[Not known]	1 (difficult to estimate)	Not preserved	6th–7th cent. (Kasser)
Papyrus	At least 22	161 (at least 171)	Not preserved (although some inscribed parchment stays survive)	6th cent. (Kehl)
Papyrus	[Modern binding]	73 (at least 75)	Modern	6th–7th cent. (Crum)

Table 5.6. Non-codex materials suggested by Robinson and others as
part of the Bodmer Papyri find

Designation(s)	LDAB No.	Language	Contents
P.Bodmer I recto	None	Greek	Land list (Panopolite nome)
P.Bodmer I verso	7335 and 2073	Greek	*Iliad* Books 5 and 6
P.Bodmer XXVIII	7072	Greek	Satyr play
P.Bodmer XLVIII	9939	Greek	*Iliad* 1.45–58
P.Bodmer XLIX	2389	Greek	*Odyssey* Books 9 and 10
P.Köln 9.362	1949	Greek	Scholia to *Odyssey* 1
P.Köln 12.468	2074	Greek	*Odyssey* Books 3–4
P.Köln inv. 901	8	Greek	Achilles Tatius
P.Duk. inv. 772			
P.Köln 9.359	4651	Greek	Cynic diatribes? Ethnographic treatise?
P.Köln 13.499	3842	Greek	Plutarch, *Life of Caesar*
P.Gen. inv. 272, 504, and 477			
P.Duk. inv. 773			
P.Gen. inv. 271	3866	Greek	Cynic diatribes
P.Duk. inv. 777			
P.Köln inv. 907			

The leaf of Isocrates thus was part of the find, but as it was waste
papyrus used for stuffing in the cover of one of the codices, it is not
really a part of the collection in the same way as the main group of
codices.[49] Thus, P.Bodmer XXVIII may also have come from a cover
of one of the codices, or it may have origins completely distinct from

Size and Preservation	Material	Format	Proposed Dates
[Substantially preserved, at least 31 cm high]	Papyrus	Standard roll; *Iliad* written against the fibers, reuse	Recto: after 216 CE Verso: early 3rd cent. (Turner)
[Fragmentary, at least 20 cm high] 6 fragments of 3 columns	Papyrus	Standard roll	2nd cent. (Turner)
[Fragmentary] 1 fragment, 6.5 cm wide × 8.2 cm high	Papyrus	Standard roll	3rd cent. (Hurst)
[Fragmentary, about 34–36 cm high] 2 fragments of 3 columns	Papyrus	Standard roll, extracted from mummy cartonnage	3rd or 2nd cent. BCE (Hurst)
[Fragmentary, at least 18.8 cm high] fragments of 1 column	Papyrus	Standard roll, written against the fibers, reuse	3rd cent. (Henrichs) 4th cent. (Lundon)
[Fragmentary, at least 20 cm high] several fragments of 13 columns	Papyrus	Standard roll	3rd or 4th cent. (Lundon)
[Fragmentary, 29.1 cm high] several fragments of 5 columns	Papyrus	Standard roll	Early 3rd cent. (Willis) Late 3rd cent. (Henrichs)
[Fragmentary, at least 23.5 cm high] several fragments of 6 columns	Papyrus	Standard roll	Late 2nd or 3rd cent. (Willis and Maresch)
[Fragmentary, at least 26.5 cm high] several fragments of several columns	Papyrus	Standard roll	Early 3rd cent. (Lundon)
[Fragmentary, 34 cm high] several fragments of at least 19 columns	Papyrus	Standard roll	2nd cent. (Willis and Maresch)

the bulk of the codices. Either way, there is good reason to doubt that it formed part of the collection with the Bodmer codices.

Now I turn to the items from Robinson's larger list that almost certainly had nothing to do with the main find (much of Tables 5.2–5.4). As I mentioned at the outset, most of Robinson's work on the

Table 5.7. Non-codex "Pachomian material" regarded by Robinson as coming from the Bodmer Papyri find

Designation(s)	LDAB No.	Language	Contents
P.Bodmer XXXIX	322184	Coptic (Sahidic)	Pachomius, Letter 11b
P.Köln 4.174 Chester Beatty W. 145	3513	Greek	Pachomius, Letters 1–3, 7, 10, 11a
P.KölnKopt. 1 (= P.KölnÄgypt. 9)	101251	Coptic (Sahidic)	Pachomius, Letters 10–11a
P.KölnKopt. 2 (= P.KölnÄgypt. 8)	107777	Coptic (Sahidic)	Pachomius, Letter 8
Chester Beatty Ac. 1486	108130	Coptic (Sahidic)	Theodorus abbot, Letter 2
Private collection LDAB 107787	107787	Coptic (Sahidic)	Theodorus abbot, Letter 2
Chester Beatty Ac. 1494 Several unnumbered fragments in the Fondation Martin Bodmer	108131	Coptic (Sahidic)	Horsiesios, Letter 3
Chester Beatty Ac. 1495 Several unnumbered fragments in the Fondation Martin Bodmer	108132	Coptic (Sahidic)	Horsiesios, Letter 4
P.Yale inv. 1779	108426	Coptic (Sahidic)	Pss 76–77

Bodmer find was carried out during the 1970s and early 1980s, when little information was available about some of these manuscripts. This is still true for some items, but since that time, several pieces about which we knew very little have been edited and published.[50] This new information suggests that some of these items have a distinctive origin. For instance, when P.Bodmer XLIX (LDAB 2389) was published in 1986, we learned that these two small pieces of a papyrus roll of Homer's *Odyssey* were extracted from mummy cartonnage and appear to be Ptolemaic in date (third or second century BCE). Dating from centuries earlier than the codices, these pieces

Size and Preservation	Material	Format	Proposed Dates
[Well preserved] 15.4 cm wide × 11.9 cm high	Parchment	Sheet	5th–6th cent. (Bosson)
[Reassembled from fragments] 15.2 cm wide × 74 cm high	Parchment	Roll (rotulus)	4th cent. (Skeat)
[Well preserved] 10 cm wide × 50 cm high	Parchment	Roll (rotulus), opisthograph	5th cent. (Quecke)
[Well preserved] 11 cm wide × 31 cm high	Parchment	Roll (rotulus)	5th cent. (Quecke)
[Irregularly shaped surface] 9–15.5 cm wide × 57 cm high	Parchment	Roll (rotulus)	6th cent. (Quecke)
[Irregularly shaped surface] 9.4–16.6 cm wide × 52 cm high	Parchment	Roll (rotulus)	5th cent. (Krause)
[Fragmentary, about 84 cm wide × about 29 cm high]	Papyrus	Standard roll	7th cent. (Orlandi)
[Fragmentary, no data on dimensions]	Papyrus	Standard roll	7th cent. (Orlandi)
[Damaged but complete] 26 cm wide × 67 cm high	Papyrus	Roll (rotulus), opisthograph	4th or early 5th cent. (Vergote and Parássoglou)

were almost certainly not found with the Bodmer Papyri.[51] P.Bodmer XLVIII (LDAB 9939), a small fragment (6.5 cm wide by 8.2 cm high) of a papyrus roll of the *Iliad* preserving lines 45–58 of Book 1, was published in 1990. The editor of this piece believed it was purchased *before* the bulk of the papyrus and parchment codices in the collection.[52] This belief is supported by consulting the list of items already in Bodmer's collection in 1947, well before the alleged date of the main find of the Bodmer Papyri. Reference is made there already to a papyrus fragment in the collection containing *Iliad* 1.45–48, which can hardly be a coincidence.[53] In 2007, P.Bodmer XLIII

(LDAB 113751) was published. This item is a papyrus leaf from a Coptic codex containing Zostrianos, a text known from one of the Nag Hammadi codices.[54] At first glance, it offers a tantalizing connection between the Bodmer Papyri and the Nag Hammadi codices, but a closer look at the details of its publication raises doubts. First, the leaf is in fact just that, a single leaf, not a full codex. Second, it is said to have arrived in Geneva folded up into a small rectangle, which suggested to the editors that it had been used as an amulet. Third, and most importantly, it is said to have been acquired by Bodmer not with the purchases of the 1950s but "perhaps just before 1970."[55] More precise information about its purchase would be useful, but even with the information presently available, P.Bodmer XLIII should probably not be regarded as part of the Bodmer Papyri proper.

For other items, the case for exclusion is less compelling but still fairly strong. In some instances, the state of preservation raises questions. As I mentioned earlier, the Bodmer codices are generally preserved quite well, but the level of preservation of three of the items in Robinson's list is simply excellent. The Glazier codex (LDAB 107756), a parchment codex of Acts in Coptic; the Scheide codex (LDAB 107734), a parchment codex of Matthew in Coptic; and the Palau Ribes Coptic gospels (LDAB 107904, 107905, and 107760; see Figure 1.13) have been preserved remarkably well, with all their pages and even their outer covers intact and with very little overall decay. In terms of quality of production, really only P.Bodmer XIX can compare, and its state of preservation is substantially worse than that of the Glazier, Scheide, and Palau Ribes codices.[56] It is difficult to believe that the latter books could have been stored for more than a thousand years in the same conditions as the rest of the Bodmer Papyri and emerged in such an unscathed state. At the same time, it is possible that these books were simply the very best preserved items in the find and hence outside of Bodmer's price range. It is impossible to say until a more detailed search of the records of Martin Bodmer is carried out.[57]

At the other end of the spectrum, some of the poorly preserved remains in the Beatty Library that Robinson assigns to the find are also open to question. These include P.ChesterBeatty XIII (LDAB 3158) and P.ChesterBeatty XIV (LDAB 3159), papyrus fragments from two codices of the Psalms in Greek, as well as Chester Beatty

Ac. 2556 (LDAB 108078), fragmentary leaves of a Coptic codex of the letters of Pachomius. Robinson would also assign to the Bodmer find several scrappy papyrus remains copied in borderline cursive hands that have little similarity with the scripts of the generally accepted Bodmer books: P.ChesterBeatty XV (LDAB 3530), a papyrus codex containing the *Apology of Phileas* and the beginning of the Psalms in Greek; P.ChesterBeatty XVI (LDAB 5622), fragments from a papyrus codex containing a work on the magicians Jannes and Jambres; and Chester Beatty Ac. 1493 (LDAB 108402), a papyrus copy of the Apocalypse of Elijah in Coptic. Nor do these items have any direct connection to known Bodmer codices in terms of their acquisition. The same is true of another book in the Beatty Library sometimes connected to the Bodmer find (though not by Robinson): a fragmentary codex of school exercises (LDAB 5508).[58] Because so little is known about the histories of the acquisitions of these books, a possible connection to the Bodmer find cannot be completely ruled out, but as far as I know, there is little positive evidence (aside from just their presence in the Beatty collection) to connect them to the find, either.

Robinson seems to have connected other books to the find only because they were for sale on the antiquities market at roughly the same period as the Bodmer books (Table 5.4). This is the case for leaves of a Coptic codex of Paul's letters (LDAB 107795) and a Coptic papyrus codex of the Minor Prophets now at the Vatican (LDAB 107766). In neither instance is there any additional connection to the Bodmer collection. In fact, some of the other books Robinson placed in this "tentative" category have now been identified as the so-called Qarara codices, which include the famous Tchacos codex containing the Gospel of Judas. These books are now widely regarded as having been discovered in the 1970s and having come from the area of Beni Masar near Oxyrhynchus (see Chapter 3).[59] This information is itself not above suspicion, but it demonstrates some of the perils of Robinson's all-inclusive approach of suggesting that almost anything available on the antiquities market in Coptic during the 1970s and 1980s could belong to the Bodmer find.

I mentioned above that two of the fragments of papyrus rolls (P.Bodmer XLIX and P.Bodmer XLVIII) were demonstrably *not* part of the main Bodmer find. The remainder of the classical material in roll format is also doubtful (Table 5.6). As early as 1967, Kasser had segregated P.Bodmer I, the *Iliad* roll, from the Greek and Coptic codices, and he later explicitly excluded it from the find that included those codices.[60] Although Kasser himself never provided detailed argumentation for this point, two pieces of evidence suggest that he may well be correct. First, although other material in roll format has sometimes been identified as part of the find, these other rolls are extremely fragmentary. That is to say, there is nothing else like P.Bodmer I—a reasonably well-preserved Greek papyrus roll—attributed to the collection.[61] Second, as noted above in Bongard's account, P.Bodmer I was not bought through Tano, and it was said to have been in Bongard's possession already in July 1951. If Robinson is correct that the find of the Bodmer Papyri proper occurred "late in 1952," then it is most unlikely that the Homer roll is part of that discovery. Yet, because Robinson's proposed date of the find is not verifiable, neither of these points is absolutely decisive (recall that Kasser reported that Tano told him the books came to light in 1950 or 1951). Nevertheless, these problems cause me to doubt that P.Bodmer I belongs to the larger group.

I also doubt that the other material on rolls formed part of the find. P.Köln 12.468 (LDAB 2074) consists of several fragments from a papyrus roll of the *Odyssey* assigned to the third or fourth century. They are now found in the collections in Cologne and at Duke University.[62] It seems likely that these pieces traversed the same network of dealers, and, because Cologne and Duke both held material that was undoubtedly part of the Bodmer find, it is possible that these pieces ultimately derive from the same provenance, but this is not a necessary conclusion. The editors of P.Köln 12.468 connected it to the Bodmer find on the basis of its physical similarities to P.Bodmer I, but as I have noted, P.Bodmer I is not likely to have been part of the main find. Thus the case for the inclusion of P.Köln 12.468 is not strong. So also, P.Yale inv. 1779 (LDAB 108426) was included in Robinson's list on the basis of only its physical similarity to some of the Pachomian material he associated with the find (on which, see below). Nothing in the acquisition history of the Yale piece suggests a connection with the main Bodmer find.

Several other fragmentary rolls divided between the Cologne and Duke collections have also been proposed as possible Bodmer

Papyri. While they do not appear in Robinson's lists, fragments of a papyrus roll containing Plutarch's *Life of Caesar* (LDAB 3842) and fragments of a roll containing a text about Alexander the Great and cynic diatribes (LDAB 3866) do show up in the recent catalog of potential Bodmer Papyri proposed by Jean-Luc Fournet.[63] I think these pieces are unlikely to have come from the same find as the Bodmer codices. No portions of these works seem to have been present in Bodmer's collection. Furthermore, pieces of the same two rolls had been acquired in Cairo for the Bibliothèque publique et universitaire in Geneva already by 1950 or at the latest early 1951, that is to say, more than a year before the alleged date of the Bodmer find, according to Robinson.[64] Robinson did regularly include in his lists another fragmentary papyrus roll that contains what seems to be cynic diatribes or an ethnographic treatise (published as P.Köln 9.359, LDAB 4651), but nothing links this roll to the Bodmer find other than the fact that it happens to be divided between Duke and Cologne. Fragments of a papyrus roll containing scholia on the *Iliad* (P.Köln 9.362, LDAB 1949) are also included in Robinson's list of potential Bodmer Papyri. The editor of these fragments, however, has pointed out rare paleographic features in this papyrus that are also found in the writings of the archive of Aurelius Ammon, a *scholasticus*, that is to say, a highly educated man, from Panopolis. Several items that certainly belong to the archive of Ammon, which contains pieces dating between 281 and 366 CE, are also found in both the Cologne and Duke collections. It may well be that these Homeric fragments belong to this archive and not to the Bodmer Papyri.[65] Jean-Luc Fournet has suggested that the same may be true of the papyrus fragments of Achilles Tatius (LDAB 8), which are also split between Cologne and Duke. In his view, the writing of Achilles Tatius more closely resembles that found in material from the archive of Ammon.[66]

The potential of *multiple, different manuscript finds* being divided across this same group of libraries that hold Bodmer material raises an important issue that Robinson never seriously addressed. One of the pieces from Beatty's collection that Robinson tentatively assigns to the Bodmer find is a codex, of sorts, now known as P.Panop. 19. Acquired by Beatty in 1956, this "book" was constructed by pasting together the written sides of two rolls to produce a double-thick length of papyrus that was blank on both sides. This thickened papyrus roll was then cut into sheets that stacked upon one another and then folded over to form a single-quire codex.[67] The two papyrus rolls used to construct the codex were copies of official correspondence, but the codex itself contains receipts from the years 339–345 CE. More importantly, the codex is definitely part of a known archive, the so-called archive of the descendants of Alopex.[68] Curiously, Robinson mentions this fact only in passing.[69] The archive presently consists of more than thirty items—"petitions and court material, title deeds, tax receipts, contracts of lease, sale and loan"— spanning the years 308–355 CE and is clearly to be associated with Panopolis. The other parts of the archive are held in Cologne. Robinson assigned P.Panop. 19 to the Bodmer find because it was acquired by the Chester Beatty Library at the same time as material from the Bodmer find, but in fact, its presence in that lot may instead provide concrete evidence that the material Beatty acquired from Tano in 1956 came from *multiple different* ancient collections, thus complicating Robinson's assignment of other Beatty items to the Bodmer find (see the discussion above).

This observation also brings us to perhaps the most controversial group of material that Robinson ascribes to the find—the letters of Pachomius the monk and his followers (Table 5.7).[70] We know from literary sources that Pachomius established a monastery at Faw Qibli (ancient Pbow) in the 330s CE.[71] The remains of a monumental church at the site (excavated in the late 1970s and early 1980s) are only about five kilometers from the spot where Robinson believed the Bodmer Papyri were discovered.[72] Several letters of Pachomius and his followers, mostly preserved in the form of narrow strips of parchment rolled vertically (*rotuli*), were on the antiquities market in the 1950s. Robinson's case for regarding this Pachomian material as part of the Bodmer find can be summarized as follows:

1. The Pachomian material appeared on the market at the same time as the Bodmer Papyri.
2. The Pachomian material is now owned by some of the same collections that hold known Bodmer Papyri.
3. The probable location of the find near Dishna is close to the ruins of the church at Faw Qibli.

4. Adding the Pachomian letters to the other "Bodmer" material helps to bring the total number of items somewhat closer to the numbers reported by one of Bodmer's Egyptian informants, and the *rotulus*-style Pachomian rolls may have appeared similar to the roughly "ten small rolls the size of one's finger" reported by one of his informants.

The combination of these factors seems compelling at first glance, but a closer look reveals some difficulties. Number 1 need indicate only that the Pachomian material and the Bodmer find were put up for sale at the same time, regardless of whether they were discovered in the same place. As we have seen, Number 2 may simply be a characteristic of the activity of the antiquities market for papyrus and parchment manuscripts from Egypt.[73] At different times, various institutions were actively purchasing for their collections. If the Pachomian material appeared on the market in the 1950s, then it would not be at all surprising that some of the same institutions that bought from the Bodmer find also obtained material from a separate find of Pachomian material.[74] That is to say, the presence of the Pachomian letters in some of the institutions that also hold Bodmer Papyri does not necessarily mean the Pachomian material was part of the Bodmer find. Number 4 is based on hearsay and impossible to confirm, and as we saw, at least one of Robinson's informants makes no mention of rolls being a part of the Bodmer find. Thus of Robinson's four primary reasons for associating the Pachomian and Bodmer material, only Number 3 in the list above (the probable find spot near Dishna) withstands scrutiny. The overall case for the inclusion of the Pachomian material is therefore not as open-and-shut as Robinson presented it to be. In addition, the format of almost all of the Pachomian material differs from that of the certain Bodmer books, which are all codices. Only one of the Pachomian items is a codex (Chester Beatty Ac. 2556), and it consists of just two badly preserved sheets in the Chester Beatty Library that do not resemble the generally accepted Bodmer codices. Given the evidence presently available, I tend to doubt that the Pachomian material was part of the Bodmer Papyri find, although it is not possible to be definitive about this point.[75]

So much for the material that is probably to be excluded from Robinson's lists. But what of the pieces that Robinson himself (and all others) have excluded (Table 5.5)? Two items with P.Bodmer designations have distinct provenances that can clearly be traced to a period before the main find of Bodmer Papyri. P.Bodmer LVII is part of a papyrus codex containing a commentary on the Psalms by Didymus the Blind. It was part of the Tura find of 1941 (see Chapter 3). P.Bodmer LVIII is a papyrus codex containing patristic works in Coptic that was formerly part of the collection of Thomas Phillipps (1792–1872). These items are justly excluded from the find. The case against two other items is less obvious.[76] P.Bodmer XVII is a fairly well-preserved papyrus codex of Acts and the Catholic Epistles. Within its pages was found a tiny papyrus fragment of the Gospel According to Matthew copied in a similar hand (P.Bodmer L).[77] These books have never been considered as part of the main Bodmer find. Why? To be sure, the writing of the manuscripts appears to be a developed form of the Alexandrian Majuscule, and the manuscripts are usually assigned on that basis to the sixth or seventh century, considerably later than the other codices. But for Robinson, who would allow Pachomian material of the sixth and possibly seventh centuries to be part of the find, the dates of P.Bodmer XVII and P.Bodmer L should have presented no obstacle to their inclusion in the find. In his edition of P.Bodmer XVII, Kasser stated that the codex was not connected to the other codices in the collection and "was different from them in every way."[78] Yet, P.Bodmer XVII is a papyrus codex with a leather cover with page dimensions reconstructed as twenty centimeters wide by thirty-two centimeters high, taller than the other codices, but not excessively so, and in a width-to-height ratio of roughly 2 to 3 that is found among the codices that are certainly part of the find.[79] The handwriting is also not totally foreign to that of the other codices; P.Bodmer II, the Greek copy of the Gospel According to John, is sometimes classed as a form of the Alexandrian Majuscule.[80] It is true that the leather cover of P.Bodmer XVII is constructed quite differently from the other covers preserved in the collection, but all of the extant covers show differences in formation. Does the exclusion of P.Bodmer XVII have to do with the circumstances of its acquisition? According to one report, Bodmer's "agents turned up P.Bodmer XVII, a much later (seventh-century) papyrus codex of entirely different format, style and script" at a time "well after he had bought the other codices."[81] But it is difficult to see how this timing would work. The acquisition of P.Bodmer XVII seems to have taken place within the period when Bodmer was still acquiring parts of the find, such as leaves of the Menander codex (some of which are said to have arrived in Geneva "a few years" after 1958).[82] P.Bodmer XVII was published in 1961, and some parts of it were quite fragmentary. It would have taken at least several weeks and probably longer to prepare the edition; it seems very likely it was purchased while Bodmer was still buying material from the main find. None of this, of course, proves that P.Bodmer XVII was a part of the find, but it does raise the question of why everyone, especially those who maintain with Robinson that the Pachomian material was part of the find, is so certain that this codex (and P.Bodmer L) should be excluded.

Taking all these factors into consideration, my working hypothesis for the actual extent of the find is minimalist, consisting of twenty-two codices and no rolls:

> P.Bodmer II
> P.Bodmer III
> The Bodmer Menander codex (P.Bodmer XXV, IV, XXVI)
> The Bodmer composite codex (P.Bodmer V, X, XI, VII, XIII, XII, VIII)
> P.Bodmer VI
> P.Bodmer XIV–XV
> P.Bodmer XVI
> P.Bodmer XVIII
> P.Bodmer XIX (which may have at one point included P.Bodmer XLII)
> P.Bodmer XX + IX (formerly thought to be part of the Bodmer composite codex)
> P.Bodmer XXI
> P.Bodmer XXII
> P.Bodmer XXIII

P.Bodmer XXIV

The Susanna-Daniel-Thucydides codex (P.Bodmer XLV, XLVI, XLVII, XXVII)

The "Codex of Visions" (P.Bodmer XXXVIII, XXIX–XXXVII)

P.Bodmer XL

P.Bodmer XLI

Schøyen MS 193

The Barcelona-Montserrat codex

Chester Beatty Ac. 1390

Chester Beatty Ac. 1499

This list is slightly larger than Kasser's assemblage of nineteen codices. Kasser had regarded P.Bodmer XX + IX as a part of the Bodmer composite codex, but I see no solid evidence for that conclusion, so I consider these leaves to represent a separate codex.[83] Also, it appears that no compelling argument can be mounted against the inclusion of Chester Beatty Ac. 1390, the papyrus codex containing Greek mathematical exercises and a portion of the Gospel According to John in Coptic, and Ac. 1499, a mostly blank codex with a Greek-Latin lexicon of Paul's letters and Greek conjugations. They were apparently bought by Beatty in 1956 as parts of the same lots that included known Bodmer material—Ac. 1389 (= P.Bodmer XXI) and Ac. 2555, which included fragments of P.Bodmer II and P.Bodmer XX.[84] Even though no portion of Ac. 1390 and Ac. 1499 was ever found in the Bodmer collection (which did, at one point, own pieces of the Barcelona-Montserrat codex and the Schøyen MS 193), these two Beatty codices are the kinds of books that Martin Bodmer, with his interest in assembling a collection of *Weltliteratur*, would not have been especially eager to acquire.[85] Since it appears that Bodmer received material from Tano on consignment, one could easily imagine Bodmer rejecting these books, leaving them available for Tano to sell to Beatty. Again, this is not to say that all other items are to be definitively excluded. But the items on this restricted list are almost certainly all from the same find and formed part of a single ancient collection at the time of their deposition in antiquity. This is the corpus that I examine.

Physical Aspects of the Bodmer Books

Even this pared-down list represents a substantial collection. A rich description of all these books is thus outside the scope of the present study.[86] For now, I just want to give a sense of what this collection looked like. The books for the most part survive in a good state of preservation, and there is reason to believe that some were even better preserved at the time of their discovery but suffered on the antiquities market.[87] In comparison with other collections we have seen, the Bodmer group is marked by its variety in terms of material (both papyrus and parchment are well represented), language (Greek, Coptic, and Latin), and construction (both single- and multi-quire codices). More than one recent scholar has been impressed by the differences in the collection, concluding that the assemblage must be the result of books with disparate origins being brought together in antiquity. This is surely a possibility, and these authors are right to note the differences, but when one looks more broadly across the range of collections of ancient codices, what stands out about the Bodmer find are the similarities among subgroups of the books.

In terms of format, the codices can be classified into three groups. Kasser had recognized this already in his 1991 article, and the codices I have added to his list can be placed into these divisions as well (compare this relative regularity with the variety of formats among the Beatty Biblical Papyri). A considerable group among the Bodmer find consists of basically square codices, with a width of between eleven and sixteen centimeters. Figure 5.2 shows these eleven codices as a group.[88] The group includes both papyrus and parchment books, with material written in Greek, Latin, and Coptic. Within this grouping, different codices show particular similarities in size, proportion, and layout of text. P.Bodmer II and P.Bodmer XVIII are especially close in regard to these features. A two-column layout is shared by a pair of the Coptic codices, P.Bodmer XIX and Schøyen MS 193. A number of these codices also display a similar method of binding, that is, the link-stitch at two independent pairs of sewing stations (P.Bodmer II, the composite codex, P.Bodmer VI, P.Bodmer XVI, and P.Bodmer XIX). An examination of the preserved book-blocks shows some of the similarities within this group as well as the idiosyncrasies of the individual construction techniques (Figure 5.3).

Figure 5.2. Bodmer codices with basically square dimensions. Top (left to right):
P.Bodmer II, P.Bodmer XVIII, P.Bodmer XIX, P.Bodmer XXII; middle (left
to right): P.Bodmer V (part of the composite codex), P.Bodmer XX + IX, the
Barcelona-Montserrat Greek-Latin codex, P.Bodmer XVI;

10 cm

bottom (left to right): Schøyen Collection MS 193, P.Bodmer VI, P.Bodmer XLV
(part of the Bodmer Susanna-Daniel-Thucydides codex).

Figure 5.3. Intact bookblocks of P.Bodmer II (top) and P.Bodmer XVIII.
(Images courtesy of the Fondation Martin Bodmer, Cologny-Geneva.)

The quires of the (secondary) binding of P.Bodmer II remain partially visible along the damaged spine. Although the leaves of P.Bodmer II and those of P.Bodmer XVIII are very similar on a two-dimensional level, some aspects of the construction of the codices are rather different. The quires of P.Bodmer XVIII appear to have been sewn with the link-stitch method using a single thread (that is to say, a method consistent with the rebinding of P.Bodmer II but not its original binding, which employed two separate threads in two independent pairs of sewing stations); and although most of the front and back covers of P.Bodmer XVIII were removed before its acquisition, it is clear from the remains that the covers were sewn together at the spine, resulting in a visibly concave bookblock, as opposed to the damaged but quite uniform spinal edge of P.Bodmer II.[89]

At the level of scripts, three of the codices in the squarish group share especially similar handwriting. P.Bodmer II can be compared with the Greek script of P.Bodmer XX and with the Coptic script of Schøyen MS 193 (Figure 5.4). This similarity is telling. P.Bodmer II has regularly been considered the earliest codex of this group. It is generally assigned to the early third century, and at the time of its publication, media outlets did not hesitate to claim even greater antiquity. The headline in the *New York Times* of December 30, 1956, declared that the manuscript was "Dated 150 A.D.," a date that many scholars would endorse later.[90] Yet, in terms of both its handwriting and its format, P.Bodmer II is completely at home aside these two manuscripts, at least one of which (P.Bodmer XX, the *Apology* of Phileas) was copied no earlier than 305 CE.[91] It seems quite possible that the antiquity of P.Bodmer II has been exaggerated.[92]

A second easily discernable group within the larger collection has a height of about twenty-four to twenty-eight centimeters and a width that is roughly half that height. There are four codices in this group: the Menander codex, P.Bodmer XIV–XV (the Gospels According to Luke and John, sold from the Bodmer collection and donated to the Vatican Library, where it is now known as Papyrus Hanna 1 Mater Verbi), P.Bodmer XXIV (the Psalms in Greek, sold from the Bodmer collection and now part of the Museum of the Bible Collection in Washington, D.C.), and Chester Beatty Ac. 1390 (Figure 5.5). At least three of these four codices also share a construction technique: The Menander codex, P.Bodmer XIV–XV, and

Figure 5.4. Detail of the scripts of P.Bodmer II, P.Bodmer XX,
and Schøyen Collection MS 193.

(Images courtesy of the Fondation Martin Bodmer, Cologny-Geneva;
and the Schøyen Collection, Oslo and London.)

the Psalms codex are all single-quire papyrus constructions. Chester Beatty Ac. 1390 is also a papyrus book, and only one quire is presently extant, but its contents (mathematical exercises in Greek and a portion of the Gospel According to John in Coptic) leave open the possibility that additional quires once existed. This format and size are also known from the Nag Hammadi codices, several of which closely resemble these codices in terms of format (that is to say,

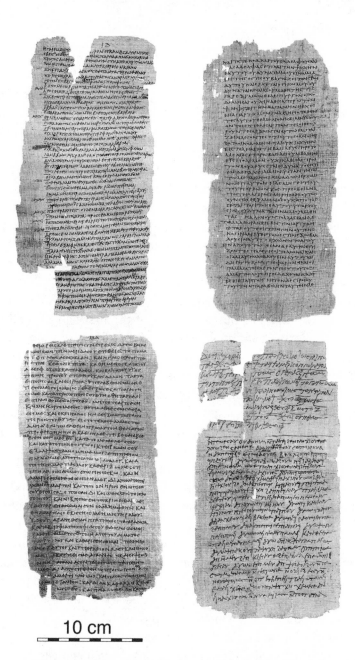

Figure 5.5. Bodmer codices with width about half the height. Top (left to right): The Bodmer Menander codex and Papyrus Hanna 1 Mater Verbi (formerly P.Bodmer XIV–XV); bottom (left to right): P.Bodmer XXIV (now Museum of the Bible MS.000170) and Chester Beatty Ac. 1390.

single-quire papyrus codices between about 26 and 30 cm high and half as wide).[93] Chester Beatty Ac. 1390 and the Menander codex are routinely assigned to the fourth century.[94] Once more, Greek codices with "biblical" material have been assigned the earliest dates. Both P.Bodmer XIV–XV (Gospels According to Luke and John) and P.Bodmer XXIV (Psalms) have been assigned dates as early as the second century solely on the basis of their handwriting.[95] But again, there is reason to distrust such early datings. In addition to the fact that codices of a very similar format and construction technique are known to have been produced in the fourth century, the handwriting of P.Bodmer XIV–XV has close parallels among samples that can be securely dated to the fourth century.[96] Figure 5.6 provides a side-by-side comparison of P.Bodmer XIV–XV with samples from two letters from an archive of the first half of the fourth century (P.Herm. 4 and 5). The stakes for trying to obtain a proper date for this particular manuscript are quite high. Textual critics of the New Testament have described this manuscript as "the most significant" New Testament papyrus so far discovered, largely because of the early date assigned to it by its original editors and the fact that its text is very much like that of the Codex Vaticanus.[97] When it was published and believed to be as old as the late second century, P.Bodmer XIV–XV was thought to overturn the commonly held opinion that the second and third centuries were a period when the text of the New Testament was relatively fluid and unstable. Yet, in terms of its format, construction, and handwriting, P.Bodmer XIV–XV is at home in the fourth century with many of the other Bodmer Papyri. As far as the date of the Psalms codex, we may be able to have a firmer knowledge in the near future, as I am informed that this book has been subjected to radiocarbon analysis by its new owners, and the results will soon be published.[98]

The third group consists of codices with a width that is roughly two-thirds the height. This group includes seven codices: P.Bodmer III, P.Bodmer XXI, P.Bodmer XXIII, the Codex of Visions, P.Bodmer XL, P.Bodmer XLI, and Chester Beatty Ac. 1499. As Figure 5.7 suggests, this group is less well-defined than the other two. The group is diverse in terms of language (Greek, Coptic, and Latin are all represented) and material (both papyrus and parchment examples are present). In regard to dates, two of these codices offer some

P.Herm. 4 and 5   (P.Bodmer XIV-XV)

Figure 5.6. Detail of the scripts of P.Herm. 4 and 5 and
Papyrus Hanna 1 Mater Verbi (formerly P.Bodmer XIV–XV).

Figure 5.7. Bodmer codices with width about two-thirds the height.
Top (left to right): Chester Beatty Ac. 1499, P.Bodmer XXI, P.Bodmer XXIII,
and P.Bodmer XL; bottom (left to right): the Bodmer Codex of Visions,
P.Bodmer XLI, and P.Bodmer III.

10 cm

(Images of P.Bodmer III, XXI, XXIII, XL, XLI, and the Codex of Visions
courtesy of the Fondation Martin Bodmer, Cologny-Geneva; image of Chester Beatty
Ac. 1499 © The Trustees of the Chester Beatty Library, Dublin, photographed by the Center
for the Study of New Testament Manuscripts.)

relatively objective evidence. The economic information in the documentary papyri removed from the cover of P.Bodmer XXIII establishes a *terminus post quem* for the construction of this codex in the first half of the fourth century. The contents of the Codex of Visions (a narrative set in a heavenly court with officials mirroring those in the contemporary imperial court) establish a *terminus post quem* for this codex in the middle decades of the fourth century (though some paleographers have preferred a fifth-century date for the copying of this codex).[99] The other codices lack objective criteria for dating, but each of them has been assigned to dates ranging between the fourth and fifth centuries, although Pasquale Orsini has recently assigned P.Bodmer XL (parchment leaves of the Song of Songs in Coptic) to the sixth century.[100]

This grouping by size is a convenient means for dividing and discussing the codices, but there are also similarities that cut across these groups. The two lists of words (one found in the Barcelona-Montserrat codex and one in Chester Beatty Ac. 1499) share a three-column layout. In his recent paleographic analysis of the Bodmer Papyri, Orsini has pointed out close connections between the handwriting of the Barcelona-Monserrat codex and that of the Menander codex.[101] It may also be noted that the Codex of Visions contains a text titled "The Vision of Dorotheos, the son of Quintus the Poet," and the Barcelona-Montserrat codex has two dedications to a person named Dorotheos, though few scholars would equate these two individuals.[102] And finally, although decorations in Greek manuscripts of this era tend to be highly stereotypical, the Codex of Visions and the Barcelona-Montserrat codex do happen to use some quite similar decorative motifs (Figure 5.8).[103] Beyond these paleographic similarities, we may have an instance of the same copyist at work in different codices. If it is correct that P.Bodmer VIII circulated as a part of a different codex before being bound together with the other works in the composite codex, then we have an example of a single writer copying parts of two codices (it is widely agreed that the copyist of P.Bodmer VIII also copied P.Bodmer X, XI, and VII in the composite codex).[104] At the same time, we also find within single books the work of multiple copyists (or at least samples of writing copied in different hands, whether by a single copyist or multiple copyists), not only in the composite codex but in at least

Figure 5.8. Decorative elements from the Barcelona-Montserrat Greek-Latin codex (left) and the Bodmer Codex of Visions (right).

(Images courtesy of the Abadia de Montserrat Collection © Abadia de Montserrat; and the Fondation Martin Bodmer, Cologny-Geneva.)

eight of the other codices as well, not to mention the work of correctors and the marginal glosses of readers.[105]

These groups of physical similarities crisscrossing the corpus suggest a relatively restricted temporal and geographic range for the production of these books.[106] The Bodmer Papyri are sometimes described as dating from the second to the sixth century, but as we have seen, it is entirely possible that the bulk of the material that actually made up the collection could be placed in narrower confines between, say, the late third century to the early fifth century. In the instances when it is possible to establish a reliable *terminus post quem* (P.Bodmer XX, P.Bodmer XXIII, and the Codex of Visions), that date falls squarely in the fourth century. In light of the foregoing analysis, my working hypothesis for the Bodmer find is that it is a collection that began to be formed in the fourth century. This may have happened as a result of multiple smaller collections being brought together or as a result of local production, or (more likely) a combination of the two. It is possible (but in my view unlikely) that some of the books may have been produced before the fourth century. The bulk of the collection appears to me to be a product of the fourth and fifth centuries, and I imagine a date of deposition in the late fifth or sixth century. None of this can be proved at present, but these hypotheses at least rest on a sensible review of all the available evidence.

The Proposed Social Settings

Who owned the codices in antiquity? For Robinson, the answer was clear. His case for a Pachomian monastic setting for the collection is by far the most developed argument for a specific ancient context of the Bodmer books. Several points converge in support of Robinson's theory: the alleged find spot near Dishna in the vicinity of the church at Faw Qibli, the presence of Pachomian letters in the same collection of repositories that contain material generally acknowledged to be from the main Bodmer find, and the statements in archival records in Barcelona and the Chester Beatty Library associating the materials with a Pachomian monastery and the area of Dishna.[107] As Robinson has also pointed out, basic literacy was emphasized in the rules of the Pachomian order, and the presence of books is taken for granted in the rules.[108] Thus, the biblical material would certainly be at home in such a setting, and some of the educational material would also make sense in such a context.

Yet, Robinson's thesis is not without difficulties. As we have seen, the case for the Pachomian letters being part of the same find as the Bodmer books is not as clear-cut as Robinson made it appear. Similarly, the information from dealers (or, more likely a single dealer, Tano) connecting the find to a Pachomian site is open to suspicion. In addition, Robinson had little to say about the classical texts in the collection. While he overestimated the amount of classical material in the collection as a whole, Robinson simultaneously minimized the importance of the very classical material that was most likely part of the collection. He pushed the Menander codex into the background by suggesting that it was never really a working part of the Christian library, but rather a "relic."[109] But the Menander codex seems to have been produced in the fourth century.[110] When, exactly, did it become a relic? And what of the other classical material? Here the history of publication comes into play. The publishing of isolated, individual texts rather than whole codices has obscured the fact that the other classical material in codex form is actually *bound together* with clearly Christian works. The Bodmer Thucydides (P.Bodmer XXVII), published in 1975, is part of the same manuscript that included portions of the "biblical" books of Susanna and Daniel published separately six years later. The works are copied in

Figure 5.9. An intact bifolium of the Bodmer Susanna-Daniel-Thucydides
codex showing Dan 1:5–1:10 and the beginning of Book VI of Thucydides,
copied in distinctly different hands.

(Image courtesy of the Fondation Martin Bodmer, Cologny-Geneva.)

different hands but in the same quire, which makes it clear we are
dealing with a unitary codex and not a later compilation (Figure 5.9).
The Barcelona-Montserrat codex (LDAB 552) contains excerpts
from Cicero's Catiline orations and a hymn to the Virgin Mary,
Latin hexameters on Alcestis, a mythological drawing, and other
texts. Thus, the classical works in the assemblage do not appear to
be "relics" at all. They are being copied simultaneously with clearly
Christian material.[111] They are an integral part of the collection.
This observation extends even further, into the actual composition
of some of the Christian material, namely the Codex of Visions
(LDAB 1106), which includes hexameters of the sort one encoun-
ters in the Greek and Roman rhetorical training regimen but on
Christian rather than classical topics.[112]

For Fournet, the presence of non-Christian literature, especially

that of the comic playwright Menander, renders a monastic provenance unlikely and a Pachomian origin extremely dubious.[113] Yet, we
do know with certainty that later Christian monks in Egypt did read
and copy Menander. Among the materials excavated at the Monastery of Epiphanius in Thebes was a chunk of limestone on which
someone had copied selected lines from Menander's works in alpha-
betical order by the first letter of the first word of each line.[114] So it
would seem that the presence of classical literature in general and
Menander in particular would not render a monastic setting impossible. Thus, if Robinson is correct about both the extent and the
setting of the collection, then perhaps we need to broaden our view
of monastic education curricula and reading habits in fourth- and
fifth-century Egypt. But, despite the confidence with which Robinson put forward his thesis, his proposition is not the only possible
setting for the Bodmer find.

The classical material perhaps would be less conspicuous in a
nonmonastic educational setting in a developed urban area. Even if
the once popular association of the Bodmer find with Panopolis can
no longer be maintained, an urban educational setting remains a
possibility. One could imagine such a school in Tentyra, for example.
In addition to the presence of grammatical and lexical tools among
the Bodmer Papyri, the kinds of mistakes found in, for instance, the
Menander codex are not inconsistent with a school setting.[115] And if
the *ethopoiia* on Christian themes in the Codex of Visions would be
at home in either a monastic or a nonmonastic setting, the *ethopoiia*
on classical mythological themes in the Latin hexameters on Alcestis in the Barcelona-Montserrat codex would be somewhat strange
in a monastic context. Indeed, what speaks most in favor of a school
setting is probably the presence of Latin material in the assemblage.
Latin texts are not at all common in the extant remains of early
Egyptian monastic life.[116] Such works would be a better fit in a nonmonastic urban school. Yet, some of the materials in the collection
would appear somewhat curious in a nonmonastic context. Coptic
biblical books in diverse dialects, which might be explained as copies
made of books brought from different regions by people coming to
join a monastery, seem to me less easy to understand in a school setting. And if Robinson's inventory is correct, the specifically Pacho-

mian materials would certainly stand out. But of course, the adherents of this nonmonastic educational setting would deny that the Pachomian letters are part of the same find.

If we move the discussion from the theoretical to the material and attempt to compare the Bodmer books with some of the other surviving collections of Christian books, the Bodmer group stands out for its heterogeneous nature. Biblical scholars have often grouped the Bodmer Papyri together with the Beatty Biblical Papyri, largely because both collections were thought to contain "early" copies of the texts of the New Testament. Yet, the Bodmer assemblage, with its combinations of various languages and writing surfaces, presents a profile that differs considerably from the Beatty Biblical Papyri, which are all written in Greek on papyrus. Perhaps even more striking are the combinations of texts found in the Bodmer Papyri. While the Beatty Biblical Papyri in some ways mirror what would become some of the standard collections of "New Testament" texts (Paul's letters, Revelation on its own, the four gospels), the Bodmer books bring together all sorts of different material. The diverse contents of the Bodmer composite codex (LDAB 2565, that is, P.Bodmer V, X, XI, VII, XIII, XII, and VIII) have been analyzed from a variety of angles.[117] In addition to the combinations of classical and Christian material mentioned above, we also find intriguing pairings of strictly Christian works in other codices: the Gospel According to John and Genesis in P.Bodmer III, and the Gospel According to Matthew and Romans in P.Bodmer XIX. We do not see anything like this in the Beatty Biblical Papyri.

What about the Nag Hammadi hoard? These twelve papyrus codices (plus one tractate) are all written in Coptic. The books are said to have been discovered in a jar near the cliffs of Jabal al-Tarif, quite close to the proposed find spot of the Bodmer Papyri near Dishna (see Figure 5.1). The Nag Hammadi codices are usually dated to the second half of the fourth century on the basis of dated papyri used to stiffen the covers of the codices.[118] The most recent research on the Nag Hammadi find makes a strong case that the books were produced by Pachomian monks, on the basis of, among other things, the inscribed papyri from the covers.[119] As already noted, some of these books bear a close resemblance in terms of format to some of the Bodmer books, such as P.Bodmer XIV–XV, the Menander codex, and the Psalms codex. Given the possibility that these two groups of books were found in very close proximity and seem to come from the same time period, it is tempting to wonder whether they might be somehow associated. Yet, the two groups of books also show important differences. Although specialists in the Nag Hammadi corpus have subtle ways of subdividing the codices in terms of their physical aspects (such as the constructions of their covers and their handwriting), in the broad sweep of early Christian codices in Egypt, the Nag Hammadi group seems remarkable for its overall uniformity.[120] Similarly, in terms of contents, the Nag Hammadi books consist almost entirely of material that is generally described as "gnostic" or "demiurgical," although it is worth remembering that Codex VI (LDAB 107746) does contain "classical" material in the form of an excerpt from Plato's *Republic* translated into Coptic. Again, experts classify the individual tractates in various ways (such as Sethian, Valentinian, and Thomasine), but there does seem to be a fairly close family resemblance among these books in terms of shared vocabulary and cosmological interests.[121] Once again, then, I would argue that the Bodmer collection, with its mix of languages, contents, writing surfaces, and sizes, seems to be a rather more diverse assemblage.

As a final piece of comparative evidence, we may broaden the temporal scope and look a bit later in time to the large hoard of material associated with Dioscorus of Aphrodito.[122] These manuscripts came into the public eye in 1907 with Gustave Lefebvre's publication of a Greek papyrus codex of Menander (LDAB 2745).[123] Lefebvre said that he discovered the Menander manuscript at the top of a broken jar in a house in Kom Ishqaw, an area about equidistant between Asyut and Akhmim (see Figure 5.1). Under the Menander codex was a wealth of private papers—the personal archive of Dioscorus of Aphrodito, which contained material in Greek, Coptic, and Latin, with dates ranging from the fifth century to about 585 CE. The Dioscorus archive is largely documentary, but it does contain literary and educational materials, such as hexameter verses, acrostic poems, Greek conjugations, rhetorical exercises, and a Greek-Coptic lexicon.[124] The bulk of the literary materials consists of Dioscorus's own compositions.[125] The contents of the material are not dissimilar to some of the Bodmer Papyri, even if the Dioscorus material is definitely distinct in terms of both script and format. When this find is placed for comparison beside the Bodmer collection, the primary question about the Dioscorus archive is, Where are the biblical books? Dioscorus surely knew his scriptures well; his own compositions contain both biblical and classical allusions.[126] In fact, it is almost certain that some of Dioscorus's books are lost to us. Although Lefebvre's published account gave the impression that the house containing the archive of Dioscorus was basically undisturbed when he arrived to excavate, recent archival research suggests that he did not discover a pristine site, but rather one that had already been pillaged by illicit diggers.[127] So it is quite likely that there was more than just the Menander codex among the papers of Dioscorus. Once again, however, the illicit antiquities trade obscures our view.

Thus, there is some overlap in terms of contents with what we find in the Bodmer collection. But is it at all appropriate to compare the Bodmer collection to a personal archive? Granted, no known personal archive from the region would suggest ownership of books like the Bodmer Papyri. Nevertheless, I think it is a question at least worth considering. We have already seen that the extent of the Bodmer find is not a settled matter. The collection as it is known to us was heavily shaped by the aesthetics of both Martin Bodmer and Chester Beatty. I alluded to this point earlier, and I wish to emphasize it again. Bodmer was building a collection of world literature, and Beatty appears to have had an interest in the technological history of the book.[128] Would either of them have even *wanted* to acquire strictly documentary material if it were offered to them as part of the find? We of course cannot know, but this is a possibility that we should entertain as we think through potential circumstances for the production and use of the Bodmer collection.

None of these corpora of texts provides an exact analogue for the Bodmer collection, and neither a monastic nor a school setting perfectly accounts for the diverse contents of the Bodmer Papyri. And other possibilities do exist. Rodolphe Kasser, who edited so many of the Coptic Bodmer texts, mused that the assemblage of books may have been brought together by at least two different types of figures—one "a rich landowner, with a taste for old favourites and the new writings of the time, indeed a kind of Martin Bodmer of the 5th or 6th century," and another, "more likely candidate," "a *scriptorium* teacher, progressively building up a respectable and varied library to suit the needs and tastes of his customers and pupils."[129] Gianfranco Agosti, while doubting that a Pachomian library would contain the amount of classical material we find in the Bodmer collection, nevertheless describes the setting from which the books emerged as "quasi-monastic . . . in the broadest possible sense."[130] Alberto Camplani has suggested the books might have been collected by a precursor to "one of the forms of collective laity that we see emerging during the fifth century."[131] Laura Miguélez-Cavero has combined elements from earlier hypotheses, suggesting that the books belonged to a "religious community" in Panopolis.[132] The list could go on.

Until some semblance of a consensus is reached on the contents of the Bodmer Papyri, its ancient context will continue to remain in question. The discovery that the waste papyrus used in the cover of P.Bodmer XXIII included a document mentioning a person likely to be from Dendera suggests that the books were probably found in that region. Given the evidence presently available, I now lean toward a monastic milieu, but it must be remembered that our knowledge of fourth-century monasticism is imperfect, and if the Bodmer Papyri were to be regarded as the contents of a monastery library, they would become an important source of knowledge for early monastic practice (the risk of circular argumentation is easy to see). In any event, the various other possibilities cannot be definitively ruled out. The goal of this chapter has been to provide an overview of what we can know with a degree of certainty and how we can know it. That is to say, I hope I have given a clearer picture of what the evidence is and exactly where the (many) points of ambiguity and disagreement lie.

But the uncertainty surrounding this corpus should not inhibit the study of these books. It is of course important to carefully study the individual texts of the Bodmer collection, as scholars have done quite well over the past sixty years. It is also important, however, to look beyond the individual texts to consider the whole books that carry these individual texts. This kind of contextualization can only enrich our understandings of the texts. And even if the exact contents of the find cannot presently be established as firmly as we might like, there is wide agreement that a core set of the codices has at least a degree of archaeological connection. Paying more attention to how the individual books fit into this larger grouping promises to yield still more insights into the social world of Christians in Egypt.

CHAPTER SIX

Excavating Christian Litter and Literature at Oxyrhynchus

A S FLINDERS PETRIE OVERSAW excavations of the Egyptian city of Koptos in the winter of 1893–1894, he was likely formulating the principles of modern archaeology that he would lay out a decade later in no uncertain terms:[1] "The unpardonable crime in archaeology is destroying evidence which can never be recovered; and every discovery does destroy evidence unless it is intelligently recorded. Our museums are ghastly charnel-houses of murdered evidence; the dry bones of objects are there, bare of all the facts of grouping, locality, and dating which would give them historical life and value."[2]

Accompanying Petrie on the Koptos expedition was Bernard P. Grenfell (1870–1926), freshly graduated from Queen's College, Oxford. After learning the craft of overseeing a dig in Egypt, Grenfell returned there in 1895, and he persuaded his friend and fellow graduate of Queen's Arthur S. Hunt (1871–1934) to join the expedition, which was sponsored by the Egypt Exploration Fund.[3] The goal of their project was unique for the time—a mission dedicated not to finding monumental architecture or statuary but specifically to searching out papyri in Egyptian towns. And there is perhaps an echo of a lesson learned from Petrie in Grenfell's reasoning for undertaking this new project: "The superior attractions of temples and tombs for the excavator have caused the sites of towns to be left, except in a few notable cases, to native diggers, whether for nitrous earth or for antiquities, with the result that many of the most valuable objects found never even reach the dealers' shops, while all the historical information concerning their date and *provenance* is lost."[4]

Over the next decade, Grenfell and Hunt would together explore several towns in search of papyri, but their names are most closely linked to the city of Oxyrhynchus, which they began to excavate in the winter of 1896–1897.[5] The modern town of Al Bahnasa marks the site of ancient Oxyrhynchus, a city located about 180 kilometers south of Cairo and just west of the Nile, separated from the great river by the Bahr Yusuf, "Joseph's Canal" (see the map in the front matter and Figure 6.1).[6] Oxyrhynchus was occupied continuously throughout the Roman era, though it seems to have been abandoned for a period between the late seventh century through the ninth century.[7] As Grenfell noted, the prospect of finding early Christian manuscripts made Oxyrhynchus an especially attractive site for this undertaking:

> I had for some time felt that one of the most promising sites in Egypt for finding Greek manuscripts was the city of Oxyrhynchus. . . . Above all, Oxyrhynchus seemed to be a site where fragments of Christian literature might be expected of an earlier date than the fourth century, to which our oldest manuscripts of the New Testament belong; for the place was renowned in the fourth and fifth centuries on account of the number of its churches and monasteries, and the rapid spread of Christianity about Oxyrhynchus, as soon as the new religion was officially recognized, implied that it had already taken a strong hold during the preceding centuries of persecution.[8]

And so, on December 20, 1896, Grenfell and Hunt arrived at Oxyrhynchus. The material they collected over the next decade has so far yielded fragments of well over a hundred Christian books dating from perhaps as early as the latter part of the second century

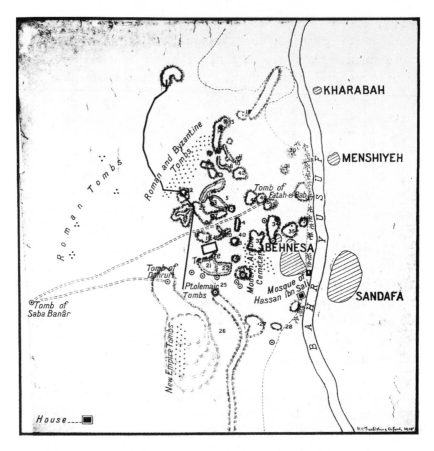

Figure 6.1. Plan produced in 1908 showing the modern town of Bahnasa
on the Yusuf canal, with the numerous ancient rubbish mounds where the papyri
were excavated marked with numbers.

(Image courtesy of the Egypt Exploration Society.)

through the sixth or seventh century. Still more pieces emerged from
the later excavations at Oxyrhynchus by others, especially Italian
teams under the leadership of Ermenegildo Pistelli and Evaristo
Breccia. And what has been so far published is only a portion of
what was found. The work of the excavators of Oxyrhynchus thus
provides us with a sizable corpus of Christian manuscripts with a
secure geographical provenance and allows us glimpses of the precise
archaeological contexts of many important early Christian manuscripts. But these glimpses are often not as precise as we might like.

In what follows, I trace what we can know of the excavations of Grenfell and Hunt and then examine the Christian literary material that they and their successors found.

From Excavation to Publication: The Work of Grenfell and Hunt

After searching the remains of the town and its cemeteries with little success, Grenfell and Hunt turned their attention to the many high mounds of rubbish that dotted the landscape (see Figure 6.1). It was here, in the midst of several centuries' worth of accumulated trash, that success came in a swift and spectacular fashion. Grenfell relates the story:

> On January 11th we sallied forth at sunrise with some seventy workmen and boys, and set them to dig trenches through a mound near a large space covered with piles of limestone chips, which probably denotes the site of an ancient temple, though its walls have been all but entirely dug out for the sake of the stone. The choice proved a very fortunate one, for papyrus scraps at once began to come to light in considerable quantities. . . . Later in the week Mr. Hunt, in sorting the papyri found on the second day, noticed on a crumpled uncial fragment written on both sides the Greek word ΚΑΡΦΟΣ ("mote"), which at once suggested to him the verse in the Gospels concerning the mote and the beam. A further examination showed that the passage in the papyrus really was the conclusion of the verse, "Thou hypocrite, cast out first the beam out of thine own eye, and then shalt thou see clearly to pull out the mote that is in thy brother's eye;" but that the rest of the papyrus differed considerably from the Gospels, and was, in fact, a leaf of a book containing a collection of sayings of Christ, some of which, apparently were new. . . . The following day Mr. Hunt identified another fragment as containing the first chapter of St. Matthew's Gospel. The evidence both of the handwriting and of the dated papyri with which they were found makes it

certain that both the "Logia" and the St. Matthew fragment
were written not later than the third century, and they are,
therefore, a century older than the earliest manuscripts of
the New Testament.[9]

The "Logia" would later be identified as the Gospel According to
Thomas (P.Oxy. 1.1, LDAB 4028). The discovery of early Christian
writings older by a century than any then known, and of completely
unknown sayings of Jesus that predated the earliest manuscripts of
the New Testament, was "the fulfilment of a late Victorian dream."[10]
Upon their return to England, Grenfell and Hunt promptly published the "Logia" in an inexpensive pamphlet that sold briskly and
helped to finance subsequent expeditions. Newspapers and maga-
zines gave the story ample coverage, to which I will return.[11]

Grenfell and Hunt spent the next five winters digging elsewhere
in Egypt before returning to Oxyrhynchus in 1903. They excavated
at Oxyrhynchus for the next four winters, amassing what is probably
the world's largest collection of papyri. Grenfell oversaw teams of
up to two hundred workers digging the trash mounds, while Hunt
tried to keep pace flattening, cleaning, and packing the finds. Some
sense of their excavation practices can be gleaned from one of Grenfell's public lectures:

> The method of digging a mound on a large scale is extremely
> simple. The workmen are divided into groups of 4 or 6, half
> men, half boys, and in the beginning are arranged in a line
> along the bottom of one side of a mound, each group having
> a space two metres broad and about 3 metres long assigned to
> it. At Oxyrhynchus the level at which damp has destroyed all
> papyrus is in the flat ground within a few inches of the sur-
> face, and in a mound this damp level tends to rise somewhat,
> though of course not nearly so quickly as the mound rises
> itself. When one trench has been dug down to the damp level,
> one proceeds to excavate another immediately above it, and
> throw the earth into the trench which has been finished, and
> so on right through the mound until one reaches the crest,
> when one begins again from the other side. The particular
> mixture of earth mixed with straw and bits of wood in which

papyrus is found, and which is to the papyrus digger what quartz is to the gold-seeker, sometimes runs in clearly marked strata between other layers of cinders, bricks or all kinds of debris containing no papyrus, but in many of the mounds at Oxyrhynchus papyri are found continuously down to a depth of five or even eight metres. As a rule the well preserved documents are discovered within 3 metres of the surface; in the lower strata the papyri tend to be more fragmentary, though our trenches in a few mounds have reached 9 metres at the highest parts before coming to the damp level.[12]

That papyri seem to be preserved only in a particular type of matrix should give us pause. Grenfell elaborates on this point elsewhere: "The papyri tend to run in layers rather than to be scattered through several feet of rubbish, and as a rule were associated with the particular kind of rubbish composed largely of pieces of straw and twigs which the natives call *afsh*," which usually "disappeared within four metres of the surface" of the ground because of moisture.[13] This observation is an important reminder that the texts recovered from Oxyrhynchus represent just a portion of what was thrown away (which itself no doubt represents just a portion of the writing that once existed at the site).

After the papyri were extracted, they were taken to Hunt's tent, where he divided them into boxes. At times, this task could become overwhelming because of the sheer amount of papyrus being recovered. As Grenfell wrote of their first season's work:

The flow of papyri soon became a torrent which it was difficult to cope with. Each lot found by a pair, man and boy, had to be kept separate; for the knowledge that papyri are found together is frequently of the greatest importance for determining their date, and since it is inevitable that so fragile a material should sometimes be broken in the process of extricating it from the closely-packed soil, it is imperative to keep together, as far as possible, fragments of the same document. We engaged two men to make tin boxes for storing the papyri, but for the next ten weeks they could hardly keep pace with us. . . . We came upon a mound which had a thick

layer consisting almost entirely of papyrus rolls . . . the difficulty was to find enough baskets in all Behneseh to contain
the papyri. At the end of the day's work no less than thirty-
six good-sized baskets were brought in . . . several of them
stuffed with fine rolls three to ten feet long, including some
of the largest Greek rolls I have ever seen. As the baskets
were required for the next day's work, Mr. Hunt and I started
at 9 p.m. after dinner to stow away the papyri in some empty
packing-cases which we fortunately had at hand. The task
was only finished at three in the morning and on the following night we had a repetition of it.[14]

Some choice manuscripts were claimed by Egyptian authorities and
left in Cairo, but the vast majority were shipped back to Oxford. A
recent study by Alexander Jones provides some insight into the fate
of the papyri after their arrival in Oxford:

Later, but still in Grenfell and Hunt's time in the early decades of [the twentieth] century, fragments that appeared
to be substantial and well enough preserved to merit further
work were extracted from the original boxes, flattened, and
filed in packets in a new series of boxes, each packet apparently corresponding to one of the former boxes, and each
new box therefore containing the "best" pieces from several.
This partition of the fragments into two series of boxes, a
main series containing larger pieces (but also numerous small
bits, perhaps found intermingled with the others) and a series
of "scrap" boxes, survives still.[15]

The statement "each packet apparently corresponding" to one of
the former boxes is later clarified by the observation that "most records of the correspondences between the new and old boxes are
lost." Thus, determining the season and precise place that a given
fragment was found is sometimes challenging, unless Grenfell and
Hunt made specific remarks stating unambiguous contexts for finds.[16]
    And despite their stated concern for context and provenance,
publications by Grenfell and Hunt are almost always frustratingly
vague about the details of where exactly specific pieces were found

and what else was found in their general vicinity. Worse still, interspersed with the pieces published in *The Oxyrhynchus Papyri* series are pieces Grenfell purchased from dealers, and not all of them are clearly identified as such.[17] Their lackluster record keeping is sometimes attributed to their race against *sebakhîn*, or looters.[18] Yet, this seems not to have been a concern for most of their time at Oxyrhynchus. Upon returning to Oxyrhynchus six years after the initial campaign of 1896–1897, Grenfell wrote in a letter back to the Egypt Exploration Fund: "As a matter of fact, there is not a great deal to fear from casual plundering. . . . During our six years' absence very little plundering has taken place."[19] It is not until their fourth season (1904–1905) that they express concern about plundering ("the dealers are at length turning their attention to Behnesa"), and it is not until the report of the sixth (1906–1907) and final season that Grenfell and Hunt mention the presence of *sebakhîn* at Bahnasa.[20] The more likely reason for their hectic working pace and less-than-ideal record keeping was a shortage of money. Their annual reports to the Egypt Exploration Fund regularly conclude with requests for continued financial support, and Grenfell's letters from that time express similar concerns.[21] In Egypt, their goal was to extract as much papyrus as possible for the fund in as short a space of time as possible, while still making an effort to retain some contextual knowledge of the finds. Back in England, the objective was to publish the material as quickly as possible so that subscribers to the fund would be regularly provided with a volume from the *Graeco-Roman Memoirs* series, which presented the finds of Grenfell and Hunt from Oxyrhynchus and elsewhere. Under these circumstances, it is unsurprising that so little contextual archaeological information was published.

But Grenfell and Hunt did keep at least some records containing more information than what they published. Beginning with Volume 40 of *The Oxyrhynchus Papyri*, inventory numbers were published along with the fragments.[22] These numbers can (sometimes) tell us the season in which particular pieces were excavated. There is also a different series of combinations of numbers and letters written on many of the papyri themselves that have only recently been decoded.[23] Furthermore, mention is occasionally made of a notebook containing a variety of information about the excavations, and the notebook is said to include some of Grenfell's general obser-

vations about the site. Elsewhere, the notebook is described as recording the work of the 1902–1903 season and helping clarify the
inventory numbers Grenfell and Hunt assigned to the papyri. Still
other sources mention a notebook in Hunt's handwriting with a key
to the numbering system on the plan of Oxyrhynchus produced by
Grenfell and Hunt.[24] For now, this notebook remains unpublished,
and the details of the contents are known to only a handful of Oxford savants. We await the publication of this important material,
which may well add some clarity to the history of excavations at
Oxyrhynchus.

In any event, on some occasions, even Grenfell and Hunt's casual
remarks in their publications do provide just enough information to
reconstruct the context of some of the finds. For example, through
a cunning bit of detective work, AnneMarie Luijendijk was able to
establish that P.Oxy. 2.209 (LDAB 3025), a school copy of the first
verses of Romans written in a labored Greek hand, belonged to the
archive of a man named Aurelius Leonides, who was a flax trader in
Oxyrhynchus during the early fourth century.[25] This is a rare instance in which we can identify and actually know a little bit about
an owner of an early Christian text, even if it is just a single small
excerpt from an epistle.

Would that we had that kind of information for all the other
fragmentary texts found at Oxyrhynchus! The material unearthed
by Grenfell and Hunt spans the whole spectrum of Greek writing
from an Egyptian town in the Roman era. On the literary side, they
found what are often our oldest copies of known classical authors and
works as well as copies of authors and works that had been lost since
the medieval age. Among nonliterary pieces, they deciphered all
manner of documents of everyday life—personal letters, business letters, official correspondence, receipts, tax records, bills of sale, wills,
marriage contracts, and much more. As they edited and published
these texts over twenty years, Grenfell and Hunt became masters of
nearly every branch of classical studies, from the niceties of Greek
lyric poetry to the nitty-gritty of the taxation system of Byzantine
Egypt. Their editions of papyri appeared with commendable regularity, especially considering that between 1896 and 1907, they spent
most of their winters excavating.

The high level of their scholarship is all the more impressive since they also dedicated time to publicity and fundraising.[26] The early Christian papyri of Oxyrhynchus played a special role in this respect, forming an important part of the public face of the Graeco-Roman Branch of the Egypt Exploration Fund. I already mentioned the affordable editions of the "Logia" produced only six weeks after the papyrus itself reached England, in which Grenfell and Hunt portray themselves as something quite distinct from ivory tower scholars: "Oxyrhynchus offered a peculiarly attractive field for explorers who, like ourselves, make the recovery of Greek papyri, with all the manifold treasures they may bring, their principal aim."[27] According to the annual report of the Egypt Exploration Fund for 1897–1898, the "Logia" pamphlet was "a very profitable venture," which "formed a good basis on which to build up our new Branch."[28] Meanwhile, Grenfell and Hunt were involved in an accompanying publicity push in the summer of 1897, sitting for studio portraits and retelling the story of their first excavation season with the addition of various "human interest" elements (Figure 6.2). Grenfell wrote an article for the American illustrated monthly *McClure's Magazine*, which largely reproduces the text of the introduction to the "Logia" pamphlet but also includes extra details, such as a portrayal of the children they employed:

> As the papyrus digging was relatively light work, I had more boys than men diggers, the former being not only easier to manage and more trustworthy, but quite as keen about the work as the men, which is rather remarkable, seeing that all their earnings go to their parents. But I should think nearly every boy in the district who could walk wanted to be taken on to the work. Some of the tiny applicants looked as though they had only recently left their cradles, if they had ever known such luxuries, which, of course, they had not. One of the smartest workers of all was also the smallest, a little chap about eight years old, who had a wonderful eye for the right kind of soil for finding papyri. I am afraid some tender-hearted persons would have thought me a very brutal task master, if they could have seen some of these children lifting and carrying away heavy baskets of rubbish all day, clothed, perhaps, if the weather was hot, in nothing but a cap on

their heads and a piece of string round their waists. But I think the same persons would have retracted their opinion, if they could, at the end of the day's work, have seen the said infants racing each other home over the sand dunes, while I plowed my way painfully in the rear.[29]

In another illustrated newspaper, a particular child was singled out as "the boy who found the logia" (Figure 6.3). Their later excavation

HOW WE FOUND THE "LOGIA."

IN spite of the number of excavations which have been conducted in Egypt during the last twenty years, comparatively little has yet been done for the scientific exploration of the many ancient town ruins with which the country is studded, especially along the edge of the desert. The superior attractions of temples and tombs for the excavator have caused the sites of towns to be left, except in a few notable cases, to native diggers, whether for nitrous earth or for antiquities, with the result that many of the most valuable objects found never even reach the dealers' shops, while all the historical information concerning their date and *provenance* is lost.

A. S. HUNT, M.A.
Sometime Craven Fellow in the University of Oxford.

BERNARD P. GRENFELL, M.A.
Sometime Craven Fellow in the University of Oxford.

Figure 6.2. Portraits of Arthur S. Hunt and Bernard P. Grenfell accompanying Grenfell's article in *McClure's Magazine*, July 1897.

Figure 6.3. Drawing of one of the child laborers from Oxyrhynchus
accompanying a story on Grenfell and Hunt in the *Daily Graphic*, July 21, 1897.
(Image courtesy of the British Library, London, UK/Bridgeman Images.)

seasons were covered in the media as well, although not in such detail.[30] Subsequent finds of previously unknown gospels brought more
short, affordable pamphlets published in 1904 and 1908 that circulated widely.[31] Grenfell and Hunt also regularly lectured to public
audiences even after their excavations had concluded.[32]

The most reliable reports suggest that Grenfell and Hunt recovered a total of about half a million papyrus and parchment items,
ranging from small fragments to substantial portions of long rolls.[33]
It is difficult to know how this figure translates into numbers of actual independent texts. In many cases, a single fragment represents
all that remains of a manuscript. Yet, Hunt at one point mentioned
spending several weeks flattening and sorting "some thirty thousand
pieces of various sizes" that constituted the second large find of literary papyri from the 1905–1906 season, which was eventually con-
solidated into about thirty-five different papyrus rolls.[34] In any event,

for a full accounting of the Oxyrhynchus materials, we must also consider the manuscripts unearthed during later excavations at the site undertaken by Flinders Petrie in the 1920s, Italian teams between 1910 and 1914, and again between late 1927 and 1934, as well as finds from more recent excavations.[35] It is thus hard to state firmly what proportion of the total number of excavated texts has been published, but even so, what has been published constitutes a significant collection of texts.[36] Up to April 2016, the P.Oxy. series had published 5,289 numbered items. Many more will no doubt appear in coming years.

The Christian Books of Oxyrhynchus

Because Oxyrhynchus thrived for centuries after Constantine, a large amount of Christian material is preserved from the site. I leave aside the fascinating Christian documents (letters, contracts, etc.) found at Oxyrhynchus. A number of these classes of texts have been the subject of systematic treatments in recent years.[37] My focus here continues to be on the Christian books, which have received somewhat less attention as a group.[38] But even giving an overview of just the Christian books from Oxyrhynchus is not as straightforward as it might seem. All the terms need clarification: How certain are we that a given book came from Oxyrhynchus? What counts as "Christian"? And what counts as "a book"?

For the purposes of this survey, I searched the Leuven Database of Ancient Books in April 2016 for "Oxyrhynchus" and "Christian"; the search yielded 229 items.[39] The Oxyrhynchite provenance of some of these items is dubious (they were bought on the antiquities market, and there is no clear connection to Oxyrhynchus other than a dealer's word), so I left them aside. More difficult is the question of what is meant by "Christian" books.[40] Are they books produced by Christians? or books owned and/or read by Christians? Both are legitimate possibilities, but that kind of information is rarely possible to recover. Who can say whether this or that copy of the *Iliad* might have belonged to a Christian? Thus, the Leuven Database results are limited to books with identifiably Christian content or, in the case of the *Kestoi* of Julius Africanus, an identifiably Christian author. And even in this smaller corpus, an argument could be made that some of the items are "Jewish" rather than "Christian."[41] For example, P.Oxy. 7.1007 (LDAB 3113) is a fragment of a leaf from a Greek parchment codex of Genesis. The word ΘΕΟC is contracted in the usual way (ΘC̄), but the divine name, generally translated as ΚΥΡΙΟC and contracted as Κ̄C̄ in Christian manuscripts, is instead replaced by a double paleo-Hebrew letter yod. Should this manuscript be regarded as Christian (as the codex form and the *nomen sacrum* contraction suggest)? Or, might it be Jewish (as the use of Hebrew characters seems to imply)? I have left ambiguous examples like this one in my data set and also added two ambiguous items that the Leuven Database classifies as Jewish. I regard them as more likely Christian than Jewish: P.Oxy. 4.656 (LDAB 3094), a papyrus codex of Genesis in Greek that apparently does not contract *nomina sacra*, and a codex of the works of Philo of Alexandria (LDAB 3540) that only occasionally employs *nomina sacra*.[42] Many of the items in the Leuven Database results are single sheets of papyrus or parchment containing a fascinating variety of prayers or magical incantations (the lines between these two designations are sometimes thin) that use Christian phrases or symbols. Because they are not proper books, I have also left aside almost all of these items, but some of them, such as P.Oxy. 34.2684 (LDAB 2846), do, I think, fit a loose definition of a book, in this case a sheet from a miniature codex containing verses from the Letter of Jude (Figure 6.4). Although I do not treat most of these texts here, they serve as important reminders that for

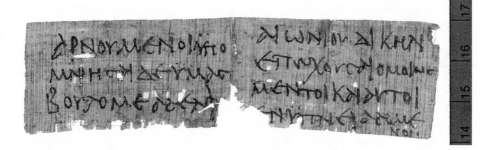

Figure 6.4. P.Oxy. 34.2684, a sheet from a miniature papyrus
codex containing the Letter of Jude.

(Image courtesy of the Egypt Exploration Society and Imaging Papyri Project,
University of Oxford.)

ancient Christians, writings were not just for conveying theological truths; they had the power to heal, protect, and perform other powerful actions.[43]

Thus, having taken account of these adjustments, the resulting set consists of 152 books (that is to say, rolls or codices) that seem to me to be Christian productions that can be securely connected to Oxyrhynchus (see the appendix). This number (and indeed all the numbers that follow) should be regarded as constantly in flux, pending the publication of more texts and further study of the texts that have already been published. And there are further reasons for being cautious with statistics based on papyrological evidence. Roger Bagnall's warning bears repeating: "We can never trust patterns of documentation without subjecting them to various sorts of criticism. It is not only arguments from silence that are suspect, but arguments from scarcity or abundance. The documentary record is irreparably lumpy, mainly because of patterns of deposition, preservation, discovery, and editorial choice."[44] In the case of Oxyrhynchus, every part of this warning should be kept in mind: Deposition—we are dealing with trash. How much does what people threw out reflect the reading materials that people *did not* throw out? Preservation—not every scrap of Christian material that was deposited in the trash heaps has been recovered. How much Christian literature fell into parts of the trash heaps outside the *afsh* that so helpfully preserved papyrus? Discovery—not every scrap of Christian material that survived in the trash heaps was recovered by archaeologists. How many Christian pieces over the years have been destroyed by illicit diggers or sold on the antiquities market? And finally, editorial choice—it is difficult to know how well the published corpus reflects the texts yet to be published. It is not publicly known, for example, how many more Christian texts sit unpublished in boxes at Oxford.

So, with all these caveats in mind, I can now pose the question: What does the corpus of 152 Christian books found at Oxyrhynchus look like? One obvious way of classifying the material is by language. The vast majority of the fragments are Greek. There is a single fragment of a parchment leaf in Latin, from the book of Genesis, P.Oxy. 8.1073 (LDAB 3203).[45] Several small fragments of Syriac writing can be assigned with confidence to Oxyrhynchus. They appear to be parts of two separate, highly fragmentary papyrus rolls containing

Christian (possibly Manichaean) texts and seem to have been found during the 1904–1905 season.[46] Only two Coptic fragments certainly from Oxyrhynchus have been published, but more are awaiting publication.[47] The remainder of the items are written in Greek.

In terms of contents, we may classify the materials by genre. I recognize the roughness of some of these assignments, but for now, I will live with this imprecision in order to avoid imposing potentially anachronistic "canonical" categories. I list the pieces in decreasing order of frequency.

Gospels (42 items)
Gospel According to Matthew (15 copies)
Gospel According to John (14 copies)
Gospel According to Thomas (3 copies)
Gospel According to Luke (2 copies)
Gospel According to Mary (1 copy)
Gospel According to Mark (1 copy)
Unknown gospels (6 items)[48]

Hebrew scriptures (Septuagint and Old Latin; 26 items)
Psalms (7 copies)
Genesis (4 Greek copies, 1 Latin copy)
Exodus (2 copies)
Leviticus (2 copies)
Judith (2 copies)
Tobit (2 copies)
Amos (1 copy)
Ecclesiastes (1 copy)
Joshua (1 copy)
Job (1 copy)
Sirach (1 copy)
Wisdom of Solomon (1 copy)

Letters (23 items)
Romans (4 Greek copies, 1 Coptic copy)
James (4 copies)
Hebrews (3 copies)

Galatians (3 copies)
1 Peter (2 copies)
1 Corinthians + Philippians (1 copy)
1 Corinthians (1 copy)
2 Corinthians (1 copy)
1 John (1 copy)
1–2 Thessalonians (1 copy)
Jude (1 copy)

Patristic sermons/expositions (23 items)
Melito of Sardis, *On Passover* (1 copy)
Aristides, *Apology* (1 copy)
Justin Martyr, *First Apology* (1 copy)
Irenaeus, *Against Heresies* (1 copy)
Julius Africanus, *Kestoi* (1 copy)
Basil of Seleucia, Oration 22 (1 copy)
Pseudo-Chrysostom, *De decollatione praecursoris* (1 copy)
Theophilus of Alexandria, *On Contrition* (1 copy)
Cyril of Alexandria, *Festal Letter* (1 copy)
Unknown Jewish-Christian dialogue (1 copy)
Unknown onomasticon (1 copy)
Unknown miscellaneous sermons/expositions (12 items)

Revelatory literature (19 items)
Shepherd of Hermas (10 copies)
Revelation (5 copies)
Sophia of Jesus Christ (1 copy)
1 Enoch (1 copy)
Revelation of Baruch (1 copy)
6 Ezra (1 copy)

Acts and legends (8 items)
Acts of the Apostles (3 copies)
Acts of John (1 copy)
Acts of Peter (1 copy)
Acts of Paul (1 copy)
Acts of Paul and Thecla (1 copy)
Nativity of Mary (1 copy)

Martyrdoms (4 items)
Martyrdom of Dioscorus (1 copy)
Martyrdom of Mamas (1 copy)
Martyrdom of Christine (1 copy)
Martyrdom of Pamoun (1 copy)

Testimonia collections (2 items)
A codex containing selections of Exodus and Susanna
A codex containing selections from Jeremiah, Amos, and the Psalms

Mixed books (1 item)
A codex of Exodus and Revelation[49]

Church order (1 item)
A Greek codex of the Didache

Church calendar (1 item)
A Coptic codex[50]

Hymn with musical notation (1 item)
A reused roll with a Christian hymn[51]

Philo of Alexandria (1 item)
A papyrus codex of the writings of Philo[52]

This mix of texts is interesting, but it is partially deceptive. Some of these fragments surely came from larger collections that included more than just the preserved text. For example, extant page numbers on P.Oxy. 13.1598 (LDAB 3017) indicate that these fragments of the Thessalonian correspondence occupied pages 207–210 in this book, which likely means that we are dealing with a codex that contained much more material, probably a larger collection of Paul's letters. On the other hand, some of these fragments may not have contained the whole text with which they are usually associated. This may be the case for one or more copies of the Shepherd of Hermas (P.Oxy. 50.3527 and 50.3528, LDAB 1098 and 1095, respectively), which could well be copies of only one part of that composite text.[53]

Nevertheless, this listing does provide us with a good sense of the variety of Christian material that was read (or at least thrown out) at Oxyrhynchus.

Turning to the physical aspects of these manuscripts, I note first that the vast majority of the writing (120 items) is on papyrus, with parchment a distant second (32 items). The parchment items are all codices. These fragments are copied in various types of writing, spanning the spectrum from fine literary productions to quite crudely copied pieces. At one end of the spectrum we have formal samples, like the carefully executed Biblical Majuscule of P.Oxy. 65.4444 (LDAB 3179), a parchment codex of the Wisdom of Solomon (Figure 6.5). At the other end of the spectrum are pieces like P.Oxy. 10.1230 (LDAB 2791), a fragment of a papyrus codex of Revelation written in a hand displaying several cursive tendencies (Figure 6.6). Within the corpus we find representatives of most of the named styles of writing discussed in Chapter 2. Especially well represented are pieces written in the so-called Formal Mixed style. Figure 6.7 illustrates two well-executed examples: one of the copies of the Gospel According to Thomas (P.Oxy. 4.655, LDAB 4029) and a leaf of a papyrus codex of the *Apology* of Aristides (P.Oxy. 15.1778, LDAB 338).[54] Some forty pieces of the Christian material might be classified as resembling this type of writing to a greater or lesser degree.

Turning to the question of formats, Table 6.1 shows the breakdown of the database into codices and rolls. The codex is the favored format by a large margin. This pattern fits well with the received wisdom, both about the Christian preference for the codex format and the overall switch in usage from roll to codex from the second through the fifth centuries. The only class of literature in which rolls outnumber codices is patristic sermons and exegesis. Of the twenty-five rolls, seven are reused; that is to say, the Christian material has been copied on the back of a roll previously used for another purpose.[55] Most famously, P.Oxy. 4.657 and PSI 12.1292 (LDAB 3018) are parts of a roll containing the letter to the Hebrews that was copied on the back of a Latin copy of an epitome of Livy. This piece also happens to be the most substantially intact Christian book that has survived from Oxyrhynchus. Figure 6.8, showing all the frames in the British Library along with a fragment recovered in later Italian excavations superimposed, demonstrates the sizable remains. The

Figure 6.5. P.Oxy. 65.4444, fragment of a leaf of a parchment codex containing the Wisdom of Solomon, copied in a Biblical Majuscule.

Figure 6.6. P.Oxy. 10.1230, fragment of a leaf of a papyrus codex containing Revelation, copied in a hand with cursive tendencies.

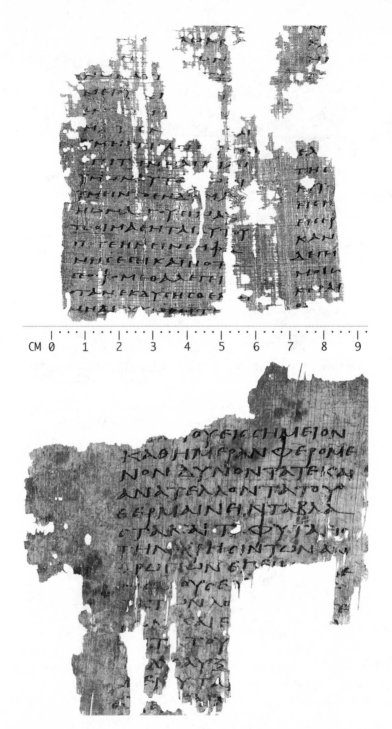

Figure 6.7. Examples of the Formal Mixed style of script from Oxyrhynchus:
P.Oxy. 4.655 (Houghton Library MS Gr SM4367), fragment of a papyrus
roll containing the Gospel According to Thomas (top); and P.Oxy. 15.1778,
fragmentary leaf of a papyrus codex containing the *Apology* of Aristides (bottom).

(Images courtesy of the Houghton Library, Harvard University; and the Egypt
Exploration Society and Imaging Papyri Project, University of Oxford.)

Table 6.1. Formats of Christian books at Oxyrhynchus

	Rolls	Codices	Total
Gospels	5	37	42
Hebrew scriptures (Septuagint and Old Latin)	2	24	26
Epistles	1	22	23
Patristic sermons/expositions	12	11	23
Revelatory literature	2	17	19
Acts and legends	0	8	8
Martyrdoms	2	2	4
Testimonia collections	0	2	2
Mixed books	0	1	1
Church order	0	1	1
Church calendar	0	1	1
Hymn	1	0	1
Philo of Alexandria	0	1	1
Total	25	127	152

figure is, however, somewhat misleading in that it does not give a good sense of the probable length of the original roll. In the gap between the upper and lower clusters of fragments, we can calculate that eleven columns are missing. The average column-to-column width of the extant portions is about 20 centimeters. So, the text of Hebrews would have occupied well over 5 meters, and there is reason to believe that Hebrews was preceded in this roll by another text. The columns were numbered, and the earliest number (on the column that begins with Heb 2:14) is MZ (= 47). If forty-six columns preceded Hebrews, that would mean another 9.2 additional meters, for a roll of at least 14.2 meters with a height of 26.3 centimeters. Thus, if Hebrews was the last text copied on the roll, when rolled up, this piece would have been somewhere between the size of a wine bottle and a typical two-liter bottle of soda.[56]

For the codices in the data set, we can make a few general observations. Many different formats are represented, ranging from books with heights less than 10 centimeters (generally regarded as miniature codices) to those with heights ranging from 20 to 30 centimeters. Few among the Christian codices at Oxyrhynchus could be properly described as "large" (that is, more than about 30 cm in height), but it is fair to say that some Christian codices from Oxy-

11 columns
missing
(ca. 2.2 meters)

Almost 2 full
columns missing
(ca. 40 cm)

0 cm   50 cm   100 cm

Figure 6.8. P.Oxy. 4.657 (British Library Papyrus 1532 verso) + PSI 12.1292 (fragment added to upper right frame), fragments of a papyrus roll containing Hebrews.

(Images courtesy of the British Library, London, UK/Bridgeman Images; the PSI online project, the Istituto Papirologico G. Vitelli, and the Cairo Museum.)

rhynchus would be considered luxury productions by most standards.[57] The first item that comes to mind is P.Oxy. 15.1780 (LDAB 2788), a copy of the Gospel According to John executed in a clear and regular Biblical Majuscule. The height of the page is 25.6 centimeters, and Turner estimated the width as 16 centimeters.[58] In 2006, a copy of the Martyrdom of Pamoun was published (P.Oxy. 70.4759, LDAB 10692; Figure 6.9). It is a neatly written and generously spaced example of the Alexandrian Majuscule, according to its editor, or of the Biblical Majuscule according to the Leuven Database (again we see the paleographic classification problem).[59] Portions of the upper and lower margins remain, and the editor estimates a page 22 centimeters wide by 30.5 centimeters high. So, this would be a large-format codex. Also noteworthy is an especially thick codex containing some of the works of Philo of Alexandria (LDAB 3540). Although Philo was Jewish, this codex of his works

Figure 6.9. P.Oxy. 70.4759, a leaf of a papyrus codex
containing the Martyrdom of Pamoun.

(Image courtesy of the Egypt Exploration Society and Imaging Papyri Project,
University of Oxford.)

employs some (though not all) of the standard *nomina sacra* contractions and is thus seemingly, though not definitely, a Christian product. In terms of page dimensions, the book is not especially large at 15 centimeters wide by 17.5 cm high, but extant page numbers indicate that the book would have been quite thick, at least 291 pages (the highest surviving page number), but more probably at least 374 pages.[60]

At the other end of the size spectrum are miniature codices, that is, books with heights less than 10 centimeters.[61] These pieces tend to be on parchment rather than papyrus. The type and size of writing on these small codices can vary quite widely, as the two examples in Figure 6.10 demonstrate. P.Oxy 5.840 (LDAB 5831) is 8.8 centimeters high by 7.4 centimeters wide, and the copyist has managed to fit twenty-two lines on one side and twenty-three lines on the other. P.Oxy. 7.1010 (LDAB 3181) is 8.4 centimeters high by 5.6 centimeters wide and contains half as many lines per page and is copied in a larger, considerably more legible hand.

The foregoing examples show that we can *sometimes* recover reasonably good codicological data from these manuscripts, but most of the Oxyrhynchus Christian literary pieces are very fragmentary. For every nice, nearly complete leaf we have, there are many more tiny scraps from which little reliable codicological data can be gathered. This makes good sense, given that these materials were excavated from trash heaps. As AnneMarie Luijendijk has shown, several of these books were discarded as whole books (that is to say, we are not talking about a stray leaf that fell out of a book).[62] But these whole books were torn into pieces before being discarded. So, for example, we have fragments of the inner and outer bifolia of P.Oxy. 2.208 and 15.1781, parts of a single-quire codex of the Gospel According to John from Oxyrhynchus (LDAB 2780), suggesting that the whole codex was discarded, not just a random leaf. But even when it can be demonstrated that such codices were likely thrown out whole, what we most often find in the trash heaps are discontinuous scraps.

Given this pattern, the recently published codex of Acts, P.Oxy. 74.4968 (LDAB 119313), stands out. Here we have a couple of very nicely preserved leaves and six more fragmentary consecutive pages from two quires, and even portions of the binding structures. This

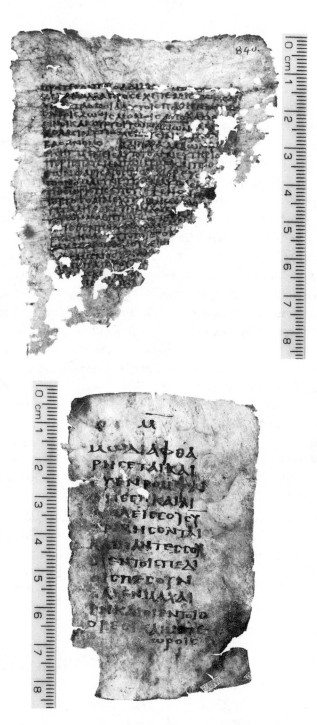

Figure 6.10. P.Oxy. 5.840 (Bodleian Library, Ms. Gr. Th. g 11) (top), a leaf of a parchment codex containing an unknown gospel, and P.Oxy. 7.1010 (Bodleian Library, Ms. Gr. Bibl. g 3) (bottom), a leaf of a parchment codex of 6 Ezra.

(Images courtesy of the Bodleian Libraries, University of Oxford.)

is out of keeping with the way the other pieces were preserved. And there may be a good reason for this. As the editors of the piece note, "The box in which the fragments were stored contained miscellaneous material only partly from Oxyrhynchus, so that the provenance of 4968 is subject to doubt."[63] Given the level of its dissimilarity to the other Christian codices in terms of preservation, I think there is good reason to suspect that it did not come from the trash heaps of Oxyrhynchus (and I have accordingly left it out of my tallies).[64]

Finally, I come to the question of dates. As I noted at the outset, in broad terms, we can say that the Christian materials at Oxyrhynchus date from perhaps as early as the end of the second century to as late as the seventh century. When we attempt to be more precise, we face a number of challenges. Only a handful of the Christian literary manuscripts from Oxyrhynchus are relatively securely datable. In Chapter 2, I described P.Oxy. 3.412 (LDAB 2550) in some detail. This papyrus roll contains the *Kestoi* written by Julius Africanus, a friend of Origen. From the contents of the *Kestoi*, we know the text was written after 227 CE. But this particular roll was cut up and reused, and there is a copy of a will of one Aurelius Hermogenes on the back with a date in the short-lived reign of the emperor Tacitus, who ruled from 275 to 276. So this piece is an example of an informal round hand probably datable within a fifty-year period. There are also at present four copies of martyrdoms from Oxyrhynchus, and these pieces have a *terminus post quem* of the year when the martyr died. That is the current extent of the relatively securely dated Christian books from Oxyrhynchus.[65] For the rest of the corpus, we rely on paleographic dates, which are always open to revision.[66]

In Table 6.2, I present a chronological arrangement of the Christian books from Oxyrhynchus using the century dates assigned in the Leuven Database. For manuscripts that are assigned date ranges that cross centuries (second to third, third to fourth, etc.), I have simply split the total numbers of these groups and distributed half to the earlier century and half to the later century, adding the extra to the earlier century when the tally is odd.[67] Using the dates given by the Leuven Database has both benefits and drawbacks. On the positive side, these dates take account of scholarship subsequent to the original editions of the manuscripts. The drawback is that on

Table 6.2. Christian manuscripts from Oxyrhynchus by century (CE)

	1st	2nd	3rd	4th	5th	6th	7th	8th
Christian manuscripts	0	6	58	46	26	13	3	0
"New Testament" manuscripts	0	3	26	18	12	4	0	0
Non–"New Testament" manuscripts	0	3	31	29	14	10	2	0

occasion, dates given do not reflect published scholarship but are instead based on correspondence from paleographers to the editors of the database. For example, P.Oxy. 60.4009 (LDAB 4872), an unknown gospel sometimes identified as the Gospel According to Peter, was assigned by its editors to the second century. The Leuven Database assigns it to the fourth century on the strength of a letter from the paleographer Pasquale Orisini.[68] Such large disparities between the dates of the original editors and more recent scholarship are relatively rare, and when they do occur, they are usually accompanied by reference to published scholarship. Thus, while any chronological arrangement of manuscripts based on paleography will be problematic, relying on the Leuven Database seems the lesser of many evils. The first row of Table 6.2 gives the overall data for "Christian" manuscripts. Just a handful of books are assigned to the second century, while the third and fourth centuries account for more than two-thirds of the Christian books so far published from Oxyrhynchus. The total decreases markedly for the fifth century, and Christian books all but disappear in the seventh century. These numbers could be broken down further in a variety of ways. For now, I choose just one further shuffling of the data to show the benefits and drawbacks of these sorts of exercises. Up to this point I have avoided "canonical" divisions of this corpus to circumvent the risk of anachronism, but the fact of the matter is that such canonical classifications have formed part of the scholarly apparatus that has generated our knowledge about these texts from the moment they were published. So, it may be illuminating to investigate the material under such headings to see whether trends can be detected. The second and third rows of Table 6.2 thus divide the corpus into "New Testament" manuscripts and all other Christian books.

Organizing the data in this way raises questions. There are sixty-three New Testament books, about 41 percent of the total number of Christian books so far published from Oxyrhynchus, but the percentage fluctuates somewhat over the centuries, from 50 percent in the second century to 30 percent in the sixth century. Where are the Greek New Testament texts of the sixth century? Why do they trickle out when other Christian literature persists? There are a few plausible answers. Maybe they just did not get thrown out. Maybe there was a shift to Coptic for New Testament manuscripts. Both are possibilities, but it seems that relatively little Coptic material was recovered from Oxyrhynchus.[69] Perhaps the most surprising aspect of this presentation of the data is the decrease in overall numbers between the third and the fourth centuries. The differences in the totals for these centuries in Table 6.2 show that almost all of the decrease in numbers from the third to the fourth century comes from a drop-off in copies of what we would call New Testament manuscripts (a 31 percent drop for New Testament manuscripts and a 6.5 percent drop for other Christian manuscripts). Given Constantine's rise to power in the early part of the fourth century and the subsequent toleration and promotion of Christian practices, would we not expect *more* production of New Testament texts during the fourth century? At the very least we would expect the rates of production and survival to remain basically constant, as we seem to see with the rest of Christian literature. Perhaps these numbers are simply due to the random chances of survival and preservation. Yet, it seems strange that at the very point at which we have a historical reason to suspect both a greater production of Christian manuscripts and a greater chance of survival for those manuscripts, the numbers of *this one particular grouping* drop off.

To really explore this problem, detailed paleographic reassessment of all the pieces would need to be carried out. That task is outside the scope of this discussion. What I can note are two broad trends in dating that deserve some attention. First, I pointed out in Chapter 2 that our database of literary manuscripts with relatively secure dates (either a firm *terminus ante quem* or *terminus post quem*) is dominated by material on rolls. Christian materials, and especially the texts we now call the New Testament, tend to be copied on codices. Thus, this material (a corpus consisting almost entirely of codices) would seem to be especially susceptible to being "pulled early" by comparison with dated literary material (a corpus consisting almost entirely of rolls). Second, what is striking about the Christian materials from Oxyrhynchus that have been assigned to early dates is the lack of reference to any securely datable manuscripts. Take, for example, the original editions of P.Oxy. 50.3523 (LDAB 2775, Gospel According to John) and P.Oxy. 64.4404 (LDAB 2935, Gospel According to Matthew), which were both assigned on paleographic grounds to the second century by their original editors without reference to any securely dated documents or datable manuscripts. In fact, the only manuscripts discussed are other Christian manuscripts also dated only by paleography. This observation does not mean that the second-century dates assigned by the editors are necessarily incorrect. It only serves to draw attention to the strangely circular character of the discussion.[70]

But it is important to keep reminding ourselves not to be seduced by these numbers games, as interesting as they may be. For at least some of the numbers appear less perplexing when considered in terms of the overall trends for preservation at Oxyrhynchus. When we look at all the preserved literature from Oxyrhynchus that has so far been published, we see an extreme peak in the second century (866 rolls and 36 codices = 902 books), followed by a drop in the third century (577 rolls and 128 codices = 705 books) and a sharp drop in the fourth century (60 rolls and 113 codices = 173 books).[71] These numbers could be the result of changes in literary output over the centuries, or changes in conditions of preservation. Recall Grenfell's description of the *afsh*, the particular matrix in the trash heaps that preserved papyrus. Perhaps, for whatever reason, the waste that created this material was simply more plentiful when manuscripts of the second century were thrown out. We have no way of knowing. But even if these larger trends of preservation explain the overall decline of surviving Christian books from the third century to the fourth century, the sharper decline of New Testament manuscripts would still remain anomalous.

Our survey of the Christian books from Oxyrhynchus has been

helpful in gaining a sense of what has been so far published from the material collected there. But even in this more ideal situation, when we know where these texts were found, archaeological problems remain. Grenfell and Hunt (and later Pistelli and Breccia) gathered this material from trash heaps in and around the city. This much we know. But this knowledge provokes a chain of related questions: How well does the published portion of the Christian manuscripts represent the full number of Christian manuscripts that were excavated? How well does what was excavated represent the whole of what survived antiquity in the trash heaps (that is to say, how much was destroyed or stolen during excavations)? How well did the material that survived to the twentieth century represent what was originally thrown out in the trash heaps in antiquity? And finally, how did that trash reflect the actual reading habits of the residents of Oxyrhynchus? Were these books from the libraries of a few individuals? Or was book ownership more widespread? And what of the fact that these manuscripts *were trash*? We have always known this, but it is only recently that scholars have paid serious attention to this phenomenon.[72] What does it mean to toss into the garbage books that might have been thought of as scripture?

These are challenging questions, but I do not think throwing up our hands in despair is the appropriate response. Papyrologists will continue publishing new pieces. Scholars will continue chipping away at the difficult problems that surround these papyri. We have seen reasons to hope for progress in untangling at least some of the archaeological questions. The inventory numbers (when they are known) can tell us the season that material was excavated. Grenfell's unpublished notebook is said to provide clues to the particular mounds excavated in a given season. The passing remarks of Grenfell and Hunt about particular finds may yield more information. Just as was the case with the Beatty Biblical Papyri and the Bodmer Papyri, we are left with more questions than answers. But with the Christian texts from Oxyrhynchus, there is at least some promise that we might have the raw materials to produce some satisfying answers in the future.

CHAPTER SEVEN

Fabricating a Second-Century
Codex of the Four Gospels

T HROUGHOUT THIS BOOK WE have seen numerous examples of the problems that can arise when working with
early Christian manuscripts: misinformation about provenance, repetition of dubious "facts" about manuscripts,
overconfidence in assigning dates, media sensationalism, and more.
Several of these problems come together in spectacular fashion in
connection with a group of fragmentary papyrus leaves containing small portions of the Gospels According to Luke and Matthew
(LDAB 2936). Numerous respected scholars have given in to the
temptation to build grand theories upon these small papyrus scraps,
which simply cannot bear the weight placed upon them.

From Fragments to Codex

Although the first of the fragments that concern us came to light in
the late nineteenth century, the best place to begin the story is in the
middle, at a lecture given by the papyrologist Colin H. Roberts in
1962.[1] The topic is a certain papyrus codex discovered in Egypt:

> In 1889, as a result of excavations in the ancient city of Kop-
> tos (now Quft) in Upper Egypt, a find of an unusual nature

came into the hands of French archaeologists. While a
Graeco-Roman house was being uncovered, it was noticed
that one of the walls gave a hollow ring when tapped; it was
opened up and in a carefully prepared niche was found a
papyrus codex. It had clearly not been touched since it was
first placed there; it was complete and still had attached to it
its original and rather primitive binding. The contents were
identified as two treatises of the Graeco-Jewish scholar Philo
(who flourished in the first half of the first century A.D.)
by the French Dominican scholar Père Scheil. . . . [Arthur]
Hunt, always a conservative and cautious judge of a hand,
assigned [the codex] to the third century A.D.

In fact, this codex of Philo is among the best-preserved papyrus
books to have survived from antiquity. It is now part of the collection of the Bibliothèque nationale de France (LDAB 3541).[2] And
there was still more that made this particular codex special. Roberts
continues:

But this is not quite the end of the story. Stuck in the inside
binding of the codex were found some torn scraps of papyrus; they had been glued together to form papier mâché as
padding for the leather binding (an obvious and common
practice). These, when cleaned and edited, turned out to contain fragments of the Third Gospel written in a singularly
handsome hand, with two columns to the page. Their editor, writing in 1938 and with no reference to the date of the
Philo codex from which they came, assigned them to the
fourth century. But if the Philo, as the experts agree, belongs
to the third century, clearly the discarded papyrus MS used
as stuffage for the binding cannot conceivably be later; in
fact, the hand in which the Gospel fragments were written
is of a type common in both [the] third and fourth centuries,
and these fragments carry some unmistakable evidence of
being written earlier than the fourth century.

Finally, Roberts also described the context in which the codex was hidden away in antiquity, to lie undisturbed for centuries until its discovery:

> But why should a complete codex have been buried in this deliberate fashion in the first place? It is worth noting that, though the text is that of a Jewish philosopher, the MS is Christian; the presence of certain abbreviations peculiar to Christian scribes [the *nomina sacra*] is conclusive.... Towards the end of the third century the last and most thorough-going of the persecutions by the state broke over the Church, that of Diocletian, known as the Great Persecution.... One of the principal objects of the persecution ... was the destruction of the sacred and liturgical books of the Christians. The Philo codex carried the undeniable stigma of the proscribed religion; so its owner bricked it up out of sight of the police. That he failed to claim it may suggest that there was other evidence against him, and that he did not survive the persecution. Such an explanation would suit admirably the evidence of the handwriting, and it is difficult to think of any circumstances in a later age which would call for such concealment.

In brief, then, the situation according to Roberts is as follows: We have a papyrus codex of Philo, the covers of which were stiffened using fragments of pages of a papyrus codex of the Gospel According to Luke; New Testament scholars now refer to these scraps of Luke as "𝔓4" (Figure 7.1). The handwriting of the Philo codex is assigned to the third century, so the fragments of Luke, which were waste material by the time of the construction of the Philo codex, must have been copied even earlier than that. The Philo codex was reportedly excavated from a hole in a wall in a house in Koptos, where it was deposited during the Diocletianic persecutions. Thus, we have a very rare example of a fairly early New Testament papyrus not from Oxyrhynchus with a relatively secure archaeological context.

Now, if we move back in time to 1953, we find the same Colin Roberts publishing three small fragments from a papyrus codex of

Figure 7.1. Ms. Suppl. grec 1120 [2], leaf of a papyrus codex
containing the Gospel According to Luke.

(Image courtesy of the Bibliothèque nationale de France, Paris.)

cm 1

Figure 7.2. Papyrus Gr. 17, fragments of a leaf from a papyrus codex
containing the Gospel According to Matthew.
(Image courtesy of the President and Fellows of Magdalen College Oxford.)

Matthew kept in Magdalen College at Oxford.[3] These papyri are
known to New Testament scholars as "𝔓64" (Figure 7.2). Roberts
assigned these fragments on the basis of their handwriting to "the
later second century." Four years later, Ramón Roca-Puig, a Span-
ish papyrologist, edited two more small fragments from a codex of
Matthew in a collection in Barcelona ("𝔓67"), assigning them to a
period "not later than the third century" (Figure 7.3).[4] Eric Turner
then recognized that all of these fragments of Matthew were written
in the same hand, and so in 1962 Roca-Puig produced a second edition in which he assigned the Barcelona fragments to the second
half of the second century.[5]

Now, if we move ahead in time to 1979, we find that Roberts
then returned to these fragments of Matthew. In light of similarities
first pointed out by Kurt Aland, Roberts now claimed that the Oxford and Barcelona fragments of Matthew were all part of the same

Figure 7.3. P.Monts.Roca inv. 1, fragments of leaves from a papyrus codex
containing the Gospel According to Matthew.
(Image courtesy of the Abadia de Montserrat Collection © Abadia de Montserrat.)

manuscript as the Luke fragments in Paris. Roberts wrote, "There can in my opinion be no doubt that all these fragments come from the same codex which was reused as packing for the binding of the late third century codex of Philo."[6] Roberts also reasserted the provenance for the codex of Philo: It was "written in the later third century and found in a jar which had been walled up in a house at Coptos, . . . preserved intact with its binding. We may surmise that its owner concealed it with the intention of removing it from its hiding-place when danger had passed, either when Coptos was besieged and sacked by Diocletian in A.D. 292 or later in his reign during the last and severest of the persecutions."[7] So, now we have a manuscript that contained *both* the gospel of Matthew *and* the gospel of Luke, and it apparently has a surprisingly precise archaeological context—the leather cover of the codex of Philo that was found (now in a jar) in a house in Koptos—with a secure *terminus ante quem* during the period of Diocletian. This is becoming a more impressive book.[8]

From Codex to Icon: Popular Media Interest
and Two More Gospels

Yet, so far this story is pretty mundane. As we have seen with the
Beatty Biblical Papyri and the Bodmer Papyri, it is not unusual for
parts of the same codex to be divided among different holding institutions. It was not until the mid-1990s that these fragments became
truly exceptional. On Christmas Eve 1994, the *Times* ran a front-
page story carrying the title "Oxford papyrus is eyewitness record of
the life of Christ." The Oxford papyrus in question was the fragmentary leaf of Matthew at Magdalen College. Nearly two full pages
in the *Times* gave voice to the case of Carsten Thiede (1952–2004),
who argued that the Matthew fragments dated not to the late second century, as Roberts had claimed, but to "the mid-first century."[9]
The Christmas Eve news story appeared in anticipation of an academic article to be published by Thiede in *Zeitschrift für Papyrologie
und Epigraphik* in 1995.[10] This article spelled out Thiede's ideas more
fully. First, he argued that the Paris fragments of Luke were part of
a different book that was copied "considerably later (by up to one-
hundred years)." The fragments of Matthew from Oxford and Barcelona were then said to date from "the first century, perhaps (though
not necessarily) predating AD 70." Thiede's "argument" (I use the
term loosely) for this new date was purely paleographic, based on
asserted similarities with Greek writings from Nahal Hever and
Qumran in Palestine and Herculaneum in Italy. Thiede's article drew
swift rebuttals from the academic community, with a subsequent
issue of *Zeitschrift für Papyrologie und Epigraphik* publishing a thorough, point-by-point refutation by Klaus Wachtel.[11] Undaunted,
and indeed buoyed by the ongoing publicity, Thiede and the author
of the original column in the *Times* copublished a popular book re-
asserting and elaborating Thiede's claims and attacking his critics.[12]
Thiede's proposals again failed to persuade any experts, but the tac-
tic of making his case in the media and the popular press drew world-
wide attention to his claims.[13] Thiede's ideas were featured in the
New York Times, on the cover of *Der Spiegel*, and in many other prominent media outlets.[14]

In the following year, another article in a major biblical studies
journal kept the spotlight on these fragments. The papyrologist The-

odore Skeat (1907–2003) laid out a thesis that is in some ways just as astonishing as the claims made by Thiede. Skeat was convinced that these fragments were once part of a codex that contained all four gospels.[15] Thus, like Roberts, Skeat believed that all the fragments of Matthew and the fragments of Luke must have come from the same codex. But Skeat went even further. In a long and detailed discussion, he tried to extrapolate numbers of letters that would have appeared on individual pages of the Matthew fragments to demonstrate that the codex could not have contained only Matthew and Luke and that it must have been a single-quire construction. According to Skeat, the codex must have contained something else between the gospels of Matthew and Luke, and there was no doubt about what that "something else" must be: "We come to the conclusion that another Gospel or Gospels must have intervened at this point; and since a codex containing three gospels is unthinkable, the only possible conclusion is that the manuscript *originally contained all four Gospels*."[16] Skeat was not deterred by the fact that codices with three gospels are known, as are codices that mix gospels and other literature.[17]

Skeat also offered the fullest paleographic discussion of the fragments and made a vigorous argument that this four-gospel codex was datable to the second century. At the same time, however, he observed that "the general appearance of the script" could be described in the very terms used to characterize the writing of Codex Sinaiticus, which is generally thought to have been copied in the middle of the fourth century.[18] Skeat also spent several paragraphs puzzling over how Frederic Kenyon could have assigned the Luke fragments to the fourth century but the Philo codex to the third century.[19] This point is important, and I return to it shortly.

Later that same year, our fragments of Matthew and Luke featured prominently in another article in the same journal. In the printed version of his presidential address to the Society for New Testament Studies, Graham Stanton, Lady Margaret's Professor of Divinity at Cambridge, fully accepted Skeat's arguments and pushed them still further. He wrote: "Skeat has now shown beyond reasonable doubt that 𝔓64+𝔓67+𝔓4 are from the same single-quire codex, probably our earliest four-Gospel codex which may date from the

late second century. . . . The codex was planned and executed me-
ticulously: the skill of the scribe in constructing it is most impressive. . . . This codex does not look at all like an experiment by a
scribe working out ways to include four gospels in one codex: it
certainly had predecessors much earlier in the second century."[20]
For Stanton, then, we have not just one, but *multiple* luxury codices
containing all four canonical gospels, and they were circulating not
just at the end of the second century, but much earlier in the century
as well! We have come a long way from five small fragments of Matthew's gospel and a few damaged leaves of Luke.

The papers by Skeat and Stanton provoked several responses.
The two most important appeared in *New Testament Studies*. Peter
Head addressed Skeat's mathematical calculations of letters per page
and demonstrated that because of the fragmentary nature of the evidence, Skeat could not possibly achieve the precision he claimed.[21]
Shortly after that, Scott Charlesworth, in a very detailed analysis,
pointed out that Skeat's argument that the fragments all came from
one single-quire codex had neglected the one crucial type of evidence that could be almost decisive for such an argument—the directions of the fibers of the individual leaves. It turns out that on
some of the fragments of Matthew, the horizontal fibers precede the
vertical, and on others, the vertical precede the horizontal. So, for
example, one of the Barcelona fragments contains Matt 3:9 written
on the vertical fibers and Matt 3:15 on its reverse written along
the horizontal fibers, but the other fragment contains Matt 5:20–22
written along the horizontal fibers and on its reverse Matt 5:25–28
written against the vertical fibers. Thus, the center of a quire most
likely intervened between these fragments. The same alternating
pattern is true of the leaves of Luke, which shows that both the Matthew fragments and the Luke fragments probably came from multi-
quire codices.[22] So, Skeat's four-gospel, single-quire codex theory of
these fragments has not carried the day, but the question of whether
the Matthew and the Luke fragments might come from the same
multi-quire codex remains open.[23] And there is still broad agreement
that the Luke fragments (and perhaps the Matthew fragments) come
from a known archaeological context (the house in Koptos) and have
a secure *terminus ante quem* in that they were used to construct the

covers of a codex of Philo that was deposited in the house in Koptos
during the reign of Diocletian. Yet, these "facts" turn out to be ques-
tionable as well. We are now ready to go back to the very beginning
of this story.

The Relationship of the Philo Codex and
the Fragmentary Leaves of Luke

Jean-Vincent Scheil (1858–1940) was a scholar of the ancient Near
East. He is best remembered as a pioneer in Elamite studies and for
his edition and translation of Hammurabi's Code, but he also had an
early interest in Egyptology. In December 1890, at the age of thirty-
two, he made his first trip to Egypt as part of the French archaeological mission in Cairo.[24] While there, he happened to obtain the
leather-bound papyrus codex of Philo of Alexandria that we have been
discussing. In his publication of this Philo codex, Scheil gave some
details of the book's acquisition and a description of its physical state
at that time:

> The papyrus, the contents of which we publish here, was
> found at Coptos in Upper Egypt in 1889. Doubtless consid-
> ered in ancient times as a very precious thing, it was en-
> closed and sealed in a niche. The hollow sound of the wall
> drew attention to this location. Upon opening it, its secret
> was revealed: two treatises of Philo of Alexandria. . . . In its
> hiding place, the book must have been very compressed;
> concrete is encrusted on the exterior; the sheets adhered
> strongly in a single mass and were also held to each other by
> many small grains of salt, products of centuries of condensa-
> tion in the plant tissue. The 44 very fragile leaves were num-
> bered and divided into quires of 10, 10, 12 and 12 leaves. . . .
> Following the forty-fourth leaf, as a clump, I think, and to
> fill up the capacity of the cover, there were several fragments
> of leaves adhering together and coming from a collection of
> gospels, one of them carrying κατα μαθθαιον, and the others
> fragments of St. Luke. The end of the last treatise with its
> subscript title [i.e., page 89] was found following, on the in-
> side cover.[25]

Two key details emerge from this account. First, we hear of a fragment with the words κατα μαθθαιον, "according to Matthew." In fact,
this fragment contains the full title "Gospel According to Matthew"
and appears to be the remains of a title page. But the handwriting
of this title page is not the same as that of the Luke fragments or
the Matthew fragments in Oxford and Barcelona. It is thus unclear
whether this leaf was part of the same manuscript as the Luke fragments.[26] But what is truly remarkable is that Scheil actually stated
(as long ago as 1893!) that the gospel fragments were *not* stuffed in
the leather cover at all. Rather, he informs us with considerable precision that the fragmentary leaves of Luke were found between page
88 and the last page of the Philo codex, page 89, which was glued to
the inside of the back cover. Indeed, to this day, the last page of the
Philo codex, page 89, remains pasted to the inside of the back cover
(Figures 7.4 and 7.5). So, the idea that the gospel fragments were
used as stuffing in the covers was simply an inference on the part of
Roberts in 1963. Indeed, before 1963, other scholars had assumed
on the basis of Scheil's description that the Luke fragments were
slipped in among the leaves of the Philo codex. This is why an authority such as Frederic Kenyon assigned the Philo codex to the
third century while at the same time placing the copying of the Luke
fragments in the fourth century. Kenyon described the leaves of Luke
as "attached to" the manuscript of Philo.[27] Only *after* Roberts did
scholars begin to use the Philo codex as a *terminus ante quem* for the
Luke fragments.

How did Roberts come to his mistaken conclusion, which nearly
all subsequent scholars have followed? To begin with, Scheil's description is less than crystal clear. As far as I know, Scheil described
the relationship between the Luke fragments and the Philo codex
in three different ways. First, the description I have already mentioned: "A la suite du quarante-quatrième feuillet, en guise de bourre,
je pense, et pour remplir la capacité de la couverture, se trouvaient
plusieurs fragments de feuillets collés ensemble, et provenant d'un
Évangéliaire, l'un d'eux portant κατα μαθθαιον, et les autres, des fragments de saint Luc. La fin du dernier traitè et sa suscription se trouvent à la suite, sur la couverture intérieure." (Following the forty-
fourth leaf, as a clump, I think, and to fill up the capacity of the
cover, there were several fragments of leaves adhering together and

Figure 7.4. The closed leather cover of Bibliothèque nationale de France Ms. Suppl. grec 1120, a papyrus codex containing works by Philo of Alexandria.

(Image adapted from Jean-Vincent Scheil, "Deux traités de Philon," *Mémoires publiés par les membres de la Mission Archéologique Française au Caire* 9.2 [1893], Plate 4; courtesy of the Bibliothèque nationale de France, Paris.)

coming from a collection of gospels, one of them carrying κατα μαθθαιον, and the others fragments of St. Luke. The end of the last treatise with its subscript title [i.e., page 89] was found following, on the inside cover.)[28]

Later in the same work, Scheil characterized the relationship in different terms: "Ce fragment, écrit en trés belles onciales, se trouvait à la suite des traités de Philon." (This fragment, written in very neat uncials, was found following the treatises of Philo.)[29] And in his

Figure 7.5. The open leather cover of the Philo codex (Ms. Suppl. grec 1120) showing the last page (89) still pasted to the inside of the back cover (partially obscured by protective mesh).

(Image courtesy of the Bibliothèque nationale de France, Paris.)

publication of the fragments of Luke in 1892, Scheil had described the relationship in still another way: "Je présente aux lecteurs de cette nouvelle Revue quelques fragments de l'Évangile selon saint Luc, recueillis au cours de ma mission d'Égypte (1891). Le texte en est écrit en capitales grecques, sur un papyrus provenant de *Coptos* et se trouvant joint à un autre plus considérable contenant deux traités de *Philon d'Alexandrie* écrits en onciales." (I present to the readers of this new journal some fragments of the Gospel According to Luke, gathered during my mission in Egypt [1891]. The text is written in Greek capitals, on a papyrus from Koptos and found attached to another more substantial [manuscript] containing two treatises of Philo of Alexandria written in uncials.)[30]

None of these descriptions is really adequate, and Scheil's speculation about the reason for the inclusion of the Luke fragments ("in order to fill up the capacity of the cover") is confusing. It seems most likely that he thought the leather cover was too big to hold just the treatises of Philo, and the Luke leaves were added simply to fill up the extra space. Roberts may have been correct to guess that the gospel leaves came from the cover, but it would have to have been the front cover, since the last page of Philo is still glued to the back cover. But if that is the case, then someone must have tampered with the codex because Scheil specifically said that he found the gospel leaves between pages 88 and 89 of the Philo codex. I think it more likely that the Luke pages were just slipped in for safekeeping in antiquity.

Is there other evidence for this kind of practice? We seem to have an analogous case in the Nag Hammadi codices.[31] In one of the early photographs of Nag Hammadi Codex VI taken before the codices were disassembled, it is possible to see the edge of a page sticking out near the front cover (see Figure 1.3). Looking more closely, we can just make out the first letters of the last few lines (Figure 7.6). This pattern of letters does not match any of the leaves of Codex VI. In fact, these letters belong to what we now call Codex XIII, which is actually just a few leaves containing a single tractate. These leaves were stashed away between the front cover and the first pages of Codex VI.[32] The consistent pattern of rotting beginning from the inserted leaves of Codex XIII and continuing on to the first pages of Codex VI confirms that the extra leaves were placed there in antiquity.

If something similar did in fact happen with the leaves of Luke in the Philo codex, our thinking about the relationship in terms of dating between the Philo codex and the leaves of Luke would need revision.[33] Most scholars regard Nag Hammadi Codex XIII as basically contemporary with Codex VI.[34] Perhaps the Philo codex and the leaves of Luke should also be thought of as contemporaries. Alternatively, the Luke leaves could have been copied later and simply worn out from use more quickly than the Philo codex into which they were later inserted. The bottom line is that because Scheil reports that the gospel leaves were found among the leaves of the Philo codex and not in the binding, there is not necessarily any specific chronological relationship between the dates of the two manuscripts.

The Provenance of the Philo Codex

What about Roberts's claim that the Philo codex has a secure *terminus ante quem* because it was hidden away in the wall of a house in

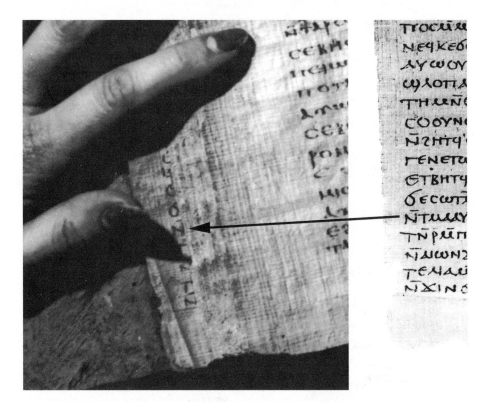

Figure 7.6. Detail of leaf of Nag Hammadi Codex XIII inside Codex VI (left)
and after separation and mounting (right).

(Images adapted from a photograph by Jean Doresse [left] and James M. Robinson [ed.], *The
Facsimile Edition of the Nag Hammadi Codices: Codices XI, XII and XIII* [Leiden: Brill, 1973],
114 [right]); courtesy of the Institute for Antiquity and Christianity Records, Special
Collections, Claremont Colleges Library, Claremont, California.)

Koptos in the year 292 or shortly thereafter? Jerome's *Chronicle* does
tell us that Koptos revolted and was "utterly destroyed" under Diocletian, but that was hardly the end of the city.[35] In fact, Koptos recovered and thrived during the fourth century and beyond. It held
sufficient prestige to become the seat of a bishop probably as early
as the second quarter of the fourth century, and the remains of an
impressive church and baptistery with construction phases in the
fifth or sixth century are still present.[36] The real decline of the town
did not occur until the ninth and tenth centuries, meaning that
Koptos would have endured other tribulations when someone might
well have stashed away a valued book. At the very least, the Sasanian

invasion in the first quarter of the seventh century and the Arab invasion in the second quarter of that century come to mind. Thus, Roberts's proposal of a *terminus ante quem* for the Philo codex and the Luke fragments in the late third century is not tenable. But all of this is a moot point, since there is a distinct possibility that the codex did not even come from Koptos at all.

To understand why, we must move ahead almost a half century from Scheil's publications. In 1938, Jean Merell (1904–1986), a young Czech scholar, was working on writing an introduction to early Christian papyri. While he was examining manuscripts in Paris, he discovered some additional fragments of the same manuscript of Luke that Scheil had published.[37] Merell contacted Scheil to ask about them. The result was further details about Scheil's acquisition of the codex. Merell reported as follows: "Last June, Father Scheil told me that, having bought a codex containing two treatises of Philo of Alexandria at Luxor in 1891, he had had the good fortune of finding there fragments of our biblical papyrus."[38] Thus, it becomes clear that Scheil did not actually *find* the book in a niche in a house in Koptos; he *bought* the book at Luxor. Perhaps this could have been surmised from the fact that Scheil places the "discovery" of the codex in 1889, but his own first arrival in Egypt came in late 1890. In any event, the details of the story of the alleged discovery of the codex must have come from a local antiquities dealer. So then, was the book actually found in a hollow wall in a house in Koptos? We simply cannot know.

So where does that leave us? The notice that the Philo codex was purchased at Luxor is of interest. In his 1953 article on the Magdalen College Matthew fragments, Roberts made the following statement about their acquisition: "The fragments were purchased by the Reverend Charles B. Huleatt in Luxor in 1901." We do not know where or exactly when the Barcelona fragments were bought, but Roberts also noted that Huleatt seems to have at one point possessed additional pieces of the same manuscript: "It is probable that there were further fragments of the same leaf since a letter by Mr. Huleatt to the Librarian refers to purchases of fragments from the same manuscript in successive years, but nothing beyond what is published below is now extant in the Library."[39] The period of ten years between Scheil's purchase of the Philo codex and Huleatt's purchase of the Matthew fragments does not seem very long when compared with the interval of more than twenty years between the purchases of different parts of the Chester Beatty Ezekiel-Daniel-Susanna-Esther codex.[40] But on the basis of the evidence presently available, all we can confidently say is that the possibility exists that all of the pieces may have originated from a single dealer in Luxor and perhaps from a single codex that contained Matthew and Luke. Pushing beyond this conclusion about provenance is simply speculation.

The Date of the Matthew and Luke Fragments

What about the date of the fragments? Our archaeological context and our secure *terminus ante quem* proved to be chimerical. In this case, as in so many others, we are forced to turn to paleographic analysis. How have the experts evaluated these fragments? Again, the 1953 article by Roberts provides some useful information: "The fragments were correctly identified by their purchaser, and assigned by him to the third century A.D.; a note in the Librarian's report for 1901 reads: 'Mr. Huleatt supposes them to be of the third century; but Dr. Hunt who recently examined the fragments thinks they may be assigned with more probability to the fourth century.' Only the belief that Hunt's dating in 1901 was substantially incorrect would excuse a detailed study of such minute fragments."[41]

In this article, as we have seen, Roberts concluded that the Matthew fragments dated to the late second century. In 1979, when he asserted that both the Matthew fragments and the leaves of Luke came from a single book datable to the second century, Roberts described this second-century date as a matter of agreement among paleographers.[42] That was untrue in 1979, and it remains untrue now. In 1977, no less an authority than Eric Turner had assigned the Luke fragments to the third century, even allowing for the possibility of a fourth-century date.[43] Many opinions about the date of the fragments have been expressed over the years, and the range runs from the first century to the sixth century. Not all of these opinions are of equal value. As we have seen, Thiede's proposed first-century date was based on wishful thinking. The sixth-century date that Scheil originally assigned to the fragments of Luke has been universally rejected. Even leaving aside these extremes, there is still a fairly wide range of proposed dates. Taking into consideration only the acknowledged experts, we have Pasquale Orsini and Willy Clarysse suggesting a date of 175–200 CE, an unrealistically narrow window.[44] Skeat's comparison with the examples of the Biblical Majuscule collected by Guglielmo Cavallo led him to endorse Roberts's assignment of the fragments to the late second century.[45] The twenty-eighth edition of the Nestle-Aland *Novum Testamentum Graece* describes the Matthew fragments as "ca. 200" and the Luke fragments as third century.[46] Peter Parsons has opted for the third century.[47] Turner's opinion varied, sometimes assigning the Matthew fragments as early as the second century and sometimes allowing a date as late as the fourth century for the Luke fragments.[48] Hunt placed the Magdalen College fragments in the fourth century. Even Kenyon, who generally preferred to date biblical manuscripts at the early end of the spectrum of possible dates, nevertheless placed the Luke fragments in the fourth century, both in his handbook on paleography published in 1899 and in correspondence with Jean Merell in 1938.[49] More recent scholars have tended to simply dismiss the inconvenient opinions of Hunt and Kenyon. Skeat, for example, characterized the spectrum of paleographic opinions as follows: "To sum up: on the basis of the foregoing, the only real difference of opinion regarding the dating of P4 and P64+P67 is whether they are to be described as 'late 2nd century' or '*circa* 200.'"[50] The assessments of Hunt and Kenyon from the first half of the twentieth century simply disappear. It is sometimes argued that experts dated manuscripts later in those early days simply because of a lack of sufficient comparative evidence.[51] But with this kind of handwriting, the so-called Biblical Majuscule, the earliest relatively datable examples, P.Oxy. 4.661 and P.Ryl. 1.16, had already been published in 1904 and 1911, respectively. Kenyon, at least, had the relevant evidence at hand in 1938 and still assigned the Luke fragments to the fourth century.

Yet, when one examines Roberts's 1953 article, the impression it gives is that Roberts immediately recognized that Hunt was obviously wrong and that these fragments had an appearance specifically characteristic of the second century. As Roberts wrote at that time, "Only the belief that Hunt's dating in 1901 was substantially incorrect would excuse a detailed study of such minute fragments." But in fact, in his paleographic discussion of the Matthew fragments *Roberts did not offer a single securely dated parallel to justify his redating*. He simply asserted that the fragments were "demonstrably earlier" than a copy of Homer that Wilhelm Schubart had assigned to the third century—also on the basis of paleography. Only later, in an appendix to Roca-Puig's edition, did Roberts offer more securely dated parallels: P.Oxy. 4.661 (LDAB 474), a small part of a papyrus roll of epodes assigned to the late second century because it was reused for a document that was written, according to Grenfell and Hunt, "not later than the beginning of the third century"; and P.Dura 2, two small fragments of a roll of Appian that certainly predate 256 CE since they were recovered from Dura-Europos (LDAB 303).[52]

But there is more to the story. Even Roberts changed opinions about the date of the Matthew fragments quite drastically. He apparently first examined the fragments at the request of the Magdalen College librarian in 1951. At that time, he prepared a short memo that identified the fragments as preserving portions of chapter 26 of Matthew's gospel (Figure 7.7).[53] He also offered an evaluation of the date: "Manuscript to be dated probably in 2nd half of 3rd [century], early 4th [century] not excluded." Is this to be attributed simply to an attitude of deference to the datings proposed by Huleatt and Hunt? That is possible, but I have my doubts. A decade later in his 1962 lecture, before he decided that the Matthew and Luke fragments came from the same codex, Roberts had described the Luke fragments thus: "The hand in which the Gospel fragments were written is of a type common in both third and fourth centuries, and these fragments carry some unmistakable evidence of being written earlier than the fourth century."[54] How much earlier, Roberts left unclear, but there was no mention of the second century in that article. The fact of the matter is that this kind of writing is extremely difficult to date with precision. Recall the case of P.Ryl. 1.16 from Chapter 2. This fragment of a papyrus roll of a comedy written in the Biblical Majuscule style was reused for a letter (published separately as P.Ryl. 2.236) dated to January 256 (see Figure 2.3). The original editor, Arthur Hunt, assigned the comedy to the late second century. Turner assigned it to about 150, and Cavallo assigned it to about 225. Thus, even in this optimal scenario, where one end of the date range is absolutely fixed, the experts disagree by seventy-five

3 fragments from a page of a [papyrus]
codex of St. Matthew's Gospel: there
were 2 cols. to the page, and
verso (across fibres) precedes recto
(along fibres). Average of 16 letters to line

Fr. (i) has on verso   XXVI. 7,8
——— ——— recto   XXVI. 31
Fr. ii ——— verso   XXVI. 10,11
——— ——— recto   XXVI. 32,33
Fr. iii ——— verso   XXVI. 14,15
——— ——— recto   XXVI. 22,23

MS to be dated probably in 2e half
of 3rd c. : early 4th c. not
excluded.

C. H. Roberts

9 . v . 51

Figure 7.7. Memo of Colin H. Roberts reporting on the Magdalen
College fragments of Matthew, May 9, 1951.

(Image courtesy of the President and Fellows of Magdalen College Oxford.)

years. Is it really surprising, then, that experts give a range of well over a century for our gospel fragments? Is there any way to narrow this range of possible dates?

Perhaps, but we need to move beyond paleography. One feature common to both the fragments of Matthew and those of Luke is a pattern of textual division by means of *ekthesis* (the opposite of indentation). Is it possible to determine anything about the date of the fragments on the basis of this type of textual division? In the writings of ancient Christian authors, one finds a few mentions of divisions into *stichoi*, or sense clauses, in Christian manuscripts beginning in the early third century, but the pattern of division in our fragments seems to be something rather more advanced than sense clauses.[55] These are paragraphs. Similar techniques of division of the text are known to occur in manuscripts generally assigned to the fourth and fifth centuries, like Codex Sinaiticus (LDAB 3478), Codex Bezae (LDAB 2929), and the Freer codex of the gospels (LDAB 2985).[56] Now, for Roberts, the presence of such textual division in the Matthew fragments proved that this kind of textual division went all the way back to the second century.[57] But because paleographic dating is so uncertain, the inference should probably work in the opposite direction: the presence of developed textual divisions should, if anything, make us lean toward a rather later date for these fragments, although not much stress can be placed on this kind of argumentation.

Don Barker has recently proposed that the range of possible dates for the production of these fragments of Matthew and Luke runs from the middle of the second century to the middle of the fourth century.[58] This is a sensible evaluation. A second-century date is not impossible. These fragments may represent both an early example of the Biblical Majuscule type of hand and an early example of this system of textual division. They may also represent both an early example of the multi-quire papyrus codex and an early example of a multi-gospel codex. *But it is equally possible that these fragments were copied in the third or even the fourth century, when all of these characteristics are more common.* There is just a lot of uncertainty surrounding various aspects of these fragments. What does seem certain is that they hardly form a secure foundation upon which to build theories about second-century Christian scribal practice or the development of the codex or the emergence of a four-gospel canon.

What lessons can be taken away from this strange story? Probably the most obvious point is the degree to which scholars are susceptible to the overwhelming temptation to weave fragmentary bits of papyrological evidence into coherent, even compelling stories, whether it is Roberts's inventive tale of someone secretively hiding away the Philo codex in a jar during the persecutions of Diocletian, or Skeat's confidence that the fragments of Matthew and Luke could only be explained in one way ("the only possible conclusion is that the manuscript *originally contained all four Gospels*"), or Stanton's claim that the fragments *prove* the existence of multiple four-gospel codices circulating in the early second century. Difficulties are smoothed over, inconvenient facts are ignored, and new details are added to fill in the many blanks. Because so little remains and so many questions must stay open, undisciplined speculation can flow more freely. Fragments like these can be marshaled to support all sorts of theories.[59]

And again, issues of assigning dates have come to the fore. Even if we set aside the specious claims of Thiede and focus only on the serious discussion of the date of these fragmentary leaves, it becomes clear just how subjective the paleographic method of assigning dates is. There seems to be no way to deal with the fact of the uncertain date of these fragments. The tantalizing *possibility* that the fragments *might* date to as early as the second century all too easily slides into a misguided confidence that they *must* date to this period. Some of these problems could be at least partially addressed by radiocarbon analysis. Again, however, institutions have little to gain by subjecting their prized biblical manuscripts to testing that could undercut their allegedly early dates, which are their claim to fame. But the main point to take away from this episode is that the first step toward the production of reliable knowledge about these early Christian manuscripts is to be honest about what we *do not* know.

Epilogue: The Future of Ancient Christian Books

WHILE MUCH OF THIS book has had a cautionary, if not negative tone ("we can't know this"), I think I have made my case that closer attention to the archaeology of early Christian manuscripts does pay dividends. When we know that a given manuscript likely was found with other books, or when we know that a manuscript has potentially informative features beyond its handwriting (such as binding, evidence of use, and repairs), it is always a good idea to take that context and information into consideration when evaluating the manuscript. And, of course, when we don't know any of these things, it is always a good idea to be transparent about that.

Issues of dating have recurred throughout this study. In terms of practical historical outcomes of our survey, I think it is safe to say that although a few Christian books *may* be as old as the second century, none of them *must* be that old, not even the celebrated fragment of the fourth gospel in the John Rylands Library.[1] The drive to have older and older Christian manuscripts, however, shows no signs of abating. In 2012, rumors began to swirl on the Internet about the existence of a fragment of the Gospel According to Mark that was removed from mummy cartonnage (which, like covers of books, was sometimes made of pasted layers of papyrus) and was datable to the first century.[2] We await the publication of this papyrus to see what the actual evidence is for this dating. An uncannily similar claim was

269

made about a papyrus published in the 1980s, which also involved Mark's gospel, mummy cartonnage, and a first-century date.[3] This other "first-century Mark" was pretty clearly a *pia fraus*.[4] Let us hope the new "first-century Mark" has more substance.

"First-century Mark" aside, the problem of assigning dates to Greek literary manuscripts of the early Christian period is not going away. Paleography can provide a general guide to the date of a manuscript of the Roman era, but it simply cannot deliver the precision and certainty that some of its practitioners claim. Radiocarbon analysis, if executed well and reported responsibly, could illumine these debates considerably, but I am not terribly optimistic. During the course of my work, I approached numerous institutions with queries about carrying out radiocarbon analysis. A small number expressed interest, but the majority cited total nondestruction policies with regard to their holdings. Any analysis that causes damage to a manuscript is not permitted. I can see the appeal of having a simple, blanket policy like this. Yet, a more careful cost-benefit analysis seems desirable. If an institution owns ten leaves of a codex, or a meter-long papyrus roll with wide margins containing a good deal of blank space, is the avoidance of radiocarbon dating simply to preserve the sanctity of the ancient object really justifiable? I think not. The flip side of the coin is that institutions that own manuscripts potentially have a lot to lose with the results of radiocarbon analysis. For example, if a given object's chief value for an institution lies in its being "the earliest" example of something, radiocarbon analysis, because of its association with "hard science," presents the potential threat of undercutting the claim to fame. Humanistic scholars of art history or paleography may be freely allowed to opine about the date of an artifact, but because "science" is, for better or worse, viewed as producing authoritative knowledge, scientific analysis poses a risk for institutions that has nothing to do with physical damage to the object. It is not surprising that these sorts of issues can on occasion bring the interests of scholars into conflict with the interests of owners and curators of the objects of scholarly inquiry. I do not see an easy solution to this impasse, but I think there is value in simply making the conflict of interests explicit.

And the topic of conflicts of interest brings us to the other leit-motif of this book: the commercial trade in ancient artifacts. The antiquities market has cast a shadow over this whole study, obscuring the archaeological knowledge that we most wish to access. The market is the enemy of archaeologists, but at the same time, it is often the source of their objects of study. But the loss of contextual knowledge is not the only deleterious effect of the market. What I have been talking about when I have spoken of a collection's "acquisition" of a manuscript is usually the movement of that artifact out of Egypt to a collection in a more affluent nation. A host of cultural heritage issues are at stake. What is to be done about this?

Again, there are no easy answers, but I would be happy to see the following two things happen. First of all, scholars need to take a more serious interest in "museum archaeology," that is, understanding the histories of collections: When and how were materials acquired? Who was involved? If the materials were purchased, who were the dealers? The more answers we have to these kinds of questions, the greater the chances of reassembling dispersed finds and more clearly seeing exactly how artifacts ended up in their current locations.[5] For this to happen, collections need to be open to having scholars work through their records to try to sort out these problems. My second recommendation is also directed to curators of manuscripts: Digitize. Many collections have already made digital images of their manuscripts widely available, and the results can be spectacular.[6] Nothing can replace autopsy inspection of a manuscript— tilting a glass-framed papyrus just so or subtly shifting a raking light across a parchment codex to catch an unexpected detail. But ideally, anyone with an Internet connection should be able to access high-resolution images of manuscripts. Spending these past few years intensively studying early Christian books has made me keenly aware that such study is a group effort. The increased availability of images of manuscripts will help to grow an international team of people who can make progress in a field where secure knowledge is a hard-won battle.

Appendix
Christian Books from Oxyrhynchus

THIS LIST WAS CURRENT as of the end of 2016. The books below are grouped by genre. Within each genre, the pieces are grouped in descending order by number of extant copies (which are then arranged by date, according to the Leuven Database), and unidentified works are listed last. The headings are fairly self-explanatory. In the "Publication" column, I generally list only one identification number; if other parts of the manuscript have been published elsewhere (indicated by "etc."), the details can be found at the relevant LDAB entry. In the "Format" column, "Roll (r)" indicates a reused roll.

Gospels (42 items)

Publication	LDAB No.	Text	Language	Material	Format	LDAB Date (Century)
P.Oxy. 50.3523	2775	John	Greek	Papyrus	Codex	2nd
P.Oxy. 2.208 etc.	2780	John	Greek	Papyrus	Codex	3rd
P.Oxy. 10.1228	2779	John	Greek	Papyrus	Roll	3rd
P.Oxy. 15.1780	2788	John	Greek	Papyrus	Codex	3rd
P.Oxy. 65.4445	2781	John	Greek	Papyrus	Codex	3rd
P.Oxy. 65.4446	2782	John	Greek	Papyrus	Codex	3rd
P.Oxy. 65.4447	2783	John	Greek	Papyrus	Codex	3rd
P.Oxy. 65.4448	2784	John	Greek	Papyrus	Codex	3rd
P.Oxy. 71.4803	112358	John	Greek	Papyrus	Codex	3rd
P.Oxy. 71.4805	112360	John	Greek	Papyrus	Codex	3rd
P.Oxy. 13.1596	2785	John	Greek	Papyrus	Codex	3rd to 4th
P.Oxy. 6.847	2787	John	Greek	Parchment	Codex	4th
P.Oxy. 71.4804	112359	John	Greek	Papyrus	Codex	4th
P.Oxy. 71.4806	112361	John	Greek	Papyrus	Codex	4th to 5th
P.Oxy. 64.4404	2935	Matthew	Greek	Papyrus	Codex	2nd
P.Oxy. 64.4403	2938	Matthew	Greek	Papyrus	Codex	3rd
P.Oxy. 34.2683 etc.	2937	Matthew	Greek	Papyrus	Codex	3rd
P.Oxy. 1.2	2940	Matthew	Greek	Papyrus	Codex	3rd
P.Oxy. 64.4401	2939	Matthew	Greek	Papyrus	Codex	3rd
P.Oxy. 24.2384	2942	Matthew	Greek	Papyrus	Codex	4th
P.Oxy. 64.4402	2943	Matthew	Greek	Papyrus	Codex	4th
P.Oxy. 24.2385	2947	Matthew	Greek	Papyrus	Codex	4th

P.Oxy. 66.4494	7156	Matthew	Greek	Papyrus	Codex	4th
P.Oxy. 9.1170	2951	Matthew	Greek	Papyrus	Codex	5th
P.Oxy. 10.1227	2949	Matthew	Greek	Papyrus	Codex	5th
PSI 1.1	2956	Matthew	Greek	Papyrus	Codex	5th
P.Oxy. 64.4406	2957	Matthew	Greek	Papyrus	Codex	5th to 6th
P.Oxy. 9.1169	2958	Matthew	Greek	Parchment	Codex	5th to 6th
P.Oxy. 3.401	2955	Matthew	Greek	Parchment	Codex	5th to 6th
P.Oxy. 1.1	4028	Gospel According to Thomas	Greek	Papyrus	Codex	2nd to 3rd
P.Oxy. 4.655	4029	Gospel According to Thomas	Greek	Papyrus	Roll	3rd
P.Oxy. 4.654	4030	Gospel According to Thomas	Greek	Papyrus	Roll (r)	3rd
P.Oxy. 24.2383	2852	Luke	Greek	Papyrus	Codex	3rd
P.Oxy. 66.4495	7157	Luke	Greek	Papyrus	Codex	3rd
P.Oxy. 1.3	2913	Mark	Greek	Parchment	Codex	5th to 6th
P.Oxy. 50.3525	5406	Gospel According to Mary	Greek	Papyrus	Roll	3rd
P.Oxy. 76.5072	140276	Unknown gospel	Greek	Papyrus	Codex	2nd to 3rd
P.Oxy. 2.210	5222	Unknown gospel	Greek	Papyrus	Codex	3rd
P.Oxy. 41.2949	5111	Unknown gospel	Greek	Papyrus	Roll (?)	3rd
P.Oxy. 10.1224	5727	Unknown gospel	Greek	Papyrus	Codex	4th
P.Oxy. 60.4009	4872	Unknown gospel	Greek	Papyrus	Codex	4th
P.Oxy. 5.840	5831	Unknown gospel	Greek	Parchment	Codex	4th to 5th

Hebrew scriptures (Septuagint and Old Latin; 26 items)

P.Oxy. 15.1779	3106	Psalms	Greek	Papyrus	Codex	3rd
P.Oxy. 10.1226	3139	Psalms	Greek	Papyrus	Codex	3rd to 4th
P.Oxy. 11.1352	3156	Psalms	Greek	Parchment	Codex	4th
P.Oxy. 6.845	3199	Psalms	Greek	Papyrus	Codex	4th to 5th

Publication	LDAB No.	Text	Language	Material	Format	LDAB Date (Century)
P.Oxy. 73.4931	117811	Psalms	Greek	Papyrus	Codex	5th
P.Oxy. 75.5021	128923	Psalms	Greek	Papyrus	Codex	5th
P.Oxy. 78.5127	171874	Psalms (amulet?)	Greek	Parchment	Codex	5th
P.Oxy. 4.656	3094	Genesis	Greek	Papyrus	Codex	2nd to 3rd
P.Oxy. 9.1166	3114	Genesis	Greek	Papyrus	Roll	3rd
P.Oxy. 7.1007	3113	Genesis	Greek	Parchment	Codex	3rd
P.Oxy. 9.1167	3186	Genesis	Greek	Papyrus	Codex	4th
P.Oxy. 8.1073	3203	Genesis	Latin	Parchment	Codex	5th
P.Oxy. 8.1074	3096	Exodus	Greek	Papyrus	Codex	3rd
P.Oxy. 65.4442	3118	Exodus	Greek	Papyrus	Codex	3rd
P.Oxy. 11.1351	3133	Leviticus	Greek	Parchment	Codex	3rd
P.Oxy. 10.1225	3185	Leviticus	Greek	Papyrus	Roll	4th
PSI 2.127	3230	Judith	Greek	Papyrus	Codex	3rd to 4th
P.Oxy. 75.5020	128922	Judith	Greek	Papyrus	Codex	4th
P.Oxy. 13.1594	3131	Tobit	Greek	Parchment	Codex	3rd to 4th
P.Oxy. 8.1076	3321	Tobit	Greek	Parchment	Codex	6th
P.Oxy. 6.846	3339	Amos	Greek	Papyrus	Codex	6th
P.Oxy. 17.2066	3286	Ecclesiastes	Greek	Papyrus	Codex	5th to 6th
P.Oxy. 9.1168	3184	Joshua	Greek	Parchment	Codex	4th
PSI 10.1163	3163	Job	Greek	Papyrus	Codex	4th
P.Oxy. 13.1595	3313	Sirach	Greek	Papyrus	Codex	6th
P.Oxy. 65.4444	3179	Wisdom of Solomon	Greek	Parchment	Codex	4th

Letters (23 items)

P.Oxy. 66.4497	7159	Romans	Greek	Papyrus	Codex	3rd
P.Oxy. 11.1355	3010	Romans	Greek	Papyrus	Codex	3rd
JEA 13 (1927)	107980	Romans	Coptic	Parchment	Codex	4th to 5th
PSI 1.4	3031	Romans	Greek	Parchment	Codex	5th
P.Oxy. 11.1354	3055	Romans	Greek	Papyrus	Codex	6th to 7th
P.Oxy. 9.1171	2768	James	Greek	Papyrus	Codex	3rd
P.Oxy. 10.1229	2770	James	Greek	Papyrus	Codex	3rd
P.Oxy. 65.4449	2769	James	Greek	Papyrus	Codex	3rd
PSI 1.5	2771	James	Greek	Parchment	Codex	4th to 5th
P.Oxy. 66.4498	7160	Hebrews	Greek	Papyrus	Codex (?)	3rd
P.Oxy. 4.657 etc.	3018	Hebrews	Greek	Papyrus	Roll (r)	3rd to 4th
P.Oxy. 8.1078	3019	Hebrews	Greek	Papyrus	Codex	4th
P.Oxy. 18.2157	3026	Galatians	Greek	Papyrus	Codex	4th to 5th
PSI 2.118 (now lost)	3034	Galatians	Greek	Parchment	Codex	5th
PSI 3.251	3032	Galatians	Greek	Parchment	Codex	5th
P.Oxy. 73.4934	117814	1 Peter	Greek	Papyrus	Codex	3rd to 4th
P.Oxy. 11.1353	3067	1 Peter	Greek	Parchment	Codex	4th
P.Oxy. 7.1008-1009	3016	1 Corinthians and Philippians	Greek	Papyrus	Codex	4th
P.Oxy. 72.4844	113259	1 Corinthians	Greek	Papyrus	Codex	4th
P.Oxy. 72.4845	113260	2 Corinthians	Greek	Papyrus	Codex	6th
P.Oxy. 3.402	2789	1 John	Greek	Papyrus	Codex	3rd to 4th
P.Oxy. 13.1598	3017	1-2 Thessalonians	Greek	Papyrus	Codex	2nd to 3rd
P.Oxy. 34.2684	2846	Letter of Jude	Greek	Papyrus	Codex	4th to 5th

Patristic sermons/expositions (23 items)

Publication	LDAB No.	Text	Language	Material	Format	LDAB Date (Century)
P.Oxy. 3.405	2459	Irenaeus	Greek	Papyrus	Roll	2nd to 3rd
P.Oxy. 3.412	2550	Julius Africanus	Greek	Papyrus	Roll	3rd
P.Oxy. 13.1600	2609	Melito, *On Passover*	Greek	Papyrus	Codex	4th to 5th
P.Oxy. 15.1778	338	Aristides, *Apology*	Greek	Papyrus	Codex	4th
P.Oxy. 78.5129	171876	Justin, *First Apology*	Greek	Parchment	Codex	4th
PSI 15.1453	457	Basil of Seleucia	Greek	Papyrus	Roll	6th to 7th
P.Oxy. 13.1603	3858	Ps.-Chrysostom	Greek	Papyrus	Roll	5th to 6th
P.Oxy. 31.2531	4017	Theophilus of Alexandria	Greek	Papyrus	Codex	6th
P.Oxy. 76.5074	140278	Cyril of Alexandria	Greek	Papyrus	Roll (r)	7th to 8th
P.Oxy. 17.2070	5404	Jewish–Christian dialogue	Greek	Papyrus	Roll	3rd
P.Oxy. 1.4	5506	Unknown, homily?	Greek	Papyrus	Roll	3rd
P.Oxy. 3.406	3500	Unknown, Origen?	Greek	Papyrus	Codex	3rd
P.Oxy. 17.2072	5405	Unknown, apology?	Greek	Papyrus	Codex	3rd
P.Oxy. 36.2745	3503	Unknown onomasticon	Greek	Papyrus	Roll (r)	3rd
P.Oxy. 77.5106	140275	Unknown hexameters	Greek	Papyrus	Roll	3rd
P.Oxy. 1.5	2607	Unknown, Melito?	Greek	Papyrus	Codex	3rd to 4th
JEA 2 (1915)	113511	Unknown, homily?	Syriac	Papyrus	Roll?	3rd to 4th
Manichaean texts	113512	Unknown, homily?	Syriac	Papyrus	Roll (r)	3rd to 4th
P.Oxy. 17.2068	5714	Unknown, liturgical?	Greek	Papyrus	Roll (r)	4th
P.Oxy. 13.1601	3506	Unknown, homily?	Greek	Papyrus	Codex	4th to 5th
P.Oxy. 15.1785	5998	Unknown, homily?	Greek	Papyrus	Codex?	5th
P.Oxy. 17.2074	2610	Unknown, Melito?	Greek	Papyrus	Codex	5th
P.Oxy. 17.2071	6328	Unknown, sermon?	Greek	Papyrus	Codex	6th

Revelatory literature (19 items)

P.Oxy. 50.3528	1095	Shepherd of Hermas	Greek	Papyrus	Codex	2nd to 3rd
P.Oxy. 69.4706	10575	Shepherd of Hermas	Greek	Papyrus	Roll	2nd to 3rd
P.Oxy. 50.3527	1098	Shepherd of Hermas	Greek	Papyrus	Codex	3rd
P.Oxy. 69.4705	10574	Shepherd of Hermas	Greek	Papyrus	Roll	3rd
P.Oxy. 69.4707	10576	Shepherd of Hermas	Greek	Papyrus	Codex	3rd
P.Oxy. 15.1828	1099	Shepherd of Hermas	Greek	Parchment	Codex	3rd
P.Oxy. 3.404	1101	Shepherd of Hermas	Greek	Papyrus	Codex	3rd to 4th
P.Oxy. 13.1599	1104	Shepherd of Hermas	Greek	Papyrus	Codex	4th
P.Oxy. 9.1172 etc.	1105	Shepherd of Hermas	Greek	Papyrus	Codex	4th
P.Oxy. 15.1783	1103	Shepherd of Hermas	Greek	Parchment	Codex	4th
P.Oxy. 10.1230	2791	Revelation	Greek	Papyrus	Codex	4th
P.Oxy. 66.4499	7161	Revelation	Greek	Papyrus	Codex	3rd to 4th
P.Oxy. 66.4500	7162	Revelation	Greek	Parchment	Codex	3rd
P.Oxy. 8.1080	2793	Revelation	Greek	Parchment	Codex	4th
P.Oxy. 6.848	2799	Revelation	Greek	Parchment	Codex	5th to 6th
P.Oxy. 8.1081	5620	Sophia of Jesus Christ	Greek	Papyrus	Codex	4th
P.Oxy. 17.2069	1087	Enoch	Greek	Papyrus	Codex	4th
P.Oxy. 3.403	3471	Revelation of Baruch	Greek	Papyrus	Codex	4th to 5th
P.Oxy. 7.1010	3181	6 Ezra	Greek	Parchment	Codex	4th

Acts and legends (8 items)

P.Oxy. 13.1597	2853	Acts of the Apostles	Greek	Papyrus	Codex	3rd
PSI 10.1165	2854	Acts of the Apostles	Greek	Papyrus	Codex	4th
P.Oxy. 66.4496	7158	Acts of the Apostles	Greek	Papyrus	Codex	5th
P.Oxy. 6.850	5724	Acts of John	Greek	Papyrus	Codex	4th
P.Oxy. 6.849	5677	Acts of Peter	Greek	Parchment	Codex	4th

Publication	LDAB No.	Text	Language	Material	Format	LDAB Date (Century)
P.Oxy. 13.1602	5800	Acts of Paul	Greek	Parchment	Codex	5th
P.Oxy. 1.6	5942	Acts of Paul and Thecla	Greek	Parchment	Codex	5th
P.Oxy. 50.3524	2563	Nativity of Mary	Greek	Papyrus	Codex	6th
Martyrdoms (4 items)						
P.Oxy. 50.3529	5716	Martyrdom of Dioscorus	Greek	Papyrus	Roll	4th
P.Oxy. 6.851	6067	Martyrdom of Mamas	Greek	Papyrus	Codex	5th to 6th
PSI 1.26–27	5957	Martyrdom of Christine	Greek	Papyrus	Roll (opisthograph)	6th to 7th
P.Oxy. 70.4759	10692	Martyrdom of Pamoun	Greek	Papyrus	Codex	6th to 7th
Testimonia collections (2 items)						
P.Oxy. 78.5128	171875	Exodus, Susanna	Greek	Papyrus	Codex	3rd to 4th
P.Oxy. 73.4933	117813	Jeremiah, Amos, Psalms	Greek	Papyrus	Codex	4th to 5th
Mixed books (1 item)						
P.Oxy. 8.1075 + 1079	3477, 2786	Exodus and Revelation	Greek	Papyrus	Codex (?)	3rd
Church order (1 item)						
P.Oxy. 15.1782	5826	Didache	Greek	Parchment	Codex	4th to 5th
Church calendar (1 item)						
ZNW 37 (1938)	113877	Church calendar	Coptic	Parchment	Codex	5th to 6th
Hymn with musical notation (1 item)						
P.Oxy. 15.1786	5403	Musical hymn	Greek	Papyrus	Roll (r)	3rd
Philo of Alexandria (1 item)						
P.Oxy. 9.1173 etc.	3540	Philo of Alexandria	Greek	Papyrus	Codex	3rd

Notes

Prologue

1. For the context of Freer's collecting practices and his interest in Egypt, see Gunter, *A Collector's Journey*. On Freer's purchase of the manuscripts, see the detailed investigation of Clarke, "Paleography and Philanthropy."

2. On December 19, 1906, Freer wrote to his friend Frank J. Hecker (1846–1927), "Since beginning this letter I have closed a purchase of some ancient manuscripts of exceeding interest . . . I fully intended to resist all temptations but the manuscripts carried me completely off my feet and after two days of examination assisted by two Greek scholars I fell by the wayside." All references to the correspondence and writings of Freer are drawn from the Charles Lang Freer Papers, Freer Gallery of Art and Arthur M. Sackler Gallery Archives, Smithsonian Institution, Washington, D.C. I am grateful to David Hogge for assistance in navigating the archive.

3. Charles Lang Freer Diary, December 19, 1906. Freer sent the manuscripts back to the United States in January 1907. As he was preparing to leave Egypt for Ceylon, Freer wrote that he would be shipping four cases back to Detroit, one of which included "manuscripts in Greek writing—5 volumes or parts and a few small samples of early Greek writing on *papyrus*" (letter of Charles Lang Freer to J. M. Kennedy, January 18, 1907). I do not know the fate of the papyrus mentioned in the letter.

4. See Sanders, "New Manuscripts," and Sanders, "Four Newly Discovered Biblical Manuscripts." The former is an abbreviated version of a lecture Sanders gave on December 30, 1907, at the annual meeting of the Archaeological Institute of America held in Chicago (summarized already in the *New York Times* of December 31, 1907). The latter emphasized the text-critical importance of the manuscripts.

5. These headlines are a sample of those collected in the notebooks of press clippings in the archives at the Freer Gallery. Most of the sources of the clippings are unidentified. In the case of Figure 0.1, I am reasonably certain that the source is the *Chicago Examiner*. Although I was unable to find a full copy of the January 5, 1908, issue (the Chicago Public Library, which seems to have the most complete holdings of the title, lacks this issue), a letter from Francis W. Kelsey to Freer dated January 6, 1908, begins as follows: "Dear Mr. Freer, I have just seen a copy of the Chicago Examiner of yesterday containing a full page statement in regard to the Greek manuscripts, with an illustration, which is, to say the least, amusing." No other press clipping matches this description.

6. See Sanders, *The Old Testament Manuscripts*, and Sanders (ed.), *Facsimile of the Washington Manuscript of Deuteronomy and Joshua*.

7. See Sanders, *The New Testament Manuscripts*, and Sanders (ed.), *Facsimile of the Washington Manuscript of the Four Gospels*.

8. See "New Verses Found in Gospel Papyri" and "Old Greek Bible Reveals Verses Lost for Centuries."

9. "Old Greek Bible Reveals Verses Lost for Centuries."

10. "Old Greek Bible Reveals Verses Lost for Centuries." The article of May 13 had stated that "the manuscript dates from either the fourth or the fifth century."

11. "Petrie Discusses Freer Gospel Ms."

12. Sanders, *The New Testament Manuscripts*, 139. The opinion of the British papyrologist Bernard P. Grenfell is also cited here in support of a fourth-century date (134).

13. See Sanders, *The New Testament Manuscripts*, 3–4.

14. See Sanders, *Facsimile of the Washington Manuscript of the Four Gospels*, v: "The main part of the manuscript was written in the Fourth Century, in Egypt." For a fifth-century date, see Turner, *The Typology of the Early Codex*, 28; for the possibility of a sixth-century date, see Schmid, "Reassessing the Palaeography."

15. See Schmid, "Reassessing the Palaeography."

16. See Turner, *The Typology of the Early Codex*, 26.

17. For the fifth-century date, see Harry Y. Gamble's description of the Freer Psalms codex in Brown (ed.), *In the Beginning*, 260–261.

18. Ali Arabi (ca. 1840–1932) was a well-known antiquities dealer. Europeans in search of ancient manuscripts regularly patronized his shop in Giza. See Hagen and Ryholt, *The Antiquities Trade in Egypt*, 192–195.

19. Sanders, "New Manuscripts," 49 and 55.

20. See Schmidt, "Die neuen griechischen Bibelhandschriften," 359–360: "Bei meinem letzten Aufenthalte in Ägypten konnte ich die wahre Herkunft dieser Schätze mit Sicherheit feststellen" (On my last trip to Egypt I was able to ascertain with certainty the true origin of these treasures). For the Nitrian hypothesis, see Goodspeed, "The Detroit Manuscripts."

21. Sanders, "Age and Ancient Home," 141.

22. The quotation is drawn from three pages of undated handwritten notes kept with the Ali Arabi correspondence in the Charles Lang Freer Papers at the Freer Archive. For a summary of the full memorandum, see Clarke, "Paleography and Philanthropy," 53–55.

23. See the correspondence cited in Clarke, "Paleography and Philanthropy," 53–57.

24. Freer did acquire further Greek and Coptic manuscripts, although it is generally agreed that his later acquisitions were not part of the same find as the 1906 purchase. The Greek papyrus manuscript of the Minor Prophets that Freer bought in 1916 is sometimes grouped together with the parchment books he acquired in 1906, but this papyrus book came through a different dealer, Maurice Nahman (1868–1948), and a different intermediary, Dr. David Askren (1875–1939), an American Presbyterian missionary doctor, two names that we will encounter repeatedly in this book.

25. Clarke, "Paleography and Philanthropy," 57–58.

26. See the overview of excavations in Capasso and Davoli (eds.), *Soknopaiou Nesos Project I*, 11–18.

27. On June 24, 1913, Sanders wrote to Freer: "I was also much disappointed at not finding definite proofs of Christian occupation of Dime, but I had to confess that much was the case. . . . I still hold my original opinion: 'Christian occupation of Dime very doubtful and in any case temporary'" (Charles Lang Freer Papers). For the location of the find at Theadelphia by Nahman, see the letter of Kelsey to Charles D. Walcott of October 6, 1920 (Charles Lang Freer Papers).

28. See Boak (ed.), *Soknopaiou Nesos*, v.

29. For the Coptic papyrus and ostraca, see Capasso and Davoli (eds.), *Soknopaiou Nesos Project I*, 231–247. For the ostracon with the Christian symbol (a staurogram) and the hypothesis of a monastic hermitage in the temple precinct, see Capasso, "Un *ostrakon* con staurogramma."

30. It should be noted that the current excavators of the site increasingly favor the possibility that the Freer books were in fact found at Soknopaiou Nesos. See Capasso and Davoli, "Soknopaiou Nesos Project," 76–77. The excavators' recent public presentations suggest that evidence for later Christian occupation at the site (specifically at the area identified by Ali as "the corner," that is, inside the walls of the main temple) is growing. We eagerly await the excavators' future publications.

31. There even exists a somewhat different version of the story of the purchase itself. The "canonical" account (given in Gunter, *A Collector's Journey*, 93, and Clarke, "Paleography and Philanthropy") is drawn from Freer's diaries and correspondence. The other version appeared in the *Times* of London: "Particulars as to the recent discovery of some new authentic manuscripts of the Bible are given in to-day's *Débats* by

M. Gaston Migeon, who was fortunate enough last year to discover, in company with Mr. Charles Freer, of Detroit, Michigan, among the odds and ends amassed by the Gizeh merchants certain manuscripts unearthed among the ruins of Akmin, in Upper Egypt" ("Discovery of Biblical Manuscripts"). Freer's accounts do not mention the presence of anyone aside from his interpreter. Freer's friend Gaston Migeon (1861–1930), who was then a conservator at the Louvre, did say that he was with Freer on the day of the purchase (although the placement of the purchase in January is unlikely): "Au mois de janvier 1907, M. Charles Freer, le grand industriel de Détroit (Michigan) (Etats-Unis), me rejoignait au Caire, et nous eûmes du plaisir à visiter ensemble les marchands. Il en est un bien curieux, qui occupe à Ghizeh plusieurs maisons bondées des choses les plus hétéroclites amoncelées sous une épaisse poussière. Après d'interminables palabres et de mystérieuses négociations, M. Ch. Freer parvint à se rendre possesseur de plusieurs manuscrits découverts dans les ruines d'Akmin, dans la Haute-Egypte" (Migeon, "Nouveaux manuscrits authentiques de la Bible"). For Freer's plans to meet Migeon in Cairo, see Gunter, *A Collector's Journey*, 50–51.

32. On the text of Freer's gospel manuscript, see, for example, Hurtado, *Text-Critical Methodology and the Pre-Caesarean Text*.

33. See Gunter, "Charles Lang Freer's Biblical Manuscripts," 9: "Since the opening of the Freer Gallery of Art in 1923, the manuscripts have seldom been exhibited, and several have never been displayed."

34. See the editor's introduction to Hurtado (ed.), *The Freer Biblical Manuscripts*, 1–2.

35. See, for example, Roberts, "The Codex," expanded and revised by Roberts and Skeat as *The Birth of the Codex*.

36. See Larsen, "Accidental Publication, Unfinished Texts"; Epp, "The Multivalence of the Term 'Original Text'"; and Parker, *The Living Text of the Gospels*.

37. The two most widely used texts in English are Aland and Aland, *The Text of the New Testament*, along with Metzger and Ehrman, *The Text of the New Testament*.

38. The most celebrated example is Royse, *Scribal Habits*.

39. There are also photographic albums that present pages of manuscripts with some basic details, but again, these types of books are usually focused on the handwriting of the manuscripts, and details about the archaeological context and construction of the manuscripts are not a priority. The most widely known album of early Christian manuscripts is Metzger, *Manuscripts of the Greek Bible*. Two more recent books containing a number of photographs of early Christian manuscripts unfortunately also contain a good deal of misinformation and cannot be recommended: Comfort and Barrett, *The Text of the Earliest New Testament Greek Manuscripts*, and Comfort, *Encountering the Manuscripts*. For examples of some

of the problems in these books, see Malik, *P.Beatty III* (𝔓⁴⁷), 42–44, and Nongbri, "Grenfell and Hunt," 152–153.

40. For contrasting views of the level of "professionalism" of early Christian copyists, see Haines-Eitzen, *Guardians of Letters*, and Mugridge, *Copying Early Christian Texts.* On issues of canonization, see Wallraff, *Kodex und Kanon.*

41. Codex Vaticanus and Codex Sinaiticus, the famous parchment manuscripts, have been especially well served in recent years. See Andrist (ed.), *Le manuscrit B de la Bible*, and McKendrick et al. (eds.), *Codex Sinaiticus.*

42. Hurtado appropriately cites as an important predecessor to his own work Roberts, *Manuscript, Society and Belief,* which was a landmark study published in 1979. The evidence upon which Roberts built his arguments is now somewhat dated.

43. Hurtado, *The Earliest Christian Artifacts*, 17.

44. Bagnall, *Early Christian Books in Egypt*, 1.

45. Hurtado, *The Earliest Christian Artifacts*, 16, and Bagnall, *Early Christian Books in Egypt*, 1–50.

46. Bagnall, *Early Christian Books in Egypt*, 2.

47. Chapter 7 of this book explores an example of this phenomenon in great detail, but a shorter example can be given here. Although the Gospel According to John is not clearly quoted by Christian authors until near the end of the second century, it is common for biblical scholars to argue that we can be *certain* that this gospel was written much earlier because of "archaeological discoveries" of ancient manuscripts. For example, in a popular introductory textbook, a well-respected New Testament scholar writes that "the archaeological discovery of Greek manuscripts of John's Gospel in Egypt dating from the late . . . or even early second century . . . makes a late second-century date of composition impossible" (Johnson, *The Writings of the New Testament*, 466). Yet, the three manuscripts that Johnson cites to support this claim were all purchased on the antiquities market. They have no certain archaeological context, and the dates assigned to them are based only on handwriting, which cannot realistically provide such a narrow window of time. See the discussion in Chapter 2.

48. James M. Robinson, for instance, relied heavily on the reports of locals from the areas where the Nag Hammadi codices and the Bodmer Papyri were allegedly found. When some colleagues challenged the veracity of these reports, Robinson claimed that "such scholars [look] down condescendingly on the Egyptians as natives one could never trust" (Robinson, "Theological Autobiography," 138).

49. Robinson, for example, is said to have described his own research among Egyptian locals in the 1970s as follows: "Whenever I went down, I would bring the villagers a bottle of whiskey and a ten-pound note. That was big money at the time. That was my chore in tracking it down. I am not

a field archaeologist. I went from rumor to rumor, village to village" (quoted in Krosney, *The Lost Gospel*, 132).

50. See Scott, *Decoding Subaltern Politics*.

51. Goldhill, *The Buried Life of Things*, 193 and 195. On inanimate objects as agents, see, for example, Latour, *Reassembling the Social*. After a detailed and subtle discussion of actor-network theory and various other posthumanisms, Theodore R. Schatzki sensibly concludes as follows: "Objects lack the capacity to institute meaning. . . . [T]he enabling and constraining effects of objects and arrangements on activities are relative to actors' ends, projects, hopes, fears, and so on. Objects, if you will, make a contribution, but the nature of that contribution depends on us" (Schatzki, *The Site of the Social*, 105–122, quotation at 117).

52. The list of New Testament manuscripts is maintained by the Institut für neutestamentliche Textforschung (INTF). The most up-to-date version can be found online at http://ntvmr.uni-muenster.de/liste. The INTF now also uses a completely numeric system of identification for the papyri (as it long has for other classes of manuscripts), such that, for example, P.Bodmer II, a Greek codex of the Gospel According to John (LDAB 2777), is assigned the number 10066, in addition to the traditional designation, 𝔓66.

53. This observation has been made before. See, for instance, Aland and Aland, *The Text of the New Testament*, 84: "The term 'papyrus' has since [the middle of the twentieth century] held an almost magical charm, not only for the general public but for New Testament scholars as well, though with no real justification. Papyrus is merely a particular variety of writing material among others." I agree with this sentiment entirely, but the Alands themselves, at times, seem to fall prey to the seduction of the papyri. After noting the importance of one particular manuscript that happens to have been copied on papyrus, they advise that "these 'great' papyri should be introduced to students from the start because they are just as important, and in many ways more important, than the great uncial manuscripts of the New Testament" (*The Text of the New Testament*, 57–58).

54. See further the discussion in Kraus, "Pergament oder Papyrus?," translated into English with updated reflections in Kraus, *Ad Fontes*, 13–24.

55. See the list of known papyri in Gregory, *Die griechischen Handschriften*, 45–47, which provides the earlier designations of several of the fourteen items.

56. Gregory, *Die griechischen Handschriften*, 15–16. For its place in the history of scholarship, see Aland and Aland, *The Text of the New Testament*, 73–75.

57. Kenyon, *Handbook to the Textual Criticism of the New Testament*, 36–38.

58. Writing in the late second or early third century, the Christian scholar Origen refers to the whole of Christian scriptures as "the *so-called* 'Old

Testament' and *that which is called* the 'New Testament'" (*De principiis* 4.1.1). For the text, see Görgemanns and Karpp, *Origenes,* 668: *tēs te legomenēs palaias diathēkēs kai tēs kaloumenēs kainēs*). See further Kinzig, "*Kainē diathēkē,*" who argues that Marcion of Sinope may have coined the term in the middle of the second century.

59. See Nongbri, "The Construction of P.Bodmer VIII."
60. On this point, see the meditations of Clivaz, "The New Testament at the Time of the Egyptian Papyri."
61. I am happy to report that similar artifact-centered approaches are being pursued in regard to Christian books in Syriac and other languages as well. See the expansive (and open access) online resource edited by Alessandro Bausi, *Comparative Oriental Manuscript Studies.*

Chapter One. The Early Christian Book

1. I have compiled the account in this chapter with the help of several classic treatments. The fundamental study of early codicology is Turner, *The Typology of the Early Codex.* Still useful, though now dated, is the nicely illustrated account of the codex in the second edition of Schubart, *Das Buch,* 112–145. For an overview of ancient bookbinding, see Szirmai, *The Archaeology of Medieval Bookbinding.* For a sober account of the challenges and rewards of using fragmentary evidence for the reconstruction of binding techniques, see Miller, "Puzzle Me This." When synthetic discussions of early Christian manuscripts do treat the making of books, the focus is usually on preparing the page for the copying of text. The first chapter of Metzger and Ehrman, *The Text of the New Testament,* for example, is dedicated to "The Making of Ancient Books," but it has little to say about the actual construction of codices. A better summary can be found in Gamble, "Bible and Book."

2. These numbers were calculated by searching the "century" and "bookform" categories of the LDAB in October 2016. No account is taken of items classified as "sheets." The numbers were checked against the "graphing" feature of the LDAB, which produced different raw numbers (because of the algorithms used to divide the values of individual pieces assigned dates like "second century to fourth century") but nearly identical percentages. The percentages of codices I calculated are somewhat higher than those reported in 1983 by Roberts and Skeat, *The Birth of the Codex,* 36–37: In the first century, codices account for 1 percent, in the second century 2 percent, in the third century 17 percent, in the fourth century 70 percent, and in the fifth century 89 percent. We may account for these differences by noting both the updated data set of the LDAB and the fact that Roberts and Skeat restricted themselves to non-Christian books containing literature (that is, they left out books containing grammatical exercises, etc.).

3. See, for example, Haines-Eitzen, *Guardians of Letters*, 20: "My principal concern is with ancient scribes, particularly those who copied Christian literature during the second and third centuries"; and Hurtado, *The Earliest Christian Artifacts*, 16: "We limit our definition of 'earliest' Christian manuscripts to those that can be dated with some confidence to the second and third centuries." So also Blumell and Wayment (eds.), *Christian Oxyrhynchus*, treat material only "from the second through the fourth century" (8), but they do reflect on the difficulties of dating material (12).

4. I address this point in greater detail in my discussion in Chapter 6 of the Christian material from Oxyrhynchus.

5. The alleged "Christian preference for the codex," or the observation that Christians seemed to adopt the codex earlier than other Romans, was already noted with some frequency in the 1930s; see, for example, Kenyon, *Books and Readers*, 95–100. The hypothesis took on the status of fact after the publication of Roberts, "The Codex." It may be well to point out that our earliest *securely datable* Christian texts are rolls, P.Dura 10 (LDAB 3071), copied at some point before 256 CE, and P.Oxy. 3.412 (LDAB 2550), likely copied between 227 CE and 276 CE (both discussed at length in Chapter 2).

6. Theories on the origin and early spread of the codex abound, and they will not be dealt with here. Many treatments of this question seem to me to rely on a problematic data set that has assigned Christian codices dates that are generally too early. For sensible overviews of the many issues involved, see van Haelst, "Les origines du codex," and Bagnall, *Early Christian Books in Egypt*, 70–90.

7. See, for example, van Haelst, "Les origines du codex," 14: "L'origine matérielle, physique du codex est la tablette à écrire." Roberts and Skeat began their study of the codex with a similar assertion: "There has never been any doubt about the physical origin of the codex, namely that it was developed from the wooden writing tablet" (*The Birth of the Codex*, 1). But a prominent historian of bookbinding disagrees, commenting on the words of Roberts and Skeat: "The certainty with which the validity of this statement is taken for granted is in marked contrast with the lack of any substantial evidence or explanation as to the exact nature of this genetic relationship. Yet the assumption is being repeated again and again without any sign of intellectual discomfort about the weakness of the argument" (Szirmai, "Wooden Writing Tablets," 31).

8. The passages from Martial (in Books I and XIV of the epigrams) receive detailed treatment in Roberts and Skeat, *The Birth of the Codex*, 24–29. Another piece of early evidence might be provided by the letter of 2 Timothy, attributed to the apostle Paul, which at 4:13 mentions "the books, especially the parchment ones" (*ta biblia malista tas membranas*). The attribution of the letter to Paul, however, is challenged by some scholars

who would date the composition of the letter in the second century. See the classic study of Harrison, *The Problem of the Pastoral Epistles.*

9. See Nicholls, "Parchment Codices in a New Text of Galen."

10. The document, P.Petaus 30, was published as part of the archive of Petaus, but it is not entirely clear that the letter is actually part of the archive. On the archive in general, see the online Trismegistos summary at http://www.trismegistos.org/arch/archives/pdf/182.pdf. On P.Petaus 30 specifically, see Turner, *The Papyrologist at Work*, 37–38.

11. P.Oxy. 1.30, a leaf of a parchment codex containing a historical work in Latin (LDAB 4472), is sometimes assigned a date as early as the beginning of the second century or even the first century (on the basis of its handwriting). See Mallon, "Quel est le plus ancien exemple?"

12. For the production of papyrus, we have an ancient source in Pliny the Elder, as well as many modern treatments. The classic discussion is Lewis, *Papyrus in Classical Antiquity.* More recently, see the summary of evidence in Bülow-Jacobsen, "Writing Materials in the Ancient World."

13. For the papyrus roll, the fundamental studies are Johnson, *Bookrolls and Scribes in Oxyrhynchus*, and Turner, "The Terms Recto and Verso," at 27–53. On the dimensions of rolls, see Johnson, *Bookrolls and Scribes in Oxyrhynchus*, 86–87 and 141–152.

14. There are a few examples of narrow rolls that were rolled not horizontally from right to left, but rather vertically, from bottom to top, a form sometimes referred to in scholarship as a *rotulus*. This usage of the term *rotulus* seems to have originated with Turner, "The Terms Recto and Verso," 27–53.

15. Many writers use the term "opisthograph" to refer to a reused roll. This strikes me as imprecise. When Pliny the Younger wrote of his uncle's opisthograph commentaries (*Ep.* 3.5.17), he referred to works written continuously on the front and back of the rolls. This is not the same as the reuse of the back of an old roll sometime after the copying of the front of the roll. The two activities should be distinguished. On the phenomenon of reused rolls, see Lama, "Aspetti di tecnica libraria ad Ossirinco."

16. One result of this is that the rolls from which the sheets of a well-preserved codex were cut can often be reconstructed, which can be extremely helpful in settling questions about the construction of the codex. See, for example, Emmel, "A Question of Codicological Terminology."

17. The leaves of the Manichaean codices of Medinet Madi (LDAB 107976, 107977, 108111, 108112 + 108140, 108137, 108138, and 108139) seem to have been prepared from purpose-made sheets rather than sheets cut from a premade roll. This was, at any rate, the conclusion of Ibscher ("Der Kodex," 13).

18. For an in-depth description of the processes involved in producing

parchment, see Reed, *Ancient Skins.* For more recent developments in the understanding of the ancient production of parchment, see the essays in Rück (ed.), *Pergament.*

19.　　For the data on Codex Sinaiticus, see Parker, *Codex Sinaiticus,* 7–8 and 44. The four Greek Bibles that scholars presume were at one time "complete" (meaning that they are suspected to have contained some form of what are now commonly called the Old and New Testaments) are the Codex Sinaiticus, the Codex Vaticanus (LDAB 3479), the Codex Alexandrinus (LDAB 3481), and the Codex Syri Rescriptus (LDAB 2930). Did many other complete Bibles exist and simply fail to survive? It is hard to know, but one recent investigator is highly doubtful: "Nichts berechtigt zu der Annahme, dass die wenigen erhaltenen Exemplare nur die Spitze des Eisbergs sind und einst dutzende oder gar hunderte davon im Umlauf waren. Die allermeisten Bibelhandschriften enthielten und enthalten kleinere Schriftgruppen" (Wallraff, *Kodex und Kanon,* 38).

20.　　The most recent and thorough treatment of ancient Egyptian inks is Christiansen, "Manufacture of Black Ink." On parchment and metallic inks, see Reed, *Ancient Skins,* 156. In addition to writing surfaces and inks, other materials used in the bookblock would include the cord or thread used for binding, which could be composed of either vegetal matter (such as linen) or animal matter (finely twisted leather).

21.　　The terms "recto" and "verso" can be confusing, especially when it comes to papyrus codices, because early papyrologists accustomed to working with rolls sometimes used the term "recto" to refer to the face of the papyrus showing horizontal fibers, while at other times when working with codices they would use the term "recto" to refer to the side of the papyrus that preserved the right-hand page, regardless of its fiber orientation. Papyrologists tend now to refer to the faces of a piece of papyrus simply by noting on which side the fibers run horizontally (in the direction of writing, →) and on which side the fibers run vertically (perpendicular to the direction of writing, ↓), often using arrows to clarify the meaning. See the excellent discussion in Turner, "The Terms Recto and Verso."

22.　　Gregory, "The Quires in Greek Manuscripts," 29–30.

23.　　See the brief codicological summary in Galiano, "Notes on the Madrid Ezekiel Papyrus." For updates on this codex, see Torallas Tovar and Worp (eds.), *Greek Papyri from Montserrat (P.Monts.Roca IV),* 97–107.

24.　　See the discussions in Ibscher, "Der Kodex," and Robinson, "The Future of Papyrus Codicology."

25.　　For lists of different quire formations in early codices, see Turner, *The Typology of the Early Codex,* 61–64.

26.　　For the data on the Jeremiah codex (LDAB 108176), see Kasser, *Papyrus Bodmer XXII,* 7–8. For the construction of the British Library codex (Ms. Or. 7594, LDAB 107763), see Emmel, "A Question of Codicological Terminology."

27. See Robinson, "The Construction of the Nag Hammadi Codices," and the discussion in Szirmai, *The Archaeology of Medieval Bookbinding*, 7–14.

28. There is evidence for other methods of binding early Christian codices with multiple quires, such as the Chester Beatty codex of the gospels and Acts (LDAB 2980), a papyrus codex assigned to the third century that seems to be composed of single-sheet quires stab-bound by two separate cords of thread, an unparalleled technique for a papyrus codex containing literature, as far as I know (see the discussion of this codex in Chapter 4). The use of single-sheet quires and the positions of the holes for the binding threads bear more resemblance to what papyrologists usually call "notebooks," such as the leather notebook in the Berlin collection (P 7358 + 7359) and the "Harris Homer" (LDAB 2419). An example of a more typical multi-quire codex that seems to have been rebound using the stabbing method is the Bodmer composite codex (LDAB 2565). See the discussion in Nongbri, "The Construction of P.Bodmer VIII." In both the case of the Beatty codex of the gospels and Acts and the Bodmer composite codex, the physical evidence drives me to the conclusion that the stabbing method was probably used, but a multi-quire codex bound in such a way seems like it would have been very awkward to use.

29. My summary is drawn from the description in Szirmai, *The Archaeology of Medieval Bookbinding*, 16, supplemented by the studies in van Regemorter, *Binding Structures in the Middle Ages*. The statements of Turner about the binding of multi-quire codices are misleading (*The Typology of the Early Codex*, 55, followed by Hurtado, *The Earliest Christian Artifacts*, 84).

30. Several different stitching variations are described and schematically illustrated in Szirmai, *The Archaeology of Medieval Bookbinding*, 16–17.

31. Ibscher claimed that no multi-quire codex predated the fourth century, a position that few papyrologists would accept today (Ibscher, "Der Kodex," 11–12). Nevertheless, I think Ibscher was correct that the multi-quire codex was a conceptual outgrowth of the single-quire codex, and indeed the technology of the multi-quire codex presupposes the prior existence of single-quire codices. Turner's apparent doubts on this point (*The Typology of the Early Codex*, 99) do not seem warranted.

32. The fullest discussion of the structure of Nag Hammadi Codex I can be found in Robinson (ed.), *The Facsimile Edition of the Nag Hammadi Codices: Codex I*, xvii. I am grateful to Stephen Emmel for discussing the construction of this codex with me and clarifying several points with reference to a scale model of Codex I in his possession.

33. Emmel, "The Nag Hammadi Codices Editing Project," 20, note 28. See further Robinson, *The Facsimile Edition of the Nag Hammadi Codices: Introduction*, 39–40.

34. The "Harris Homer" (LDAB 2419), for example, has an average of about fifty lines per page. A complete codex of the *Iliad* with that layout would

occupy some 314 pages. Single-quire codices of approximately this size are known, such as a Coptic codex of Paul's letters (LDAB 107795), which probably had about 300 pages, but they are extremely rare.

35.   Papyrus that is finely made and smoothed can deceive even experts and can lead to errors in reconstructing the quires of a codex. For an example of two respected papyrologists differing on the fiber orientations of a papyrus leaf, see Turner, "The Terms Recto and Verso," 26–27. Turner faults Victor Martin for incorrectly identifying the fiber orientation of the last leaf of P.Bodmer XX (LDAB 220465), but after inspecting the leaf myself under high magnification, I can say with confidence that it was Turner himself who was deceived.

36.   For scribal preparations, see, for example, Turner, *Greek Manuscripts of the Ancient World*, 4–13.

37.   Turner (*The Typology of the Early Codex*, 74) cites two examples from among the Bodmer Papyri, P.Bodmer II (copyist progressively expanding writing to take up more space) and P.Bodmer XIV–XV (copyist progressively contracting writing to conserve space). On the question of the order of copying and binding in P.Bodmer II, see Nongbri, "The Limits of Palaeographic Dating."

38.   See Pietersma, *Two Manuscripts of the Greek Psalter*, 1.

39.   See Milne and Skeat, *Scribes and Correctors of the Codex Sinaiticus*, 72.

40.   One item sometimes cited as evidence of the copying of codices before binding is the Bodmer Menander codex (LDAB 2743), which was said to contain a bifolium with a line of writing (on page 14) that extended through the right margin, beyond the central fold, into the left margin of the conjoined folio (page 51) (Kasser and Austin, *Papyrus Bodmer XXV*, 11), but after close inspection of the folia in question, I am not completely convinced that the bifolium has broken cleanly along the line of the central fold. The codex thus does not provide unambiguous evidence for inscribing before binding.

41.   A collection of data (now in need of a systematic update) can be found in Paap, Nomina Sacra *in the Greek Papyri*.

42.   See Roberts, *Manuscript, Society and Belief*, 74–78.

43.   For a relatively recent effort at clarifying the origins of the phenomenon (with a good bibliography of earlier studies), see Hurtado, "The Origin of the *Nomina Sacra*."

44.   The encaustic (wax) painting on the wooden boards of the Freer codex is thought to have been applied in the seventh century. See the description in Brown (ed.), *In the Beginning*, 268–269. On wooden covers in general, see Sharpe, "The Earliest Bindings with Wooden Board Covers."

45.   See the discussion of leather covers in Szirmai, *The Archaeology of Medieval Bookbinding*, 28–30.

46.   See Kasser, *Papyrus Bodmer XVI*, 7–8.

47.   Just how long early codices stayed in use is a difficult question. One ex-

pert estimates that for medieval codices, "even the sturdiest binding when used extensively will inevitably wear out in 25 or 50 years" (Szirmai, *The Archaeology of Medieval Bookbinding*, 137). George W. Houston's recent study of the remains of (non-Christian) book collections in the Roman world claimed that the useful life of some papyrus rolls "clearly could last for half a millennium" (Houston, *Inside Roman Libraries*, 175). I have elsewhere given reasons to take this claim with a grain of salt; see Nongbri, Review of Houston, *Inside Roman Libraries*. In the end, Houston more cautiously concludes that "the evidence from our collections indicates that a usable lifetime of about 100 to 125 years was common and can reasonably be considered the norm; a small but significant number of manuscripts were still usable some 300 years after they were first created" (257). This seems more plausible, and it is not out of keeping with the data of the Bodmer Papyri that I take up in Chapter 5.

48. See further Nongbri, "The Limits of Palaeographic Dating," 31–32.

49. It is helpful to know that this method of repair was used on leaves of papyrus codices. Often the presence of thread with smaller fragments leads to the conclusion that the fragment must be an amulet. For example, the editor of P.Oxy. 64.4406 (LDAB 2957), a fragment of a papyrus leaf of the Gospel According to Matthew, identified it as an amulet only because of the presence of a thread woven through it. It seems much more likely to me that P.Oxy. 64.4406 is simply a fragment of a codex leaf that was repaired with thread.

50. A number of the Bodmer codices show evidence of rebinding. See the discussion in Chapter 5.

51. See the description in Kasser, *Papyrus Bodmer XIX*, 7–17.

52. Ibscher's work on the Manichaean codices from Medinet Madi is reasonably well documented. See Ibscher, "Die Handschriften." Ibscher wrote a section called "Die Handschrift" in each of the following publications: Polotsky, *Manichäische Homilien*, ix–xiv; Allberry, *A Manichaean Psalm-Book*, viii–xviii; and Polotsky and Böhlig, *Manichäische Handschriften der Staatlichen Museen Berlin: Kephalaia*, 1, v–xiv. Ibscher's work on the Beatty Biblical Papyri is not, to my knowledge, systematically reported, but some observations can be found in Ibscher, "Der Kodex." Finally, Ibscher's notes on the Berlin papyrus codex of Proverbs in Coptic (LDAB 107968) can be found in "Beschreibung der Handschrift."

53. For a detailed discussion of the reasoning for the reconstruction, see Quecke, *Das Johannesevangelium saïdisch*, 7–18. Furthermore, parts of the leather at the spine may be a modern reconstruction that took place before the book arrived in Barcelona. See Albarrán Martínez and Nodar Domínguez, "Escribir la palabra de Dios," 27–29.

54. For an in-depth treatment of conservation practices, see Fackelmann, *Restaurierung von Papyrus*. For a more recent overview with updated bibliography, see Frösén, "Conservation of Ancient Papyrus Materials."

55. See Kasser and Wurst (eds.), *The Gospel of Judas*, 11.

56. See, for example, Kordowska, "Conservation Work on Three Coptic Manuscripts."

57. The question of who manufactured early Christian books is difficult, not least because there are probably several quite different answers. Previous discussions have centered on whether the earliest manuscripts were produced in "scriptoria" under some sort of ecclesiastical authority or in "private" settings free from such authority. There is no compelling evidence either way because both the terms "scriptorium" and "private" are difficult to pin down in the Roman era. A more productive approach has recently been modeled by Chrysi Kotsifou, who has gathered the data of documentary papyri and ostraca that discuss the production of codices during the fourth to seventh centuries (Kotsifou, "Books and Book Production," and Kotsifou, "Bookbinding and Manuscript Illumination").

58. See now the thorough study of Mugridge, *Copying Early Christian Texts*.

Chapter Two. The Dating Game

1. A convenient online tool, the Date Converter for Ancient Egypt, can perform these conversions: http://aegyptologie.online-resourcen.de/Date _Converter/Roman_Emperors.

2. The "indiction" mentioned here refers to another, overlapping system of dating by cycles of fifteen years. See Bagnall and Worp, *Chronological Systems of Byzantine Egypt*.

3. Recently published Ethiopic and Coptic versions of the story of Phileas provide us with this precise date. For details, see Bausi, "The Coptic Version of the *Acta Phileae*."

4. Albert Pietersma, who edited a different papyrus copy of the *Apology of Phileas*, argued that the texts of both the papyrus copies were derived from an earlier version of the text, suggesting some distance between the date of the martyrdom and the production of the Bodmer copy. See Pietersma, *The Acts of Phileas Bishop of Thmuis*, 13–23.

5. For a helpful and cautious discussion, see Turner, "The Terms Recto and Verso."

6. This letter, P.Ryl. 2.236, is part of a large collection of documents known as the Heroninos Archive. It is one of several literary manuscripts in this archive reused for documentary purposes. For an overview of the archive, see Rathbone, *Economic Rationalism and Rural Society*.

7. For "about 150," see Turner, "Recto and Verso," at 106, note 3. For 220–225, see Cavallo, *Ricerche sulla maiuscola biblica*, 46. It is difficult to estimate how old a manuscript would be before it would be reused for another purpose. The article by Turner surveyed papyri that contained dated documents on both sides and presented examples in which the interval between first use and reuse ranged between less than a year and

almost one hundred years. For further discussion, see Turner, "Writing Material for Businessmen."

8. The editors of this papyrus, Grenfell and Hunt, thought that the orations were copied "probably not more than a generation later" than the report on the front of the papyrus (see the introduction to P.Oxy. 11.1366, p. 111).

9. On Julius Africanus and the *Kestoi*, see the introductory material in Wallraff et al. (eds.), *Iulius Africanus Cesti*, esp. xi–xxxii.

10. On the reconstruction of Nero's baths and their christening as *Thermae Alexandrinae*, see *Scriptores Historiae Augustae Alexander Severus* 25.3–8. For the date of 227 CE, see Jerome's Chronicle under the 251st Olympiad: *thermae alexandrianae romae aedificatae*; text from Helm (ed.), *Eusebius Werke siebenter Band*, 215.

11. The will was published separately as P.Oxy. 6.907. For further details on the will and other papyri probably associated with it, see Bagnall, "An Owner of Literary Papyri."

12. See Grenfell and Hunt's commentary on P.Oxy. 6.907, pp. 247–253.

13. The very fact that these manuscripts from Oxyrhynchus were discarded as trash does, however, raise interesting questions. See Luijendijk, "Sacred Scriptures as Trash."

14. For a good overview of these excavations, see Hopkins, *The Discovery of Dura-Europos*.

15. Kraeling, *A Greek Fragment of Tatian's Diatessaron*. The identification of this fragment as part of Tatian's *Diatessaron* is by no means certain. See Parker, Taylor, and Goodacre, "The Dura-Europos Gospel Harmony."

16. Kraeling claimed that the paleographic range for the fragment would extend back as far as the beginning of the third century (*A Greek Fragment of Tatian's Diatessaron*, 6). Parker, Taylor, and Goodacre argue that the manuscript was most likely copied in the late second century ("The Dura-Europos Gospel Harmony," 194–199).

17. Other examples would be the carbonized papyri at Herculaneum, which must have been copied before the eruption of Vesuvius in 79 CE. On these manuscripts, see Sider, *The Library of the Villa dei Papiri at Herculaneum*.

18. The most up-to-date and comprehensive general introductions to Greek paleography are in Italian: Crisci and Degni, *La scrittura greca dall'antichità*, and Cavallo, *La scrittura greca e latina dei papiri*. A condensed version of the material in Cavallo's book can be found in that author's "Greek and Latin Writing in the Papyri." Still very valuable is the introductory discussion in Turner, *Greek Manuscripts of the Ancient World*, 1–23, and the exemplary discussions of the Minor Prophets roll from Naḥal Ḥever by Peter J. Parsons in "The Scripts and Their Date."

19. See the cautious comments of Turner in *Greek Manuscripts of the Ancient World*, 20: "For the Roman period my conclusion . . . is that several 'styles' of writing were simultaneously in use. Contemporary with each

other, they cross-fertilize and hybridize easily. Study of these reciprocal influences is rewarding, provided only that the investigator is not trying to prove a derivation of one 'style' from another."

20. Paleography is sometimes characterized by its practitioners as a "science." Evaluating that claim, of course, depends on determining exactly what is meant by the word "science." See the discussion of Canart, "La paléographie est-elle un art ou une science?" What is more certain in terms of social history is that the modern academic discipline of paleography emerged out of the aesthetic interests and connoisseurship of elite circles in the eighteenth and nineteenth centuries. See Treharne, "The Good, the Bad, theUgly."

21. On this terminology, see Cavallo, *La scrittura greca e latina dei papiri*, 14, and Turner, *Greek Manuscripts of the Ancient World*, 1–4.

22. Roberts, *Greek Literary Hands*, xii.

23. For literary material copied in documentary hands, see, for example, the first twelve columns of British Library Pap. 131, a copy of Aristotle's *Constitution of Athens* (LDAB 391, images available online at British Library, Digitised Manuscripts, http://www.bl.uk/manuscripts/FullDisplay .aspx?ref=Papyrus_131). Good examples of documents written in a more formal literary hand are P.Herm. 4 and 5, which are discussed in Chapter 5.

24. I have in mind especially the "chancery script of Subatianus Aquila," which is easily recognizable and clearly a style to which some writers aspired. I am aware of the pitfalls of attributing "aims" and "aspirations" to copyists, but in this instance, we possess a well-executed writing exercise, P.Ryl. 1.59 (LDAB 718), in which a line of Demosthenes is copied out repeatedly in this hand. For details, see Turner, "A Writing Exercise from Oxyrhynchus," who observes "the fact that a budding chancery scribe should practise by copying a line of Demosthenes seems to confirm that principle of the absence in the ancient world of a sharp division between bookhands and documentary hands" (238).

25. Thus, for the period after the ninth century, when dated colophons become more common, paleographers of Greek literary manuscripts can offer more confident estimates of dates of undated manuscripts.

26. Even in the case of Greek cursives from the Roman era, however, some caution is necessary. Spending time perusing the many images of cursive Greek papyri on the PapPal website (http://www.pappal.info/), which are searchable by date, demonstrates the varieties of handwriting present at any given time and the duration of different types of writing. Turner has noted "how little truth there is in the facile, often repeated dictum that cursive, quickly written handwritings are easier to date than literary hands" ("Writing Material for Businessmen," 164).

27. Some paleographers distinguish among "stylistic classes" (writings shar-

ing a general framework, form, and structure of some but not all letters), "styles" (a seemingly tighter grouping than the stylistic class), and "canons" (well-defined styles with set rules that persist "over a period of several centuries"). For this schema, see Cavallo, "Fenomenologia 'libraria' della maiuscola greca." For an application of this schema to papyrus copies of New Testament texts, see Orsini and Clarysse, "Early New Testament Manuscripts and Their Dates," 448. For reasons that will be outlined later, I find this terminology somewhat vague and not very helpful. I therefore use more traditional vocabulary.

28. For Turner's classification, see *Greek Manuscripts of the Ancient World*, 20–23.

29. See Cavallo, "Osservazioni paleografiche," 209–220.

30. See Cavallo, *Ricerche sulla maiuscola biblica* and the more recent treatment of Orsini, *Manoscritti in maiuscola biblica*.

31. See Cavallo, "*Grammata Alexandrina*."

32. On the "severe style," see Funghi and Messeri Savorelli, "Sulla scrittura di P.Oxy. II 223 + P. Köln V 210." For the "sloping ovigal majuscule," see Cavallo, *La scrittura greca e latina dei papiri*, 111–116.

33. All of the samples pictured in Figure 2.10 have at one time or another been classified by Turner as Informal Round.

34. Incredibly, there has been a recent call to abandon this approach of focusing on securely datable comparanda and attempting instead "to expand the analytical perspective for using undated manuscripts" to establish dates for other undated manuscripts. For this blind-leading-the-blind approach to paleography, see Porter, "Recent Efforts to Reconstruct Early Christianity" (quotation at 79).

35. The classic example of this approach is Cavallo's *Ricerche sulla maiuscola biblica*, which should be read together with the review by Parsons, Review of Cavallo *Ricerche sulla maiuscola biblica*.

36. See the appreciative but incisive critique of Cavallo by Parsons, "The Palaeography of the Herculaneum Papyri."

37. It is interesting to note in this regard that in his classic study of the Biblical Majuscule, Cavallo on some occasions uses minute paleographic details as indicators of date and on other occasions uses those same details as indicators of geographic origin. See Cavallo, *Ricerche sulla maiuscola biblica*, 84–105.

38. For writing professionals with attested careers of thirty or so years, see Claytor, "Heron, Son of Satyros." For a possible instance of a copyist with a career of "not less than 49 years," see Revel Coles's introduction to P.Oxy. 67.4608, p. 215.

39. For example, Rafaella Cribiore has discussed the fourth-century archive of Aurelia Charite, a landowner in Hermopolis, among whose papers survive samples of both her own handwriting and that of her mother.

Cribiore draws attention to the similarities in the hands and suggests that Aurelia Charite was taught to write by her mother. See Cribiore, *Writing, Teachers, and Students*, 15.

40. We see this ability demonstrated in writing exercises, such as P.Oxy. 31.2604, which shows the same poetic line copied out in different writing styles that we generally associate with different dates. For other similar exercises, see P.Köln 4.175 and P.Oxy. 68.4669.

41. Sayce, "The Greek Papyri," 24. There had been earlier announcements of the papyrus in the press. A syndicated article mentioning the discovery of the papyrus appeared in the *New York Times* in 1888 ("Finds in the Fayum"). Interestingly, in this article, the papyrus is said to date from "about the second or third century." A search of Petrie's unpublished journals and diaries yielded no further details on the archaeological context of the discovery, though the overall profile of the Hawara cemetery indicates that a burial date later than the third century is most unlikely.

42. Thompson, *Handbook of Greek and Latin Palaeography*, 110.

43. Kenyon, *The Palaeography of Greek Papyri*, 101–103.

44. Few paleographers today would find P.Lond. 2.141 and the Hawara Homer comparable. See the discussion in Turner, *Greek Manuscripts of the Ancient World*, 3–4.

45. Thompson, *An Introduction to Greek and Latin Palaeography*, 141–147.

46. Kenyon had been more cautious in this regard in 1899: "Though it would be rash to express a definite judgement merely on the strength of a few facsimiles, it is worthwhile suggesting a doubt whether [the Ambrosian *Iliad*] may not be considerably older than the fifth century, the date to which it is now assigned" (*The Palaeography of Greek Papyri*, 121). By 1912, however, Maunde Thompson wrote of general agreement on a third-century date (*An Introduction to Greek and Latin Palaeography*, 198–199).

47. In the middle of the twentieth century, a fourth-century date for the Ambrosian *Iliad* was typical. See Calderini, *Ilias Ambrosiana*, xiii. For a review of scholarship and argument for a late-fifth or early-sixth-century date, see Cavallo, "Considerazioni di un paleografo," 70–85.

48. See, for example, the discussion of the Hawara Homer in Turner, *Greek Manuscripts of the Ancient World*, 38.

49. Cavallo, "Osservazioni paleografiche," 216: "L'elegante armonia delle forme, inoltre, riporta senz'altro ad un periodo di intensa vita culturale del mondo greco. Si sa che l'appassionato filellenismo di Adriano si fece promotore di quella «Renaissance des Hellenentums» che assicurò alla cultura greca il primo posto nell'impero; furono cosi creati i presupposti per quella fioritura della grecità che caratterizza il periodo degli Antonini. Poiché le manifestazioni grafiche sono intimamente legate ai fenomeni culturali in quanto, necessariamente, ne costituiscono un riflesso, è certo che alla rinascita dei valori della civiltà greca è dovuto, in

generale, l'impulso calligrafico che cosi largamente pervade la scrittura letteraria del II secolo. L'«onciale romana», nelle sue forme piu perfette, rappresenta forse l'espressione piu alta di questo impulso. . . . È quasi certo quindi che manoscritti quali il P. Oxy. XXIII 2354, il P. Oxy. I 20, l'Iliade di Hawara, il P. Tebt. II 265 e il P. Vindob. G. 19797 vadano attribuiti all'età degli Antonini. . . . Con lo spirare del II secolo, differenti fattori culturali e mutate tendenze tecniche e di gusto segnano il declino e quindi la scomparsa dell' «onciale romana». Per documentarne la fase di decadenza si possono citare il P. Ryl. III 514 (testo non identificato), nel quale l'angolo di scrittura risulta piu aperto e, soprattutto, il P. Oxy. XXXII 2624 (lirica corale). Quest'ultimo è di fondamentale interesse paleografico in quanto mostra l'impossibilità di tenere in vita un canone quando non corrisponda piu al clima culturale che lo ha espresso."

50. Cavallo, "Osservazioni paleografiche," 219, note 55.
51. Cavallo, "Considerazioni di un paleografo," 78: "La maiuscola rotonda era . . . una reviviscenza quindi voluta in un ambiente pagano e conservatore, ricercata per creare una continuità ideale con il libro della tradizione classica in una epoca in cui ne era ormai vicina la tragica scomparsa. L'«Iliade Ambrosiana» mostra che la funzione assegnata, tra i secoli V e VI, alla maiuscola rotonda fu dunque quella di far rivivere, al livello grafico, l'Antico contro il Bizantino destinato a trionfare."
52. See Carlini, "Amicus Plato," 42, note 5.
53. Willis, "A New Fragment of Plato's *Parmenides*."
54. Turner, *The Typology of the Early Codex*, 3.
55. P.Oxy. 2.246 is cited by Cavallo at "Osservazioni paleografiche," 213.
56. See the editor's introduction to P.Oxy. 50.3529, p. 22.
57. Parsons, "The Scripts and Their Date," 23.
58. Del Corso, "Lo 'stile severo' nei P.Oxy." Other Oxyrhynchus papyri (such as the many published in the PSI series) are not part of his survey.
59. Orsini and Clarysse have described as severe style the following additional New Testament manuscripts from Oxyrhynchus: P.Oxy. 1.2 (P1, LDAB 2940), P.Oxy. 4.657 (P13, LDAB 3018), P.Oxy. 7.1008 and 7.1009 (P15 + 16, LDAB 3016), P.Oxy. 65.4446 (P107, LDAB 2782), P.Oxy. 66.4494 (P110, LDAB 7156), and P.Oxy. 66.4499 (P115, LDAB 7161); see Orsini and Clarysse, "Early New Testament Manuscripts," 457. Orsini and Clarysse also describe a second group containing five New Testament papyri from Oxyrhynchus as showing the alternation of thick and thin strokes in addition to the characteristics of the severe style (457).
60. For a survey of documentary rolls reused for literature at Oxyrhynchus, see Lama, "Aspetti di tecnica libraria ad Ossirinco."
61. It has been suggested that the copyist of the roll in Del Corso's list with the latest *terminus post quem* (P.Oxy. 7.1016, LDAB 3811, after 235 CE) also copied one of the codices on the list, P.Oxy. 57.3885 (LDAB 4105). See Funghi and Messeri Savorelli, "P.Oxy. VII 1016 e P.Oxy. LVII 3885."

62. See the data presented in Chapter 1 above.

63. There is a small corpus of codices that were constructed by pasting together the written sides of used documentary rolls to make a double-thick length of blank papyrus and then cutting this thickened papyrus into sheets that were folded for use in codices. On this group, see Bagnall, "Public Administration and the Documentation of Roman Panopolis," 1–12.

64. If the dates assigned to the reused rolls Lama has inventoried are basically correct, the phenomenon of reusing the backs of documentary rolls for literary texts seems to have died out (at least in Oxyrhynchus) during the course of the third century (of the 182 items in her catalog, only four pieces are assigned a date as late as "III/IV"; all the rest are earlier). See the data collected in Lama, "Aspetti di tecnica libraria ad Ossirinco," 61–71. Thus, using these relatively datable samples to assign paleographic dates to codices rests on the assumption that particular types of handwriting died out along with the roll format (which, as we see from Del Corso's list, is a false assumption).

65. Of the thirty-nine somewhat datable samples of writing from the first four centuries CE compiled by C. H. Roberts in 1956, only two are drawn from codices (and one from "a rough notebook"). See Roberts, *Greek Literary Hands*, 10–24.

66. The problem becomes somewhat less severe as we move later in time (the fourth century and beyond), when literary writing and documentary writing begin to become more easily comparable thanks to what Jean-Luc Fournet has called "la littérarisation des documents" and "la documentarisation de la littérature." See Fournet, *Ces lambeaux*, 76–84.

67. I borrow the phrase from Foster, "Bold Claims, Wishful Thinking."

68. For a clear and accessible account of the use of radiocarbon analysis and other forms of radiometric dating, see Macdougall, *Nature's Clocks*. For more detailed and nuanced discussions, see Taylor and Bar-Yosef, *Radiocarbon Dating*, and Ramsey, "Radiocarbon Dating." My summary draws from these sources.

69. An especially clear explanation of this equation can be found in Macdougall, *Nature's Clocks*, 79–80.

70. In addition to tree rings, core samples from sedimentary lakes can also provide data for calibrating radiocarbon dates. See Ramsey et al., "Developments in the Calibration and Modeling of Radiocarbon Dates."

71. Macdougall, *Nature's Clocks*, 77.

72. The letter is preserved in a manuscript in the Bibliothèque nationale de France (Ms. Champagne 154). The Latin text can be consulted in Chevalier, *Étude critique sur l'origine du St Suaire de Lirey-Chambéry-Turin*, Appendix G, vii–xii. An English translation can be found in Thurston, "The Holy Shroud and the Verdict of History."

73. Damon et al., "Radiocarbon Dating of the Shroud of Turin," 614.

74. A variety of theories seeking to undermine the radiocarbon analysis of the shroud were raised almost as soon as the results were published, but these theories were discredited early on. See Gove, "Dating the Turin Shroud." As more such theories arose, specialists convincingly responded. See, for example, Long, "Attempt to Affect the Apparent ^{14}C Age of Cotton." For a full and up-to-date account of the shroud, see Nicolotti, *Sindone*.

75. For a recent, sound overview of the motley world of Dead Sea Scrolls scholarship, see Collins, *The Dead Sea Scrolls*.

76. A few scholars maintained that the scrolls were medieval in date. See, for example, Zeitlin, "The Hebrew Scrolls."

77. See Bonani et al., "Radiocarbon Dating of the Dead Sea Scrolls," and Bonani et al., "Radiocarbon Dating of Fourteen Dead Sea Scrolls."

78. See Jull et al., "Radiocarbon Dating of Scrolls." Both the Zürich results and the Arizona results have been republished with updated calibrations in Taylor and Bar-Yosef, *Radiocarbon Dating*, 40.

79. Bonani et al., "Radiocarbon Dating of the Dead Sea Scrolls," 29, and Jull et al., "Radiocarbon Dating of Scrolls," 17. A more useful characterization of the results is provided by Gregory L. Doudna: "For about 80 percent of the [samples that underwent radiocarbon analysis] there was overlap between some part of the radiocarbon date possibility range and paleographic date estimates" ("Carbon-14 Dating," 1.120.). The whole situation was aptly summarized by Dennis Pardee, who commented that the radiocarbon analysis of the scrolls "shows that the paleographers weren't out to lunch. On the other hand, it does not show that their claim to be able to date manuscripts within 25 years is supported." The comment is reported in Wise et al. (eds.), *Methods of Investigation of the Dead Sea*, 452–453.

80. Eshel, "Some Paleographic Success Stories," 48–49.

81. To take one example, Joseph M. Baumgarten claimed that on paleographic grounds 4Q266, a copy of the Damascus Document, "may be dated to the first half of the first century B.C.E." ("The Laws of the *Damascus Document*," 57). The Arizona radiocarbon analysis of 4Q266 yielded a range of 45 BCE–120 CE with a 95 percent probability (40 BCE–125 CE in the more recent calibration in Taylor and Bar-Yosef, *Radiocarbon Dating*, 40). This does not necessarily mean that Baumgarten's paleographic date is wrong (again, radiocarbon date ranges are a matter of probability), but the radiocarbon analysis has hardly "confirmed" this paleographic date.

82. Given the difficulties we have seen above with Greek paleography, the degree of confidence with which paleographers of Hebrew and Aramaic assign dates to undated pieces is shocking, especially in light of the relatively minute pool of securely datable samples to use for comparison.

83. Using the more recent calibration data, Taylor and Bar-Yosef calculate

a date range for 1QIsa[a] of 215–85 BCE, with a 71 percent probability (*Radiocarbon Dating*, 40), making a date of 250–225 BCE less probable but at the same time introducing a previously excluded probability of a later date (say, 110–85 BCE).

84. See Rasmussen et al., "The Effects of Possible Contamination," and Rasmussen et al., "Reply to Israel Carmi."

85. This papyrus carries the designation XḤev/Se 8a. For details on the text, see Cotton and Yardeni, *Aramaic, Hebrew and Greek Documentary Texts from Naḥal Ḥever*, 34–37.

86. See Jull et al., "Radiocarbon Dating of Scrolls," 13–15.

87. See, for example, the article in the *New York Times* by Wilford and Goodstein, "'Gospel of Judas' Surfaces After 1,700 Years."

88. Kasser, Meyer, and Wurst, *The Gospel of Judas from Codex Tchacos*, 184.

89. A query to A. J. Timothy Jull of the University of Arizona in July 2014 received no reply.

90. Krosney, *The Lost Gospel*, 269–275.

91. For the problems of Krosney's presentation, see Askeland, "Considering the Radiometric Dating of the Tchacos Codex." My thanks to Christian Askeland for sharing with me a copy of this chapter in advance of its publication. A summary of the chapter is available online in Askeland, "Radiometric Dating of the Gospel of Judas."

92. This point was first noted by Head, "The Gospel of Judas and the Qarara Codices."

93. See Askeland, "Considering the Radiometric Dating of the Tchacos Codex."

94. For a summary of paleographic opinions, see Head, "The Gospel of Judas," 11.

95. See Stiles, "UA Radiocarbon Dates Help Verify Coptic Gospel of Judas Is Genuine."

96. For further details, see Cockle, "Restoring and Conserving Papyri," 150.

97. Clark, "Pigment Identification by Spectroscopic Means."

98. See, for example, Pappas, "Truth Behind Gospel of Judas Revealed in Ancient Inks."

99. See DeConick, "Gospel of Judas Dated to 280 CE." The version of the news story she cites can now be found at Fox News Science, http://www.foxnews.com/science/2013/04/08/truth-behind-gospel-judas-revealed-in-ancient-inks/.

100. See "Ink Analysis: The Gospel of Judas."

101. See the critical comments on the use of ink analysis in the debate surrounding the so-called Gospel of Jesus's Wife in Krutzsch and Rabin, "Material Criteria and Their Clues for Dating," 362–364.

102. Cockle, "Restoring and Conserving Papyri," 150.

103. What would be useful is the creation of a database by systematically

analyzing the ink of explicitly dated papyri in order to create chemical profiles of the inks used in different time periods. Such a procedure still would not produce exact dates for undated manuscripts, but it would make the analysis of ink at least somewhat more informative.

104. See Goler et al., "Characterizing the Age of Ancient Egyptian Manuscripts."

Chapter Three. Finding Early Christian Books in Egypt

1. See *A Report from the Committee Appointed to View the Cottonian Library*, 11. The popular version of these events has the renowned classical scholar Richard Bentley (1662–1742) escaping the fire "coming out in his night-gown and large wig, with the Alexandrian Old Testament Manuscript under his arm" (Nichols, *Literary Anecdotes of the Eighteenth Century*, 9.592). As Alexandrinus was bound in multiple volumes, it is possible that Casley and Bentley each rescued a portion of the work.

2. See Weitzmann and Kessler, *The Cotton Genesis*, 8 and 31–34.

3. See McKendrick, "The Codex Alexandrinus." The usual description of Cyril Lucar simply presenting Alexandrinus as a "gift" glosses over a somewhat messy political situation and minimizes the use of Alexandrinus as a diplomatic tool. See the accounts of Spinka, "Acquisition of the Codex Alexandrinus by England," and Davey, "Fair Exchange? Old Manuscripts for New Printed Books." The British ambassador at Constantinople, Thomas Roe (1581–1644), brokered the acquisition of the codex, and according to the assessment of Spinka, "the methods of securing his ends in the search for likely manuscripts used by this engaging and genial English ambassador cannot be pronounced strictly scrupulous" (23).

4. See the discussion in Weitzmann and Kessler, *The Cotton Genesis*, 3–6.

5. Codex Vaticanus is known to have been in Italy at least as early as 1481 and perhaps as early as 1475, at which time it began to appear in catalogs of the Vatican Library. For details, see Devreesse, *Le Fonds grec de la Bibliothèque Vaticane*, 73 and 82. Codex Bezae appears to have been consulted at the Council of Trent in 1546. For details, see Scrivener, *Bezae Codex Cantabrigiensis*, viii.

6. We know little of the circumstances of Bruce's acquisition of the codex. According to Bruce, the codex was "dug up at Thebes." See Bruce, *Travels to Discover the Source of the Nile*, 5.7. I owe this reference to Crégheur, "Pour une nouvelle histoire," 49–50. A later writer gave a more elaborate account: "When Mr. Bruce was at Medînăt tăboû or Thebes, in Upper Egypt, he purchased a Coptic manuscript which had been found in the ruins near that place, in the former residence of some Egyptian monks." See Robins, *A Catalogue of a Valuable Collection of Oriental Literature*, 35.

7. Unfortunately, we know nothing of the provenance of the codex before Askew bought it, allegedly in 1772. The report of this purchase in a letter from Carl Gottfried Woide to Johann David Michaelis (June 28, 1773) is terse: "Dr. Askew had chanced to buy it in a bookshop" (see Buhle, *Literarischer Briefwechsel von Johann David Michaelis, Dritter Theil,* 69). Earlier in his life (1746–1749), Askew had spent time in Constantinople, Mount Athos, and Italy and was at that time actively acquiring books. It seems at least possible that he acquired his Coptic codex during that trip. For a contemporary account of his book collection, see "Nachricht von dem Büchervorrath des Herrn Dr. Anton Askew." For his travels, see Welford, *Men of Mark 'twixt Tyne and Tweed,* 1.115–120.

8. In 1774, the Askew codex was identified as being even older than the Codex Alexandrinus by Woide, "Sur le Dictionnaire Cophte," 339–340. Compare Woide's comments with those of Michaelis in the letter mentioned above (Buhle, *Literarische Briefwechsel,* 73).

9. Davoli, "Papyri, Archaeology, and Modern History," citing Earle, "Egyptian Cotton and the American Civil War."

10. Bailey, "*Sebakh,* Sherds and Survey."

11. See Read, *The Faddan More Psalter.*

12. On Codex Sinaiticus (LDAB 3478), see Parker, *Codex Sinaiticus.* For the discovery of a palimpsest containing the Old Syriac of the gospels from the same monastery (LDAB 117850), see Soskice, *The Sisters of Sinai.*

13. That distinction between licit and illicit excavation is not as clear-cut as it might appear. The authorities and laws governing excavation and export in Egypt changed through the decades, as did enforcement of those laws. For overviews, see Khater, *Le régime juridique des fouilles et des antiquités en Egypte,* and more recently Hagen and Ryholt, *The Antiquities Trade in Egypt,* 133–146.

14. Finds of specifically Christian manuscripts could be more widely contextualized in terms of manuscript discoveries from Roman Egypt in general, but such an undertaking is outside the scope of this book. For a broader survey of finds of ancient books in Egypt current up to the early 1930s, see Preisendanz, *Papyrusfunde und Papyrusforschung.* For a less detailed but more recent account, see Cuvigny, "The Finds of Papyri."

15. Askren's fascinating story is waiting to be written. For some of the details, see Nongbri, "The Acquisition of the University of Michigan's Portion" (the date of Askren's death is given incorrectly there as 1940 at 95, note 7).

16. For a thorough description of the Hamuli Coptic books, see the catalog of Depuydt, *Catalogue of Coptic Manuscripts.*

17. David L. Askren to Francis W. Kelsey, February 11, 1915, Folder 2, Box 82, Kelsey Museum of Archaeology Papers 1890–1979, Bentley Historical Library, University of Michigan. The letter is mentioned in a biography of J. P. Morgan's librarian, Belle da Costa Greene, where it is

attributed to "David Askins." See Ardizzone, *An Illuminated Life*, 275–276 and 518, note 75.

18. Friedrich Zuker (1881–1973) was a German classical philologist and archaeologist. The diaries of his excavations in 1909 and 1910 are available in Zucker and Schubart, "Die berliner Papyrusgrabungen in Dîme."

19. Stomati Scopelitis also reportedly sold (unrelated) papyri to Germans in later years; see Hagen and Ryholt, *The Antiquities Trade in Egypt*, 262. Fanous Monsour is unknown to me outside of this reference, and I have not been able to track down any additional information about him.

20. This is the same Ali Arabi who sold Charles Lang Freer his famous biblical manuscripts.

21. Maurice Nahman (1868–1948) was chief cashier at the Crédit foncier égyptien from 1908 to 1925. He was also one of Cairo's leading antiquities dealers, and many major finds of early Christian manuscripts passed through his hands. See Hagen and Ryholt, *The Antiquities Trade in Egypt*, 253–255.

22. Morgan actually purchased the books from a group of owners in Paris (Nahman is not named among them) in December 1911, and the price was said to be in the range of $200,000 U.S. For details, see Depuydt, *Catalogue of Coptic Manuscripts*, 1.lx. Just how much Morgan paid was a matter of considerable speculation in the media. The *New York Times* ran multiple articles on the question with headlines like "Morgan Bibles Really Priceless: Facts About the Coptic MSS. for Which the Financier Was Said to Have Overpaid" (March 10, 1912).

23. A sensationalist account of a contemporary (1911) newspaper captures the orientalist overtones of much of the press coverage of such discoveries: "The collection has just been received by Mr. Morgan from Paris, where its purchase from the antiquaries who rescued the sheaves of ancient manuscripts from the Arabs was made. Prof. Henry Hyvernat of the Catholic University of America, who is one of the best known authorities on Coptic literature and who was instrumental in gathering from Arab vandals codex after codex of almost priceless vellum, has done preliminary work upon the collection. . . . It was due to the energy of M. Chassinat, head of the French Institute of Archaeology at Cairo, and Prof. Hyvernat that the fugitive bundles of manuscripts were all brought together again. This was only accomplished after six months of labor and at the frequent risk of the lives of the two enthusiasts. To them is due the credit of having preserved the most complete collection of Coptic manuscripts extant" ("Rare Coptic Manuscripts Secured by J. P. Morgan").

24. A letter to Charles Lang Freer dated May 10, 1910, from the Kalebdjian brothers (antiquities dealers with offices in Cairo and Paris) stated that the codices ("about fifty pieces") had been gathered in a safe place, although "four or five manuscripts were seized by the Service of Antiqui-

ties," and "the local police displays the greatest energy in order to take hold of such manuscripts." The brothers then invited Freer to view the manuscripts in Paris in June to consider purchasing them (Kalebdjian Frères to Charles Lang Freer, May 10, 1910, Folder 14, Box 15, Kelsey Museum of Archaeology Papers 1890–1979, Bentley Historical Library, University of Michigan). This information supplements the account of the marketing of the manuscripts given in Depuydt, *Catalogue of Coptic Manuscripts*, 1.lix–lx.

25. For a complete listing, see Depuydt, *Catalogue of Coptic Manuscripts*, 1.lxxxii–lxxxviii.

26. See Hyvernat, *A Check List of Coptic Manuscripts in the Pierpont Morgan Library*, xi–xii.

27. See Nongbri, "Finding Early Christian Books at Nag Hammadi and Beyond."

28. Bouriant, "Fragments grecs du livre d'Énoch," 93–94. For further details on the codex and extrapolations about its discovery, see van Minnen, "The Greek *Apocalypse of Peter.*"

29. See Bouriant, "Fragments grecs du livre d'Énoch," 94: "Les fragments reproduits dans le volume pourraient cependant être d'une epoque plus ancienne que celle où vivait le moine dans le tombeau duquel ils ont été déposés" (The fragments reproduced in the volume could, however, be from an age before the life of the monk in whose tomb they were buried). Elsewhere in the cemetery (it is not clear exactly where), a second book was found (a mathematical papyrus codex assigned to the sixth century, LDAB 6240). No association with a corpse is mentioned. See Baillet, "Le papyrus mathématique d'Akhmîm," 2.

30. See, for example, "The Gospel According to Peter," which ran on p. 5 in the *Times* on December 2, 1892. An early book on the Gospel According to Peter reflected on the theme even more romantically: "The dead have long been giving up their secrets, but it is only in recent times that we have been able to realise the fact that the tombs of Egypt may contain many a precious work, now known to us but in name" ([Cassels], *The Gospel According to Peter*, 1).

31. "Zum Schlusse will ich noch bemerken, dass auf Grund meiner persönlichen Nachforschungen die Handschrift zuerst bei einem arabischen Antikenhändler in Achmim aufgetaucht ist. Sie war, wie ich weiter erfuhr, eingehüllt in Federn in einer Mauernische gefunden worden. Wir dürfen daher mit Sicherheit annehmen, dass sie aus dem Gräberfelde von Achmim oder wenigstens aus der Umgebung der Stadt stammt" (Schmidt, *Die alten Petrusakten*, 2).

32. "Im Januar dieses Jahres wurde Hrn. Dr. Reinhardt in Kairo von einem Antikenhändler aus Achmim eine umfangreiche Papyrushandschrift angeboten, die nach dessen Angaben von einem Fellahen in einer Mauer-

nische gefunden sein sollte" (Schmidt, "Ein vorirenaeisches gnostisches Originalwerk," 839, my emphasis).

33. Reports of subsequent finds of Christian books did make reference to the Akhmim codex. An announcement of the Smith sisters' discovery of the Sinaitic Syriac codex of the gospels (LDAB 117850) opened with this line: "It will be remembered that last year Professor Hanak [i.e., Harnack] surprised the theological world by his discovery in an Egyptian tomb of a fragment of the Gospel and Apocalypse of St. Peter" ("Discovery of a Syrian Text of the Gospels"; the reference to Harnack playing a role in the discovery is, of course, mistaken). This is not to suggest that the codex containing the Gospel According to Peter was still fresh on everyone's mind in 1903. Other discoveries from Egypt, like the Oxyrhynchus sayings of Jesus published in 1897, had by that time come to overshadow it. On the early reception of the Gospel According to Peter, see Foster, "The Discovery and Initial Reaction to the So-Called Gospel of Peter."

34. Budge, *By Nile and Tigris*, 2.372–374.

35. See Bell, "Mr. Bell's Description of the Papyrus Fragments." I am grateful to Peter Toth of the British Library for confirming that these documents remain unpublished and await further study.

36. Frederic Kenyon had dated the cursive writing after Acts to the middle of the fourth century with a high degree of confidence (Budge, *Coptic Biblical Texts*, lv–lvii), but more recently, it has become clear that this type of writing persisted at least as late as the last quarter of the fifth century. See Orsini, "La maiuscola biblica copta," 133–134.

37. Although Petrie's archaeological methods would not meet modern standards, they were revolutionary at the beginning of the twentieth century. See Petrie, *Methods and Aims in Archaeology*.

38. The so-called Edfu manuscripts are a good illustration of Budge's method of encouraging digging by natives and then buying parts of what they found: "My publication of the complete text of the Coptic version of the Psalter in the dialect of Upper Egypt from a papyrus codex helped to increase the demand for Coptic manuscripts and antiquities, and the natives began to seek out and excavate the ruins of Coptic monasteries and churches all over the country. I had paid several visits to Edfû from Aswân in 1886, 1887 and 1888, and had seen several Coptic tombs cleared out, and from what I saw there and from what I read I became convinced that a very large Christian community must have flourished there between the fourth and the eleventh centuries. It was evident that this community maintained churches and monasteries, and that the priests and monks who lived at Edfû must have possessed manuscripts containing Biblical and Patristic texts. Between 1887 and 1900 the 'finds' of Egyptian antiquities, both predynastic and dynastic, were so numerous

and important that I could not induce the natives to turn their attention to Edfû until the winter of 1902–3. Then we dug up several memorial inscriptions and important architectural fragments. . . . In 1907 the dealers in Upper Egypt formed themselves into a company, and under an arrangement with [Gaston Maspero (1846–1916), the director of the Egyptian Service of Antiquities] they continued the excavations which I began in 1903, and discovered many good Coptic inscriptions. Best of all, they succeeded in finding the place in the neighbouring hills where the monks of Edfû and Asnâ had hidden their manuscripts, probably when the Arabs under Al-Yâzûrî ravaged Upper Egypt between 1153 and 1158. Here they discovered a large number of manuscripts written in the Coptic dialect of Upper Egypt and one small manuscript written in Nubian. Some of the company of dealers sold the MSS. which were their shares of the 'find' to a gentleman who resold them to the British Museum, and I acquired the remaining thirteen volumes in 1907–8" (Budge, *By Nile and Tigris*, 2.369–371).

39. In one instance, Budge wrote of going to Egypt in 1892 and, among many other activities, stopping at a structure that was being dug out by locals near the White Monastery in Sohag. After looking around the site, Budge was asked by the natives to fund the rest of the clearing of this structure. Budge "agreed to the proposal of the natives, and told them I expected them to find me something very good in return for the outlay." When Budge returned to the site in 1895, he reported that "several natives came towards me, clapping their hands and signing joyfully; as soon as I saw what they had to show me I felt that they had good cause for rejoicing." In clearing out the structure, they had found a box constructed out of inscribed stone slabs, and inside this box they claimed to have found "two large books with papyrus leaves, bound in stout leather-covered boards also made of papyrus." See the account in Budge, *By Nile and Tigris*, 2.328–342 (quotations at 333 and 340). These books turned out to be a copy of the Psalms in Coptic (LDAB 108024) and a collection of Coptic homilies (LDAB 107789). See Budge, *The Earliest Known Coptic Psalter*, and Budge, *Coptic Homilies in the Dialect of Upper Egypt*.

40. Krosney, *The Lost Gospel*, 9–27, quotation at 10.

41. Indeed, some generally quite critical scholars have been relatively uncritical in using this story to interpret the use of the codices. See, for example, DeConick, "The *Gospel of Judas*," 98–99.

42. A welcome voice of skepticism is provided by Jenott, *The Gospel of Judas*, 103–105.

43. Krosney, *The Lost Gospel*, 24.

44. Krosney, *The Lost Gospel*, 26.

45. Emmel seems to have regarded even this report as suspicious, noting that "it is difficult to know how seriously to take such information" (quoted in Robinson, *The Secrets of Judas*, 54–57, at 56). One of the Greek codices

(LDAB 10719) contains mathematical material, and its contents appear to be connected with the Oxyrhynchite nome, so the assignment of the find to the general area of Oxyrhynchus may be correct (see the report of Bagnall in Krosney, *The Lost Gospel*, 298).

46. For the first description, see Gabra, "Zur Bedeutung des koptischen Psalmenbuches," 37. For the second, see Gabra, *Der Psalter im oxyrhynchitischen (mesokemischen/mittelägyptischen) Dialekt*, 23. For the third, see Brown, *In the Beginning*, 74. Brown's source for this more elaborate description is unclear. She cites Gabra, *Cairo*, but Gabra here describes the book again only as having been found "in a shallow grave under a young girl's head" (110).

47. Petrie, "The Discovery of the Papyrus," ix.

48. Occasionally, a tomb or the like is given as provenance for a Christian book and then retracted. For example, the original editors of the Cologne miniature parchment codex containing a biography of Mani in Greek (LDAB 5804) at first claimed that the book came from "a grave in Oxyrhynchus" (Henrichs and Koenen, "Ein griechischer Mani-Codex," 100). This suggestion was later retracted and replaced by the claim that the book had spent about fifty years in a private collection in Luxor, and that before that, its place of discovery was unknown (Koenen, "Zur Herkunft des Kölner Mani-Codex").

49. See the comments of Cuvigny, "The Finds of Papyri," 44–45. The reason it is sometimes claimed that burial with books was common in Roman Egypt probably has to do with a particularly high-profile example, namely the Hawara Homer (see the discussion of this piece in Chapter 2).

50. Despite periodic pleas to the contrary, in fact nothing suggests that any Christian material was found among the Jewish texts in the caves at Qumran. For a sober overview, see Collins, *The Dead Sea Scrolls*.

51. Munier, "Tourah."

52. Guéraud, "Note préliminaire sur les papyrus d'Origène découverts à Toura."

53. This visit seems to have taken place at the end of September 1941, after the Cairo Museum had secured a large portion of the find. See the account in Guéraud and Nautin, *Origène*, 19.

54. Guéraud, "Note préliminaire," 86: "J'ai visité la carrière peu après la trouvaille, avec M. Drioton, directeur général du Service des Antiquités. Nous avons interrogé le contremaître européen, le raïs (surveillant) égyptien, et l'un des ouvriers qui avaient assisté à la découverte. Ils nous ont montré l'endroit où se trouvaient les papyrus: dans l'une des galeries, à 20 ou 25 mètres de son débouché sur la rotonde. La lente dégradation de la roche au cours des siècles accumule dans les galeries une masse de poussière et de débris de pierre qui forment un talus le long de chaque paroi. C'est, nous a-t-on dit, en déblayant cet amoncellement,

haut à cet endroit d'un mètre environ, que les ouvriers tombèrent sur une masse de papyrus déposés presque au pied même de la paroi, entassés tous ensemble (et non pas dispersés dans les débris) mais sans aucune espèce de protection ni rien qui fît croire à une cachette aménagée avec quelque soin."

55. Guéraud, "Note préliminaire," 87: "Questionné sur ce qu'ils ont fait aussitôt les papyrus découverts, l'ouvrier a dit qu'ils avaient prévenu le raïs, qui a prévenu le contremaître, qui a prévenu la police. La police est venue et a trouvé tous les papyrus, auxquels personne n'avait touché. Elle les a emportés, et on ne sait pas ce qu'elle a fait ensuite."

56. Guéraud, "Note préliminaire," 87: "Cette histoire, qui rappelle en son genre celle de la charta Borgiana, compte au moins un élément tout à fait invraisemblable: c'est qu'il ait pu se trouver de nos jours, à dix kilomètres du Caire, des gens ignorant la valeur marchande des papyrus."

57. Guéraud and Nautin, *Origène*, 15–21, at 17. The details of this account differ in small ways from that given by Guéraud in his "Note préliminaire."

58. For the dating of the handwriting of the Tura codices, see, for example, Kehl, *Der Psalmenkommentar*, 17, note 4.

59. For Nahman's role, see Guéraud and Nautin, *Origène*, 18.

60. For the state of affairs in the mid-1960s, see Koenen and Doutreleau, "Nouvel inventaire des papyrus de Toura," 565.

61. See Mackay and Griggs, "The Recently Rediscovered Papyrus Leaves of Didymos the Blind," and Harker, "Didymos the Blind Sees the Light of Day."

62. The manuscripts that lingered on the antiquities market suffered by being soaked in water and manipulated in other ways. See Guéraud, "Note préliminaire," 89–90.

63. It is possible that the books came from the nearby Monastery of Arsenius (Dayr al-Qusayr). See Koenen and Müller-Wiener, "Zu den Papyri."

64. The evidence for this find and the marketing of these books has been gathered in Robinson, *The Manichaean Codices of Medinet Madi*.

65. The story merited two columns in the *Times*. See Thompson, "Mani and the Manichees."

66. On the identity of Manichaeans as Christians, see the discussion in Nongbri, *Before Religion*, 66–73, and the literature cited there.

67. For Rolf Ibscher's sneeze, see Robinson, *The Manichaean Codices of Medinet Madi*, 156.

68. Schmidt's early evaluation is found in a letter from Chester Beatty's librarian, John Wooderson, to "Mr. Corble," June 6, 1930: "Prof. Schmidt thinks that it comes from Akhmim" (Chester Beatty Library Archives, CBP 592).

69. Schmidt and Polotsky, "Ein Mani-Fund in Ägypten," 8–9. The relevant section of the article is reprinted in Robinson, *The Manichaean Codices of*

Medinet Madi, 56–57: "Den gesamten Fund muß mein Gewährsmann noch vor Augen gehabt haben, denn nach beiläufiger Mitteilung, die er mir jetzt beim Besuch im März 1932 machte, lagen die Papyrusbücher, jedes von kahlen Deckeln in Holz umgeben, in einer Holzkiste, die in einem früheren Wohnhause aufgefunden wurde. Die Holzkiste soll zerfallen gewesen sein, so daß eine Aufbewahrung sich nicht lohnte. Es hat den Anschein, als ob dem Antikenhändler im Fajûm der ganze Fund von den arabischen Findern angeboten wurde, dieser aber sich nicht getraute, sein Geld allein in diesen unansehnlichen Papyrusbüchern anzulegen, weshalb er den Fund mit anderen Händlern teilte. Damit wird auch eine Beobachtung von Dr. Ibscher bestätigt, daß die Mani-Handschriften infolge ihrer feuchten Lagerung in absehbarer Zeit dem Zerfall nahegebracht wären, also nicht in der trockenen Wüstenerde gelegen haben können. Denn die Keller der Häuser von Medînet Mâdi waren der Feuchtigkeit von oben und unten ausgesetzt, so daß die Papyri von Salzkristallen vollständig durchsetzt werden konnten."

70. For the churches of Kellis, see Bowen, "The Fourth-Century Churches at Ismant el-Kharab." A synthesis of the evidence for the Manicheans at Kellis is currently under way in a doctoral dissertation by Mattias Brand at Leiden University ("The Manichaeans of Kellis").

71. Hope et al., "Dakhleh Oasis Project," 5. For the publication of the tablet, see Gardner, *Kellis Literary Texts, Volume 1,* 8–30.

72. For editions of these texts, see Bagnall (ed.), *The Kellis Agricultural Account Book,* and Worp and Rijksbaron (eds.), *The Kellis Isocrates Codex.* For the archaeological context of the area of discovery, see the discussion in Hope, "The Find Context of the Kellis Agricultural Account Book."

73. See Hope, "The Archaeological Context," 156–161. For the edition of the codex, see Gardner, *Kellis Literary Texts, Volume 2,* 94–110.

74. Hope, "The Archaeological Context," 161. Many of the documentary papyri from this area were also assembled from fragments found in different rooms. See the discussion in Worp, *Greek Papyri from Kellis,* 3–7.

75. See Luijendijk, "Sacred Scriptures as Trash." For another instance of a Christian text found in a house in a probable trash context, see Schwendner, "A Fragmentary Psalter from Karanis and Its Context."

76. The excavation report and texts are published in Winlock, Crum, and Evelyn White, *The Monastery of Epiphanius.* An overview of the literary material is provided at 1.196–208.

77. See the discussion in Winlock, Crum, and Evelyn White, *The Monastery of Epiphanius,* 1.xxii–xxiii.

78. For the inventory of what was found in this context, see Winlock, Crum, and Evelyn White, *The Monastery of Epiphanius,* 1.31–32, note 5.

79. Górecki, "Sheikh Abd el-Gurna," 266. For details of the books' condition upon discovery, see Kordowska, "Conservation Work on Three Coptic Manuscripts."

80. Doresse, *The Secret Books of the Egyptian Gnostics*, caption to frontispiece.

81. Doresse *Les livres secrets des gnostiques d'Égypte*, 137.

82. Doresse, *The Secret Books of the Egyptian Gnostics*, 133

83. See Robinson, "From the Cliff to Cairo," 25–26.

84. Robinson's publications on the discovery of the codices are numerous. Much of the information he collected and published in different venues has been gathered in Robinson, *The Nag Hammadi Story*. For a critical overview of Robinson's account, see Goodacre, "How Reliable Is the Story of the Nag Hammadi Discovery?"

85. The documentary, called *The Gnostics*, originally aired in November 1987 on Channel 4 (UK). This episode can be viewed on YouTube. The quotation here is drawn from the transcription in Goodacre, "How Reliable Is the Story of the Nag Hammadi Discovery?," 311, with minor adjustments. The ellipses indicate points at which narration or other interviews are interspersed in the course of Muhammad 'Ali's story. Also excised from the quotation is a segment during which Muhammad 'Ali looks through the autumn 1979 issue of *Biblical Archaeologist* and identifies both a picture of himself and a picture of the general location of the find: "That's where I found the books, on the *jabal*, the mountain." The claim that he was digging for *sebakh* is dubious. The rubble at the base of the cliffs is hardly a promising site for finding ancient mud-brick and organic remains.

86. See the evidence gathered in Goodacre, "How Reliable Is the Story of the Nag Hammadi Discovery?," 308 and 313–314.

87. Robinson, "From the Cliff to Cairo," 35–36. A very similar statement appears in Robinson's 2009 article in the *Journal of Coptic Studies*, "The Discovery of the Nag Hammadi Codices," 11.

88. See Robinson's summary in the *Göttinger Miszellen*, "The First Season of the Nag Hammadi Excavation," 72–73.

89. Mina, "Le papyrus gnostique," 129, and Robinson, *The Nag Hammadi Story*, 1.93.

90. See the summary of Robinson and Van Elderen, "The First Season of the Nag Hammadi Excavation," 19–21.

91. For instance, T 1, located close to the boulder identified by Muhammad 'Ali, was excavated: "Cave 1 was nearby, and was also excavated. It involved an extensively disturbed burial with many bones in the debris in front of the cave. The cave itself was small and undressed, with bones in the west and south alcoves. The few sherds found in the cave were Byzantine and perhaps New Kingdom." Similarly, excavation of T 8, about 330 meters north of T 1, yielded coins of the sixth and seventh centuries and excerpts from the Psalms in Coptic painted on a wall (Robinson and Van Elderen, "The First Season of the Nag Hammadi Excavation," 20).

92. Tano's acquisition of the Nag Hammadi codices is outlined in great detail most recently in Robinson, *The Nag Hammadi Story*, 1.1–349.

93. See Emmel, "[Research Note on the Codicology of Nag Hammadi Codex I]." Some parts of the find remain separated. The leather cover of Codex I is now owned by the private collector Martin Schøyen, and a small portion of a leaf of Codex III is in Yale's Beinecke Library.

Chapter Four. A Discovery "Which Threw All Others in the Shade"

1. Letter of Arthur E. R. Boak to Frank E. Robbins, December 20, 1931, Box 1, Folder 8, Institute for Archaeological Research Papers, Bentley Historical Library, University of Michigan. Further excerpts from this letter are published in Nongbri, "The Acquisition of the University of Michigan's Portion," 99–100. The notion that "the natives burned" part of the find is a trope that goes back to the very earliest European encounters with Egyptian papyri. For the earliest such report known to me, see Schow, *Charta papyracea graece scripta musei Borgiani Velitris*, iii–iv: "diripiebant Turcae, earumque fumo (nam odorem fumi aromaticum esse dicunt) sese oblectabant" (the Turks tear them up; they are delighted by the smoke, for they say its smell is aromatic).

2. On Askren's role in the 1915 purchases by J. P. Morgan, Jr., and Freer, see Depuydt, *Catalogue of Coptic Manuscripts*, 1.lxxiv–lxxvii.

3. Frederic Kenyon is chiefly remembered both as a pioneer in the early days of papyrology, editing and translating Aristotle's *Athenian Constitution* (LDAB 391) and many other papyri in the 1890s, and as the long-time director of the British Museum from 1909 to 1930. After his work on the Beatty Biblical Papyri, Kenyon dabbled in the fields of Christian apologetics and theology. For the former, see Kenyon, *The Bible and Modern Scholarship*, in which he set out "to restore confidence in the Bible as a guide to truth and a basis for the conduct of life," and for the latter, see Kenyon, *The Reading of the Bible as History, as Literature and as Religion*.

4. Kenyon, "The Text of the Bible."

5. Kenyon, *The Story of the Bible*, 112.

6. Kenyon generally described the Numbers-Deuteronomy codex as "not later than the first half of the second century," although he occasionally gave a more specific date, claiming that it was "written about A.D. 120–50." See Kenyon, *The Story of the Bible*, 14.

7. There are eleven codices but twelve Roman numerals because Kenyon originally thought Codex IX and Codex X were two different books. It later became clear that they were part of the same codex. Rather confusingly, this series of Roman numerals has been extended to include other

materials in the Chester Beatty collection that are not part of the same find. Thus, "P.ChesterBeatty XIII" and beyond, while containing "biblical" material, are not part of the Chester Beatty Biblical Papyri proper.

8.   Kenyon, *The Chester Beatty Biblical Papyri.*

9.   For details of Beatty's biography, see Wilson, *The Life and Times of Sir Alfred Chester Beatty.*

10.   On Beatty as a collector, see Horton, *Alfred Chester Beatty.*

11.   I rely here on Horton, "The Chester Beatty Biblical Papyri," and Nongbri, "The Acquisition of the University of Michigan's Portion."

12.   The text is cited in Horton, "The Chester Beatty Biblical Papyri," 154.

13.   Some statements in this portion of Horton's otherwise exemplary account of Beatty's acquisitions are incorrect ("The Chester Beatty Biblical Papyri," 155–156). A gap of about a year in the archival material relating to Kenyon in the Chester Beatty Library coupled with a lack of access to the Michigan records seems to have led to a few mistaken conclusions. These issues are sorted out below and in greater detail in Nongbri, "The Acquisition of the University of Michigan's Portion."

14.   See Horton, "The Chester Beatty Biblical Papyri," 153. That Beatty was working primarily with Nahman is confirmed in the archival materials from the University of Michigan.

15.   See Gerstinger, "Ein Fragment des Chester Beatty-Evangelienkodex."

16.   See von Erffa, "Esai. 19, 3 sqq.," 109–110.

17.   See Bell and Roberts, *A Descriptive Catalogue of the Greek Papyri in the Collection of Wilfred Merton*, 1.v–1.vi and 1.6–1.12.

18.   Enoch E. Peterson to Arthur E. R. Boak, March 9, 1930, Box 5, Folder 7, Institute for Archaeological Research Papers, Bentley Historical Library, University of Michigan. Longer excerpts from this letter can be found in Nongbri, "The Acquisition of the University of Michigan's Portion," 95.

19.   Arthur E. R. Boak to Campbell Bonner, January 4, 1931 [this must be an error for 1932], Box 1, Folder 8, Institute for Archaeological Research Papers, Bentley Historical Library, University of Michigan. Fuller citation of this letter can be found in Nongbri, "The Acquisition of the University of Michigan's Portion," 100–101.

20.   For a more detailed account of these dealings, see Nongbri, "The Acquisition of the University of Michigan's Portion," 101–102.

21.   I take this opportunity to correct a statement in my earlier article "The Acquisition of the University of Michigan's Portion." At p. 103, I had deduced the most likely date of purchase as 1936, but a subsequent search of archival records at Princeton placed the purchase firmly in the summer of 1935. A letter of October 1, 1935, from H. W. Dodds (then president of Princeton University) to John H. Scheide reveals the following: "On Saturday Allan Johnson [1881–1955] appeared in this office with a package wrapped in an old French newspaper. On removing the

string he disclosed twenty leaves of what he considered to be a third century Greek version of Ezekiel and the oldest Greek version in existence. Undoubtedly he has written you a full description. The leaves are in excellent condition and the writing so clear that anyone in a Freshman Greek course could read the text." The Scheide Ezekiel leaves were thus purchased before October 1935. A reply from Scheide to Dodds dated October 4, 1935, provides another clue as to the date of the purchase: "I am just in receipt of your letter of October 1st informing me that Professor Johnson has delivered to you the leaves of papyri which he and [Edmund Harris Kase, 1905–1999] secured in Egypt, and I am delighted to have you tell me in what fine condition they are and that the University is willing to become the custodian of them. I am sure that Professors Johnson and Kase have laid us all under lasting obligation to them for their kindness in undertaking so trying a trip at so unseasonable a time of year." The "unseasonable" time for a visit to Egypt would no doubt be summer. Both these letters are found in Princeton's Seeley G. Mudd Manuscript Library (Princeton University Archives, Department of Rare Books and Special Collections, Princeton University Library; Scheide, John H; 1935–1941; Office of the President Records: Jonathan Dickinson to Harold W. Dodds Subgroup; Box 147, Folder 2). In a letter to Scheide dated February 24, 1936, Johnson, who had already completed a transcription of the Greek text of the leaves, expressed the hope that some difficulties in the text could be resolved when "the rest of Ezekiel gets out of the hands of the dealer." He also noted that he had "no further word from Askren, and I suppose he thinks it wise to leave the dealer alone until he grows more reasonable, if ever." This letter was found together in a folder in the Scheide Library labeled "Scheide Collection 17.1," along with Johnson's typescript of the transcription of the Ezekiel leaves.

22. On the leaves bought in the 1950s and 1960s, see Fernández-Galiano, "Nuevas páginas del códice 967," and Roca-Puig, "Daniele." My thanks to Sofía Torallas Tovar for informing me that the Barcelona and Madrid portions of the Ezekiel-Daniel-Susanna-Esther codex were likely acquired in the 1950s and 1960s. At some point between 1954 and 1965, the papyrus collection at Cologne also acquired parts of this codex. See the "Vorwort" to Hamm, *Der Septuaginta-Text des Buches Daniel*.

23. Kenyon, "The Text of the Bible," 13.

24. Kenyon, *The Chester Beatty Biblical Papyri*, fasciculus I, 5.

25. Schmidt, "Die neuesten Bibelfunde aus Ägypten," 285–286: "Als ich im Frühjahr 1930 . . . einen kurzen Aufenthalt in Kairo nahm, wurden mir zahlreiche, zum Teil prachtvoll erhaltene, Papyrusblätter in griechischer Sprache von Händlern vorgelegt, die bei genauerer Prüfung sich als Stücke aus AT- und NTlichen Bibelhandschriften erwiesen. Freilich ein Ankauf von meiner Seite war durch die phantastischen Forderungen von

vornherein ausgeschlossen. . . . [A]llem Anschein nach der ganze Fund, wie auch sonst der Fall, unter die verschiedenen Händler verteilt worden war, so daß ein Ankauf unverhältnismäßig große Mittel erforderte, um nur einen bedeutenden Anteil sich zu sichern. Diese so bedauernswerte Zerreißung wurde bestätigt bei einem Besuche im Fajûm, wo mir weitere Blätter zu noch exorbitanteren Preisen angeboten wurden. Die Gefahr, daß der Fund in alle Winde zerstreut würde, war beseitigt, als ich zu meiner besonderen Freude die Kunde erhielt, daß A. Chester Beatty, ein bekannter Privatsammler, den größten Teil der Blätter erworben und nach London übergeführt hätte."

26. Schmidt, "Die neuesten Bibelfunde aus Ägypten," 292–293: "Die Feststellung eines Fundortes ist ja stets eine höchst schwierige, da der Finder sowohl wie der Händler das größte Interesse an der Verwischung aller Spuren hat, um nicht von der Behörde oder der Museumsverwaltung zur Rechenschaft gezogen zu werden. Trotzdem habe ich die Nachforschung nach dem geheimnisvollen Fundorte bei meinem letzten Aufenthalt fortgesetzt und konnte zunächst bei meinem alten vertrauten Gewährsmann, der selbst eine Reihe Blätter besessen hatte, das Geständnis erreichen, daß das Fajûm, an das man in erster Linie denkt, nicht in Frage käme. Ein Fundort in Oberägypten ist ausgeschlossen durch die Händlergruppe, in deren Besitz die Blätter gelangt waren. Jedenfalls konnte der Fundort nicht weitab vom Fajûm liegen. So glaube ich einen wichtigen Fingerhinweis in der Erklärung meines Gewährsmanns zu besitzen, wenn er die Erreichung der Fundstätte dahin umschrieb, daß ich von Bûsch, einer Eisenbahnstation zwischen Wasta und Benisuêf (115 km von Kairo), mich östlich an das Nilufer begeben und über den Nil nach der Ortschaft 'Alâlme übersetzen müsse. 'Alâlme ist die Ortschaft, von der eine Straße zu dem Antonius- und Pauluskloster am Roten Meere geht und von der nördlich das alte Antoniuskloster liegt und noch weiter nördlich ebenfalls am Ostufer der Flecken Atfiḥ, das alte Aphroditopolis, aus dem Antonius, der Begründer des ägyptischen Mönchtums, stammt. Hier müssen Kirchen und Klöster vorhanden gewesen sein, die in alter Zeit die christlichen heiligen Schriften auf Papyrus besaßen und die nach deren Abnutzung sie auf Pergament übertragen haben."

27. Schmidt, "Die Evangelienhandschrift der Chester Beatty-Sammlung," 225–226: "Bedauerlicherweise hat K. zu meinen Nachforschungen über den Fundort keine Stellung genommen, ja meinen Artikel überhaupt nicht erwähnt. Noch in diesem Frühjahr habe ich den Fajûmer Händler von neuem ausgefragt und die gleiche Auskunft erhalten, derzufolge eine Ortschaft 'Alâme auf dem Ostufer des Nils in der Gegend von Atfiḥ, dem alten Aphroditopolis, als Fundort anzusehen ist. Auf diese entlegene Gegend wäre wohl schwerlich ein Händler gekommen, wenn der Finder nicht tatsächlich von dort nach dem Fajûm gereist wäre. Die mir wohlbekannten Angaben eines Kairener Zwischenhändlers sind irreführend.

Beiläufig bemerkte der Händler, daß die Papyrusbücher in einem Topf aufgefunden wären. Dadurch wird meine These vollauf bestätigt, daß es sich bei diesem Funde um abgenutzte, defekte Kodizes handelt, die als heilige Schriften nicht vernichtet werden durften, sondern der Erde in Töpfen übergeben wurden, wie man auch wichtige Dokumente in Krügen aufzubewahren pflegte. Derartige Bücherfunde in Gefäßen sind in Ägypten keine Seltenheit. . . . Die Finder haben scheinbar die kleinsten Fetzen aus dem Topfe zusammengelesen und nicht als wertlos weggeworfen, da nach Mitteilung von Dr. Ibscher zahllose Stücke mitegeben sind, die jeder Zusammenfügung spotten. Wir werden auf weiteren Zuwachs an Material daher wohl verzichten müssen, abgesehen von ca. sechs Blättern, die sich noch heute im Besitze eines Händlers befinden, weil seine Forderungen zu exorbitant sind. Nach meiner Kenntnis handelt es sich hierbei um ATliche Stücke."

28. On the Cairo *genizah*, see Reif, *A Jewish Archive from Old Cairo*.

29. See Seider, "Aus der Arbeit der Universitätsinstitute," 161: "Schmidt berichtete noch von zahlreichen gefährlichen Fälschungen: 'Bei unserem früheren Agenten entdeckte ich ein ganzes Lager. Er war tief getroffen, als ich alles für gefälscht erklärte.'" I am grateful to Malcolm Choat for drawing this report to my attention. For an additional example of the unreliability of Schmidt's assertions about provenance, see Hagen and Ryholt, *The Antiquities Trade in Egypt*, 175.

30. Indeed, it is difficult to find any information at all about the history of 'Alâlme. The 1914 edition of Baedeker's guide, usually a fairly thorough source for identifying small towns around the Nile, gives the following information about the region between Wasta and Beni Suef: "On the [west bank of the Nile] the mountains recede a little, but on the [east] bank their steep and lofty spurs frequently extend down to the river in rising picturesque forms. None of the Nile-villages before Benisueif need be mentioned. On the [east] bank stands the Coptic convent of Deir Mar Antonios, from which a caravan-route leads to the Red Sea" (Baedeker, *Egypt and the Sûdân*, 225).

31. On the identification of Pispir, see Amélineau, *La géographie de l'Égypte à l'époque copte*, 353–354, and Timm, *Das christlich-koptische Ägypten in arabischer Zeit*, 2.742–749.

32. Perhaps this is the reason that Schmidt did not mention previous archaeological work at the site of Aphroditopolis. The most recent organized work had taken place in 1911 and 1912, when John de Monins Johnson (1882–1956) had searched the area with the specific goal of finding papyri on behalf of the Egypt Exploration Society. As far as I know, the only published records of the excavations are two short reports: Johnson, "Excavations at Atfieh," and Johnson, "Graeco-Roman Branch." Already in 1911 Johnson noted that the ancient sites near the town "were known to have suffered more than ordinarily in recent years from the

depredations of the fellahin" ("Excavations at Atfieh," 6). Johnson's initial impression at the site seemed to confirm this: "The first prospect was the melancholy one of many years' promiscuous plundering and *sebakh*-digging carried on unhindered" (6). After two months of work, Johnson had uncovered a number of pharaonic and Ptolemaic graves in different burial areas, coming away with "a fair measure of useful papyrus cartonnage" (13) from the mummies. He returned for a brief period during 1912, and in neither report does he mention ruins of monasteries, nor papyri or other artifacts from the Roman era or later. The evidence for early Christian remains in the area is thin. See the summary of literary evidence in Timm, *Das christlich-koptische Ägypten*, 1.251–256.

33. Some or all of the caves where the Dead Sea Scrolls were found near Qumran are occasionally claimed to have functioned as *genizot*, but as with most matters relating to the scrolls, there is disagreement. For an informed and even-handed assessment, see Taylor, "Buried Manuscripts and Empty Tombs."

34. Sanders, *A Third-Century Papyrus Codex of the Epistles of Paul*, 13 and 29.

35. Arthur E. R. Boak to Campbell Bonner, January 4, 1931 [this must be an error for 1932], Box 1, Folder 8, Institute for Archaeological Research Papers, Bentley Historical Library, University of Michigan. Fuller citation of this letter can be found in Nongbri, "The Acquisition of the University of Michigan's Portion," 100–101.

36. Schmidt's theory is not entirely undercut by this report. Taylor notes that *genizot* were for temporary storage and that Jewish manuscripts were in fact interred in cemeteries after their removal from the *genizah*. See Taylor, "Buried Manuscripts and Empty Tombs," 269–270.

37. See Horton, "The Chester Beatty Biblical Papyri," 157–158. The memorandum now carries the label "CBP 1566" in the Beatty Library. The full text of the report and images of the pages can be found in Nongbri, "The Acquisition of the University of Michigan's Portion," 107–109 and Figures 1–4. I have been unable to learn anything about the identity of Shaker Farag.

38. No such notes were present in the Beatty Library archives.

39. The memorandum concludes with a curious note: "The coffin on which the three jars were found was of wood and broken, and close to the coffin a glass lamp was found. Plain glass (not coloured) with date of glass on the outside of the lamp." Glass lamps of various sorts were fairly common in the Roman world, but I know of none that was stamped with dates. It occurs to me that "date" here may also mean the dried fruit. Glass bottles made in the withered shape of a date were also common, but again, I am not aware of glass lamps decorated with dates.

40. Kenyon, *The Story of the Bible*, 112–113.

41. For a discussion of the Coptic glosses, see Crum, "The Coptic Glosses."

42. In the 1930s, Crum was more confident, claiming that "the dialect ex-

emplified is pure Fayyûmic and a significant indicator of the writer's home. . . . Fayyûmic, free from any Saʿidic contamination, is unlikely to have come from any place to the east of the Nile" (Crum, "The Coptic Glosses," x and note 3).

43. Eric Turner once favored this hypothesis. See his *Greek Papyri*, 201. I have given reasons to doubt that the two corpora were part of the same find in Nongbri, "The Acquisition of the University of Michigan's Portion," 109–112.

44. For instance, in the handbook of Richard Seider, the provenance of all the Beatty biblical codices is given without discussion in the following form: "Fundort: Aphroditopolis (Mittelägypten)" (*Paläographie der griechischen Papyri*, 2.86, 2.118, and throughout). An exception to the rule is van Haelst, *Catalogue des papyrus littéraires juifs et chrétiens*, 30–31.

45. See Parker, *An Introduction to the New Testament Manuscripts and Their Texts*, 1–10.

46. See Kenyon, *The Chester Beatty Biblical Papyri*, fasciculus II. Given the speed with which Kenyon produced this edition, it is perhaps not surprising that some corrections to his text were necessary. There was talk of producing a new edition in the 1950s, but nothing seems to have come of this. See Horton, "The Chester Beatty Biblical Papyri," 160.

47. Kenyon, *The Chester Beatty Biblical Papyri*, fasciculus I, 16.

48. Thus as late as 1954, Kenneth W. Clark could state that "the most influential factor in recent criticism is the general view that the Neutral text [i.e., the text represented by Codex Vaticanus] is itself a derived text which has passed through a process of revision" ("The Effect of Recent Textual Criticism," 37). For more detail on the role of these papyrus manuscripts in debates about the text of the New Testament documents, see Nongbri, "Reconsidering the Place of Papyrus Bodmer XIV–XV," 434–437.

49. Kenyon, *The Chester Beatty Biblical Papyri*, fasciculus II, x.

50. Orsini and Clarysse, "Early New Testament Manuscripts and Their Dates," classification at 457 and date at 470. The shapes of individual letters can certainly find parallels among the examples of the severe style securely dated to that period (P.Oxy. 7.1012, LDAB 5448, comes to mind), but the square modulus of the letters in the Beatty codex, and the lack of pronounced vertical variation between letters characteristic of the severe style, would seem to bring the Beatty codex nearer to the hand of the Freer gospels, which also shows a decided slope to the right, in overall appearance.

51. Cavallo has stated that the Chester Beatty gospels codex was a product "probabilmente della fine del III secolo" (*Ricerche sulla maiuscola biblica*, 118–119).

52. Codices often referred to as "notebooks" include the so-called Harris Homer (which is not really "literary" in that it was inscribed only on the

right-hand pages, and the left pages were left blank and later used for
the partial copying of a grammatical work; LDAB 2419), a leather sheet
with records of work done and payments made in the Berlin collection
(Berliner Papyrus-Sammlung P 7358 + 7359), and P.Ness. 8–9, a papyrus
codex composed of eight single-sheet quires containing a Greek glossary of some kind and the *Twelve Chapters on Faith* ascribed to Gregory
Thaumaturgus (LDAB 589). All three of these "notebooks" were stab
bound.

53. Many of the Aphrodito codices are made up of single sheets and date to
the eighth century. See the evidence gathered in Gascou, "Les codices
documentaires égyptiens."

54. I base this statement on the dimensions of the Glazier codex (LDAB
107756), which has 112 leaves and was likely originally about 2.6 centimeters thick without its covers. See Sharpe, "The Earliest Bindings with
Wooden Board Covers," 3 and 6.

55. Kenyon wrote two introductions to this codex, one after Beatty's first purchase and a second after Beatty acquired the forty-six additional leaves.
See Kenyon, *The Chester Beatty Biblical Papyri*, fasciculus III and fasciculus III *Supplement.*

56. See Ibscher, "Der Kodex," 12–13. Ibscher concluded that the manufac-
turer of the codex trimmed the sheets progressively shorter as they were
cut from the roll, but his estimate of a ten-centimeter difference between the innermost and outermost sheets of the Pauline Epistles codex
is probably too large.

57. See Kenyon, *The Chester Beatty Biblical Papyri*, fasciculus III *Supplement*,
xiv–xv.

58. Wilcken, "The Chester Beatty Biblical Papyri," 113.

59. See Sanders, *A Third-Century Papyrus Codex of the Epistles of Paul*, 13: "I
agree that the manuscript belongs to the third century, but I would hesitate to put emphasis on the first half of the century." Sanders proposed
a fanciful scenario in which the better-preserved among the Beatty codices were considered later than those that were less well preserved. No
evidence supports such a supposition.

60. See Cavallo, "*Grammata Alexandrina*," 34 and 50.

61. Grenfell and Hunt, *Fayûm Towns and Their Papyri*, 220–221.

62. Turner, *The Typology of the Early Codex*, 20 and 148.

63. Kim, "Palaeographical Dating of P[46] to the Later First Century," 248–
257. For a thoughtful rebuttal of all of Kim's disparate lines of argument,
see Pickering, "The Dating of the Chester Beatty-Michigan Codex of
the Pauline Epistles."

64. Pickering, "The Dating of the Chester Beatty-Michigan Codex of the
Pauline Epistles," 221. Kim's dating is also objectionable on nonpaleo-
graphic grounds. James Royse has pointed out that Beatty Codex II "has
as many as eight conflations, usually readings somehow combining a

reading found in the Western tradition ... with one found in the Alexandrian tradition. ... Such readings suggest that [the codex] is late enough that both these traditions had already arisen (at least in some early form), and thus a first century date would appear extremely implausible" (Royse, *Scribal Habits*, 201).

65. See Orsini and Clarysse, "Early New Testament Manuscripts and Their Dates," 458 for the assignment of style and 470 for the assignment of date.

66. See the discussion of Epp, "Issues in the Interrelation of New Testament Textual Criticism and Canon," 495–502.

67. See Ebojo, "A Scribe and His Manuscript."

68. See Malik, *P.Beatty III (𝔓47)*.

69. Kenyon, *The Chester Beatty Biblical Papyri*, fasciculus III, xi–xii.

70. Turner, *The Typology of the Early Codex*, 64 (but compare p. 87, where the Beatty Revelation codex is simply "third century," and p. 148, where "third century?" is the designation); Malik, *P.Beatty III (𝔓47)*, 41–58; Orsini and Clarysse, "Early New Testament Manuscripts and Their Dates," 458 and 470.

71. Kenyon, *The Chester Beatty Biblical Papyri*, fasciculus IV. These two books have since been reedited by Pietersma, *Chester Beatty Biblical Papyri IV and V*.

72. Kenyon, *The Chester Beatty Biblical Papyri*, fasciculus IV, ix.

73. Pietersma, *Chester Beatty Biblical Papyri IV and V*, ix.

74. Kenyon, *The Chester Beatty Biblical Papyri*, fasciculus IV, ix.

75. See Cavallo, *La scrittura greca e latina dei papiri*, 89, and Turner, *The Typology of the Early Codex*, 18, 64, and 165 (third to fourth century); 76 (fourth century).

76. See Kenyon, *The Chester Beatty Biblical Papyri*, fasciculus V, 71, note 17; and 99.

77. Kenyon, *The Chester Beatty Biblical Papyri*, fasciculus V, ix.

78. For the range of opinions on the Hyperides papyrus, see Kenyon, *The Palaeography of Greek Papyri*, 85–88. For a more recent assessment, see Cavallo, "La scrittura greca libraria tra i secoli I a.C.–I d.C.," 25.

79. Kenyon, *The Bible and Modern Scholarship*, 18.

80. Turner, "Some Questions," 438.

81. The other parallels proposed by Turner were PSI 13.1337, a record of a trial before the prefect Appius Sabinus (after 250 CE); P.Oxy. 8.1100, which records an edict of the prefect Subatianus Aquila from the year 206 CE; PSI 12.1248, a letter of the year 235 CE; and SB 5.7696, another record of a trial before Appius Sabinus published by Skeat and Wegener, "A Trial Before the Prefect of Egypt Appius Sabinus."

82. P.Oxy. 17.2105 had itself been misdated by its original editor. Turner related the story: The papyrus "is the edict of a prefect read by Hunt as Petronius Honoratus, prefect in A.D. 148. In 1967 Dr. John Rea reread

this name as that of Maevius prefect in A.D. 231–36, i.e., almost ninety years later! The hand can in fact be easily paralleled from documents of the middle of the third century, e.g., P. Oxy. ix 1200 (A.D. 266). This example is especially instructive since it is the error of an outstanding palaeographer; and concerns a documentary hand, a type of writing which it has often been claimed is easier to date with confidence than a book hand. Any practicing palaeographer will be able to think of similar errors in which he has himself been caught out and will be humble in consequence" (*The Typology of the Early Codex*, 3).

83. Roberts, *Manuscript, Society and Belief*, 78–81, at 81. Nevertheless, in 1983, Roberts and Skeat included the Beatty Numbers-Deuteronomy codex in their list of Christian books that in their opinion "may be assigned to the second century" (Roberts and Skeat, *The Birth of the Codex*, 40).

84. Turner, "Some Questions," 438.

85. Kenyon, *The Chester Beatty Biblical Papyri*, fasciculus VI, viii.

86. Kenyon, *The Chester Beatty Biblical Papyri*, fasciculus VI, xiii.

87. Crisci, "Note sulla più antica produzione di libri cristiani."

88. Turner, *The Typology of the Early Codex*, 20 and 100.

89. Kenyon, *The Chester Beatty Biblical Papyri*, fasciculus I, 8–9.

90. Wilcken, "The Chester Beatty Biblical Papyri," 113.

91. Kenyon, *The Chester Beatty Biblical Papyri*, fasciculus VII, viii.

92. See Johnson, Gehman, and Kase, *The John H. Scheide Biblical Papyri*, 5.

93. The reference comes in a review of Richard Seider's handbook (Cavallo, "Note sulla scrittura greca libraria dei papiri," 75). Seider, however, assigns a date of "third to fourth century" for the leaves of Ezekiel but a date at the beginning of the third century for the leaves of Daniel! See Seider, *Paläographie der griechischen Papyri*, 2.122–123 and 2.143. Turner also noted this oddity and favored the later date (Turner, Review of Seider's *Paläographie der griechischen Papyri, Band 2*, 712). Elsewhere, however, Cavallo has assigned this codex to the middle of the third century. See Cavallo, "*Grammata Alexandrina*," 50.

94. Roberts, *Manuscript, Society and Belief*, 79, note 1.

95. The second leaf has been reedited: Pietersma, "The 'Lost' Folio of the Chester Beatty *Ecclesiasticus*."

96. Kenyon, *The Chester Beatty Biblical Papyri*, fasciculus VI, xiv.

97. See Turner, *The Typology of the Early Codex*, 181, and Cavallo and Maehler, *Greek Bookhands of the Early Byzantine Period*, 10–11.

98. The only codex that was not edited by Kenyon, this volume was published by Campbell Bonner of the University of Michigan. See Bonner, *The Last Chapters of Enoch in Greek*, and Bonner, *The Homily on the Passion by Melito Bishop of Sardis*.

99. A codex found in Akhmim (LDAB 1088) contained earlier chapters of Enoch, and subsequently, a nearly complete Greek text of Melito's ser-

mon was discovered among the Bodmer Papyri (P.Bodmer XIII, LDAB 2565).

100. See Kenyon, *The Chester Beatty Biblical Papyri*, fasciculus I, 9, and fasciculus VIII, 12. Bonner also assigned the codex to the fourth century, though without fully assenting to the comparison with LDAB 5590; see Bonner, *The Last Chapters of Enoch in Greek*, 12–13.

101. For this and other excerpts from the letter, see Horton, "The Chester Beatty Biblical Papyri," 154–155.

102. I draw information about these books from the editions of Kristen De Troyer in Minutoli and Pintaudi (eds.), *Papyri Graecae Schøyen*.

103. I have not had the benefit of studying these manuscripts in person. I wonder whether it might be possible that the two Schøyen manuscripts come from a single codex. Codices with multiple sets of page numbers restarting at "1" are known (such as the Bodmer composite codex, LDAB 2565), and the slight variation in the dimensions of the extant Schøyen leaves is within the limits of tolerance for ancient papyrus codices. See Turner, *The Typology of the Early Codex*, 23.

104. In general, the remains of codices from Oxyrhynchus do not preserve this many leaves. One exception is P.Oxy. 74.4968 (LDAB 119313), which is several papyrus leaves from two quires of a codex of Acts. But, as the editors of the piece note, these leaves came from a box of material with mixed provenance and so may not actually be from Oxyrhynchus.

105. De Troyer would place the Schøyen manuscripts in the late second century or early third century, citing other authorities: "Guglielmo Cavallo dates the papyrus between the end of the second and the beginning of the third century C.E., more precisely, ca. 210–215 C.E. This date has been confirmed by Detlef Fraenkel and Udo Quast" (P.Schøyen 1.23, p. 92). Cavallo provided a longer paleographic description classifying the handwriting of these manuscripts as a type of Alexandrian Majuscule and concluding by stating, "si puo assegnare il nostro codice di papiro con la piu alta probabilita ad una data intorno al tardo II o inizio del III secolo d.C." (we can assign our papyrus codex with the highest probability to a date around the late second century or the beginning of the third century CE) (P.Schøyen 1.23, p. 92). I am not sure of the source of the impossibly narrow five-year span "ca. 210–215" CE.

106. See Dospěl Williams, "'Into the Hands of a Well-Known Antiquary of Cairo.'"

107. The paleography of magical papyri is only beginning to be explored. See Nodar and Torallas Tovar, "Paleography of Magical Handbooks."

Chapter Five. An Elusive Collection

1. Today, parts of the Bodmer Papyri are found in the following institutions (in addition to the Fondation Martin Bodmer): The Chester Beatty

Library, the University of Cologne papyrus collection, the Duke University papyrus collection, the Abbey of Montserrat, the Vatican Library, the VanKampen Collection, the Museum of the Bible, and the collection of Martin Schøyen (others would add even more locations: the university library of Geneva, the Palau Ribes collection, the Pierpont Morgan Library, the Beinecke Library at Yale, and the Princeton University Library).

2. In 2000, the K. G. Saur publishing house produced a ten-volume set of reprints of items published in the *Papyrus Bodmer* series along with photographic plates of the books (many of which were not included in the original editions). See Bircher (ed.), *Bibliotheca Bodmeriana*.

3. For an up-to-date listing of the "P.Bodmer" items listed by number, see Nongbri, "The Bodmer Papyri: An Inventory of 'P.Bodmer' Items."

4. When this chapter was nearly complete, the 2015 volume of the journal *Adamantius* appeared. It contained several articles dedicated to various aspects of the Bodmer Papyri. Two articles in particular contain projects that partially overlap with my own: Fournet, "Anatomie d'une bibliothèque," and Schubert, "Les Papyrus Bodmer." We all have identified a similar set of problems in the study of the collection, although we sometimes resolve these problems in rather different ways.

5. Again, the 2015 issue of *Adamantius* contains works relevant to this topic. On the codicology of the Bodmer books, see Buzi, "Qualche riflessione." On the paleography, see Orsini, "I Papiri Bodmer." Other individual books did emerge from the antiquities market in states of preservation similar to, or even better than, the Bodmer Papyri. See, for instance, the Glazier codex (LDAB 107756) of the Pierpont Morgan Library, a Coptic text of Acts on parchment that was extraordinarily well preserved with its wooden covers. Good color images can be found in Kebabian, "The Binding of the Glazier Manuscript." It should be noted, however, that at least one scholar (James M. Robinson) considers it possible that the Glazier codex was part of the Bodmer find.

6. Robinson, *The Story of the Bodmer Papyri*.

7. See, for example, Robinson, *The Story of the Bodmer Papyri*, 141. For a similar assessment of the book, see Schubert, "Les Papyrus Bodmer," 41.

8. See Kraus, *A Rare Book Saga*, 272: "Dr. Bodmer rose to the first rank of collectors in 1931 when he bought a Gutenberg Bible for a price rumored to be £30,000—not the inflation riddled, devalued pound of today but the old prewar value of $5, thus making it the highest price paid for a printed book up to that time."

9. For Bodmer's conception of world literature, see Bodmer, *Eine Bibliothek der Weltliteratur*; Bodmer, "Ansprachen anläßlich der Einweihung der Bibliotheca Bodmeriana," 9–20, esp. 16; and Méla, *Legends of the Centuries*, 41–50.

10. Bongard's account is given in Méla, *Legends of the Centuries*, 34–35. Robinson's 2011 book makes no mention of this source.

11. On Tano, see Merrillees, *The Tano Family*, and Hagen and Ryholt, *The Antiquities Trade in Egypt*, 266–267.

12. Méla, *Legends of the Centuries*, 35. This individual from Luxor is identified in an editorial aside as Mahmoud Mohasseb, "an industrialist from Luxor." In fact, this person may also have been a trader in antiquities, a descendant of the well-known antiquities dealer Muhammad Mohassib (1843–1928). See Hagen and Ryholt, *The Antiquities Trade in Egypt*, 245–247. In regard to P.Bodmer II, an alternate story exists of Bodmer acquiring at least part of the codex himself in 1955. See Zimmermann, *Neutestamentliche Methodenlehre*, 73: "Ein Sohn des Herrn Bodmer mir mitteilte, konnte sein Vater bei einem Aufenthalt in Ägypten im Jahre 1955 die Handschrift von einer ihm befreundeten koptischen Familie erwerben" (A son of Mr. Bodmer informed me that during a stay in Egypt in 1955, his father was able to acquire the manuscript from a Coptic family that had befriended him).

13. Kasser, "Status quaestionis 1988 sulla presunta origine dei cosiddetti Papiri Bodmer," 193: "Ha affermato con tutta sicurezza che il luogo di questa scoperta non fu nei dintorni di Nag Hammadi, ma in quelli di Assiut" (She has affirmed with all certainty that the location of this discovery was not in the surroundings of Nag Hammadi but in those of Asyut).

14. Letter from William H. Willis to James M. Robinson, February 25, 1980, cited in Robinson, *The Story of the Bodmer Papyri*, 37.

15. Martin, *Papyrus Bodmer I*.

16. Only a part of P.Bodmer II had been acquired before 1956. During 1956, Bodmer was able to get more of the codex, thus a second volume was published in 1958 and reprinted with facsimile plates of the whole in 1962.

17. This single codex was published separately as P.Bodmer V (Nativity of Mary), P.Bodmer X (apocryphal correspondence of Paul and the Corinthians), P.Bodmer XI (11th Ode of Solomon), P.Bodmer VII (Jude), P.Bodmer XIII (Melito's paschal sermon), P.Bodmer XII (a hymn), and P.Bodmer VIII (1–2 Peter). For further details, see Nongbri, "Recent Progress," 171–172.

18. Kasser and Testuz were emphatic about this point in their original edition. See Kasser and Testuz, *Papyrus Bodmer XXIV*, 7: "Nous ne savons pas de quelle partie de l'Egypte provient le Papyrus Bodmer XXIV. Une seule chose est sûre: il ne fait pas partie du lot comprenant les P. Bodmer, grecs ou coptes, II à XVI et XVIII à XXIII, et, pas davantage, il n'est de la même origine que le P. Bodmer I ou le P. Bodmer XVII" (We do not know from what part of Egypt P.Bodmer XXIV originated. Only

one thing is certain: It was not part of the lot composed of P.Bodmer II to XVI and XVIII to XXIII, nor was it of the same origin as P.Bodmer I or P.Bodmer XVII). Yet, in 1991, Kasser did include P.Bodmer XXIV as a part of the ancient collection. No reason is given for the change. See Kasser's entry for "Bodmer Papyri," in Atiya (ed.), *The Coptic Encyclopedia*, 8.48–53.

19.   For this theory, see especially Turner, *Greek Papyri*, 52. I do not know the exact geographic information on the land register. This document ("P.Bodmer I recto") is said to have been published in an extremely small print run in 2010: Derda, *P. Bodmer I Recto*. As of July 2017, no library to which I have access possessed a copy, so I have not been able to consult this work.

20.   See Cribiore, "Higher Education in Early Byzantine Egypt," 51; Martin and Primavesi, *L'Empédocle de Strasbourg*, 43–51; and Bagnall, *Egypt in Late Antiquity*, 103–104, which cites relevant earlier literature. A systematic statement of this thesis was promised by Joseph van Haelst in 1991, but it never appeared. See Kasser, Cavallo, and van Haelst, "Appendice," 105–106, note 5.

21.   This theory was put forward by Turner, *Greek Papyri*, 52 and 201. It was floated again as recently as 2009. See Martinez, "The Papyri and Early Christianity," 612, note 26. For reasons to doubt the theory, see Nongbri, "The Acquisition of the University of Michigan's Portion," 109–111.

22.   See, for example, Kasser, "Bodmer Papyri," 8.48.

23.   See Kasser, "Les dialectes coptes," 81: "Le manuscrit qui nous l'a fait connaître semble avoir été trouvé un peu à l'est (nord-est) de Nag' Hammādi."

24.   See Reverdin, "Les Genevois et Ménandre," 9: "Pendant longtemps, on n'eut que des indications assez vagues sur leur provenance. Peu avant de mourir, toutefois, l'antiquaire qui les avait vendus, leva le secret; il révéla que ces papyrus provenaient d'un village proche de Nag'Hammâdi, en Haute Egypte, localité rendue célèbre par la découverte, vers la même époque, de textes gnostiques coptes; qu'il avait acquis tout le lot, à l'exception de quelques fragments, détachés au moment de la découverte, et qu'il l'avait vendu, sans en rien distraire, à M. Bodmer. Il s'agit, selon toute vraisemblance, de ce qui subsiste de la bibliothèque d'un couvent" (For a long time, we had only vague indications about their provenance. Shortly before dying, however, the dealer who had sold them unveiled the secret: He revealed that these papyri came from a village near Nag Hammadi in Upper Egypt, a place made famous by the discovery of Coptic gnostic texts at about the same time and that he had acquired the whole lot with the exception of a few fragments and that he had sold it, without diverting anything, to Mr. Bodmer. This is, in all likelihood, what remains of the library of a monastery).

25.   See Kasser, "Status quaestionis 1988," 191–192: "Poche settimane prima

della sua morte, l'antiquario che ha fornito la quasi totalità della raccolta ha confidato all'autore del presente 'status quaestionis' che tutti questi documenti furono trovati verso l'anno 1950 o 1951 a 'Dabba' o 'Debba' (Ed-Debba, 5 km ad est, leggermente nord-est, di Nag Hammadi. Certo, si sa che normalmente gli antiquari non danno informazioni autentiche sull'origine della loro merce. Ma dato che costui era in legami di amicizia con l'autore, stava per morire e sapeva che questa informazione era di massima importanza per la scienza, si può considerare verosimile che abbia parlato con sincerità" (Just a few weeks before his death, the dealer who supplied almost the whole collection confided in the author of the present "status quaestionis" that all these manuscripts were found in the year 1950 or 1951 at Dabba or Debba [Ed-Debba, 5 km east, slightly north-east of Nag Hammadi]. Of course, it is well known that normally antiquities dealers do not provide true information about the origins of their goods. But given that this man was in the bonds of friendship with the author, he was about to die, and he knew that this information was of the highest importance to scholarship, it can be considered likely that he spoke with sincerity). In 2000, Kasser noted that he still trusted the dealer's information: "There is thus every reason to take at face value what the merchant later said about 'Ed-Debba' as the place of the find" (Kasser, "Introduction," 1.lvi).

26. As far as I know, Robinson first published this information in 1977: Van Elderen and Robinson, "The Second Season of the Nag Hammadi Excavation," 52–54. He published numerous more detailed accounts in the following years: "The Discovering and Marketing of Coptic Manuscripts"; "The First Christian Monastic Library"; "The Pachomian Monastic Library" (printed in both the *Occasional Papers of the Institute for Antiquity and Christianity* and *Manuscripts of the Middle East*); "The Manuscript's History and Codicology"; and "Introduction: AC. 1390."

27. Robinson, *The Story of the Bodmer Papyri*, 108–110. I distill what follows from Robinson's dense account, pp. 108–129.

28. Robinson, *The Story of the Bodmer Papyri*, 113 and 135.

29. Robinson, *The Story of the Bodmer Papyri*, 116.

30. See the account and sources cited in Robinson, *The Story of the Bodmer Papyri*, 35–39, but also note Doutreleau's own somewhat doubtful assessment of his own memories after twenty years at *The Story of the Bodmer Papyri*, 42, note 101, and 45, note 112.

31. Letter from Doutreleau to James M. Robinson, August 31, 1976, cited in Robinson, *The Story of the Bodmer Papyri*, 37, note 84: "The Bodmer Papyri came almost all from Tano's, and . . . Mr. Bodmer was ignorant of their origin. Tano, who knew much more on this topic, said nothing about it to the purchasers. It is in chatting with him that I learned what I have already said."

32. See Willis, "The New Collections of Papyri at the University of Mis-

sissippi." The dealer from whom Mississippi purchased the Crosby-Schøyen codex and its portion of P.Bodmer XXII has been identified as Maguid Sameda. See Robinson, *The Story of the Bodmer Papyri*, 41–42, note 99.

33. In addition to the details about the Barcelona-Montserrat codex collected by Robinson (*The Story of the Bodmer Papyri*, 99–101), see now the more extensive account in Gil and Torallas Tovar, *Hadrianus*, 17–27, which presents a letter written in 1955 from Sylvestre Chaleur, director of the Institut Copte in Cairo, to Roca-Puig claiming that the provenance of the Barcelona-Montserrat codex was "the monastery of St. Pachom."

34. See Shore, *Joshua I–VI and Other Passages in Coptic*, 7.

35. See Robinson's account in *The Story of the Bodmer Papyri*, 63. I have adjusted his citations of the registry notes after checking the originals in Dublin. Robinson has nothing to say about the claim that this book (and presumably the others) was found in a cemetery.

36. See Robinson, *The Story of the Bodmer Papyri*, 127 and 162.

37. The connection between the Barcelona-Montserrat codex and the Pachomian monastery in the records of Roca-Puig may ultimately derive from the same source: Roca-Puig's correspondence also indicates dealings with Phocion Tano, who may well have been the seller of the codex. See Gil and Torallas Tovar, *Hadrianus*, 29–30.

38. See the letter from Jean Doresse cited in Robinson, *The Story of the Bodmer Papyri*, 38–39, note 90.

39. Robinson raised the possibility of miscommunication in the case of Bongard's claim that Tano told her the place of the find was "Mina" or "Minia" near Asyut: "In fact the local Copts of the Dishnā region offer the popular etymology to the effect that Abū Manā' derives from the name of the Coptic saint, Mina, which may help to explain the garbled report by Mlle Bongard" (Robinson, *The Story of the Bodmer Papyri*, 179). It is a clever explanation, but it still would not explain the alleged connection to Asyut.

40. For this list, see Di Bitonto Kasser, "P.Bodmer LI recto," 112–113.

41. See the edition in Fournet, "Anatomie d'une bibliothèque," 25–40.

42. In earlier publications, I was more ambivalent on the question of the find spot, as I knew that the documents from the cover of P.Bodmer XXIII were in the process of publication (this was announced already in 1998; see Di Bitonto Kasser, "P.Bodmer LI recto," 112–113), but I was not yet aware of any specific geographic associations of that material. The matter is not completely settled, but the weight of evidence does make the region of Dishna the most likely find spot.

43. See the literature cited in note 26 above.

44. Robinson, *The Story of the Bodmer Papyri*, 169–172.

45. For a good overview of Pachomius and his movement, see Rousseau, *Pachomius.*

46. Robinson, *The Story of the Bodmer Papyri*, 8.

47. Turner, "Papyrus Bodmer XXVIII," 1–2. Turner noted, however, that the director of the Bibliothèque Bodmer at the time assured him that if these fragments did come from a binding, "they had been extracted from it before they reached the Bodmer Library" (2). Robinson, who regarded P.Bodmer XXVIII as part of the find, emphasized this point and also referred to the other rolls identified as copies of Homer in order to argue that all these rolls and P.Bodmer I formed part of the same collection (Robinson, *The Story of the Bodmer Papyri*, 27). But, as we will see, there is good reason to doubt that these other Homeric rolls were part of the find.

48. Schubert, "P. Bodmer LII."

49. Schubert also makes this point ("Les Papyrus Bodmer," 44): "Dans plusieurs cas, des fragments sont répertoriés comme des P.Bodmer, mais leur usage a été soit distinct de l'ensemble soit antérieur aux textes constituant le noyau central, et pourraient donc n'avoir rien à voir avec le gros de la collection" (In many cases, fragments are listed as "P.Bodmer," but their usage has been either distinct from the collection or before the texts that make up the nucleus, and they may therefore have nothing to do with the bulk of the collection).

50. As far as I know, there is no new information on P.Bodmer XLIV, a parchment codex of Daniel said to be written in Bohairic and assigned by Wolf-Peter Funk to a date from the tenth to the twelfth centuries and thus not to be considered part of the Bodmer find (Robinson, *The Story of the Bodmer Papyri*, 183). In 2016, Daniel Sharp examined P.Bodmer XLII and reported that it is a single fragmentary leaf of a parchment codex of 2 Corinthians in Coptic (personal communication from Sharp in August 2016). It bears a close resemblance to P.Bodmer XIX in terms of format and script and may have been a part of that codex before it was rebound to include only parts of the Gospel According to Matthew and Romans.

51. Hurst, "Papyrus Bodmer 49," 221: "Martin Bodmer l'avait sans doute acheté avant d'acquérir le lot qui fait la célébrité des papyrus Bodmer" (Martin Bodmer doubtless bought this before acquiring the lot that sealed the fame of the Bodmer Papyri).

52. See Hurst, "Papyrus Bodmer 48," 30: "Ce 'petit fragment' . . . acquis sans doute par le collectionneur Martin Bodmer avant l'achat du lot qui constitue l'essentiel des manuscrits sur papyrus de cette bibliothèque" (This "small fragment" . . . doubtless acquired by the collector Martin Bodmer before the purchase of the lot that makes up the essential manuscripts on papyrus in this library).

53. See Bodmer, *Eine Bibliothek der Weltliteratur,* 141.

54. Kasser and Luisier, "P.Bodmer XLIII."

55. Kasser and Luisier, "P.Bodmer XLIII," 251, note 3: "Selon des souvenirs personnels, peut-être juste avant 1970" (According to personal memories, perhaps just before 1970).

56. If it could be demonstrated that the leather of the present binding of the Palau Ribes codex was added in the eighteenth or nineteenth century, then this codex could be decisively excluded from the Bodmer find. See Albarrán Martínez and Nodar Domínguez, "Escribir la palabra de Dios," 27.

57. Charlotte Magnin and Cécile Neeser Hever are currently at work on studies of Martin Bodmer's correspondence and diaries.

58. This codex was published by Clarysse and Wouters, "A Schoolboy's Exercise in the Chester Beatty Library." It was attributed to the Bodmer find by Blanchard, "Sur le milieu d'origine du papyrus Bodmer de Ménandre." Blanchard based his argument on the similarities and sequences of names in the Bodmer Menander, the Beatty exercise, and another school text, P.Bouriant 1 (LDAB 2744), even going so far as to almost claim that the latter (which was published already in the 1920s!) was part of the Bodmer collection: "il me paraît donc possible de présenter le papyrus scolaire Chester Beatty et, à un moindre degré, le *P.Bouriant* 1, comme des témoins du papyrus Bodmer de Ménandre" (it seems therefore possible to me to present the Chester Beatty school papyrus and, to a lesser degree, P.Bouriant 1, as witnesses to the Bodmer Menander papyrus), 219. The similarities that Blanchard points out are impressive, but surely, if Menander was part of a school curriculum, the Bodmer Menander was only one of many manuscripts that included the *Samia-Dyskolos-Aspis* triad.

59. See Robinson, *The Story of the Bodmer Papyri,* 106–107. In a book that was apparently written later (even though it was published earlier), Robinson rejects a provenance in Upper Egypt for the Qarara codices (*Secrets of Judas,* 44), so I have left the Tchacos codex and the other Qarara codices out of Table 5.4.

60. See Kasser and Testuz, *Papyrus Bodmer XXIV,* 7, and Kasser "Bodmer Papyri," 8.48.

61. For this reason, Fournet leaves P.Bodmer I out of his "minimalist" inventory. See Fournet, "Anatomie d'une bibliothèque," 9.

62. The Bodmer Papyri (both actual and alleged) in the Duke collection have an especially complicated history. These pieces originated from the private collection of archaeologist David M. Robinson (1880–1958). On the odd history of these "Robinson Papyri," some of which still seem to be unaccounted for, see Willis, "The New Collections of Papyri at the University of Mississippi." An update from a quarter century later suggests that some of the Robinson Papyri did not end up in the Duke col-

lection and were presumably dispersed on the antiquities market; see Willis, "Duke Papyri," 44–47. This assumption would seem to be confirmed by the recently published Sappho fragments (LDAB 341738), which are said to have come from the collection of Robinson Papyri; see Obbink, "The Poems of Sappho." On the whole question, see Nongbri, "The Robinson Papyri."

63. See Fournet's catalog in "Anatomie d'une bibliothèque," 21–24.

64. Victor Martin published parts of the Plutarch roll in late 1951 and described the pieces as having been "acquired last winter from an antiquities dealer in Cairo for the Library of Geneva." This most likely refers to the winter of 1950–1951. See Martin, "Un papyrus de Plutarque," 138: "Le papyrus publié ci-après atteste qu'on lisait aussi Plutarque en Égypte dès la fin du IId siècle en tout cas. Il s'agit de débris d'un volumen contenant la Vie de Jules-César acquis l'hiver passé d'un marchand d'antiquités du Caire pour la Bibliothèque de Genève." Martin also published parts of the Alexander/cynic roll in 1959 and reported that this roll had been acquired in Cairo in 1950. See Martin, "Un recueil de diatribes cyniques," 77: "acquisition au Caire en 1950 pour le compte de la Bibliothèque publique et universitaire de Genève."

65. See John Lundon's comments in Gronewald et al. (eds.), *Kölner Papyri*, 59, note 10. So also Fournet, "Homère et les papyrus non littéraires," 126 and 152. On the archive of Aurelius Ammon, see "Archive of Aurelius Ammon, Scholasticus, Son of Petearbeschinis," Leuven Homepage of Papyrus Collections, http://www.trismegistos.org/arch/archives/pdf /31.pdf.

66. See Fournet, "Anatomie d'une bibliothèque," 11.

67. For a discussion of similarly constructed codices, see Bagnall, "Public Administration and the Documentation of Roman Panopolis," 1–12.

68. See the online summary of the archive, "Archive of Descendants of Alopex," Leuven Homepage of Papyrus Collections, http://www.tris megistos.org/arch/archives/pdf/317.pdf. Robinson makes his case for including the tax codex as a part of the Bodmer find in *The Story of the Bodmer Papyri*, 75–77.

69. See Robinson's discussion of the codex in *The Story of the Bodmer Papyri*, 74–80, esp. 75–76, and 98–99.

70. Robinson's most extensive discussion of the Pachomian material can be found in *The Story of the Bodmer Papyri*, 130–150.

71. On Pachomius and the foundation of the monastery at Pbow, see the ancient biographies of Pachomius collected in Veilleux, *Pachomian Koinonia*, 71 and 334.

72. On the church at Faw Qibli, see Grossmann and Lease, "Faw Qibli."

73. In July 2017, Dan Sharp and I were able to identify fragments of more Pachomian literature among some unsorted material at the Fondation Martin Bodmer. Thus, in addition to P.Bodmer XXXIX (letter 11b of

Pachomius), the collection also holds parts of letters 3 and 4 of Horsie-sios, which form parts of Chester Beatty Library Ac. 1494 and 1495 (LDAB 108131 and 108132). We have not yet been able to locate acquisition details for the newly identified Bodmer fragments.

74. So also Fournet, "Anatomie d'une bibliothèque," 12: "De plus, l'argument de la présence de ces textes dans les mêmes collections doit être relativisé par le fait que, dans les années 1950, ce sont les mêmes grandes collections qui sont à la recherche de papyrus: il n'est pas étonnant que ce soit vers elles qu'affluent des textes de provenances diverses" (Moreover, the argument from the presence of these texts in the same collections must be relativized by the fact that, in the 1950s, the same great collections were searching for papyri; it is not surprising that this is where texts of diverse provenances would end up). It should also be recalled that in the 1950s Bodmer was acquiring early Christian books that clearly did not belong to the main find. P.Bodmer LVII, a portion of a commentary on the Psalms by Didymus the Blind, was definitely part of the Tura find of 1941 (see Chapter 3), but it was bought by Bodmer through Bongard in 1953 from the Groppi Collection in Cairo (Méla, *Legends of the Centuries*, 34).

75. Robinson has responded to those who challenge his inclusion of the Pachomian material and other items with the main Bodmer find: "To attribute such manuscripts to the shared provenience will remain to some degree speculative. However to attribute to each a separate provenience is also speculative, in that otherwise unattested manuscript discoveries must thereby be conjectured" (*The Story of the Bodmer Papyri*, 52). This claim is a false equivalence. Such a statement presumes an exhaustive knowledge of every single illicit discovery of a manuscript anywhere in Egypt during the 1950s. It is the kind of complete knowledge that surely neither Robinson nor anyone else has ever had. It is no stretch of the imagination to infer (not "conjecture") that illicit digging turned up lots of items in different times and places that are forever lost to scholarship.

76. On P.Bodmer LVII, see Gronewald, *Didymos der Blinde;* on P.Bodmer LVIII, see Crum, *Der Papyruscodex.*

77. P.Bodmer L once may have been part of a companion codex to P.Bodmer XVII, but as it was found bonded by the decay ("collé par la pourriture") of the edges of two leaves of P.Bodmer XVII, this leaf was likely already reduced to its present state in antiquity. For discussion, see Kasser, *Papyrus Bodmer XVII*, 9–10.

78. See Kasser, *Papyrus Bodmer XVII*, 7: "La provenance exacte nous est inconnue. En tous cas, on ne peut établir aucun rapport entre ce document et les autres codices anciens (grecs ou coptes, de papyrus ou de parchemin) appartenant à la Bibliothèque Bodmer et publiés dans cette même série: d'ailleurs, [P.Bodmer XVII] se distingue d'eux en tous points" (The

exact provenance is unknown. In any case, one cannot establish any connection between this document and the other ancient codices [Greek or Coptic, papyrus or parchment] belonging to the Bibliotheca Bodmeriana and published in the same series: [P.Bodmer XVII] is distinct from them in every way).

79. The leaves of the Codex of Visions, for example, are reconstructed as 17.5 centimeters wide and 28.5 centimeters high. P.Bodmer XVII has almost exactly the same ratio and is only about 10 percent larger.

80. See Cavallo, "Greek and Latin Writing in the Papyri," 129.

81. Letter of William H. Willis to James M. Robinson, May 27, 1980, cited in Robinson, *The Story of the Bodmer Papyri*, 22, note 38.

82. Letter of Louis Doutreleau to James M. Robinson, July 28, 1976, cited in Robinson, *The Story of the Bodmer Papyri*, 45, note 112.

83. For reasons to doubt that P.Bodmer XX + IX was joined to the composite codex, see Nongbri, "Recent Progress."

84. See Robinson, *The Story of the Bodmer Papyri*, 57–62.

85. This point was noted already by Robinson, *The Story of the Bodmer Papyri*, 77.

86. Other aspects of the Bodmer books that I do not treat here, including pagination and titles, are addressed in Buzi, "Qualche riflessione," 47–59.

87. Several Bodmer Papyri show evidence of being repaired with modern tape before their arrival in Geneva.

88. This image is composite. I have made every effort to reproduce the images at a relatively true scale.

89. For details on the binding of P.Bodmer II, see Nongbri, "The Limits of Palaeographic Dating," 25–32. For a discussion of the construction of P.Bodmer XVIII, see Kasser, *Papyrus Bodmer XVIII*, 7–8.

90. For an attempt to legitimate the second-century date for P.Bodmer II, see Hunger, "Zur Datierung des Papyrus Bodmer II." For thorough criticism of Hunger's arguments, see the summary of scholarship on P.Bodmer II in Nongbri, "The Limits of Palaeographic Dating."

91. The similarity in appearance of Schøyen MS 193 ("the Crosby codex") and P.Bodmer II was noted already in the 1960s. William H. Willis commented: "The closest parallel in size, hand, quality of papyrus, and general appearance is the Bodmer *Évangile de Jean* (P. Bodmer II). . . . So similar in format are the Crosby and Bodmer codices that one would surmise that they are products of the same scriptorium" ("The New Collection of Papyri at the University of Mississippi," 387). Schøyen MS 193 has been assigned a wide variety of dates, but it has recently been subjected to radiocarbon analysis, and the publication of those results should add some important new data to the discussion. I am grateful to Hugo Lundhaug for this information.

92. For a detailed assessment of the date of P.Bodmer II, see Nongbri, "The

Limits of Palaeographic Dating." While agreeing on the possibility of a fourth-century date for P.Bodmer II, Orsini has questioned the specific comparison between P.Bodmer II and P.Bodmer XX on the grounds that the two pieces "display two different graphic types" ("tipologie grafiche differenti") and thus are not comparable (Orsini, "I Papiri Bodmer," 61, note 5). I find this line of argument unconvincing. Surely, in the broad spectrum of ancient Greek writing, these samples are sufficiently similar in appearance, both at the level of the formation of individual letters and at the level of overall appearance, to warrant comparison. I sense that the basis of our difference in opinion stems from the fact that "styles" (or "stylistic classes" or "graphic types") tend to be conceived as inherent qualities of ancient writing rather than modern systems of classification used by scholars for our own interests. See Chapter 2 above.

93. Nag Hammadi Codices II, VI, X, XI, and the loose leaves designated as Codex XIII all fall into this group.

94. Turner proposed paleographic parallels for the Menander codex dating from the fourth century (see Turner, Review of Seider's *Paläographie, Band 1*). More recently Pasquale Orsini has suggested pushing the date of the codex to the second half of the fourth century on the basis of comparisons with the Barcelona-Montserrat codex (Orsini, "I Papiri Bodmer," 65–66).

95. The original editors of P.Bodmer XIV–XV argued on slim grounds for a date of 175–225 CE (see Martin and Kasser, *Papyrus Bodmer XIV–XV*, 1.13). Colin H. Roberts asserted that the Psalms codex (P.Bodmer XXIV) was copied "in all probability in the second half of the second century a. d." See Barthélemy, "Le Psautier grec et le papyrus Bodmer XXIV," 106–107. Turner, however, preferred a third- to fourth-century date for this codex (*The Typology of the Early Codex*, 21, 59, and 171). More recently, Orsini has suggested it was copied in the first half of the third century on the basis of a comparison with the handwriting of such pieces as the Oxyrhynchus roll of Julius Africanus, P.Oxy. 3.412 (Orsini, "I Papiri Bodmer," 62).

96. For a detailed assessment of the date of P.Bodmer XIV–XV, see Nongbri, "Reconsidering the Place of Papyrus Bodmer XIV-XV."

97. See Aland and Aland, *The Text of the New Testament*, 244.

98. The radiocarbon testing results for P.Bodmer XXIV are forthcoming in Dru, "A Complex Pondering." I am grateful to Josephine Dru for supplying this information.

99. See Bremmer, "An Imperial Palace Guard in Heaven." For a paleographic assessment, see Kasser, Cavallo, and van Haelst, "Appendice," 123–124.

100. For the original dating of P.Bodmer XL, see Kasser and Luisier, "P.Bodmer XL," 154. For the sixth-century dating, see Orsini, "I Papiri Bodmer," 77.

101. Orsini, "I Papiri Bodmer," 64–66.

102. On the question of Dorotheos and the Bodmer Papyri, see Agosti, "Poesia greca nella (e della?) Biblioteca Bodmer," 94, and Gil and Torallas Tovar, *Hadrianus*, 30–31.

103. Very similar decorations can be found, for example, in the titles of the Pierpont Morgan *Iliad* (LDAB 2120).

104. Repairs to the last bifolia of P.Bodmer VIII show that at least one, and perhaps both, of these bifolia are artificial, making it quite likely that the quires of P.Bodmer VIII circulated independently of the rest of the composite codex before eventually being bound to the other works. See Nongbri, "The Construction of P.Bodmer VIII." For the paleographic identity among P.Bodmer X, XI, VII, and VIII, see the arguments of Wasserman, "Papyrus 72 and the *Bodmer Miscellaneous Codex*," 149–154, and Orsini, "I Papiri Bodmer," 63–64.

105. The Bodmer books that show the work of multiple hands are the composite codex, P.Bodmer XX + IX, the Menander codex, the Susanna-Daniel-Thucydides codex, P.Bodmer III, P.Bodmer XXI, P.Bodmer XIX, P.Bodmer XXIV, and the Codex of Visions. See further Orsini, "I Papiri Bodmer."

106. I leave aside for now similarities in the contents of the Bodmer books. Some intriguing work in this area has been carried out by Agosti, "Poesia greca nella (e della?) Biblioteca Bodmer."

107. On the church, see Grossmann and Lease, "Faw Qibli." On the Pachomian materials, see Robinson, *The Story of the Bodmer Papyri*, 130–150.

108. The relevant literature is cited in Robinson, *The Story of the Bodmer Papyri*, 152–153.

109. Robinson writes: "The fact that the late material is only in Coptic, with its implications that Greek had died out in the community whose library is involved, may explain some oddities regarding the Greek material: The non-Christian materials may no longer be recognizable as such, since they are no longer read; the fact that they were known as part of the older holdings of the library would have given them a status as relics that would account for their burial with the Christian material. In fact the repairs made on some of the older Greek codices are such as to render them largely unusable, an observation which has led to the conjecture that, at least in their case, their final use was that of a relic" (*The Story of the Bodmer Papyri*, 31). Robinson's assessment of the repairs to at least one of the Greek codices (P.Bodmer XIV–XV) is incorrect. See Nongbri, "Reconsidering the Place of Papyrus Bodmer XIV–XV," 431–432.

110. See note 94 above.

111. In fact, from one point of view, they don't really constitute a distinct grouping. I have the sense that "classical" versus "Christian" is simply a modern heuristic shorthand. It is very likely that in terms of ownership, readership, and probably copying, these copies of Cicero and Thucydides are Christian books.

112. See Fournet, "Une éthopée de Caïn."
113. See Fournet, "Anatomie d'une bibliothèque," 16–17: "J'irais même jusqu'à dire que la présence de textes profanes grecs, qui plus est des comédies, déjà étrange dans une bibliothèque monastique (et sans parallèles dans les exemples dont nous disposons), n'est pas acceptable dans le cas d'un établissement tenu par des pachômiens, réputés hostiles à la culture grecque classique" (I would even go so far as to say that the presence of secular Greek texts, comedies no less, already strange in a monastic library and unparalleled in the examples available to us, is not acceptable in an establishment run by Pachomians, who were reputedly hostile to classical Greek culture).
114. This piece is P.Mon. Epiph. 615 (LDAB 2454); see Winlock, Crum, and Evelyn White, *The Monastery of Epiphanius at Thebes*, 2.320–321. Also found at the same monastery were four limestone chunks with lines of Homer (described at 2.320). It is probably also worth mentioning the general agreement that the apostle Paul quotes from a play of Menander in 1 Cor 15:33.
115. On this point, see Blanchard, "Sur le milieu d'origine du papyrus Bodmer de Ménandre."
116. A parchment fragment of a Latin historical work (possibly Livy, LDAB 2576) found in a monastic hermitage in Nalqun is a truly puzzling exception. See Bravo and Griffin, "Un frammento del libro XI di Tito Livio?"
117. On the composite codex, see especially Wasserman, "Papyrus 72 and the *Bodmer Miscellaneous Codex*," and the update by Nongbri, "Recent Progress."
118. On the discovery of the Nag Hammadi codices, see Robinson, "The Discovery of the Nag Hammadi Codices," and the discussion of the Nag Hammadi codices in Chapter 3 above. A papyrus carrying a date of 348 CE removed from the cover of Codex VII (LDAB 107747) is the latest piece and is generally taken as a *terminus post quem* for the collection. Yet, now some specialists entertain the idea that the codices might have been produced somewhat later. See, for example, Emmel, "The Coptic Gnostic Texts as Witnesses," 38.
119. See Lundhaug and Jenott, *The Monastic Origins of the Nag Hammadi Codices*.
120. For the covers, see Robinson, "The Covers"; for the copyists, see Williams, "The Scribes of Nag Hammadi Codices."
121. See, for example, the division of the Nag Hammadi material in Layton, *The Gnostic Scriptures*.
122. For basic data on the archive, see Trismegistos Archives, http://www.trismegistos.org/arch/detail.php?tm=72. For a contextualization, see Fournet, *Hellénisme dans l'Égypte du VIe siècle*, and Fournet (ed.), *Les archives de Dioscore d'Aphrodité cent ans après leur découverte*.

123. Lefebvre, *Fragments d'un manuscrit de Ménandre*. For further details, see the summary in Cuvigny, "The Finds of Papyri," 49.

124. Bell and Crum, "A Greek-Coptic Glossary."

125. Bell and Crum judged the poetic abilities of Dioscorus harshly: "His verses, if infamous as literature, are at least of interest as illustrating the morass of absurdity into which the great river of Greek poetry emptied itself" (Bell and Crum, "A Greek-Coptic Glossary," 177).

126. See MacCoull, *Dioscorus of Aphrodito*, 21. But note the possibility that the biblical allusions come through liturgical exposure: "Of Christian influences on Dioscorus's poetry, the Scriptures take pride of place; the Psalter and the Old and New Testaments were probably the most influential, as he would have been steeped in their texts through participation in the Copto-Alexandrian liturgy" (MacCoull, *Dioscorus*, 61).

127. Cuvigny, "The Finds of Papyri," 56, note 20.

128. It is difficult to tell whether this was Beatty's conscious intention. As Charles Horton notes, "Beatty had no grand plan when he was forming his collection, or, if he did, it has remained firmly hidden" (*Alfred Chester Beatty*, 44). Yet, the website for the Chester Beatty Library aptly describes his collection as "a remarkable conspectus of the arts of manuscript production and printing" (http://www.cbl.ie/Collections/Introduction.aspx). Robinson has made a similar observation (*The Story of the Bodmer Papyri*, 76–77 and 166).

129. Kasser, "Introduction," 1.lv.

130. Agosti, "Poesia greca nella (e della?) Biblioteca Bodmer," 96.

131. Camplani, "Per un profilo storico-religioso," 134: "quelle forme di impegno laicale collettivo che vediamo emergere nel corso del V secolo."

132. See Miguélez-Cavero, *Poems in Context*, 218–223.

Chapter Six. Excavating Christian Litter and Literature at Oxyrhynchus

1. The bulk of this chapter was hammered out in extended conversations with AnneMarie Luijendijk. I am grateful for her insights on many aspects of Christian Oxyrhynchus.

2. Petrie, *Methods and Aims in Archaeology*, 48.

3. In the winter of 1895–1896, Grenfell and Hunt worked with D. G. Hogarth (1862–1927). On this season, see Montserrat, "'No Papyrus and No Portraits.'" Like Petrie, Hogarth is remembered as one of the new breed of archaeologists. Montserrat describes him thus: "In the 1890s David Hogarth was a major force in promoting both more rigorous archaeological techniques in Egypt and methodical excavations for papyri, so as to discourage the growing antiquities trade" (134). On the history of the Egypt Exploration Fund (now the Egypt Exploration Society), see James (ed.), *Excavating in Egypt*.

4. Grenfell, "The Oldest Record of Christ's Life," 1023. Reflecting back several years later, Hunt also noted financial reasons for undertaking such a project: "The flow of papyri from various districts to the antiquity-dealers was obviously proceeding. Might it not be more satisfactory, perhaps in the long run more economical, to go to the source and to dig them up for oneself instead of buying them at second or third hand and thereby encouraging an illicit traffic?" See Hunt, "B. P. Grenfell: 1869–1926," 362.

5. The earlier work of Grenfell and Hunt was published along with some of their later excavations outside Oxyrhynchus in *Fayûm Towns and Their Papyri*.

6. Writing synthetically about Oxyrhynchus has become much easier in the past decade because of two important publications. For a most enjoyable and reliable overview of the history and papyri of Oxyrhynchus, see Parsons, *City of the Sharp-Nosed Fish*. For a more detailed overview of various aspects of Oxyrhynchus, see the essays collected in Bowman et al. (eds.), *Oxyrhynchus*. Study of the Christian texts from the city (up to the fourth century) has been made much more convenient with the publication of Blumell and Wayment, *Christian Oxyrhynchus*.

7. See Coles, "Oxyrhynchus."

8. Grenfell, "Oxyrhynchus and Its Papyri," 1. The annual reports of the work undertaken by Grenfell and Hunt at Oxyrhynchus are also reproduced in Bowman et al. (eds.), *Oxyrhynchus*, 345–368.

9. Grenfell, "The Oldest Record of Christ's Life," 1027–1028.

10. Coles, "Oxyrhynchus," 7.

11. Grenfell and Hunt, *Logia Iēsou*. Within a year, the "Logia" had sold 25,800 copies. See [Cotton], "The Hon. Secretary's Report, 1897–98," 19–20. For comparison, in its initial year of publication, the first volume in *The Oxyrhynchus Papyri* series sold about 1,000 copies. See [Cotton], "The Hon. Secretary's Report, 1898–9," 20.

12. Portions of the lecture are reprinted in Turner, "The Graeco-Roman Branch," 166–167.

13. Grenfell, "Oxyrhynchus and Its Papyri," 8; Grenfell and Hunt, "Excavations at Oxyrhynchus," in the *Egypt Exploration Fund Archaeological Report* (1903–1904), 15.

14. Grenfell, "Oxyrhynchus and Its Papyri," 7–9.

15. Jones, *Astronomical Papyri from Oxyrhynchus*, 56.

16. In the early years, after Grenfell and Hunt edited the papyri, many were then "distributed" to subscribers chiefly in the United Kingdom and the United States. The arrangement was explicitly quid pro quo: According to the annual reports, these distributions were "a duty which the Committee performs with a full sense of responsibility, especially towards the subscribers in America, with whom we have entered into a formal undertaking that antiquities shall be distributed in strict proportion to sub-

scriptions received" ([Cotton], "The Hon. Secretary's Report, 1899–1900," 18). For details of the distributions, see Schork, "The Singular Circumstance of an Errant Papyrus," and Johnson, "The Oxyrhynchus Distributions in America."

17. See, for example, Hunt's preface to the fifteenth volume of *The Oxyrhynchus Papyri*. After noting that several of the papyri published in this volume came from a single large find of literary papyri in 1905–1906, he adds that others "proceed from the work of different seasons, and a few, of which the most important are 1786 and 1793, were acquired by purchase on the site of Oxyrhynchus by Professor Grenfell during his visit to Egypt in the winter of 1919–20" (Grenfell, Hunt, et al. [eds.], *The Oxyrhynchus Papyri*, 15.v).

18. See, for example, Turner, "The Graeco-Roman Branch," 166. The widespread removal of *sebakh* described by Petrie reflects the situation in 1922, after a rail line to Oxyrhynchus had been laid. See Petrie, *Tombs of the Courtiers and Oxyrhynchos*, 12–13: "An intended railway line to the oasis was begun during the war, a bridge was placed over the canal, and the start of the line laid south- and westward. This was stopped, and the material was partly used to lay a branch behind the town mounds to bring away the *sebakh*. Every day a train of 100 to 150 tons of earth runs over the bridge, to distribute it along the country. Beside this a great deal is dug and removed to the canal bank for transport in barges. During all this digging papyri are found, but apparently nothing else of importance."

19. Letter from Grenfell to Herbert Grueber (honorary treasurer of the Egypt Exploration Fund), March 9, 1903, cited in Montserrat, "News Reports," 33. Grenfell elsewhere described the state of Oxyrhynchus before their arrival in 1896: "The site of Oxyrhynchus had been very little touched by antiquity-hunters" ("The Oldest Record of Christ's Life," 1029).

20. See the reports of Grenfell and Hunt ("Excavations at Oxyrhynchus") in the *Egypt Exploration Fund Archaeological Report* for 1904–1905 (13–17) and 1906–1907 (8–11).

21. See Turner, "The Graeco-Roman Branch," 169–170. In his letter to Grueber (March 9, 1903), Grenfell observed that "it will be necessary to make a strenuous appeal this summer for funds" (cited in Montserrat, "News Reports," 33). In his annual reports to the Egypt Exploration Fund, Grenfell appealed to the patriotism of the members: "I am sure you would not wish that the work, which Dr. Hunt and I began nine years ago, should be finished by the French and Germans, the Italians and Americans" ("Dr. Bernard P. Grenfell's Address," 32).

22. For the meaning of the various parts of the inventory numbers, see Grenfell, Hunt, et al. (eds.), *The Oxyrhynchus Papyri* 42, p. xiv, and Jones, *Astronomical Papyri*, 57.

23. Michael Zellman-Rohrer, who has unraveled this system, will be publishing his findings in due course.

24. Turner mentions "a draft notebook of Grenfell containing jottings on the mounds of Bahnasa" (supplementary notes to "The Graeco-Roman Branch," 185), which seems to be the same "small black notebook containing miscellaneous memoranda" that he had mentioned decades earlier in "Roman Oxyrhynchus," 80–81, note 8. In that publication, Turner held out no great hope for the usefulness of this notebook's contents: "After close study I am forced to admit that the memoranda are inadequate for topographical description, or even to pinpoint the spots at which Grenfell and Hunt made their major finds." More recent assessments of the notebook are more optimistic. The website associated with the publication of the Oxyrhynchus papyri at Oxford describes it as follows: "A useful notebook provides the key to the numbers on the Grenfell-Hunt and conjectural plans of the site. It sets out in varying detail the dates when the different mounds were excavated or partly excavated, and occasionally gives some specific information about what was found there. . . . A. S. Hunt's handwriting is not without its own problems" ("Key to the Rubbish-Mounds of Oxyrhynchus: c.1900," http://www.papyrology.ox.ac.uk/POxy/VExhibition/the_site/notebook.html); "A little notebook [that] records their work in that second season appears to be the only survivor of its type. They must have compiled similar notes every season, and the loss of these is particularly to be regretted because a feature of this little book is the packing inventory, which has been vital in understanding the inventory-number system Grenfell and Hunt bequeathed to us and in establishing links between different parts of the collection" ("Excavation Notebook, Second Season: 1902/3," http://www.papyrology.ox.ac.uk/POxy/VExhibition/introduction/notebook.html).

25. See Luijendijk, "A New Testament Papyrus and Its Documentary Context."

26. The key study for this aspect of the work of Grenfell and Hunt is Montserrat, "News Reports."

27. Grenfell and Hunt, *Logia Iēsou*, 5. On the timing of the publication, see Turner, "The Graeco-Roman Branch," 163.

28. [Grueber], "Financial Report of the Honorary Treasurer for 1897–8," 14.

29. Grenfell, "The Oldest Record of Christ's Life," 1030.

30. See, for example, the article in the *Times* of May 14, 1906 ("A Large Find of Greek Literary Papyri") by Grenfell and Hunt.

31. See Grenfell and Hunt, *New Sayings of Jesus*, which included editions of P.Oxy. 4.654 and 4.655, as well as a revised edition of P.Oxy. 1.1; and Grenfell and Hunt, *Fragment of an Uncanonical Gospel from Oxyrhynchus*, an edition of P.Oxy. 5.840.

32. Few of the public lectures by Grenfell and Hunt were published. One example is Grenfell, "The Present Position of Papyrology."

33. Parsons, *City of the Sharp-Nosed Fish*, 17. Presumably, this estimate is more accurate than Grenfell's own assessment offered in 1920 that Volume 15 of *The Oxyrhynchus Papyri* series "probably carries us more than half-way through the publication of the total finds of literary texts from that site. With regard to non-literary papyri, however, we are not yet nearly half-way through the publication, and, in fact, with the exception of the 1897 season's finds, have made comparatively little progress in unrolling them, so that the Oxyrhynchus series is likely to exceed thirty volumes" (Grenfell, "The Present Position of Papyrology," 149). As of 2016, there are eighty-two volumes in *The Oxyrhynchus Papyri* series.

34. See Hunt's preface to Volume 8 of *The Oxyrhynchus Papyri* (Grenfell, Hunt, et al. (eds.), *The Oxyrhynchus Papyri*, 8.v). On the contents of this "second find," see Houston, *Inside Roman Libraries*, 158–171, and the cautionary comments of Nongbri, Review of Houston, *Inside Roman Libraries*.

35. For Petrie's excavations, see Petrie, *Tombs of the Courtiers and Oxyrhynchos*. On the Italian campaigns, see Pintaudi, "The Italian Excavations." Of the material from the Italian excavations, 572 pieces from Oxyrhynchus have been published so far in the *Papiri della Società Italiana* (PSI) series, 55 have been published elsewhere, and 602 are unedited (I am indebted to Guido Bastianini for supplying me with this information in a personal communication in May 2016). As far as I know few papyri have emerged from other excavations at Oxyrhynchus. See the reports in Bowman et al. (eds.), *Oxyrhynchus*, 109–138.

36. There is a widespread belief that the amount of material from Oxyrhynchus is so great that it has required "crowd sourcing" through the much-publicized Ancient Lives Project, but the actual goals and outcomes of that project are unclear, since a rather full inventory of the Oxyrhynchus material seems to exist already. More than eight hundred unpublished Oxyrhynchus manuscripts containing the *Iliad*, for example, were listed already in 2001 in West, *Studies in the Text and Transmission of the Iliad*, 86–129, esp. 87. Similarly, Jones was able to select out the astronomical papyri from the collection, which suggests an inventory (see Jones, *Astronomical Papyri from Oxyrhynchus*).

37. The year 2008 saw the publication of AnneMarie Luijendijk's book-length study, *Greetings in the Lord: Early Christians and the Oxyrhynchus Papyri*, on letters related to Bishop Sotas of Oxyrhynchus and Christian documentary papyri from Oxyrhynchus. In 2012, Lincoln H. Blumell provided a systematic discussion of all Christian letters from Oxyrhynchus in *Lettered Christians: Christians, Letters, and Late Antique Oxyrhynchus*.

38. Eldon J. Epp has made an effort to treat some of the Christian literary material from Oxyrhynchus, especially the New Testament papyri. See Epp, "The Oxyrhynchus New Testament Papyri," and Epp, "The New Testament Papyri at Oxyrhynchus." AnneMarie Luijendijk has directed

attention to the copies of the Gospel According to Thomas ("Reading the *Gospel of Thomas* in the Third Century").

39. The search on which these data are based was made on May 13, 2016.

40. The literature on early Christian identity (or more accurately acts of identification) in antiquity is massive. A good entry point is Lieu, *Christian Identity in the Jewish and Graeco-Roman World*. With specific regard to Egypt and papyrological evidence, see Choat, *Belief and Cult in Fourth-Century Papyri*.

41. There was a Jewish presence at Oxyrhynchus at various points in its history. See Epp, "The Jews and the Jewish Community in Oxyrhynchus."

42. Texts of the Septuagint present the most difficulties in this regard. I have generally been inclusive with pieces that may have been produced by Jews who did not identify as Christians. Given our changing ideas about Jewish and Christian identities, I have some doubts about the traditional ways of distinguishing Jewish and Christian copies of the Septuagint (that is to say, some codices might be Jewish, some rolls might be Christian, the use of *nomina sacra* might not be strictly Christian after the fourth century). Some Septuagint pieces, however, do seem to be of non-Christian origin. Excluded from my survey are the following: a copy of the book of Job (P.Oxy. 50.3522, LDAB 3079) assigned on the basis of its handwriting to "a date early in the first century." The early date, combined with the fact that the divine name is written in archaic Hebrew letters, strongly indicates that this papyrus was a Jewish production. Two other pieces have been assigned to either the first century or early second century, both papyrus rolls of Septuagint texts, P.Oxy. 65.4443 (LDAB 3080, a column of Esther in which the word *theos* is uncontracted) and P.Oxy. 77.5101 (LDAB 140272, a collection of fragments of Psalms with the divine name in archaic Hebrew characters). The early date and the roll format suggest that these are pre-Christian productions.

43. For recent general overviews of early Christian amulets, see de Bruyn and Dijkstra, "Greek Amulets and Formularies from Egypt Containing Christian Elements," and Jones, *New Testament Texts on Greek Amulets*.

44. Bagnall, *Everyday Writing in the Graeco-Roman East*, 141.

45. PSI 12.1272 (LDAB 3233) is a Latin fragment of Exodus purchased on the antiquities market. It may be a part of the same codex as P.Oxy. 8.1073.

46. These are LDAB 113511 and 113512. In their report for the 1904–1905 season, Grenfell and Hunt describe the area of the find: "In the northern portion of the other mound—a long range running along the desert edge—the documents near the surface were of the fourth or fifth century. . . . Another interesting feature of this range was the presence in it of a certain number of Hebrew and Syriac fragments, which, as they are not later than the fifth century, have a considerable palaeographical value" (Grenfell and Hunt, "Excavations at Oxyrhynchus" [1904–1905],

13). This is the only report of finds of Syriac material at Oxyrhynchus. See further Pedersen and Larsen, *Manichaean Texts in Syriac*, 18–20 and 88–111.

47. The Coptic pieces are a fragmentary leaf of a parchment codex containing the letter to the Romans (LDAB 107980) and leaf from a parchment codex containing a church calendar (LDAB 113877). In 2007, Sarah Clackson reported that the Sackler Library at Oxford held "at least 400 individual Coptic texts, literary and non-literary, deriving from Oxyrhynchus," though it is unclear which of these were excavated and which were purchased ("Coptic Oxyrhynchus," 332).

48. Under this heading, I have included two items that are usually (but dubiously) described as copies of the Gospel According to Peter, P.Oxy. 60.4009 and 41.2949 (LDAB 4872 and 5111, respectively). For a sound argument that there is insufficient evidence for this identification, see Foster, *The Gospel of Peter*, 57–91.

49. Hunt published the two sides of this fragment separately as P.Oxy. 8.1075 (the end of Exodus) and P.Oxy. 8.1079 (the beginning of Revelation) and regarded the piece as a roll of Exodus later reused for a copy of Revelation (thus the single fragment has two entries in the Leuven Database—3477 and 2786). Yet, since both sides of the fragment display only one column of text, this piece is just as likely to be a leaf from a codex. See Nongbri, "Losing a Curious Christian Scroll." Peter van Minnen's insistence that this piece is definitely a roll is unconvincing ("From Posidippus to Palladas," 245).

50. The Oxyrhynchite provenance of this item is not completely certain, but I have included it on the strength of Walter Crum's analysis ("Fragments of a Church Calendar," 23–32).

51. The Oxyrhynchus hymn (P.Oxy. 15.1786, LDAB 5403) was purchased by Grenfell at Bahnasa in 1920. The other side of the papyrus contains an account mentioning Oxyrhynchite villages, so its Oxyrhynchite provenance seems secure. On this item, see Cosgrove, *An Ancient Christian Hymn with Musical Notation*.

52. Fragments of the Oxyrhynchus Philo codex are in multiple collections (see the LDAB entry, 3540). The Leuven Database classifies it as "Jewish," but the codex format and use of *nomina sacra* suggest it is quite possibly a Christian construction.

53. The original editor of P.Oxy. 50.3527–3528, C. H. Roberts, made the case that these copies of the *Similitudes* circulated independently of the *Visions* and *Mandates* usually associated with the Shepherd of Hermas. For more recent discussion, see Bagnall, *Early Christian Books in Egypt*, 40–49.

54. It is possible that P.Oxy. 15.1778 is one of the items that was purchased by Grenfell rather than excavated at the site. Another part of the same manuscript has emerged from the collection of Institut für Papyrologie

at Heidelberg, and it must have been obtained on the antiquities market at some point. See Hagedorn, "Ein neues Fragment."

55. I have included the hymn (P.Oxy 15.1786) among the reused rolls because it is usually described as having been written on the "verso" of an account, but both sides are written along the fibers, so I am unsure on what grounds the assignment of "recto" and "verso" were established. I have not included P.Oxy. 10.1228 (LDAB 2779), a copy of the Gospel According to John, which is written against the fibers. Yet, what should be the front of the roll is blank. It is thus possible, but not certain, that this piece is also a reused roll. On the problems of this manuscript, see Hurtado, "A Fresh Analysis of P.Oxyrhynchus 1228 ($\mathfrak{P}$22) as Artifact." I have also not included PSI 1.26–27, which is copied on both sides of a roll but appears to be a proper opisthograph, which is to say the same writing project occupies both sides of the roll.

56. See Johnson, *Bookrolls and Scribes in Oxyrhynchus*, 150.

57. In his treatment of papyrus and parchment codices, Turner seems to regard heights of 30 centimeters as being indicative of "large" codices. See, for example, Turner, "Early Papyrus Codices of Large Size."

58. This fragment has had a colorful postexcavation life. After being unearthed during the excavations of Grenfell and Hunt, it was among the papyri distributed to the United States by the Egypt Exploration Society sometime between 1921 and 1923, and it was subsequently sold and resold at auction and became part of a traveling exhibition called *Ink and Blood* before ending up as a part of the recently formed Green Collection. Its story is detailed in Mazza, "Papyri, Ethics, and Economics."

59. This was the paleographic classification on the Leuven Database on June 15, 2016.

60. For details, see Royse, "The Oxyrhynchus Papyrus of Philo." Don Barker has proposed that P.Oxy. 11.1353 (LDAB 3067, a leaf from a parchment codex containing 1 Peter) belonged to a codex with more than eight hundred pages, on the basis of a reading of what he regards as a page number. I am unconvinced. The characters Barker reads as the page number are much more spaced out than multidigit page numbers normally are, and a codex of such small dimensions (10.1 cm wide and 13.5 cm high) with more than eight hundred pages would be unwieldy to say the least (the manuscripts Barker cites as comparanda have nowhere near that many pages). For Barker's case, see his chapter "How Long and Old Is the Codex?"

61. See Turner, *The Typology of the Early Codex*, 25.

62. Luijendijk, "Sacred Scriptures as Trash."

63. See the editors' introduction to P.Oxy. 74.4968, p. 1.

64. As I noted in Chapter 4, the generally poor state of preservation of the Oxyrhynchus codices leaves me feeling skeptical about the attribution to Oxyrhynchus of two codices purchased on the antiquities market in

1998 and now in the Schøyen collection, P.Schøyen 1.23 and 2.26 (LDAB 8119 and 8120, respectively). I have not included them in my inventory.

65. P.Oxy. 15.1780, a fragment of a papyrus leaf from a codex containing the Gospel According to John, has been subjected to radiocarbon analysis. The results are forthcoming in Dru, "A Complex Pondering."

66. For much of the latter part of the twentieth century, it was fashionable to suggest that Grenfell and Hunt thought the codex was a "late" development, and as a result they tended to assign dates to Christian codices that were later than they might have been had their dating been based on paleography alone. A few years ago, I looked into these claims in detail and found them to be baseless. That is not to say that their paleographic work is always beyond reproach, but the wholesale rejection of their assessments would require stronger arguments than those that have been adduced. See Nongbri, "Grenfell and Hunt on the Dates of Early Christian Codices."

67. I have followed this procedure for each of the rows in Table 6.2, with the result that the numbers in the "Christian manuscripts" row do not necessarily equal the sum of the numbers in the columns below.

68. See LDAB 4872, last checked June 12, 2016.

69. See note 47 above.

70. This phenomenon is also noted and discussed in some detail in Bagnall, *Early Christian Books in Egypt*, 14–15.

71. These numbers were culled from the Leuven Database on June 17, 2016.

72. Luijendijk, "Sacred Scriptures as Trash."

Chapter Seven. Fabricating a Second-Century Codex of the Four Gospels

1. Roberts, *Buried Books in Antiquity*, 11–14.

2. The Philo codex is inventoried as Suppl. Gr. 1120. Just as I was beginning my study, the codex became unavailable for consultation because of conservation needed after more than a century of neglect. I am informed that a new edition of the text of the codex is being prepared by James R. Royse.

3. Roberts, "An Early Papyrus of the First Gospel."

4. Roca-Puig, *Un papiro griego del evangelio de San Mateo*, 31–36: "no es posterior al siglo III."

5. Roca-Puig, *Un papiro griego del evangelio de San Mateo*, 2nd ed. On Turner's identification of the Magdalen and Barcelona fragments, see Roca-Puig's preface to the second edition, 10.

6. Roberts, *Manuscript, Society and Belief*, 13. The possibility that all the fragments came from the same codex was first raised by Aland, "Neue neutestamentliche Papyri II," 193–195.

7. Roberts, *Manuscript, Society and Belief*, 8.
8. Not everyone was convinced. Eric Turner, who first pointed out the similarity of the Matthew fragments in Oxford and Barcelona, never agreed that they were part of the same codex as the leaves of Luke in Paris. In his 1977 book *The Typology of the Early Codex*, he estimated different page sizes for the Matthew and Luke fragments and even assigned them different dates (second century for the Matthew fragments but third or fourth century for the leaves of Luke). The INTF at Münster, which produces the Nestle-Aland Greek New Testament, also continues to list the Matthew fragments (𝔓64 + 𝔓67) and the Luke fragments (𝔓4) as distinct codices, with the former assigned a date of "ca. 200" and the latter a date of third century.
9. d'Ancona, "Eyewitness to Christ."
10. Thiede, "Papyrus Magdalen Greek 17."
11. Wachtel, "𝔓64/67." More popularly accessible rebuttals can be found in Parker, "Was Matthew Written Before 50 CE?," and Stanton, *Gospel Truth?*, 1–32.
12. Thiede and d'Ancona, *Eyewitness to Jesus*.
13. For an analysis of the whole Thiede episode from the point of view of a papyrologist, see Bagnall, *Early Christian Books in Egypt*, 25–40.
14. See "Scraps Offer an Intriguing Clue on Jesus," and a collection of stories about Thiede's claims in *Der Spiegel* (May 27, 1996) occupying more than twenty pages (64–87).
15. Skeat, "The Oldest Manuscript?"
16. Skeat, "The Oldest Manuscript?," 15.
17. See, for example, P.PalauRib. inv. 181–183, a Coptic codex containing the Gospels According to Luke, John, and Mark (LDAB 107760 + 107904 + 107905). Among the Bodmer Papyri, we have already seen P.Bodmer III, which contains the Gospel According to John and Genesis (LDAB 107758), and P.Bodmer XIX, which contains parts of the Gospel According to Matthew and Romans (LDAB 107759).
18. Skeat, "The Oldest Manuscript?," 3–4. On the date of Codex Sinaiticus, see Parker, *Codex Sinaiticus*, 52–53.
19. Skeat, "The Oldest Manuscript?," 27–28.
20. Stanton, "The Fourfold Gospel," 327–328.
21. Head, "Is P4, P64 and P67 the Oldest Manuscript of the Four Gospels?"
22. Charlesworth, "T. C. Skeat, 𝔓64+67 and 𝔓4." Charlesworth also shows that Skeat's proposal fails even if we were to assume that the papyrus sheets of the quires were laid in an alternating pattern to yield like facing like. Given the evidence of the fiber directions of the extant fragments, Skeat's single-quire proposal could work only if we were to assume that the sheets which made up the quire were stacked in a helter-skelter manner, some with horizontal fibers up, others with vertical fibers up in an irregular pattern—not completely impossible, but also not very likely.

23. One scholar has recently attempted to adapt Skeat's thesis in light of the criticisms of Head and Charlesworth. See Hill, "Intersections of Jewish and Christian Scribal Culture."

24. On Scheil's career, see Dap and Tauran, *Le père Jean-Vincent Scheil (1858–1940)*; Roques, "Éloge funèbre du R. P. Vincent Scheil"; and Dussaud, "Notice sur la vie et les travaux de M. Vincent Scheil." The chronological information about Scheil given by Skeat ("The Oldest Manuscript?," 24–25) is a mixture of speculation and outright error.

25. Scheil, "Deux traités de Philon," iii: "Le papyrus dont nous publions ci-après le contenu fut trouvé à Coptos, dans la Haute-Égypte, en 1889. Considéré sans doute aux temps anciens comme chose très précieuse, il avait été clos et muré dans une niche. Le son creux de la muraille, à cet endroit éveilla l'attention. En ouvrant, on tira de leur secret deux traités de Philon d'Alexandrie. Le tout, du format connu presque carré in-8° des livres arabes, était relié dans une couverture de cuir, avec une languette et un cordon de cuir se ramenant sur la couverture. Dans sa cachette, le livre dut être très comprimé, le béton est comme incrusté à l'extérieur; les feuillets adhéraient fortement en une masse et étaient en outre comme chevillés les uns aux autres par quantité de petits grains de sel, produits d'une condensation séculaire dans le tissu végétal. Les feuillets d'une grande ténuité étaient au nombre de 44, numérotés; disposes en cahiers de 10, 10, 12 et 12 feuilles, cousus ensemble avec une tige herbacée très fine faisant office de fil. Entre le papyrus et le fil, afin que le premier ne fût pas endommagé par le second, on avait glissè dans le pli de petits fragments rectangulaires de parchemin. Un fragment de la même substance avait été appliqué sur la marge de la page, et devait déborder sur la tranche, en guise de signet, là où finit le premier traité. Un autre genre de signet mobile oublié par le dernier lecteur du livre, entre le vingtième et le vingt et unième feuillet, est une petite plume à barbe blanche (de ramier). A la suite du quarante-quatrième feuillet, en guise de bourre, je pense, et pour remplir la capacité de la couverture, se trouvaient plusieurs fragments de feuillets collés ensemble, et provenant d'un Évangéliaire, l'un d'eux portant κατα μαθθαιον, et les autres, des fragments de saint Luc. La fin du dernier traitè et sa suscription se trouvent à la suite, sur la couverture intérieure."

26. For further description of the leaf carrying the title of Matthew, see Gathercole, "The Earliest Manuscript Title."

27. Kenyon first assigned dates to these manuscripts in 1899. On the date of the Luke fragments, he wrote: "Luke v. 30–vi. 4, in book form (attached to MS. of Philo, *vid. infr.*). Fourth century." On the Philo codex, he wrote: "Philo, *tis ho tōn theiōn klēronomos peri geneseōs Abel:* in book form. Sixth century (? third)." See Kenyon, *The Palaeography of Greek Papyri*, 132 and 145. Scheil had originally assigned both the Philo and the Luke fragments to the sixth century. Arthur S. Hunt and others subsequently

assigned the Philo codex to the third century. See Hunt's introduction to P.Oxy. 9.1173, p. 16 (LDAB 3540).

28. Scheil, "Deux traités de Philon," iii.

29. Scheil, "Deux traités de Philon," 216.

30. Scheil, "Fragments de l'Évangile selon saint Luc, recueillis en Égypte," 113.

31. For details on the Nag Hammadi codices, see Chapter 3.

32. See Robinson, "Inside the Front Cover of Codex VI," and Williams and Jenott, "Inside the Covers of Codex VI."

33. Gathercole has also recognized that, according to Scheil, the leaves of Luke could not have been used in the construction of the back cover, noting that "the fragments did not form stuffing inside the leather back-cover. Nor were they hidden there; they were glued together ('collés ensemble'). They must therefore have formed a kind of wad to compensate for the Philo pages being too thin or conversely the leather binding being too thick: the spine of the leather cover would presumably be vulnerable if the innards were not substantial enough to fill it." Yet, Gathercole did not follow through with the logical conclusion that the Luke fragments and the Philo codex have no necessary chronological relationship. He protested the possibility of a fourth-century date for the leaves of Luke on the grounds that such a dating "does not take sufficient account of the Philo codex." See Gathercole, "The Earliest Manuscript Title," 221 and 224.

34. The Nag Hammadi codices as a group are generally dated to a period no earlier than the middle of the fourth century. The waste papyri used in the cover of Codex VII carry dates as late as 348 CE, which suggests that Codex VII, at least, was produced after that time. A more precise dating of the Nag Hammadi codices is difficult. On the whole question, see now Lundhaug and Jenott, *The Monastic Origins of the Nag Hammadi Codices*, 9–11.

35. On the meager sources for this uprising and their difficulties, see Bowman, "Two Notes." For an overview of the life of the city in the fourth century and beyond, see Gabolde (ed.), *Coptos*, 196–225.

36. A history of the church councils written by Severus ibn al-Muqaffa' in the tenth century preserves the names of Egyptian bishops who attended the Council of Nicaea in 325 and includes "Arianus, bishop of Qeft." See Leroy and Grébaut, *L'Histoire des conciles de Sévère ibn al Moqaffa'*, 489–490 and 618–619. Phoibammon, bishop of Koptos, is listed among the attendees at the Council of Ephesus in 431; see Schwartz, *Consilium Universale Ephesenum, Volumen Primum*, 6. For the remains of the baptistry and church, see Petrie, *Koptos*, 25–26 and plate 26. On the date of the church and baptistry, see Grossman, "Qift," 7.2040.

37. Merell, "Nouveaux fragments."

38. Merell, "Nouveaux fragments," 5: "Le P. Scheil me signalait, en juin

dernier, qu'ayant, en 1891, acheté à Louqsor un codex renfermant deux traités de Philon d'Alexandrie, il avait eu la bonne fortune d'y trouver des fragments de notre papyrus biblique." The remainder of Merell's discussion of the discovery of the codex is a nearly verbatim (though unattributed) direct quotation of Scheil's discussion in "Deux traités de Philon." Interestingly, Merell did not repeat Scheil's crucial final sentence ("La fin du dernier traitè et sa suscription se trouvent à la suite, sur la couverture intérieure"). Thus, anyone relying on Merell without checking Scheil might be liable to misconstrue the relationship of the gospel fragments and the Philo codex, while anyone relying on Scheil without checking Merell would be unaware that the codex was bought on the antiquities market and not discovered in situ.

39.   Roberts, "An Early Papyrus," 233.

40.   Beatty acquired his portion of the codex in 1931, and the Köln sections were not bought until after 1954. See the preface to Hamm, *Der Septuaginta-Text des Buches Daniel Kap. 1–2*.

41.   Roberts, "An Early Papyrus," 233.

42.   Roberts, *Manuscript, Society and Belief*, 13, note 2.

43.   Turner, *The Typology of the Early Codex*, 36 and 145. There is some variation in Turner's treatment of the Luke leaves. Elsewhere in the same work he describes the Luke fragments as third century full stop (pp. 22 and 92). Nowhere in his writings, as far as I am aware, did he assent to a second-century date for this piece. He did, however, apparently accept a second-century date for the Matthew fragments (*The Typology of the Early Codex*, 22, 36, 99, and 149), but elsewhere he classifies them as among "those codices which other palaeographers whose judgment I respect have assigned to c.ii or ii/iii, but which I think belong to a later date" (*The Typology of the Early Codex*, 90–91).

44.   Orsini and Clarysse, "Early New Testament Manuscripts and Their Dates," 470.

45.   Skeat, "The Oldest Manuscript?," 26–30.

46.   Strutwolf (ed.), *Novum Testamentum Graece*, 28th ed., 792 and 795.

47.   For Parsons's opinion, see Stanton, *Gospel Truth?*, 196: "In a letter to me at the beginning of May 1995 Professor Parsons mentioned that he had consulted a meeting of papyrologists about the dating of the Magdalen fragments: most opted for the third century, one doubtfully for the fourth."

48.   See note 43 above.

49.   Kenyon, *The Palaeography of Greek Papyri*, 132, and Merell, "Nouveaux fragments," 7: "Les autorités telles que M. M. F. Kenyon, l'éditeur des papyrus Chester-Beatty, P. Collart, professeur de papyrologie à la Sorbonne et A. Dain, professeur de paléographie grecque à la Sorbonne, après examen des photographies, font remonter notre manuscrit au IVᵉ siècle."

50. Skeat, "The Oldest Manuscript?," 30. In fact, Skeat does not even mention Hunt's date for 𝔓64.
51. Roberts and Skeat regularly mischaracterized the paleographic judgments of Grenfell and Hunt in this regard. For details, see Nongbri, "Grenfell and Hunt on the Dates of Early Christian Codices."
52. Roberts, "Complementary Note."
53. This memo is kept in a folder in the archives of the Magdalen College Library along with other materials relating to the fragments of Matthew. I am grateful to Dr. Robin Darwall-Smith for providing me with the opportunity to examine these materials.
54. Roberts, "Buried Books in Antiquity," 13.
55. Origen, for example, is said to have described the Johannine epistles in terms of the number of *stichoi* they contained. See Eusebius, *Church History* 6.25.10 (Schwartz, *Eusebius Werke zweiter Band*, 578).
56. Patterns of division by paragraph are also present in other papyri, such as P.Bodmer II and P.Bodmer XIV–XV, which were originally assigned to the late second or early third century, but for paleographic and codicological reasons, these books are probably more reasonably considered fourth-century productions. See Nongbri, "The Limits of Palaeographic Dating," and Nongbri, "Reconsidering the Place of Papyrus Bodmer XIV–XV."
57. Roberts, "An Early Papyrus," 234. I also find the more complicated use of textual division to aid in dating manuscripts recently proposed by Charles Hill to be similarly problematic. Presuming early dates for papyri like P.Bodmer II, P.Bodmer XIV–XV, and the fragments of Matthew and Luke, Hill contends that "the general evolution in text delimitation was from less frequent, larger sections to more frequent, smaller ones." Yet, when he notes that the pattern of divisions in P.Oxy. 50.3523, a leaf of the Gospel According to John generally assigned to the second century, matches up more nearly with the frequency of division in Codex Vaticanus and Codex Alexandrinus (usually assigned to the fourth and fifth centuries, respectively), he does not then suggest that the Oxyrhynchus fragment should perhaps be assigned a later date. Rather, he suggests that P.Oxy. 50.3523 relied on an *exemplar* that preserved a later "stage in the tradition" of the division system, implying that manuscripts with more frequent division must have existed in the second century as well, thus apparently undercutting the original basis for his proposed "evolution." See Hill, "Rightly Dividing the Word," esp. 235–236.
58. Barker, "The Dating of New Testament Papyri," 575–578.
59. For example, before carrying out his study of our fragments of Matthew and Luke, Skeat had already spelled out a thesis about the early adaptation of a four-gospel canon as the reason for the widespread adoption of the codex in an article that appeared midyear in 1994. All that was left wanting was an extant specimen of a four-gospel codex datable to the

second century (Skeat, "The Origin of the Christian Codex"). It is thus probably no accident that Skeat locates the beginning of his study of the Matthew and Luke fragments in "the summer of 1994" (Skeat, "The Oldest Manuscript?," 1).

Epilogue

1. For the history of scholarship on this small fragment, see Nongbri, "The Use and Abuse of 𝔓52." For more recent debates, see Nongbri, "Palaeography, Precision, and Publicity."

2. See, for example, Jarus, "Mummy Mask May Reveal Oldest Known Gospel."

3. See Fackelmann, "Präsentation christlicher Urtexte." Anton Fackelmann (1916–1985) was a renowned conservator of papyrus and parchment at Vienna. This article, however, is a comedy of errors and unlike anything else he wrote. In fact, the article is the work of the conservator's son, who is also named Anton. See Nongbri, "Some Answers." The manuscript in question is now part of the Schøyen Collection, MS 2630.

4. See the summary and evaluation of Rau, "Weder gefälscht noch authentisch?," 156–159, and Nongbri, "A First-Century Papyrus of Mark."

5. For foundational work in this area, see Vandorpe, "Museum Archaeology," and Clackson, "Museum Archaeology and Coptic Papyrology."

6. Out of the many worthy undertakings, I single out the amazing Codex Sinaiticus Project as an example of what can happen when there is sufficient will (and sufficient funding): http://www.codex-sinaiticus.net/en/.

Bibliography

The following archival collections kindly provided me with access to unpublished material.

The British Library, London
Charles Lang Freer Papers, Freer Gallery of Art and Arthur M. Sackler Gallery Archives, the Smithsonian Institution, Washington, D.C.
Chester Beatty Papers, the Chester Beatty Library, Dublin
Eric G. Turner Papers, Special Collections, University of Western Australia, Perth
Institute for Antiquity and Christianity Records, Special Collections, Claremont Colleges Library, Claremont, Calif.
Kelsey Museum of Archaeology Papers 1890–1979, Bentley Historical Library, University of Michigan, Ann Arbor
Magdalen College Library Archives, Magdalen College, University of Oxford
The Scheide Library and the Seeley G. Mudd Manuscripts Library, Princeton University, Princeton, N.J.

Agosti, Gianfranco. "Poesia greca nella (e della?) Biblioteca Bodmer." *Adamantius* 21 (2015): 86–97.
Aland, Kurt. "Neue neutestamentliche Papyri II." *New Testament Studies* 12 (1966): 193–210.
Aland, Kurt, and Barbara Aland. *The Text of the New Testament: An Introduction to the Critical Editions and to the Theory and Practice of Modern Textual Criticism.* Translated by Erroll F. Rhodes. 2nd rev. ed. Grand Rapids: Eerdmans, 1995.
Albarrán Martínez, María Jesús, and Alberto Nodar Domínguez. "Escribir la palabra de Dios: Aspectos bibliológicos de los bíblicos de la colección Palau Ribes." Pages 11–32 in [no editor named], *Lo que hay entre tú y no-*

sotros. Estudios en honor de María Victoria Spottorno. Córdoba: UCOPress, 2016.

Amélineau, Emile. *La géographie de l'Égypte à l'époque copte.* Paris: Imprimerie nationale, 1893.

Andrist, Patrick (ed.). *Le manuscrit B de la Bible (Vaticanus graecus 1209): Introduction au facsimilé, Actes du Colloque de Genève (11 juin 2001), Contributions supplémentaires.* Lausanne: Zèbre, 2009.

Ardizzone, Heidi. *An Illuminated Life: Belle da Costa Greene's Journey from Prejudice to Privilege.* New York: W. W. Norton, 2007.

Askeland, Christian. "Considering the Radiometric Dating of the Tchacos Codex." Forthcoming in Cole (ed.), *Interdisciplinary Dating.*

Askeland, Christian. "Radiometric Dating of the Gospel of Judas." *Evangelical Textual Criticism.* March 10, 2015. http://evangelicaltextualcriticism.blog spot.com.au/2015/03/radiometric-dating-of-gospel-of-judas.html.

Atiya, Aziz S. (ed.). *The Coptic Encyclopedia.* 8 vols. New York: Macmillan, 1991.

Baedeker, Karl. *Egypt and the Sûdân: Handbook for Travellers.* 7th ed. Leipzig: Karl Baedeker, 1914.

Bagnall, Roger S. *Early Christian Books in Egypt.* Princeton, N.J.: Princeton University Press, 2009.

Bagnall, Roger S. *Egypt in Late Antiquity.* Princeton, N.J.: Princeton University Press, 1993.

Bagnall, Roger S. *Everyday Writing in the Graeco-Roman East.* Berkeley: University of California Press, 2011.

Bagnall, Roger S. (ed.). *The Kellis Agricultural Account Book (P.Kell. IV Gr. 96).* Oxford: Oxbow, 1997.

Bagnall, Roger S. "An Owner of Literary Papyri." *Classical Philology* 87 (1992): 137–140.

Bagnall, Roger S. (ed.). *The Oxford Handbook of Papyrology.* Oxford: Oxford University Press, 2009.

Bagnall, Roger S. "Public Administration and the Documentation of Roman Panopolis." Pages 1–12 in A. Egberts, B. P. Muhs, and J. van der Vliet (eds.), *Perspectives on Panopolis: An Egyptian Town from Alexander the Great to the Arab Conquest.* Leiden: Brill, 2002.

Bagnall, Roger S., and Klaas A. Worp. *Chronological Systems of Byzantine Egypt.* 2nd ed. Leiden: Brill, 2004.

Bailey, Donald M. "*Sebakh*, Sherds and Survey." *Journal of Egyptian Archaeology* 85 (1999): 211–218.

Baillet, Jules. "Le papyrus mathématique d'Akhmîm." *Mémoires publiés par les membres de la Mission Archéologique française au Caire* 9.1 (1892): 1–89.

Barker, Don. "The Dating of New Testament Papyri." *New Testament Studies* 57 (2011): 571–582.

Barker, Don. "How Long and Old Is the Codex of Which P.Oxy. 1353 Is a Leaf?" Pages 192–202 in Evans and Zacharias (eds.), *Jewish and Christian Scripture as Artifact and Canon.*

Barthélemy, Jean-Dominique. "Le Psautier grec et le papyrus Bodmer XXIV." *Revue de Théologie et de Philosophie*, 3rd series, 19 (1966): 106–110.

Baumgarten, Joseph M. "The Laws of the *Damascus Document* in Current Research." Pages 51–62 in Magen Broshi (ed.), *The Damascus Document Reconsidered*. Jerusalem: Israel Exploration Society, 1992.

Bausi, Alessandro (gen. ed.). *Comparative Oriental Manuscript Studies: An Introduction*. https://doi.org/10.5281/zenodo.46784.

Bausi, Alessandro. "The Coptic Version of the *Acta Phileae*." *Comparative Oriental Manuscript Studies Newsletter* 8 (2014): 11–13.

Bell, Harold Idris. "Mr. Bell's Description of the Papyrus Fragments Which Formed the Cover of the Ms. Oriental No. 7594." Pages xiv–xvii in E. A. Wallis Budge, *Coptic Biblical Texts in the Dialect of Upper Egypt*. Oxford: Trustees of the British Museum, 1912.

Bell, Harold Idris, and Walter E. Crum. "A Greek-Coptic Glossary." *Aegyptus* 6 (1925): 177–226.

Bell, Harold Idris, and Colin H. Roberts. *A Descriptive Catalogue of the Greek Papyri in the Collection of Wilfred Merton, F.S.A.* 3 vols. London: Emery Walker, 1948–1967.

Bircher, Martin (ed.). *Bibliotheca Bodmeriana: La collection des Papyrus Bodmer.* 10 vols. Munich: K. G. Saur, 2000.

Blanchard, Alain. "Sur le milieu d'origine du papyrus Bodmer de Ménandre." *Chronique d'Égypte* 66 (1991): 211–220.

Blumell, Lincoln H. *Lettered Christians: Christians, Letters, and Late Antique Oxyrhynchus*. Leiden: Brill, 2012.

Blumell, Lincoln H., and Thomas A. Wayment (eds.). *Christian Oxyrhynchus: Texts, Documents, and Sources*. Waco, Tex.: Baylor University Press, 2015.

Boak, Arthur E. R. (ed.). *Soknopaiou Nesos: The University of Michigan Excavations at Dimê in 1931–32*. Ann Arbor: University of Michigan Press, 1935.

Bodmer, Martin. "Ansprachen anläßlich der Einweihung der Bibliotheca Bodmeriana, Cologny-Genf, 6. Oktober 1951." Pages 9–20 in Fritz Ernst (ed.), *Von Zürich nach Weimar: Hundert Jahre geistiges Wachstum 1732–1832*. Zurich: Artemis, 1953.

Bodmer, Martin. *Eine Bibliothek der Weltliteratur*. Zurich: Atlantis Verlag, 1947.

Bonani, Georges, Magen Broshi, Israel Carmi, Susan Ivy, John Strugnell, and Willy Wölfli. "Radiocarbon Dating of the Dead Sea Scrolls." *Atiqot* 20 (1991): 27–32.

Bonani, Georges, Susan Ivy, Willy Wölfli, Magen Broshi, Israel Carmi, and John Strugnell. "Radiocarbon Dating of Fourteen Dead Sea Scrolls." *Radiocarbon* 34 (1992): 843–849.

Bonner, Campbell. *The Homily on the Passion by Melito Bishop of Sardis with Some Fragments of the Apocryphal Ezekiel*. Philadelphia: University of Pennsylvania Press, 1940.

Bonner, Campbell. *The Last Chapters of Enoch in Greek*. London: Christophers, 1937.

Bouriant, Urbain. "Fragments grecs du livre d'Énoch." *Mémoires publiés par les membres de la Mission Archéologique française au Caire* 9.1 (1892): 93–147.

Bowen, Gillian E. "The Fourth-Century Churches at Ismant el-Kharab." Pages 65–85 in Colin A. Hope and Gillian E. Bowen (eds.), *Dakhleh Oasis Project: Preliminary Reports on the 1994–1995 to 1998–1999 Field Seasons.* Oxford: Oxbow, 2002.

Bowman, Alan K. "Two Notes." *Bulletin of the American Society of Papyrologists* 21 (1984): 33–38.

Bowman, Alan K., Revel A. Coles, Nikolaos Gonis, Dirk Obbink, and Peter J. Parsons (eds.). *Oxyrhynchus: A City and Its Texts.* London: Egypt Exploration Society, 2007.

Brand, Mattias. "The Manichaeans of Kellis: Religion, Community, and Everyday Life in Late Antique Egypt." PhD diss., Leiden University, forthcoming.

Bravo, Benedetto, and Miriam Griffin. "Un frammento del libro XI di Tito Livio?" *Athenaeum,* n.s. 66 (1988): 447–521.

Bremmer, Jan. "An Imperial Palace Guard in Heaven: The Date of the Vision of Dorotheus." *Zeitschrift für Papyrologie und Epigraphik* 75 (1988): 82–88.

Brown, Michelle P. (ed.). *In the Beginning: Bibles Before the Year 1000.* Washington, D.C.: Freer Gallery of Art and Arthur M. Sackler Gallery, 2006.

Bruce, James. *Travels to Discover the Source of the Nile.* 5 vols. Edinburgh: J. Ruthven, 1790.

Budge, E. A. Wallis. *By Nile and Tigris: A Narrative of Journeys in Egypt and Mesopotamia on Behalf of the British Museum Between the Years 1886 and 1913.* 2 vols. London: John Murray, 1920.

Budge, E. A. Wallis. *Coptic Biblical Texts in the Dialect of Upper Egypt.* Oxford: Trustees of the British Museum, 1912.

Budge, E. A. Wallis. *Coptic Homilies in the Dialect of Upper Egypt.* Oxford: Trustees of the British Museum, 1910.

Budge, E. A. Wallis. *The Earliest Known Coptic Psalter.* London: Kegan Paul, Trench, Trübner, 1898.

Buhle, Joh. Gottlieb. *Literarischer Briefwechsel von Johann David Michaelis, Dritter Theil.* Leipzig: Weidmannschen Buchhandlung, 1796.

Bülow-Jacobsen, Adam. "Writing Materials in the Ancient World." Pages 3–29 in Bagnall (ed.), *The Oxford Handbook of Papyrology.*

Buzi, Paola. "Qualche riflessione sugli aspetti codicologici e titologici dei papiri Bodmer con particolare riguardo ai codici copti." *Adamantius* 21 (2015): 47–59.

Calderini, Aristide. *Ilias Ambrosiana: Cod. F. 205 P. Inf. Bibliothecae Ambrosianae Mediolanensis.* Bern: Urs Graf, 1953.

Camplani, Alberto. "Per un profilo storico-religioso degli ambienti di produzione e fruizione dei Papyri Bodmer." *Adamantius* 21 (2015): 98–135.

Canart, Paul. "La paléographie est-elle un art ou une science?" *Scriptorium* 60 (2006): 159–185.

Capasso, Mario. "Un *ostrakon* con staurogramma da Soknopaiou Nesos." Pages
93–101 in Mario Capasso and Mario De Nonno (eds.), *Scritti paleografici e
papirologici in memoria di Paolo Radiciotti*. Lecce: Pensa, 2015.

Capasso, Mario, and Paola Davoli. "Soknopaiou Nesos Project: Archaeological Mission of the Centro di Studi Papirologici of Salento University
(Lecce) at Soknopaiou Nesos/Dime es-Seba (El-Fayyum—Egypt), Eleventh Archaeological Season, October–December 2014. http://www.museo
papirologico.eu/img/report/2014_report_eng.pdf.

Capasso, Mario, and Paola Davoli (eds.). *Soknopaiou Nesos Project I (2003–2009)*.
Pisa: Fabrizio Serra, 2012.

Capasso, Mario, and Paola Davoli. "Soknopaiou Nesos Project. Report on
Season 2012 of the Archaeological Mission of the Centro di Studi Papirologici of Salento University at Dime es-Seba (El-Fayyum, Egypt)." *Papyrologica Lupiensia* 22 (2013): 71–84.

Carlini, Antonio. "Amicus Plato . . . : A proposito di PSI XI 1200, Gorg. 447
B ss." Pages 41–45 in Rosario Pintaudi (ed.), *Miscellanea Papyrologica*. Florence: Gonnelli, 1980.

[Cassels, Walter Richard]. *The Gospel According to Peter: A Study*. London:
Longmans, Green, 1894.

Cavallo, Guglielmo. "Considerazioni di un paleografo per la data e l'origine
della 'Iliade Ambrosiana.'" *Dialoghi di archeologia* 7 (1973): 70–85.

Cavallo, Guglielmo. "Fenomenologia 'libraria' della maiuscola greca: Stile, canone, mimesi grafica." *Bulletin of the Institute of Classical Studies* 19 (1972):
131–140.

Cavallo, Guglielmo. "*Grammata Alexandrina.*" *Jahrbuch der Österreichischen
Byzantinistik* 24 (1975): 23–54.

Cavallo, Guglielmo. "Greek and Latin Writing in the Papyri." Pages 101–148
in Bagnall (ed.), *The Oxford Handbook of Papyrology*.

Cavallo, Guglielmo. "Note sulla scrittura greca libraria dei papiri." *Scriptorium*
26 (1972): 71–76.

Cavallo, Guglielmo. "Osservazioni paleografiche sul canone e la cronologia
della cosiddetta 'onciale romana.'" *Annali della Scuola normale superiore di
Pisa. Lettere, storia e filosofia* 36 (1967): 209–220.

Cavallo, Guglielmo. *Ricerche sulla maiuscola biblica*. Florence: Le Monnier, 1967.

Cavallo, Guglielmo. *La scrittura greca e latina dei papiri: Una introduzione*. Pisa:
Fabrizio Serra, 2008.

Cavallo, Guglielmo. "La scrittura greca libraria tra i secoli I a.C.–I d.C.: Materiali, tipologie, momenti." Pages 11–29 in D. Harlfinger and G. Prato
(eds.), *Paleografia e codicologia greca*. Alessandria: Edizioni dell'orso, 1991.

Cavallo, Guglielmo, and Herwig Maehler. *Greek Bookhands of the Early Byzantine Period, A.D. 300–800*. London: Institute of Classical Studies, 1987.

Charlesworth, Scott D. "T. C. Skeat, 𝔓64+67 and 𝔓4, and the Problem of Fibre
Orientation in Codicological Reconstruction." *New Testament Studies* 53
(2007): 582–604.

Chevalier, Ulysse. *Étude critique sur l'origine du St Suaire de Lirey-Chambéry-Turin*. Paris: Alphonse Picard, 1900.

Choat, Malcolm. *Belief and Cult in Fourth-Century Papyri*. Turnhout: Brepols, 2006.

Christiansen, Thomas. "Manufacture of Black Ink in the Ancient Mediterranean." *Bulletin of the American Society of Papyrologists* 54 (2017): 167–195.

Clackson, Sarah. "Coptic Oxyrhynchus." Pages 332–341 in Bowman et al. (eds.), *Oxyrhynchus: A City and Its Texts*.

Clackson, Sarah. "Museum Archaeology and Coptic Papyrology: The Bawit Papyri." Pages 1.477–1.490 in Mat Immerzeel and Jacques van der Vliet (eds.), *Coptic Studies on the Threshold of a New Millennium*. 2 vols. Leuven: Peeters, 2004.

Clark, Kenneth W. "The Effect of Recent Textual Criticism upon New Testament Studies." Pages 27–51 in W. D. Davies and David Daube (eds.), *The Background of the New Testament and Its Eschatology*. Cambridge: Cambridge University Press, 1954.

Clark, Robin J. H. "Pigment Identification by Spectroscopic Means: An Arts/Science Interface." *Comptes Rendus Chimie* 5 (2002): 7–20.

Clarke, Kent D. "Paleography and Philanthropy: Charles Lang Freer and His Acquisition of the 'Freer Biblical Manuscripts.'" Pages 17–73 in Hurtado (ed.), *The Freer Biblical Manuscripts*.

Clarysse, Willy, and Alfons Wouters. "A Schoolboy's Exercise in the Chester Beatty Library." *Ancient Society* 1 (1970): 201–235.

Claytor, W. Graham. "Heron, Son of Satyros: A Scribe in the *grapheion* of Karanis." *Zeitschrift für Papyrologie und Epigraphik* 190 (2014): 199–202.

Clivaz, Claire. "The New Testament at the Time of the Egyptian Papyri." Pages 15–55 in Clivaz and Zumstein (eds.), *Reading New Testament Papyri in Context*.

Clivaz, Claire, and Jean Zumstein (eds.). *Reading New Testament Papyri in Context / Lire les papyrus du Nouveau Testament dans leur contexte*. Leuven: Peeters, 2011.

Cockle, W. E. H. "Restoring and Conserving Papyri." *Bulletin of the Institute of Classical Studies* 30 (1983): 147–165.

Cole, Zachary J. (ed.). *Interdisciplinary Dating: Dialogues Between Manuscript Studies and Material Sciences*. Leiden: Brill, forthcoming.

Coles, Revel. "Oxyrhynchus: A City and Its Texts." Pages 3–16 in Bowman et al. (eds.), *Oxyrhynchus: A City and Its Texts*.

Collins, John J. *The Dead Sea Scrolls: A Biography*. Princeton, N.J.: Princeton University Press, 2013.

Comfort, Philip W. *Encountering the Manuscripts: An Introduction to New Testament Paleography and Textual Criticism*. Nashville: Broadman and Holman, 2005.

Comfort, Philip W., and David P. Barrett. *The Text of the Earliest New Testament*

Greek Manuscripts: A Corrected, Enlarged Edition of the Complete Text of the Earliest New Testament Manuscripts. Wheaton, Ill.: Tyndale House, 2001.

Cosgrove, Charles H. *An Ancient Christian Hymn with Musical Notation: Papyrus Oxyrhynchus 1786: Text and Commentary*. Tübingen: Mohr Siebeck, 2011.

Cotton, Hannah M., and Ada Yardeni. *Aramaic, Hebrew and Greek Documentary Texts from Naḥal Ḥever and Other Sites*. Oxford: Clarendon, 1997.

[Cotton, James S.]. "The Hon. Secretary's Report, 1897–98." Pages 16–20 in *Egypt Exploration Fund: Report of the Twelfth Ordinary General Meeting 1897–8*. London: Egypt Exploration Fund, 1898.

[Cotton, James S.]. "The Hon. Secretary's Report, 1898–9." Pages 16–21 in *Egypt Exploration Fund: Report of the Thirteenth Ordinary General Meeting, 1898–9*. London: Egypt Exploration Fund, 1899.

[Cotton, James S.]. "The Hon. Secretary's Report, 1899–1900." Pages 15–20 in *Egypt Exploration Fund: Report of the Fourteenth Ordinary General Meeting, 1899–1900*. London: Egypt Exploration Fund, 1900.

Crégheur, Eric. "Pour une nouvelle histoire de la découverte et de l'état primitif du Codex Bruce (1769–1794)." *Journal of Coptic Studies* 16 (2014): 47–68.

Cribiore, Rafaella. "Higher Education in Early Byzantine Egypt: Rhetoric, Latin, and the Law." Pages 47–66 in Roger S. Bagnall (ed.), *Egypt in the Byzantine World, 300–700*. New York: Cambridge University Press, 2007.

Cribiore, Rafaella. *Writing, Teachers, and Students in Graeco-Roman Egypt*. Atlanta: Scholars, 1996.

Crisci, Edoardo. "Note sulla più antica produzione di libri cristiani nell'oriente greco." *Segno e testo* 3 (2005): 93–145.

Crisci, Edoardo, and Paola Degni. *La scrittura greca dall'antichità all'epoca della stampa: Una introduzione*. Rome: Carocci, 2011.

Crum, Walter E. "The Coptic Glosses." Pages ix–xii in Kenyon, *The Chester Beatty Biblical Papyri: Fasciculus VI*.

Crum, Walter E. "Fragments of a Church Calendar." *Zeitschrift für die neutestamentliche Wissenschaft* 37 (1928): 23–32.

Crum, Walter E. *Der Papyruscodex saec. VI–VII der Phillippsbibliothek in Cheltenham*. Strassburg: Karl J. Trübner, 1915.

Cuvigny, Hélène. "The Finds of Papyri: The Archaeology of Papyrology." Translated by Adam Bülow-Jacobsen. Pages 30–58 in Bagnall (ed.), *The Oxford Handbook of Papyrology*.

Damon, P. E., D. J. Donahue, B. H. Gore et al. "Radiocarbon Dating of the Shroud of Turin." *Nature* 337 (1989): 611–615.

d'Ancona, Matthew. "Eyewitness to Christ." *Times* (UK). December 24, 1994, "Weekend," pp. 1 and 3.

Dap, Laurent, and Thierry Tauran. *Le père Jean-Vincent Scheil (1858–1940): Le Champollion Lorrain*. Woippy: Mettis, 2010.

Davey, Colin. "Fair Exchange? Old Manuscripts for New Printed Books."

Pages 127–134 in Robin Cormack and Elizabeth Jeffreys (eds.), *Through the Looking Glass: Byzantium Through British Eyes*. Aldershot: Ashgate, 2000.

Davoli, Paola. "Papyri, Archaeology, and Modern History: A Contextual Study of the Beginnings of Papyrology and Egyptology." *Bulletin of the American Society of Papyrologists* 52 (2015): 87–112.

de Bruyn, Theodore S., and Jitse H. F. Dijkstra. "Greek Amulets and Formularies from Egypt Containing Christian Elements: A Checklist of Papyri, Parchments, Ostraka, and Tablets." *Bulletin of the American Society of Papyrologists* 48 (2011): 163–216.

DeConick, April D. "The *Gospel of Judas:* A Parody of Apostolic Christianity." Pages 96–109 in Paul Foster (ed.), *The Non-Canonical Gospels*. London: T & T Clark, 2008.

DeConick, April D. "Gospel of Judas Dated to 280 CE." *Forbidden Gospels*. April 10, 2013. http://aprildeconick.com/forbiddengospels/2013/04/gospel-of-judas-dated-to-280-ce.html.

Del Corso, Lucio. "Lo 'stile severo' nei P.Oxy.: una lista." *Aegyptus* 86 (2006): 81–106.

"Dem deutschen Hugo Ibscher dankt die Welt die Rettung wertvollster Geschichtsdokumente in Papyrusfunden." *Illustrierter Beobachter.* February 10, 1934.

Depuydt, Leo. *Catalogue of Coptic Manuscripts in the Pierpont Morgan Library*. 2 vols. Leuven: Peeters, 1993.

Derda, Tomasz. *P. Bodmer I Recto: A Land List from the Panopolite Nome in Upper Egypt*. Warsaw: Journal of Juristic Papyrology, 2010.

Devreesse, Robert. *Le Fonds grec de la Bibliothèque Vaticane des origines à Paul V.* Vatican City: Biblioteca Apostolica Vaticana, 1965.

Di Bitonto Kasser, Anna. "P.Bodmer LI recto: esercizio di divisione sillabica." *Museum Helveticum* 55 (1998): 112–118.

"Discovery of Biblical Manuscripts." *Times* (UK). February 18, 1908.

"Discovery of a Syrian Text of the Gospels." *Daily News* (London). April 13, 1893.

Doresse, Jean. *Les livres secrets des gnostiques d'Égypte: Introduction aux écrits gnostiques coptes découverts à Khénoboskion*. Paris: Librairie Plon, 1958.

Doresse, Jean. *The Secret Books of the Egyptian Gnostics: An Introduction to the Gnostic Coptic Manuscripts Discovered at Chenoboskion*. New York: Viking, 1960.

Doresse, Jean, and Togo Mina. "Nouveaux textes gnostiques coptes découverts en Haute-Egypte: La bibliotheque de Chenoboskion." *Vigiliae Christianae* 3 (1949): 129–141.

Dospěl Williams, Elizabeth. "'Into the Hands of a Well-Known Antiquary of Cairo': The Assiut Treasure and the Making of an Archaeological Hoard." *West 86th* 21 (2014): 251–272.

Doudna, Gregory L. "Carbon-14 Dating." Pages 1.120–1.121 in Lawrence H. Schiffman and James C. VanderKam (eds.), *Encyclopedia of the Dead Sea Scrolls*. 2 vols. New York: Oxford University Press, 2000.

Dru, Josephine K. "A Complex Pondering of Probabilities: How Can a Single 14C Test Contribute to Dating a Manuscript?" Forthcoming in Cole (ed.), *Interdisciplinary Dating.*

Dussaud, René. "Notice sur la vie et les travaux de M. Vincent Scheil, membre de l'Académie." *Comptes rendus des séances de l'Académie des Inscriptions et Belles-Lettres* 85 (1941): 486–500.

Earle, Edward Mead. "Egyptian Cotton and the American Civil War." *Political Science Quarterly* 41 (1926): 520–545.

Ebojo, Edgar Battad. "A Scribe and His Manuscript: An Investigation into the Scribal Habits of Papyrus 46 (P. Chester Beatty II—P.Mich.inv. 6238)." PhD diss., University of Birmingham, 2014.

Emmel, Stephen. "The Coptic Gnostic Texts as Witnesses to the Production and Transmission of Gnostic (and Other) Traditions." Pages 33–49 in Jörg Frey, Enno Edzard Popkes, and Jens Schröter (eds.), *Das Thomasevangelium: Entstehung—Rezeption—Theologie.* Berlin: de Gruyter, 2008.

Emmel, Stephen. "The Nag Hammadi Codices Editing Project: A Final Report." *American Research Center in Egypt Newsletter* 104 (1978): 10–32.

Emmel, Stephen. "A Question of Codicological Terminology: Revisiting GB-BL Or. 7594 to Find the Meaning of 'Papyrus Fiber Pattern.'" Pages 83–111 in Walter Beltz, Ute Pietruschka, and Jürgen Tubach (eds.), *Sprache und Geist: Peter Nagel zum 65. Geburtstag.* Halle [Saale]: Druckerei der Martin-Luther-Universität Halle-Wittenberg, 2003.

Emmel, Stephen. [Research Note on the Codicology of Nag Hammadi Codex I (the Jung Codex)]. *Bulletin of the American Society of Papyrologists* 14 (1977): 56–57.

Epp, Eldon J. "Issues in the Interrelation of New Testament Textual Criticism and Canon." Pages 485–515 in Lee M. McDonald and James A. Sanders (eds.), *The Canon Debate: On the Origins and Formation of the Bible.* Peabody, Mass.: Hendrickson, 2002.

Epp, Eldon J. "The Jews and the Jewish Community in Oxyrhynchus: Socio-religious Context for the New Testament Papyri." Pages 13–52 in Thomas J. Kraus and Tobias Nicklas (eds.), *New Testament Manuscripts: Their Texts and Their World.* Leiden: Brill, 2006.

Epp, Eldon J. "The Multivalence of the Term 'Original Text' in New Testament Textual Criticism." *Harvard Theological Review* 92 (1999): 245–281.

Epp, Eldon J. "The New Testament Papyri at Oxyrhynchus in Their Social and Intellectual Context." Pages 47–68 in William L. Petersen, Johan S. Vos, and Henk J. de Jonge (eds.), *Sayings of Jesus: Canonical and Non-Canonical: Essays in Honour of Tjitze Baarda.* Leiden: Brill, 1997.

Epp, Eldon J. "The Oxyrhynchus New Testament Papyri: 'Not Without Honor Except in Their Hometown?'" *Journal of Biblical Literature* 123 (2004): 5–55.

Eshel, Esther. "Some Paleographic Success Stories." *Biblical Archaeology Review* 23.2 (March/April 1997): 48–49.

Evans, Craig A., and H. Daniel Zacharias (eds.). *Jewish and Christian Scripture as Artifact and Canon.* London: T & T Clark, 2009.

Fackelmann, Anton. "Präsentation christlicher Urtexte aus dem ersten Jahrhundert geschrieben auf Papyrus, vermutlich Notizschriften des Evangelisten Markus?" *Anagennesis: A Papyrological Journal* 4 (1986): 25–36.

Fackelmann, Michael. *Restaurierung von Papyrus und anderen Schriftträgern aus Ägypten.* Zutphen: Terra, 1985.

Fernández-Galiano, Manuel. "Nuevas páginas del códice 967 del A.T. griego (Ez 28,19–43,9)." *Studia Papyrologica* 10 (1971): 7–77.

"Finds in the Fayum: Details of Mr. Petrie's Work—A Fragment of the Iliad." *New York Times.* June 19, 1888.

Foster, Paul. "Bold Claims, Wishful Thinking, and Lessons About Dating Manuscripts from Papyrus Egerton 2." Pages 193–211 in Craig A. Evans (ed.), *The World of Jesus and the Early Church: Identity and Interpretation in Early Communities of Faith.* Peabody, Mass.: Hendrickson, 2011.

Foster, Paul. "The Discovery and Initial Reaction to the So-Called Gospel of Peter." Pages 9–30 in Thomas J. Kraus and Tobias Nicklas (eds.), *Das Evangelium nach Petrus: Text, Kontexte, Intertext.* Berlin: de Gruyter, 2007.

Foster, Paul. *The Gospel of Peter: Introduction, Critical Edition and Commentary.* Leiden: Brill, 2010.

Fournet, Jean-Luc. "Anatomie d'une bibliothèque de l'Antiquité tardive: l'inventaire, le faciès et la provenance de la 'Bibliothèque Bodmer.'" *Adamantius* 21 (2015): 8–40.

Fournet Jean-Luc (ed.). *Les archives de Dioscore d'Aphrodité cent ans après leur découverte: histoire et culture dans l'Égypte byzantine: actes du colloque de Strasbourg, 8–10 décembre 2005.* Paris: de Boccard, 2008.

Fournet, Jean-Luc. *Ces lambeaux, gardiens de la mémoire des hommes: Papyrus et culture de l'Antiquité tardive.* [Paris]: Fayard, 2016.

Fournet, Jean-Luc. "Une éthopée de Caïn dans le Codex des Visions de la Fondation Bodmer." *Zeitschrift für Papyrologie and Epigraphik* 92 (1992): 253–266.

Fournet, Jean-Luc. *Hellénisme dans l'Égypte du VIe siècle: La bibliothèque et l'oeuvre de Dioscore d'Aphrodité.* Cairo: L'Institut français d'archéologie orientale, 1999.

Fournet, Jean-Luc. "Homère et les papyrus non littéraires: le Poète dans le contexte de ses lecteurs." Pages 125–157 in Guido Bastianini and Angelo Casanova (eds.), *I papiri omerici: Atti del convegno internazionale di studi Firenze, 9–10 Giugno 2011.* Florence: Istituto Papirologico "G. Vitelli," 2012.

Frösén, Jaakko. "Conservation of Ancient Papyrus Materials." Pages 79–100 in Bagnall (ed.), *The Oxford Handbook of Papyrology.*

Funghi, Maria Serena, and Gabriella Messeri Savorelli. "P.Oxy. VII 1016 e P.Oxy. LVII 3885: uno stesso scriba." *Tyche* 7 (1992): 79–83.

Funghi, Maria Serena, and Gabriella Messeri Savorelli. "Sulla scrittura di P. Oxy. II 223 + P. Köln V 210." *Analecta papyrologica* 1 (1989): 37–42.

Gabolde, Marc (ed.). *Coptos: L'Egypte antique aux portes du désert.* Paris: Réunion des musées nationaux, 2000.

Gabra, Gawdat. *Cairo: The Coptic Museum and Old Churches.* Cairo: Egypt International, 1993.

Gabra, Gawdat. *Der Psalter im oxyrhynchitischen (mesokemischen/mittelägyptischen) Dialekt.* Heidelberg: Heidelberger Orientverlag, 1995.

Gabra, Gawdat. "Zur Bedeutung des koptischen Psalmenbuches im oxyrhynchitischen Dialekt." *Göttinger Miszellen* 93 (1986): 37–42.

Galiano, Manuel F. "Notes on the Madrid Ezekiel Papyrus." Pages 133–138 in Deborah H. Samuel (ed.), *Proceedings of the Twelfth International Congress of Papyrology.* Toronto: A. M. Hakkert, 1970.

Gamble, Harry Y. "Bible and Book." Pages 14–35 in Brown (ed.), *In the Beginning.*

Gamble, Harry Y. *Books and Readers in the Early Church: A History of Early Christian Texts.* New Haven, Conn.: Yale University Press, 1995.

Gardner, Iain. *Kellis Literary Texts, Volume 1.* Oxford: Oxbow, 1996.

Gardner, Iain. *Kellis Literary Texts, Volume 2.* Oxford: Oxbow, 2007.

Gascou, Jean. "Les codices documentaires égyptiens." Pages 71–101 in Alain Blanchard (ed.), *Les débuts du codex.* Turnhout: Brepols, 1989.

Gathercole, Simon. "The Earliest Manuscript Title of Matthew's Gospel (BnF Suppl. gr. 1120 ii 3/𝔓4)." *Novum Testamentum* 54 (2012): 209–235.

Gerstinger, Hans. "Ein Fragment des Chester Beatty-Evangelienkodex in der Papyrussammlung der Nationalbibliothek in Wien (Pap. graec. Vindob. 31974)." *Aegyptus* 13 (1933): 67–72.

Gil, Juan, and Sofía Torallas Tovar. *Hadrianus: P.Monts.Roca III.* Barcelona: L'Abadia de Montserrat, 2010.

Goldhill, Simon. *The Buried Life of Things: How Objects Made History in Nineteenth Century Britain.* Cambridge: Cambridge University Press, 2015.

Goler, Sarah, James T. Yardley, Angela Cacciola, Alexis Hagadorn, David Ratzan, and Roger Bagnall. "Characterizing the Age of Ancient Egyptian Manuscripts Through Micro-Raman Spectroscopy." *Journal of Raman Spectroscopy* (May 6, 2016). https://doi.org/10.1002/jrs.4945.

Goodacre, Mark. "How Reliable Is the Story of the Nag Hammadi Discovery?" *Journal for the Study of the New Testament* 35 (2013): 303–322.

Goodspeed, Edgar J. "The Detroit Manuscripts of the Septuagint and the New Testament." *Biblical World* 31 (1908): 218–226.

Górecki, Tomasz. "Sheikh Abd el-Gurna (Hermitage in Tomb 1152) Preliminary Report, 2005." *Polish Archaeology in the Mediterranean* 17 (2007): 263–274.

Görgemanns, Herwig, and Heinrich Karpp. *Origenes: Vier Bücher von den Prinzipien.* 2nd ed. Darmstadt: Wissenschaftliche Buchgesellschaft, 1985.

"The Gospel According to Peter." *Times* (UK). December 2, 1892.

Gove, H. E. "Dating the Turin Shroud—An Assessment." *Radiocarbon* 32 (1990): 87–92.

Gregory, Caspar René. *Die griechischen Handschriften des Neuen Testaments.* Leipzig: J. C. Hinrichs'sche Buchhandlung, 1908.

Gregory, Caspar René. "The Quires in Greek Manuscripts." *American Journal of Philology* 7 (1886): 27–32.

Grenfell, Bernard P. "Dr. Bernard P. Grenfell's Address." Pages 27–33 in *Egypt Exploration Fund: Report of the Eighteenth Ordinary General Meeting, 1903–1904.* London: Egypt Exploration Fund, 1904.

Grenfell, Bernard P. "The Oldest Record of Christ's Life." *McClure's Magazine* 9 (July 1897): 1022–1030.

Grenfell, Bernard P. "Oxyrhynchus and Its Papyri." *Egypt Exploration Fund Archaeological Report* (1896–1897): 1–12.

Grenfell, Bernard P. "The Present Position of Papyrology." *Bulletin of the John Rylands Library* 6 (1920): 142–162.

Grenfell, Bernard P., and Arthur S. Hunt. "Excavations at Oxyrhynchus." *Egypt Exploration Fund Archaeological Report* (1903–1904): 14–17.

Grenfell, Bernard P., and Arthur S. Hunt. "Excavations at Oxyrhynchus." *Egypt Exploration Fund Archaeological Report* (1904–1905): 13–17.

Grenfell, Bernard P., and Arthur S. Hunt. "Excavations at Oxyrhynchus." *Egypt Exploration Fund Archaeological Report* (1906–1907): 8–11.

Grenfell, Bernard P., and Arthur S. Hunt. *Fayûm Towns and Their Papyri.* London: Egypt Exploration Fund, 1900.

Grenfell, Bernard P., and Arthur S. Hunt. *Fragment of an Uncanonical Gospel from Oxyrhynchus.* London: Oxford University Press, 1908.

Grenfell, Bernard P., and Arthur S. Hunt. "A Large Find of Greek Literary Papyri." *Times* (UK). May 14, 1906.

Grenfell, Bernard P., and Arthur S. Hunt. *Logia Iēsou: Sayings of Our Lord from an Early Greek Papyrus.* London: Egypt Exploration Fund, 1897.

Grenfell, Bernard P., and Arthur S. Hunt. *New Sayings of Jesus and Fragment of a Lost Gospel from Oxyrhynchus.* London: Oxford University Press, 1904.

Grenfell, Bernard P., Arthur S. Hunt, et al. (eds.). *The Oxyrhynchus Papyri.* London: Egypt Exploration Society, 1898–.

Gronewald, Michael. *Didymos der Blinde: Psalmenkommentar (Tura-Papyrus) Teil V, Kommentar zu Psalm 40–44, 4.* Bonn: Habelt, 1970.

Gronewald, Michael, Giuseppina Azzarello, John Lundon, Klaus Maresch, Fabian Reiter, Gesa Schenke, and William H. Willis (eds.). *Kölner Papyri (P.Köln), Band 9.* Wiesbaden: Westdeutscher Verlag, 2001.

Grossmann, Peter. "Qift." Pages 7.2038–7.2040 in Atiya (ed.), *The Coptic Encyclopedia.*

Grossmann, Peter, and Gary Lease. "Faw Qibli—1989 Excavation Report." *Göttinger Miszellen* 114 (1990): 9–16.

[Grueber, H. A.]. "Financial Report of the Honorary Treasurer for 1897–8."

Pages 10–15 in *Egypt Exploration Fund: Report of the Twelfth Ordinary General Meeting 1897–8*. London: Egypt Exploration Fund, 1898.

Guéraud, Octave. "Note préliminaire sur les papyrus d'Origène découverts à Toura." *Revue de l'histoire des religions* 131 (1946): 85–108.

Guéraud, Octave, and Pierre Nautin. *Origène: Sur la Pâque*. Paris: Beauchesne, 1979.

Gunter, Ann C. "Charles Lang Freer's Biblical Manuscripts." Pages 6–9 in Brown (ed.), *In the Beginning*.

Gunter, Ann C. *A Collector's Journey: Charles Lang Freer and Egypt*. Washington, D.C.: Freer Gallery of Art, 2002.

Gurtner, Daniel M., Juan Hernández, Jr., and Paul Foster (eds.). *Studies on the Text of the New Testament and Early Christianity: Essays in Honor of Michael W. Holmes on the Occasion of His 65th Birthday*. Leiden: Brill, 2015.

Hagedorn, Dieter. "Ein neues Fragment zu P.Oxy. XV 1778 (Aristides, Apologie)." *Zeitschrift für Papyrologie und Epigraphik* 131 (2000): 40–44.

Hagen, Frederik, and Kim Ryholt. *The Antiquities Trade in Egypt, 1880–1930: The H. O. Lange Papers*. Copenhagen: Royal Danish Academy of Sciences, 2016.

Haines-Eitzen, Kim. *Guardians of Letters: Literacy, Power, and the Transmitters of Early Christian Literature*. New York: Oxford University Press, 2000.

Hamm, Winfried. *Der Septuaginta-Text des Buches Daniel Kap. 1–2 nach dem kölner Teil des Papyrus 967*. Bonn: Rudolf Habelt, 1969.

Harker, Brent. "Didymos the Blind Sees the Light of Day." *BYU Today* 39 (June 1985): 18–20.

Harrison, Percy Neale. *The Problem of the Pastoral Epistles*. London: Oxford University Press, 1921.

Head, Peter M. "The Gospel of Judas and the Qarara Codices: Some Preliminary Observations." *Tyndale Bulletin* 58 (2007): 1–23.

Head, Peter M. "Is P4, P64 and P67 the Oldest Manuscript of the Four Gospels? A Response to T. C. Skeat." *New Testament Studies* 51 (2005): 450–457.

Helm, Rudolf (ed.). *Eusebius Werke siebenter Band: Die Chronik des Hieronymus, erster Teil*. Leipzig: J. C. Hinrichs'sche Buchhandlung, 1913.

Henrichs Albert, and Ludwig Koenen. "Ein griechischer Mani-Codex." *Zeitschrift für Papyrologie und Epigraphik* 5 (1970): 97–216.

Hill, Charles E. "Intersections of Jewish and Christian Scribal Culture: The Original Codex Containing 𝔓4, 𝔓64, and 𝔓67 and Its Implications." Pages 75–91 in Reidar Hvalvik and John Kaufman (eds.), *Among Jews, Gentiles, and Christians in Antiquity and the Middle Ages*. Trondheim: Tapir Academic Press, 2011.

Hill, Charles E. "Rightly Dividing the Word: Uncovering an Early Template for Textual Division in John's Gospel." Pages 217–238 in Gurtner, Hernández, Jr., and Foster (eds.), *Studies on the Text of the New Testament and Early Christianity*.

Hope, Colin A. "The Archaeological Context of the Discovery of Leaves from a Manichaean Codex." *Zeitschrift für Papyrologie und Epigraphik* 117 (1997): 156–161.

Hope, Colin A. "The Find Context of the Kellis Agricultural Account Book." Pages 5–14 in Bagnall (ed.), *The Kellis Agricultural Account Book*.

Hope, Colin A., Olaf E. Kaper, Gillian E. Bowen, and Shirley F. Patten. "Dakhleh Oasis Project: Ismant el-Kharab 1991–92." *Journal of the Society for the Study of Egyptian Antiquities* 19 (1989) [1993]: 1–26.

Hopkins, Clark. *The Discovery of Dura-Europos*. New Haven, Conn.: Yale University Press, 1979.

Horton, Charles. *Alfred Chester Beatty: From Miner to Bibliophile*. Dublin: TownHouse, 2003.

Horton, Charles. "The Chester Beatty Biblical Papyri: A Find of the Greatest Importance." Pages 149–160 in Charles Horton (ed.), *The Earliest Gospels: The Origins and Transmission of the Earliest Christian Gospels*. London: T & T Clark, 2004.

Houston, George W. *Inside Roman Libraries: Book Collections and Their Management in Antiquity*. Chapel Hill: University of North Carolina Press, 2014.

Hunger, Herbert. "Zur Datierung des Papyrus Bodmer II (P66)." *Anzeiger der Österreichischen Akademie der Wissenschaften philosophisch-historische Klasse* 97 (1961): 12–23.

Hunt, Arthur S. "B. P. Grenfell: 1869–1926." *Proceedings of the British Academy* 12 (1926): 357–364.

Hurst, André. "Papyrus Bodmer 48: Iliade 1, 45–58." *Museum Helveticum* 47 (1990): 30–33.

Hurst, André. "Papyrus Bodmer 49: Odyssée 9, 455–488 et 526–556; 10, 188–215." *Museum Helveticum* 43 (1986): 221–230.

Hurtado, Larry W. *The Earliest Christian Artifacts: Manuscripts and Christian Origins*. Grand Rapids, Mich.: Eerdmans, 2006.

Hurtado, Larry W. (ed.). *The Freer Biblical Manuscripts: Fresh Studies of an American Treasure Trove*. Leiden: Brill, 2006.

Hurtado, Larry W. "A Fresh Analysis of P.Oxyrhynchus 1228 (𝔓22) as Artifact." Pages 206–216 in Gurtner, Hernández, Jr., and Foster (eds.), *Studies on the Text of the New Testament and Early Christianity*.

Hurtado, Larry W. "The Origin of the *Nomina Sacra*: A Proposal." *Journal of Biblical Literature* 117 (1998): 655–673.

Hurtado, Larry W. *Text-Critical Methodology and the Pre-Caesarean Text: Codex W in the Gospel of Mark*. Grand Rapids, Mich.: Eerdmans, 1981.

Hyvernat, Henry. *A Check List of Coptic Manuscripts in the Pierpont Morgan Library*. New York: John Pierpont Morgan Library, 1919.

Ibscher, Hugo. "Beschreibung der Handschrift." Pages xxi–xxvii in Alexander Böhlig, *Der achmimische Proverbientext nach Ms. Berol. orient. oct. 987*. Munich: Verlag Robert Lerche, 1958.

Ibscher, Hugo. "Die Handschrift." Pages viii–xviii in C. R. C. Allberry, *A Manichaean Psalm-Book*. Stuttgart: Kohlhammer, 1938.

Ibscher, Hugo. "Die Handschrift." Pages ix–xiv in Hans Jakob Polotsky, *Manichäische Homilien*. Stuttgart: Kohlhammer, 1934.

Ibscher, Hugo. "Die Handschrift." Pages v–xiv in Hans Jakob Polotsky and Alexander Böhlig, *Manichäische Handschriften der Staatlichen Museen Berlin: Kephalaia, 1. Hälfte (Lieferung 1–10)*. Stuttgart: Kohlhammer, 1940.

Ibscher, Hugo. "Die Handschriften." Pages 82–85 in Schmidt and Polotsky, "Ein Mani-Fund in Ägypten."

Ibscher, Hugo. "Der Kodex." *Jahrbuch der Einbandkunst* 4 (1937): 3–15.

"Ink Analysis: The Gospel of Judas." McCrone Group. https://www.mccrone.com/ink-analysis-the-gospel-of-judas.

James, T. G. H. (ed.) *Excavating in Egypt: The Egypt Exploration Society, 1882–1982*. London: British Museum, 1982.

Jarus, Owen. "Mummy Mask May Reveal Oldest Known Gospel." Live Science. January 18, 2015. http://www.livescience.com/49489-oldest-known-gospel-mummy-mask.html.

Jenott, Lance. *The Gospel of Judas: Coptic Text, Translation, and Historical Interpretation of "The Betrayer's Gospel."* Tübingen: Mohr Siebeck, 2011.

Johnson, Allen Chester, Henry Snyder Gehman, and Edmund Harris Kase, Jr. *The John H. Scheide Biblical Papyri: Ezekiel*. Princeton, N.J.: Princeton University Press, 1938.

Johnson, John de Monins. "Excavations at Atfieh." *Egypt Exploration Fund Archaeological Report* (1910–1911): 5–13.

Johnson, John de Monins. "Graeco-Roman Branch." *Egypt Exploration Fund Archaeological Report* (1911–1912): 12–16.

Johnson, Luke Timothy. *The Writings of the New Testament*. 3rd ed. Minneapolis: Fortress, 2010.

Johnson, William A. *Bookrolls and Scribes in Oxyrhynchus*. Toronto: University of Toronto Press, 2004.

Johnson, William A. "The Oxyrhynchus Distributions in America: Papyri and Ethics." *Bulletin of the American Society of Papyrologists* 49 (2012): 209–222.

Jones, Alexander. *Astronomical Papyri from Oxyrhynchus (P.Oxy. 4133–4300a)*. Philadelphia: American Philosophical Society, 1999.

Jones, Brice C. *New Testament Texts on Greek Amulets from Late Antiquity*. London: T & T Clark, 2016.

Jull, A. J. Timothy, Douglas J. Donahue, Magen Broshi, and Emanuel Tov. "Radiocarbon Dating of Scrolls and Linen Fragments from the Judean Desert." *Radiocarbon* 37 (1995): 11–19.

Kasser, Rodolphe. "Bodmer Papyri." Pages 8.48–8.53 in Atiya (ed.), *The Coptic Encyclopedia*.

Kasser, Rodolphe. "Les dialectes coptes." *Bulletin de l'Institut français d'archéologie orientale* 73 (1973): 71–101.

Kasser, Rodolphe. "Introduction." Pages 1.liii–1.lix in Bircher (ed.), *Bibliotheca Bodmeriana.*

Kasser, Rodolphe. *Papyrus Bodmer XVI: Exode I–XV, 21 en sahidique.* Cologny-Geneva: Bibliotheca Bodmeriana, 1961.

Kasser, Rodolphe. *Papyrus Bodmer XVII: Actes des Apôtres, Epîtres de Jacques, Pierre, Jean et Jude.* Cologny-Geneva: Bibliotheca Bodmeriana, 1961.

Kasser, Rodolphe. *Papyrus Bodmer XVIII: Deutéronome I–X, 7 en sahidique.* Cologny-Geneva: Bibliotheca Bodmeriana, 1962.

Kasser, Rodolphe. *Papyrus Bodmer XIX: Évangile de Matthieu XIV, 28–XXVIII, 20, Epître aux Romains I, 1–II, 3 en sahidique.* Cologny-Geneva: Bibliotheca Bodmeriana, 1962.

Kasser, Rodolphe. *Papyrus Bodmer XXII et Mississippi Coptic Codex II.* Cologny-Geneva: Bibliotheca Bodmeriana, 1964.

Kasser, Rodolphe. "Status quaestionis 1988 sulla presunta origine dei cosiddetti Papiri Bodmer." *Aegyptus* 68 (1988): 191–194.

Kasser, Rodolphe, and Colin Austin. *Papyrus Bodmer XXV: Ménandre: La Samienne.* Cologny-Geneva: Bibliotheca Bodmeriana, 1969.

Kasser, Rodolphe, Guglielmo Cavallo, and Joseph van Haelst. "Appendice: Nouvelle description du Codex des Visions." Pages 103–128 in Antonio Carlini (ed.), *Papyrus Bodmer XXXVIII, Erma: Il Pastore (Ia–IIIa visione).* Cologny-Geneva: Fondation Martin Bodmer, 1991.

Kasser, Rodolphe, and Philippe Luisier. "P.Bodmer XL: *Cantique des Cantiques* en copte saïdique." *Orientalia* 81 (2012): 149–201.

Kasser, Rodolphe, and Philippe Luisier. "P.Bodmer XLIII: Un Feuillet de *Zostrien.*" *Muséon* 120 (2007): 251–272.

Kasser, Rodolphe, Marvin Meyer, and Gregor Wurst. *The Gospel of Judas from Codex Tchacos.* Washington, D.C.: National Geographic Society, 2006.

Kasser, Rodolphe, and Michel Testuz. *Papyrus Bodmer XXIV: Psaumes XVII–CXVIII.* Cologny-Geneva: Bibliotheca Bodmeriana, 1967.

Kasser, Rodolphe, and Gregor Wurst (eds.). *The Gospel of Judas Together with the Letter of Peter to Philip, James, and a Book of Allogenes from Codex Tchacos: Critical Edition.* Washington, D.C.: National Geographic Society, 2007.

Kebabian, John S. "The Binding of the Glazier Manuscript of the Acts of the Apostles (IVth or IV/Vth Century)." Pages 25–30 in Hellmut Lehmann-Haupt (ed.), *Homage to a Bookman: Essays on Manuscripts, Books and Printing Written for Hans P. Kraus on His 60th Birthday.* Berlin: Gebr. Mann, 1967.

Kehl, Aloys. *Der Psalmenkommentar von Tura Quaternio IX (Pap. Colon. Theol. 1).* Cologne: Westdeutscher Verlag, 1964.

Kenyon, Frederic G. *The Bible and Modern Scholarship.* London: John Murray, 1948.

Kenyon, Frederic G. *Books and Readers in Ancient Greece and Rome.* Oxford: Clarendon, 1932.

Kenyon, Frederic G. *The Chester Beatty Biblical Papyri: Descriptions and Texts of*

Twelve Manuscripts on Papyrus of the Greek Bible. 8 fascicles in 16 vols. London: Emery Walker, 1933–1958.

Kenyon, Frederic G. *Handbook to the Textual Criticism of the New Testament.* London: Macmillan, 1901.

Kenyon, Frederic G. *The Palaeography of Greek Papyri.* Oxford: Clarendon, 1899.

Kenyon, Frederic G. *The Reading of the Bible as History, as Literature and as Religion.* London: John Murray, 1944.

Kenyon, Frederic G. *The Story of the Bible: A Popular Account of How It Came to Us.* London: John Murray, 1936.

Kenyon, Frederic G. "The Text of the Bible: A New Discovery." *Times* (UK). November 19, 1931.

Khater, Antoine. *Le régime juridique des fouilles et des antiquités en Égypte.* Cairo: L'Institut français d'archéologie orientale, 1960.

Kim, Young Kyu. "Palaeographical Dating of P^{46} to the Later First Century." *Biblica* 69 (1988): 248–257.

Kinzig, Wolfram. "*Kainē diathēkē:* The Title of the New Testament in the Second and Third Centuries." *Journal of Theological Studies* 45 (1994): 519–544.

Koenen, Ludwig. "Zur Herkunft des Kölner Mani-Codex." *Zeitschrift für Papyrologie und Epigraphik* 11 (1973): 240–241.

Koenen, Ludwig, and Louis Doutreleau. "Nouvel inventaire des papyrus de Toura." *Recherches de science religieuse* 55 (1967): 547–564.

Koenen, Ludwig, and Wolfgang Müller-Wiener. "Zu den Papyri aus dem Arsenioskloster bei Ṭurā." *Zeitschrift für Papyrologie und Epigraphik* 2 (1968): 41–63.

Kordowska, Daria. "Conservation Work on Three Coptic Manuscripts from Sheikh Abd el-Gurna." *Polish Archaeology in the Mediterranean* 18 (2006 [2008]): 311–315.

Kotsifou, Chrysi. "Bookbinding and Manuscript Illumination in Late Antique and Early Medieval Monastic Circles in Egypt." Pages 213–244 in Juan Pedro Monferrer-Sala, Herman Teule, and Sofía Torallas Tovar (eds.), *Eastern Christians and Their Written Heritage: Manuscripts, Scribes and Context.* Leuven: Peeters, 2012.

Kotsifou, Chrysi. "Books and Book Production in the Monastic Communities of Byzantine Egypt." Pages 48–66 in William E. Klingshirn and Linda Safran (eds.), *The Early Christian Book.* Washington, D.C.: Catholic University of America Press, 2007.

Kraeling, Carl H. *A Greek Fragment of Tatian's Diatessaron from Dura.* London: Christophers, 1935.

Kraus, H. P. *A Rare Book Saga: The Autobiography of H. P. Kraus.* New York: G. P. Putnam's Sons, 1978.

Kraus, Thomas J. *Ad Fontes: Original Manuscripts and Their Significance for Studying Early Christianity.* Leiden: Brill, 2007.

Kraus, Thomas J. "Pergament oder Papyrus? Anmerkungen zur Signifikanz des Beschreibstoffes bei der Behandlung von Manuskripten." *New Testament Studies* 49 (2003): 425–432.

Krosney, Herbert. *The Lost Gospel: The Quest for the Gospel of Judas Iscariot.* Washington, D.C.: National Geographic Society, 2006.

Krutzsch, Myriam, and Ira Rabin. "Material Criteria and Their Clues for Dating." *New Testament Studies* 61 (2015): 356–367.

Lama, Mariachiara. "Aspetti di tecnica libraria ad Ossirinco: Copie letterarie su rotoli documentari." *Aegyptus* 71 (1991): 55–120.

Larsen, Matthew D. C. "Accidental Publication, Unfinished Texts and the Traditional Goals of New Testament Textual Criticism." *Journal for the Study of the New Testament* 39 (2017): 362–387.

Latour, Bruno. *Reassembling the Social: An Introduction to Actor-Network-Theory.* Oxford: Oxford University Press, 2005.

Layton, Bentley. *The Gnostic Scriptures.* New York: Doubleday, 1987.

Lefebvre, Gustave. *Fragments d'un manuscrit de Ménandre.* Cairo: L'Institut français d'archéologie orientale, 1907.

Leroy, L., and S. Grébaut. *L'Histoire des conciles de Sévère ibn al Moqaffaʿ.* Paris: Firmin-Didot, 1911.

Lewis, Naphtali. *Papyrus in Classical Antiquity.* Oxford: Clarendon, 1974.

Lieu, Judith M. *Christian Identity in the Jewish and Graeco-Roman World.* Oxford: Oxford University Press, 2004.

Long, Austin. "Attempt to Affect the Apparent ^{14}C Age of Cotton by Scorching in a CO_2 Environment." *Radiocarbon* 40 (1998): 57–58.

Luijendijk, AnneMarie. *Greetings in the Lord: Early Christians and the Oxyrhynchus Papyri.* Cambridge: Harvard University Press, 2008.

Luijendijk, AnneMarie. "A New Testament Papyrus and Its Documentary Context: An Early Christian Writing Exercise from the Archive of Leonides (P.Oxy. II 209/𝔓10)." *Journal of Biblical Literature* 129 (2010): 575–596.

Luijendijk, AnneMarie. "Reading the *Gospel of Thomas* in the Third Century: Three Oxyrhynchus Papyri and Origen's *Homilies.*" Pages 241–267 in Clivaz and Zumstein (eds.), *Reading New Testament Papyri in Context.*

Luijendijk, AnneMarie. "Sacred Scriptures as Trash: Biblical Papyri from Oxyrhynchus." *Vigiliae Christianae* 64 (2010): 217–254.

Lundhaug, Hugo, and Lance Jenott. *The Monastic Origins of the Nag Hammadi Codices.* Tübingen: Mohr Siebeck, 2015.

MacCoull, Leslie S. B. *Dioscorus of Aphrodito: His Work and His World.* Berkeley: University of California Press, 1988.

Macdougall, Doug. *Nature's Clocks: How Scientists Measure the Age of Almost Everything.* Berkeley: University of California Press, 2008.

Mackay, Thomas W., and C. Wilfred Griggs. "The Recently Rediscovered Papyrus Leaves of Didymos the Blind." *Bulletin of the American Society of Papyrologists* 20 (1983): 59–60.

Malik, Peter. *P.Beatty III (𝔓⁴⁷): The Codex, Its Scribe, and Its Text*. Leiden: Brill, 2017.

Mallon, Jean. "Quel est le plus ancien exemple connu d'un manuscrit latin en forme de codex?" *Emerita* 17 (1949): 1–8.

Martin, Alain, and Oliver Primavesi. *L'Empédocle de Strasbourg (P. Strasb. gr. Inv. 1665–1666)*. Berlin: de Gruyter, 1999.

Martin, Victor. *Papyrus Bodmer I: Iliade, chants 5 et 6*. Cologny-Geneva: Bibliotheca Bodmeriana, 1954.

Martin, Victor. "Un papyrus de Plutarque." *Aegyptus* 31 (1951): 138–147.

Martin, Victor. "Un recueil de diatribes cyniques: Pap. Genev. inv. 271." *Museum Helveticum* 16 (1959): 77–115.

Martin, Victor, and Rodolphe Kasser. *Papyrus Bodmer XIV–XV: Évangiles de Luc et Jean*. 2 vols. Cologny-Geneva: Bibliotheca Bodmeriana, 1961.

Martinez, David G. "The Papyri and Early Christianity." Pages 590–622 in Bagnall (ed.), *The Oxford Handbook of Papyrology*.

Mazza, Roberta. "Papyri, Ethics, and Economics: A Biography of P.Oxy. 15.1780 (𝔓39)." *Bulletin of the American Society of Papyrologists* 52 (2015): 113–142.

McKendrick, Scot. "The Codex Alexandrinus or the Dangers of Being a Named Manuscript." Pages 1–16 in Scot McKendrick and Orlaith A. O'Sullivan (eds.), *The Bible as Book: The Transmission of the Greek Text*. London: British Library, 2003.

McKendrick, Scot, David Parker, Amy Myshrall, and Cillian O'Hogan (eds.). *Codex Sinaiticus: New Perspectives on the Ancient Biblical Manuscript*. Peabody, Mass.: Hendrickson, 2015.

Méla, Charles. *Legends of the Centuries: Looking Through a Legendary Collection*. Translated by David Macey. Paris: Éditions Cercle d'Art, 2004.

Merell, Jean. "Nouveaux fragments du Papyrus 4." *Revue Biblique* 47 (1938): 5–22.

Merrillees, Robert S. *The Tano Family: Gifts from the Nile to Cyprus*. Lefkosia: Moufflon, 2003.

Metzger, Bruce M. *Manuscripts of the Greek Bible: An Introduction to Palaeography*. New York: Oxford University Press, 1981.

Metzger, Bruce M., and Bart D. Ehrman. *The Text of the New Testament: Its Transmission, Corruption, and Restoration*. 4th ed. New York: Oxford University Press, 2005.

Migeon, Gaston. "Nouveaux manuscrits authentiques de la Bible." *Journal des débats*. February 18, 1908.

Miguélez-Cavero, Laura. *Poems in Context: Greek Poetry in the Egyptian Thebaid 200–600 AD*. Berlin: de Gruyter, 2008.

Miller, Julia. "Puzzle Me This: Early Binding Fragments in the Papyrology Collection of the University of Michigan Library." Pages 2.198–2.297 in Julia Miller (ed.), *Suave Mechanicals: Essays on the History of Bookbinding*. 2 vols. Ann Arbor: Legacy, 2013–2015.

Milne, H. J. M., and Theodore C. Skeat. *Scribes and Correctors of the Codex Sinaiticus.* London: British Museum, 1938.

Mina, Togo. "Le papyrus gnostique du Musée Copte." *Vigiliae Christianae* 2 (1948): 129–136.

Minutoli, Diletta, and Rosario Pintaudi (eds.). *Papyri Graecae Schøyen.* 2 vols. Florence: Gonnelli, 2005–2010.

Montserrat, Dominic. "News Reports: The Excavations and Their Journalistic Coverage." Pages 28–39 in Bowman et al. (eds.), *Oxyrhynchus: A City and Its Texts.*

Montserrat, Dominic. "'No Papyrus and No Portraits': Hogarth, Grenfell and the First Season in the Fayum, 1895–6." *Bulletin of the American Society of Papyrologists* 33 (1996): 133–176.

"Morgan Bibles Really Priceless: Facts About the Coptic MSS. for Which the Financier Was Said to Have Overpaid." *New York Times.* March 10, 1912.

Mugridge, Alan. *Copying Early Christian Texts: A Study of Scribal Practice.* Tübingen: Mohr Siebeck, 2016.

Munier, Henri. "Tourah." *Bulletin de la société d'archéologie copte* 7 (1941): 92–93.

"Nachricht von dem Büchervorrath des Herrn Dr. Anton Askew in London, und von einigen griechischen Handschriften, so sich darin befinden." *Brittisches theologisches Magazin* 1.4 (1770): 222–225.

"New Verses Found in Gospel Papyri." *New York Times.* May 13, 1913.

Nicholls, Matthew. "Parchment Codices in a New Text of Galen." *Greece and Rome* 57 (2010): 378–386.

Nichols, John. *Literary Anecdotes of the Eighteenth Century.* 9 vols. London: Nichols, Son, and Bentley, 1812–1816.

Nicolotti, Andrea. *Sindone. Storia e leggende di una reliquia controversa.* Turin: Einaudi, 2015.

Nodar, Alberto, and Sofía Torallas Tovar. "Paleography of Magical Handbooks: An Attempt?" Pages 59–66 in Emilio Suárez, Miriam Blanco, and Eleni Chronopoulou (eds.), *Los papiros mágicos griegos: entre lo sublime y lo cotidiano.* Madrid: Dykinson, 2015.

Nongbri, Brent. "The Acquisition of the University of Michigan's Portion of the Chester Beatty Biblical Papyri and a New Suggested Provenance." *Archiv für Papyrusforschung* 60 (2014): 93–116.

Nongbri, Brent. *Before Religion: A History of a Modern Concept.* New Haven, Conn.: Yale University Press, 2013.

Nongbri, Brent. "The Bodmer Papyri: An Inventory of 'P.Bodmer' Items." *Variant Readings.* September 24, 2017. https://brentnongbri.com/2017/09/24/the-bodmer-papyri-an-inventory-of-p-bodmer-items/.

Nongbri, Brent. "The Construction of P.Bodmer VIII and the Bodmer 'Composite' or 'Miscellaneous' Codex." *Novum Testamentum* 58 (2016): 394–410.

Nongbri, Brent. "Finding Early Christian Books at Nag Hammadi and Beyond." *Bulletin for the Study of Religion* 45 (2016): 11–19.

Nongbri, Brent. "A First-Century Papyrus of Mark (Probably Not the One You Think)." *Variant Readings*. July 21, 2017. https://brentnongbri.com /2017/07/21/a-first-century-papyrus-of-mark-probably-not-the-one-you -think/.

Nongbri, Brent. "Grenfell and Hunt on the Dates of Early Christian Codices: Setting the Record Straight." *Bulletin of the American Society of Papyrologists* 48 (2011): 149–162.

Nongbri, Brent. "The Limits of Palaeographic Dating of Literary Papyri: Some Observations on the Date and Provenance of P.Bodmer II (P66)." *Museum Helveticum* 71 (2014): 1–35.

Nongbri, Brent. "Losing a Curious Christian Scroll but Gaining a Curious Christian Codex: An Oxyrhynchus Papyrus of Exodus and Revelation." *Novum Testamentum* 55 (2013): 77–88.

Nongbri, Brent. "Palaeography, Precision, and Publicity: Further Thoughts on P.Ryl. 3.457 (P52)." Forthcoming.

Nongbri, Brent. "Recent Progress in Understanding the Construction of the Bodmer 'Miscellaneous' or 'Composite' Codex." *Adamantius* 21 (2015): 171–172.

Nongbri, Brent. "Reconsidering the Place of Papyrus Bodmer XIV–XV (𝔓75) in the Textual Criticism of the New Testament." *Journal of Biblical Literature* 135 (2016): 403–437.

Nongbri, Brent. Review of Houston, *Inside Roman Libraries*. *Journal of Early Christian Studies* 24 (2016): 136–137.

Nongbri, Brent. "The Robinson Papyri." *Variant Readings.* July 23, 2017. https:// brentnongbri.com/2017/07/23/the-robinson-papyri/.

Nongbri, Brent. "Some Answers on Fackelmann's 'First-Century Mark' Papyrus." *Variant Readings*. August 3, 2017. https://brentnongbri.com/2017/08 /03/some-answers-on-fackelmanns-first-century-mark-papyrus/.

Nongbri, Brent. "The Use and Abuse of 𝔓52: Papyrological Pitfalls in the Dating of the Fourth Gospel." *Harvard Theological Review* 98 (2005): 23–48.

Obbink, Dirk. "The Poems of Sappho: Provenance, Authenticity, and Text of the New Sappho Papyri." Pages 34–54 in Anton Bierl and André Lardinois (eds.), *The Newest Sappho: P.Sapph. Obbink and P. GC inv. 105, frs. 1–4*. Leiden: Brill, 2016.

"Old Greek Bible Reveals Verses Lost for Centuries." *New York Times*. May 18, 1913.

Orsini, Pasquale. "La maiuscola biblica copta." *Segno e testo* 6 (2008): 121–150.

Orsini, Pasquale. *Manoscritti in maiuscola biblica: Materiali per un aggiornamento*. Cassino: Università degli studi di Cassino, 2005.

Orsini, Pasquale. "I Papiri Bodmer: scritture e libri." *Adamantius* 21 (2015): 60–78.

Orsini, Pasquale, and Willy Clarysse. "Early New Testament Manuscripts and Their Dates: A Critique of Theological Palaeography." *Ephemerides Theologicae Lovanienses* 88 (2012): 443–474.

Paap, A. H. R. E. Nomina Sacra *in the Greek Papyri of the First Five Centuries A.D.: The Sources and Some Deductions.* Leiden: Brill, 1959.

Pappas, Stephanie. "Truth Behind Gospel of Judas Revealed in Ancient Inks." Live Science. April 8, 2013. http://www.livescience.com/28506-gospel -judas-ink-authenticity.html.

Parker, David C. *Codex Sinaiticus: The Story of the World's Oldest Bible.* Peabody, Mass.: Hendricksen, 2010.

Parker, David C. *An Introduction to the New Testament Manuscripts and Their Texts.* Cambridge: Cambridge University Press, 2008.

Parker, David C. *The Living Text of the Gospels.* Cambridge: Cambridge University Press, 1997.

Parker, David C. "Was Matthew Written Before 50 CE? The Magdalen Papyrus of Matthew." *Expository Times* 107 (1995): 40–43.

Parker, David C., D. G. K. Taylor, and M. S. Goodacre. "The Dura-Europos Gospel Harmony." Pages 192–228 in David G. K. Taylor (ed.), *Studies in the Early Text of the Gospels and Acts: The Papers of the First Birmingham Colloquium on the Textual Criticism of the New Testament.* Piscataway, N.J.: Gorgias, 2013.

Parsons, Peter J. *City of the Sharp-Nosed Fish: Greek Lives in Roman Egypt.* London: Weidenfeld and Nicolson, 2007.

Parsons, Peter J. "The Palaeography of the Herculaneum Papyri." *Classical Review,* n.s. 39 (1989): 358–360.

Parsons, Peter J. Review of Cavallo *Ricerche sulla maiuscola biblica. Gnomon* 42 (1970): 375–380.

Parsons, Peter J. "The Scripts and Their Date." Pages 19–26 in Emanuel Tov (ed.), *The Greek Minor Prophets Scroll from Naḥal Ḥever.* Oxford: Clarendon, 1990.

Pedersen, Nils Arne, and John Møller Larsen. *Manichaean Texts in Syriac.* Turnhout: Brepols, 2013.

Petrie, William M. Flinders. "The Discovery of the Papyrus." Pages ix–x in Herbert Thompson, *The Gospel of St. John According to the Earliest Coptic Manuscript.* London: British School of Archaeology in Egypt, 1924.

Petrie, William M. Flinders. *Koptos.* London: Bernard Quaritch, 1896.

Petrie, William M. Flinders. *Methods and Aims in Archaeology.* London: Macmillan, 1904.

Petrie, William M. Flinders. *Tombs of the Courtiers and Oxyrhynchos.* London: British School of Archaeology in Egypt, 1925.

"Petrie Discusses Freer Gospel Ms." *New York Times.* May 14, 1913.

Pickering, Stuart. "The Dating of the Chester Beatty-Michigan Codex of the Pauline Epistles ($\mathfrak{P}^{46}$)." Pages 216–227 in T. W. Hillard, R. A. Kearsley, C. E. V. Nixon, and A. M. Nobbs (eds.), *Ancient History in a Modern University, Volume 2: Early Christianity, Late Antiquity and Beyond.* Grand Rapids, Mich.: Eerdmans, 1998.

Pietersma, Albert. *The Acts of Phileas Bishop of Thmuis (Including Fragments of the Greek Psalter)*. Geneva: Cramer, 1984.

Pietersma, Albert. *Chester Beatty Biblical Papyri IV and V: A New Edition with Text-Critical Analysis*. Toronto: Samuel Stevens Hakkert, 1977.

Pietersma, Albert. "The 'Lost' Folio of the Chester Beatty *Ecclesiasticus*." *Vetus Testamentum* 25 (1975): 497–499.

Pietersma, Albert. *Two Manuscripts of the Greek Psalter in the Chester Beatty Library Dublin*. Rome: Biblical Institute Press, 1978.

Pintaudi, Rosario. "The Italian Excavations." Pages 104–108 in Bowman et al. (eds.), *Oxyrhynchus: A City and Its Texts*.

Porter, Stanley E. "Recent Efforts to Reconstruct Early Christianity on the Basis of Its Papyrological Evidence." Pages 71–84 in Stanley E. Porter and Andrew W. Pitts (eds.), *Christian Origins and Greco-Roman Culture: Social and Literary Contexts for the New Testament*. Leiden: Brill, 2013.

Preisendanz, Karl. *Papyrusfunde und Papyrusforschung*. Leipzig: Karl W. Hiersemann, 1933.

Quecke, Hans. *Das Johannesevangelium saïdisch: Text der Handschrift PPalau Rib. Inv.-Nr. 183*. Barcelona: Papyrologica Castroctaviana, 1984.

Ramsey, Christopher Bronk. "Radiocarbon Dating: Revolutions in Understanding." *Archaeometry* 50 (2008): 249–275.

Ramsey, Christopher Bronk, Michael Dee, Sharen Lee, Takeshi Nakagawa, and Richard A. Staff. "Developments in the Calibration and Modeling of Radiocarbon Dates." *Radiocarbon* 52 (2010): 953–961.

"Rare Coptic Manuscripts Secured by J. P. Morgan." *Sun* (New York). December 31, 1911. Reprinted as "The Pierpont Morgan Collection of Coptic Manuscripts." *Catholic University Bulletin* 18 (1912): 186–190.

Rasmussen, Kaare L., Johannes van der Plicht, Frederick H. Cryer, Gregory Doudna, Frank M. Cross, and John Strugnell. "The Effects of Possible Contamination on the Radiocarbon Dating of the Dead Sea Scrolls I: Castor Oil." *Radiocarbon* 43 (2001): 127–132.

Rasmussen, Kaare L., Johannes van der Plicht, Gregory Doudna, Frank M. Cross, and John Strugnell. "Reply to Israel Carmi (2002): 'Are the ^{14}C Dates of the Dead Sea Scrolls Affected by Castor Oil Contamination?'" *Radiocarbon* 45 (2003): 497–499.

Rathbone, Dominic. *Economic Rationalism and Rural Society in Third-Century A.D. Egypt: The Heroninos Archive and the Appianus Estate*. Cambridge: Cambridge University Press, 1991.

Rau, Eckhard. "Weder gefälscht noch authentisch? Überlegungen zum Status des geheimen Markusevangeliums als Quelle des antiken Christentums." Pages 139–186 in Jörg Frey and Jens Schröter (eds.), *Jesus in apokryphen Evangelienüberlieferungen: Beiträge zu außerkanonischen Jesusüberlieferungen aus verschiedenen Sprach- und Kulturtraditionen*. Tübingen: Mohr Siebeck, 2010.

Read, Anthony. *The Faddan More Psalter: Discovery, Conservation and Investigation.* [Dublin]: National Museum of Ireland, 2011.

Reed, Ronald. *Ancient Skins, Parchments and Leathers.* London: Seminar Press, 1972.

Reif, Stefan C. *A Jewish Archive from Old Cairo: The History of Cambridge University's Genizah Collection.* Richmond, Surrey: Curzon, 2000.

A Report from the Committee Appointed to View the Cottonian Library. London: R. Williamson and W. Bowyer, 1732.

Reverdin, Olivier. "Les Genevois et Ménandre." Pages 9–18 in Louis Gaulis and André Hurst, *Ménandre, Théâtre: La Samienne, Cnémon le misanthrope, Le bouclier.* Lausanne: Éditions de l'Aire, 1981.

Roberts, Colin H. *Buried Books in Antiquity.* Arundell Esdaile Memorial Lecture 1962. Letchworth: Garden City Press, 1963.

Roberts, Colin H. "The Codex." *Proceedings of the British Academy* 40 (1954): 169–204.

Roberts, Colin H. "Complementary Note." Pages 59–60 in Roca-Puig, *Un papiro griego del evangelio de San Mateo,* 2nd ed.

Roberts, Colin H. "An Early Papyrus of the First Gospel." *Harvard Theological Review* 46 (1953): 233–237.

Roberts, Colin H. *Greek Literary Hands: 350 B.C.–A.D. 400.* Oxford: Clarendon, 1956.

Roberts, Colin H. *Manuscript, Society and Belief in Early Christian Egypt.* Oxford: Oxford University Press, 1979.

Roberts, Colin H., and Theodore C. Skeat. *The Birth of the Codex.* Oxford: Oxford University Press, 1983.

Robins, George. *A Catalogue of a Valuable Collection of Oriental Literature, Collected by James Bruce, of Kinnaird.* [London]: Smith and Robins, 1842.

Robinson, James M. "The Construction of the Nag Hammadi Codices." Pages 170–190 in Martin Krause (ed.), *Essays on the Nag Hammadi Texts in Honour of Pahor Labib.* Leiden: Brill, 1975.

Robinson, James M. "The Covers." Pages 71–86 in Robinson (ed.), *The Facsimile Edition of the Nag Hammadi Codices: Introduction.*

Robinson, James M. "The Discovering and Marketing of Coptic Manuscripts: The Nag Hammadi Codices and the Bodmer Papyri." Pages 2–25 in Birger A. Pearson and James E. Goehring (eds.), *The Roots of Egyptian Christianity.* Philadelphia: Fortress, 1986.

Robinson, James M. "The Discovery of the Nag Hammadi Codices." *Biblical Archaeologist* 42 (1979): 206–224.

Robinson, James M. "The Discovery of the Nag Hammadi Codices." *Journal of Coptic Studies* 11 (2009): 1–21.

Robinson, James M. (ed.). *The Facsimile Edition of the Nag Hammadi Codices: Codex I.* Leiden: Brill, 1977.

Robinson, James M. (ed.). *The Facsimile Edition of the Nag Hammadi Codices: Introduction.* Leiden: Brill, 1984.

Robinson, James M. "The First Christian Monastic Library." Pages 371–378 in
    Włodzimierz Godlewski (ed.), *Coptic Studies: Acts of the Third International
    Congress of Coptic Studies*. Warsaw: Éditions scientifiques de Pologne, 1990.

Robinson, James M. "The First Season of the Nag Hammadi Excavation: 27
    November–19 December 1975." *Göttinger Miszellen* 22 (1976): 71–79.

Robinson, James M. "From the Cliff to Cairo: The Story of the Discoverers
    and the Middlemen of the Nag Hammadi Codices." Pages 21–58 in Ber-
    nard Barc (ed.), *Colloque international sur les textes de Nag Hammadi (Québec,
    22–25 août 1978)*. Louvain: Peeters, 1981.

Robinson, James M. "The Future of Papyrus Codicology." Pages 23–70 in
    Robert McLachlan Wilson (ed.), *The Future of Coptic Studies*. Leiden: Brill,
    1978.

Robinson, James M. "Inside the Front Cover of Codex VI." Pages 74–87 in
    Martin Krause (ed.), *Essays on the Nag Hammadi Texts in Honour of Alexan-
    der Böhlig*. Leiden: Brill, 1972.

Robinson, James M. "Introduction: AC. 1390." Pages 2–32 in William Brashear,
    Wolf-Peter Funk, James M. Robinson, and Richard Smith (eds.), *The
    Chester Beatty Codex AC. 1390*. Leuven: Peeters, 1990.

Robinson, James M. *The Manichaean Codices of Medinet Madi*. Eugene, Ore.:
    Cascade Books, 2013.

Robinson, James M. "The Manuscript's History and Codicology." Pages xix–
    xlvii in James E. Goehring (ed.), *The Crosby-Schøyen Codex MS 193 in the
    Schøyen Collection*. Leuven: Peeters, 1990.

Robinson, James M. *The Nag Hammadi Story*. 2 vols. Leiden: Brill, 2014.

Robinson, James M. "The Pachomian Monastic Library at the Chester Beatty
    Library and the Bibliothèque Bodmer." *Manuscripts of the Middle East* 5
    (1990–1991): 26–40.

Robinson, James M. "The Pachomian Monastic Library at the Chester Beatty
    Library and the Bibliothèque Bodmer." *Occasional Papers of the Institute for
    Antiquity and Christianity* 19 (1990): 1–27.

Robinson, James M. *The Secrets of Judas: The Story of the Misunderstood Disciple
    and His Lost Gospel*. Rev. ed. San Francisco: HarperSanFrancisco, 2007.

Robinson, James M. *The Story of the Bodmer Papyri: From the First Monastery's
    Library in Upper Egypt to Geneva and Dublin*. Eugene, Ore.: Cascade Books,
    2011.

Robinson, James M. "Theological Autobiography." Pages 117–150 in Jon R.
    Stone (ed.), *The Craft of Religious Studies*. New York: St. Martin's, 1998.

Robinson, James M., and Bastiaan Van Elderen. "The First Season of the Nag
    Hammadi Excavation 27 November–19 December 1975." *American Re-
    search Center in Egypt Newsletter* 96 (1976): 18–24.

Roca-Puig, Ramón. "Daniele. Due semifogli del codice 967." *Aegyptus* 56
    (1976): 3–18.

Roca-Puig, Ramón. *Un papiro griego del evangelio de San Mateo*. [Sabadell]: Caja
    de Ahorros de Sabadell Biblioteca, 1956.

Roca-Puig, Ramón. *Un papiro griego del evangelio de San Mateo.* 2nd ed. Barcelona: [Grafos], 1962.

Roques, Mario. "Éloge funèbre du R. P. Vincent Scheil, membre de l'Académie." *Comptes rendus des séances de l'Académie des Inscriptions et Belles-Lettres* 84 (1940): 372–385.

Rousseau, Philip. *Pachomius: The Making of a Community in Fourth-Century Egypt.* Berkeley: University of California Press, 1985.

Royse, James R. "The Oxyrhynchus Papyrus of Philo." *Bulletin of the American Society of Papyrologists* 17 (1980): 155–165.

Royse, James R. *Scribal Habits in Early Greek New Testament Papyri.* Leiden: Brill, 2008.

Rück, Peter (ed.). *Pergament: Geschichte, Struktur, Restaurierung, Herstellung.* Sigmaringen: Thorbecke, 1991.

Sanders, Henry A. "Age and Ancient Home of the Biblical Manuscripts in the Freer Collection." *American Journal of Archaeology* 13 (1909): 130–141.

Sanders, Henry A. (ed.). *Facsimile of the Washington Manuscript of Deuteronomy and Joshua in the Freer Collection.* Ann Arbor: University of Michigan Press, 1910.

Sanders, Henry A. (ed.). *Facsimile of the Washington Manuscript of the Four Gospels in the Freer Collection.* Ann Arbor: University of Michigan Press, 1912.

Sanders, Henry A. "Four Newly Discovered Biblical Manuscripts." *Biblical World* 31 (1908): 138–142.

Sanders, Henry A. "New Manuscripts of the Bible from Egypt." *American Journal of Archaeology* 12 (1908): 49–55.

Sanders, Henry A. *The New Testament Manuscripts in the Freer Collection Part I: The Washington Manuscript of the Four Gospels.* New York: Macmillan, 1912.

Sanders, Henry A. *The Old Testament Manuscripts in the Freer Collection Part I: The Washington Manuscript of Deuteronomy and Joshua.* New York: Macmillan, 1910.

Sanders, Henry A. *A Third-Century Papyrus Codex of the Epistles of Paul.* Ann Arbor: University of Michigan Press, 1935.

Sayce, Archibald. "The Greek Papyri." Pages 24–37 in William M. Flinders Petrie, *Hawara, Biahmu, and Arsinoe.* London: Field and Tuer, 1899.

Schatzki, Theodore R. *The Site of the Social: A Philosophical Account of the Constitution of Social Life and Change.* University Park: University of Pennsylvania Press, 2002.

Scheil, Jean-Vincent. "Deux traités de Philon." *Mémoires publiés par les membres de la Mission Archéologique Française au Caire* 9.2 (1893): iii–viii ("Préface"), 151–215 (text of Philo), 216 ("Fragment d'Évangile"), Plates I–IV.

Scheil, Jean-Vincent. "Fragments de l'Évangile selon saint Luc, recueillis en Égypte." *Revue Biblique* 1 (1892): 113–115.

Schmid, Ulrich. "Reassessing the Palaeography and Codicology of the Freer Gospel Manuscript." Pages 227–249 in Hurtado (ed.), *The Freer Biblical Manuscripts.*

Schmidt, Carl. *Die alten Petrusakten im zusammenhang der apokryphen Apostellitteratur.* Leipzig: J. C. Hinrichs'sche Buchhandlung, 1903.

Schmidt, Carl. "Die Evangelienhandschrift der Chester Beatty-Sammlung." *Zeitschrift für die neutestamentliche Wissenschaft* 32 (1933): 225–232.

Schmidt, Carl. "Die neuen griechischen Bibelhandschriften." *Theologische Literaturzeitung* 33 (1908): 359–360.

Schmidt, Carl. "Die neuesten Bibelfunde aus Ägypten." *Zeitschrift für die neutestamentliche Wissenschaft* 30 (1931): 285–293.

Schmidt, Carl. "Ein vorirenaeisches gnostisches Originalwerk in koptischer Sprache." *Sitzungsberichte der königlich preussischen Akademie der Wissenschaften zu Berlin* 36 (1896): 839–847.

Schmidt, Carl, and Hans Jakob Polotsky. "Ein Mani-Fund in Ägypten: Originalschriften des Mani und seiner Schüler." *Sitzungsberichte der preussischen Akademie der Wissenschaften Phil.-Hist. Klasse* (1933): 4–90.

Schork, R. J. "The Singular Circumstance of an Errant Papyrus." *Arion* 16 (2008): 25–48.

Schow, Nicolao. *Charta papyracea graece scripta musei Borgiani Velitris.* Rome: A. Fulgonium, 1788.

Schubart, Wilhelm. *Das Buch bei den Griechen und Römern.* 2nd ed. Berlin: de Gruyter, 1921.

Schubert, Paul. "Les Papyrus Bodmer: contribution à une tentative de délimitation." *Adamantius* 21 (2015): 41–46.

Schubert, Paul. "P. Bodmer LII: Isocrate, *A Nicoclès 16–22.*" *Museum Helveticum* 54 (1997): 97–105.

Schwartz, Eduard. *Consilium Universale Ephesenum, Volumen Primum.* Berlin: de Gruyter, 1927.

Schwartz, Eduard. *Eusebius Werke zweiter Band: Die Kirchengeschichte, zweiter Teil.* Leipzig: J. C. Heinrichs'sche Buchhandlung, 1908.

Schwendner, Gregg. "A Fragmentary Psalter from Karanis and Its Context." Pages 117–136 in Evans and Zacharias (eds.), *Jewish and Christian Scripture as Artifact and Canon.*

Scott, James C. *Decoding Subaltern Politics: Ideology, Disguise, and Resistance in Agrarian Politics.* London: Routledge, 2013.

"Scraps Offer an Intriguing Clue on Jesus." *New York Times.* January 21, 1995.

Scrivener, Frederick H. *Bezae Codex Cantabrigiensis, Being an Exact Copy, in Ordinary Type, of the Celebrated Uncial Graeco-Latin Manuscript of the Four Gospels, and Acts of the Apostles.* Cambridge: Deighton, Bell, 1864.

Seider, Richard. "Aus der Arbeit der Universitätsinstitute: Die Universitäts-Papyrussammlung." *Heidelberger Jahrbücher* 8 (1964): 142–203.

Seider, Richard. *Paläographie der griechischen Papyri.* 3 vols. Stuttgart: A. Hiersemann, 1967–1990.

Sharpe, John Lawrence. "The Earliest Bindings with Wooden Board Covers: The Coptic Contribution to Binding Construction." Pages 2.455–2.478 in Carlo Federici and Paola F. Munafò (eds.), *International Conference on*

Conservation and Restoration of Archival and Library Materials. 2 vols. Rome: Istituto centrale per la patologia del libro, 1999.

Shore, A. F. *Joshua I–VI and Other Passages in Coptic Edited from a Fourth-Century Sahidic Codex in the Chester Beatty Library, Dublin.* Dublin: Hodges Figgis, 1963.

Sider, David. *The Library of the Villa dei Papiri at Herculaneum.* Los Angeles: J. Paul Getty Museum, 2005.

Skeat, Theodore C. "The Oldest Manuscript of the Four Gospels?" *New Testament Studies* 43 (1997): 1–34.

Skeat, Theodore C. "The Origin of the Christian Codex." *Zeitschrift für Papyrologie und Epigraphik* 102 (1994): 263–268.

Skeat, Theodore C., and E. P. Wegener. "A Trial Before the Prefect of Egypt Appius Sabinus, c. 250 A.D. (P.Lond.inv. 2565)." *Journal of Egyptian Archaeology* 21 (1935): 224–247.

Small, Sam W., Jr. "Marvelous Story of the Discovery of an Authentic Manuscript of the Bible." *Chicago Examiner.* January 5, 1908.

Soskice, Janet. *The Sisters of Sinai: How Two Lady Adventurers Discovered the Hidden Gospels.* New York: Vintage, 2010.

Spinka, Matthew. "Acquisition of the Codex Alexandrinus by England." *Journal of Religion* 16 (1936): 10–29.

Stanton, Graham N. "The Fourfold Gospel." *New Testament Studies* 43 (1997): 317–346.

Stanton, Graham N. *Gospel Truth? New Light on Jesus and the Gospels.* London: HarperCollins, 1995.

Stiles, Lori. "UA Radiocarbon Dates Help Verify Coptic Gospel of Judas Is Genuine." *University of Arizona, UA News.* March 30, 2006. https://uanews .arizona.edu/story/ua-radiocarbon-dates-help-verify-coptic-gospel-judas -genuine.

Strutwolf, Holger (ed.). *Novum Testamentum Graece.* 28th rev. ed. Stuttgart: Deutsche Bibelgesellschaft, 2012.

Szirmai, J. A. *The Archaeology of Medieval Bookbinding.* Aldershot: Ashgate, 1999.

Szirmai, J. A. "Wooden Writing Tablets and the Birth of the Codex." *Gazette du livre medieval* 17 (1990): 31–32.

Taylor, Joan E. "Buried Manuscripts and Empty Tombs: The Qumran *Genizah* Theory Revisited." Pages 269–315 in Aren M. Maeir, Jodi Magness, and Lawrence H. Schiffman (eds.), *"Go Out and Study the Land" (Judges 18:2): Archaeological, Historical and Textual Studies in Honor of Hanan Eshel.* Leiden: Brill, 2012.

Taylor, R. E., and Ofer Bar-Yosef. *Radiocarbon Dating: An Archaeological Perspective.* 2nd ed. Walnut Creek, Calif.: Left Coast, 2014.

Thiede, Carsten Peter. "Papyrus Magdalen Greek 17 (Gregory-Aland 𝔓64): A Reappraisal." *Zeitschrift für Papyrologie und Epigraphik* 105 (1995): 13–20.

Thiede, Carsten Peter, and Matthew d'Ancona. *Eyewitness to Jesus: Amazing*

New Manuscript Evidence About the Origin of the Gospels. New York: Doubleday, 1996.

Thompson, Edward Maunde. *Handbook of Greek and Latin Palaeography.* New
York: D. Appleton, 1893.

Thompson, Edward Maunde. *An Introduction to Greek and Latin Palaeography.*
Oxford: Clarendon, 1912.

Thompson, Herbert. "Mani and the Manichees: New Light on an Old Creed,
a Box in Egypt." *Times* (UK). April 20, 1933.

Thurston, Herbert. "The Holy Shroud and the Verdict of History." *Month: A
Catholic Magazine* 101 (January 1903): 17–29.

Timm, Stefan. *Das christlich-koptische Ägypten in arabischer Zeit.* 7 vols. Wiesbaden: Dr. Ludwig Reichert Verlag, 1984–2007.

Torallas Tovar, Sofía, and Klaas A. Worp (eds.). *Greek Papyri from Montserrat
(P.Monts.Roca IV).* Barcelona: Publicacions de l'Abadia de Montserrat, 2014.

Treharne, Elaine. "The Good, the Bad, the Ugly: Old English Manuscripts
and Their Physical Description." Pages 261–284 in Matthew T. Hussey
and John D. Niles (eds.), *The Genesis of Books: Studies in the Scribal Culture
of Medieval England in Honour of A. N. Doane.* Turnhout: Brepols, 2011.

Turner, Eric G. "Early Papyrus Codices of Large Size." Pages 309–312 in *Proceedings of the XIV International Congress of Papyrologists, Oxford 24–31 July
1974.* London: Egypt Exploration Society, 1975.

Turner, Eric G. "The Graeco-Roman Branch." Pages 161–178 in James (ed.),
Excavating in Egypt.

Turner, Eric G. *Greek Manuscripts of the Ancient World.* 2nd ed. London: Institute of Classical Studies, 1987.

Turner, Eric G. *Greek Papyri: An Introduction.* 2nd ed. Oxford: Clarendon,
1980.

Turner, Eric G. *The Papyrologist at Work.* Durham, N.C.: Duke University
Press, 1973.

Turner, Eric G. "Papyrus Bodmer XXVIII: A Satyr-Play on the Confrontation
of Heracles and Atlas." *Museum Helveticum* 33 (1976): 1–23.

Turner, Eric G. "Recto and Verso." *Journal of Egyptian Archaeology* 40 (1954):
102–106.

Turner, Eric G. Review of Seider's *Paläographie der griechischen Papyri, Band 1.*
Gnomon 41 (1969): 505–507.

Turner, Eric G. Review of Seider's *Paläographie der griechischen Papyri, Band 2.*
Gnomon 43 (1971): 710–712.

Turner, Eric G. "Roman Oxyrhynchus." *Journal of Egyptian Archaeology* 38
(1952): 78–93.

Turner, Eric G. "Some Questions About the Typology of the Codex." Pages
427–438 in Emil Kießling and Hans-Albert Ruprecht (eds.), *Akten des XIII.
Internationalen Papyrologenkongresses.* Munich: C. H. Beck'sche Verlagsbuch-
handlung, 1974.

Turner, Eric G. "The Terms Recto and Verso: The Anatomy of the Papyrus

Roll." Pages 1–71 in *Actes du XVe Congrès International de Papyrologie*. Brussels: Fondation Égyptologique Reine Élisabeth, 1978.

Turner, Eric G. *The Typology of the Early Codex*. Philadelphia: University of Pennsylvania Press, 1977.

Turner, Eric G. "A Writing Exercise from Oxyrhynchus." *Museum Helveticum* 13 (1956): 236–238.

Turner, Eric G. "Writing Material for Businessmen." *Bulletin of the American Society of Papyrologists* 15 (1978): 163–169.

Vandorpe, Katelijn. "Museum Archaeology or How to Reconstruct Pathyris Archives." *Egitto e Vicino Oriente* 17 (1994): 289–300.

Van Elderen, Bastiaan, and James M. Robinson. "The Second Season of the Nag Hammadi Excavation, 22 November–29 December 1976." *American Research Center in Egypt Newsletter* 99–100 (1977): 36–54.

van Haelst, Joseph. *Catalogue des papyrus littéraires juifs et chrétiens*. Paris: Publications de la Sorbonne, 1976.

van Haelst, Joseph. "Les origines du codex." Pages 12–35 in Alain Blanchard (ed.), *Les débuts du codex*. Turnhout: Brepols, 1989.

van Minnen, Peter. "From Posidippus to Palladas: What Have Literary Papyri Done for Us?" *Journal of Juristic Papyrology* 43 (2013): 243–261.

van Minnen, Peter. "The Greek *Apocalypse of Peter*." Pages 15–39 in Jan N. Bremmer and István Czachesz (eds.), *The Apocalypse of Peter*. Leuven: Peeters, 2003.

van Regemorter, Berthe. *Binding Structures in the Middle Ages*. Translated by Jane Greenfield. London: Maggs Bros., 1992.

Veilleux, Armand. *Pachomian Koinonia, Volume One: The Life of Saint Pachomius and His Disciples*. Kalamazoo, Mich.: Cistercian Publications, 1980.

Vezin, Jean. "La réalisation matérielle des manuscrits latins pendant le haut Moyen Âge." Pages 15–51 in Albert Gruys and J. P. Gumbert (eds.), *Codicologica 2: Éléments pour une codicologie comparée*. Leiden: Brill, 1978.

von Erffa, H. "Esai. 19, 3 sqq." *Studi Italiani di Filologia Classica*, n.s. 12 (1935): 109–110.

Wachtel, Klaus. "𝔓64/67: Fragmente des Matthäusevangeliums aus dem 1. Jahrhundert?" *Zeitschrift für Papyrologie und Epigraphik* 107 (1995): 73–80.

Wallraff, Martin. *Kodex und Kanon: Das Buch im frühen Christentum*. Berlin: de Gruyter, 2013.

Wallraff, Martin, Carlo Scardino, Laura Mecella, and Christophe Guignard (eds.). *Iulius Africanus Cesti: The Extant Fragments*. Translated by William Adler. Berlin: de Gruyter, 2012.

Wasserman, Tommy. "Papyrus 72 and the *Bodmer Miscellaneous Codex*." *New Testament Studies* 51 (2005): 137–154.

Weitzmann, Kurt, and Herbert L. Kessler. *The Cotton Genesis: British Library Codex Cotton Otho B. VI*. Princeton, N.J.: Princeton University Press, 1986.

Welford, Richard. *Men of Mark 'twixt Tyne and Tweed*. 3 vols. London: Walter Scott, 1895.

West, Martin L. *Studies in the Text and Transmission of the Iliad*. Munich: K. G. Saur, 2001.

Wilcken, Ulrich. "The Chester Beatty Biblical Papyri." *Archiv für Papyrusforschung* 11 (1935): 112–114.

Wilford, John Noble, and Laurie Goodstein. "'Gospel of Judas' Surfaces After 1,700 Years." *New York Times*. April 6, 2006.

Williams, Michael A. "The Scribes of Nag Hammadi Codices IV, V, VI, VIII and IX." Pages 334–342 in Marguerite Rassart-Debergh and Julien Ries (eds.), *Actes du IVe Congrès Copte*, vol. 2. Louvain-la-Neuve: Université Catholique de Louvain, Institut Orientaliste, 1992.

Williams, Michael A., and Lance Jenott. "Inside the Covers of Codex VI." Pages 1025–1052 in Louis Painchaud and Paul-Hubert Poirier (eds.), *Coptica-Gnostica-Manichaica: Mélanges offerts à Wolf-Peter Funk*. Louvain: Peeters, 2006.

Willis, William H. "Duke Papyri: A History of the Collection." *Library Notes* 51–52 (May 1985): 34–48.

Willis, William H. "The New Collections of Papyri at the University of Mississippi." Pages 381–392 in Leiv Amundsen and Vegard Skånland (eds.), *Proceedings of the IX International Congress of Papyrology*. Oslo: Norwegian Universities Press, 1961.

Willis, William H. "A New Fragment of Plato's *Parmenides* on Parchment." *Greek, Roman and Byzantine Studies* 12 (1971): 539–552.

Wilson, A. J. *The Life and Times of Sir Alfred Chester Beatty*. London: Cadogan Publications, 1985.

Winlock, H. E., Walter E. Crum, and H. G. Evelyn White. *The Monastery of Epiphanius at Thebes*. 2 vols. New York: Publications of the Metropolitan Museum of Art Egyptian Expedition, 1926.

Wise, Michael O., Norman Golb, John J. Collins, and Dennis G. Pardee (eds.). *Methods of Investigation of the Dead Sea Scrolls and the Khirbet Qumran Site: Present Realities and Future Prospects*. New York: New York Academy of Sciences, 1994.

Woide, Carl Gottfried. "Sur le Dictionnaire Cophte qu'il va publier à Oxford." *Journal des Sçavans* (June 1774): 323–343.

Worp, K. A. *Greek Papyri from Kellis: I (P.Kell.G.) Nos. 1–90*. Oxford: Oxbow, 1995.

Worp, K. A., and A. Rijksbaron (eds.). *The Kellis Isocrates Codex (P.Kell. III Gr. 95)*. Oxford: Oxbow, 1997.

Zeitlin, Solomon. "The Hebrew Scrolls: A Challenge to Scholarship." *Jewish Quarterly Review*, n.s. 41 (1951): 251–275.

Zimmermann, Heinrich. *Neutestamentliche Methodenlehre: Darstellung der historisch-kritischen Methode*. 7th ed. Stuttgart: Katholisches Bibelwerk, 1982.

Zucker, Friedrich, and Wilhelm Schubart. "Die berliner Papyrusgrabungen in Dîme und Medînet Mâdi 1909/10." *Archiv für Papyrusforschung* 21 (1971): 5–55.

Index of Subjects

For references to individual ancient books, see the Index of Manuscripts.

385

Index of Manuscripts

Page numbers in *italics* contain pictures. Manuscripts published in papyrological series are listed under those conventional abbreviations (thus, "P.Oxy. 3.412" rather than "London, British Library Papyrus 2040"). Manuscripts with well-known names are listed under those names (thus, "Codex Sinaiticus" rather than "London, British Library Add. Ms. 43725").